Worldwide Acclaim for Sudoku

"Diabolically addictive."
   —*New York Post*

"A puzzling global phenomenon."
   —*The Economist*

"The biggest craze to hit *The Times* since the first crossword puzzle was published in 1935."
   —*The Times* of London

"The latest craze in games."
   —BBC News

"Sudoku is dangerous stuff. Forget work and family—think papers hurled across the room and industrial-sized blobs of correction fluid. I love it!"
   —*The Times* of London

"Sudoku are to the first decade of the twenty-first century what Rubik's Cube was to the 1970s."
   —*The Daily Telegraph*

"Britain has a new addiction. Hunched over newspapers on crowded subway trains, sneaking secret peeks in the office, a puzzle-crazy nation is trying to slot numbers into small checkerboard grids."
   —Associated Press

"Forget crosswords."
   —*The Christian Science Monitor*

Also Available

Sudoku Easy Presented by Will Shortz, Volume 1
Sudoku Easy to Hard Presented by Will Shortz, Volume 2
Sudoku Easy to Hard Presented by Will Shortz, Volume 3
The Ultimate Sudoku Challenge Presented by Will Shortz
Sudoku for Your Coffee Break Presented by Will Shortz
Sudoku to Boost Your Brainpower Presented by Will Shortz
Will Shortz Presents Sun, Sand, and Sudoku
Will Shortz's Favorite Sudoku Variations
Kakuro Presented by Will Shortz
Will Shortz Presents Easy Kakuro
Will Shortz Presents Sudoku for Stress Relief
Will Shortz Presents Sudoku for Your Bedside
Will Shortz Presents Sudoku for the Weekend
Will Shortz Presents Quick Sudoku Volume 1
Will Shortz Presents Easiest Sudoku

For Sudoku Lovers: 300 Puzzles in Just One Book!

The Giant Book of Sudoku Presented by Will Shortz
Will Shortz Presents The Monster Book of Sudoku
Will Shortz Presents The Super-Colossal Book of Sudoku

Try These Convenient, Portable Volumes

Pocket Sudoku Presented by Will Shortz, Volume 1
Pocket Sudoku Presented by Will Shortz, Volume 2
Pocket Sudoku Presented by Will Shortz, Volume 3
Pocket Sudoku Presented by Will Shortz, Volume 4
Summertime Pocket Sudoku Presented by Will Shortz
Summertime Pocket Kakuro Presented by Will Shortz
Will Shortz Presents Vacation Sudoku
Will Shortz Presents Quick and Easy Sudoku

WILL SHORTZ PRESENTS ULTIMATE
SUDOKU

1000 WORDLESS CROSSWORD PUZZLES

EDITED BY
WILL SHORTZ

PUZZLES BY
PZZL.COM

ST. MARTIN'S GRIFFIN
NEW YORK

The puzzles in this volume have previously appeared in *The Giant Book of Sudoku Presented by Will Shortz; The Ultimate Sudoku Challenge Presented by Will Shortz; Sudoku to Boost Your Brainpower Presented by Will Shortz; Will Shortz Presents Sun, Sand, and Sudoku; Will Shortz Presents Simple Sudoku Volume 1; Will Shortz Presents Sudoku for Your Bedside; Will Shortz Presents Sudoku for Stress Relief; Will Shortz Presents Quick Sudoku Volume 1; Will Shortz Presents Sudoku for the Weekend* and *Will Shortz Presents Easiest Sudoku.*

www.stmartins.com

ISBN-13: 978-0-312-34563-1
ISBN-10: 0-312-34563-1

First Edition: August 2006

10 9 8 7 6 5 4 3 2 1

Introduction

Throughout the history of puzzles and games, many of the biggest successes have come as complete surprises, because they've broken all the "rules."

Parker Bros. famously turned down the rights to the game Monopoly in 1934, because it had "52 design errors." It was too complicated, they said, it had too many pieces, and it took too long to play. So the inventor, Charles B. Darrow, produced and sold 5,000 handmade copies of Monopoly, they quickly sold out, and—once Parker Bros. finally bought the rights—it became the biggest game hit of 1935.

Similarly, the "experts" initially pooh-poohed Scrabble, Trivial Pursuit, crossword puzzles, and many other game and puzzle successes over the years.

Hardly anyone thought sudoku would be popular when it was introduced in Britain in late 2004 and the U.S. in 2005. The public was not interested in number puzzles, according to conventional wisdom. Yet we all know what happened. In less than a year, sudoku has become one of the most popular puzzles in history. Virtually every newspaper has made room for a daily sudoku, sudoku books have been bestsellers for six straight months, and sudoku tournaments have been held across the country and around the world. *The Language Report* named "sudoku" the Word of the Year for 2005.

The craze goes on and, to everyone's surprise, shows little sign of abating.

What's So Great About Sudoku?

The appeal of sudoku comes partly from the simplicity of the rules, which can be stated in a single sentence, and the compactness of the grid, just 9 × 9 squares—combined with some unexpectedly subtle logic. Even longtime enthusiasts may not understand all the techniques needed to work it. Sudoku packs a lot of punch for so small a feature.

Sudoku is a flexible puzzle. It can be easy, moderate, or hard, and you can select the level according to your skills and mood. And the amount of time needed to solve one—generally between 10 and 30 minutes, for most people for most puzzles—is about perfect in order to feed a daily addiction. If sudoku took less time, it wouldn't pose enough challenge, and if it took more, you might lose interest or simply not be able to fit sudoku into your schedule.

Like crosswords, sudoku puzzles have blank squares that are inviting to fill in. It's said nature abhors a vacuum. We as human beings seem to have a natural compulsion to fill up empty spaces. A sudoku addict has difficulty turning a page that has empty puzzle squares begging to be completed.

Sudoku also provides an appealing rhythm of solving. Generally the first few numbers are easy to enter. Then, in the harder examples at least, you can get stymied and maybe a bit frustrated. Once you make the critical breakthrough (or breakthroughs), though, the final numbers can come quickly, giving you a rush and a heady sense of achievement—often tempting you to start another sudoku immediately. Hence the addictiveness of sudoku, which is the "crack cocaine" of puzzles.

New Challenges

On the following pages are 1000 absolutely top quality sudoku puzzles rated easy (#1–#450), moderate (#451–#650), demanding (#651–830), and very challenging (#831–#1000). Every one has been checked, rechecked, and then re-rechecked to ensure that it has a unique solution, and that it can be solved using step-by-step logic. You never have to guess here.

As usual, all the puzzles in this book were created by my colleague Peter Ritmeester and the staff of PZZL.com. Try them. And as one correspondent wrote me recently, you, too, will go "sudoku kuku."

—Will Shortz

How to Solve Sudoku

A sudoku puzzle consists of a 9 × 9-square grid subdivided into nine 3 × 3 boxes. Some of the squares contain numbers. The object is to fill in the remaining squares so that every row, every column, and every 3 × 3 box contains each of the numbers from 1 to 9 exactly once.

Solving a sudoku puzzle involves pure logic. No guesswork is needed—or even desirable. Getting started involves mastering just a few simple techniques.

Take the example on this page (in which we've labeled the nine 3 × 3 boxes A to I as shown). Note that the boxes H and I already have 8's filled in, but box G does not. Can you determine where the 8 goes here?

5	8	6					1	2
				5	2	8	6	
2	4		8	1				3
			5		3		9	
				8	1	2	4	
4		5	6			7	3	8
	5		2	3			8	1
7					8			
3	6				5			

A	B	C
D	E	F
G	H	I

The 8 can't appear in the top row of squares in box G, because an 8 already appears in the top row of I—and no number can be repeated in a row. Similarly, it can't appear in the middle row of G, because an 8 already appears in the middle row of H. So, by process of elimination, an 8 must appear in the bottom row of G. Since only one square in this row is empty—next to the 3 and 6—you have your first answer. Fill in an 8 to the right of the 6.

Next, look in the three left-hand boxes of the grid, A, D, and G. An 8 appears in both A and G (the latter being the one you just entered). In box A, the 8 appears in the middle column, while in G the 8 appears on the right. By elimination, in box D, an 8 must go in the leftmost column. But which square? The column here has two squares open.

The answer is forced by box E. Here an 8 appears in the middle row. This means an 8 cannot appear in the middle row of D. Therefore, it must appear in the top row of the leftmost column of D. You have your second answer.

In solving a sudoku, build on the answers you've filled in as far as possible—left, right, up, and down—before moving on.

For a different kind of logic, consider the sixth row of numbers—4, ?, 5, 6, ?, ?, 7, 3, 8. The missing numbers must be 1, 2, and 9, in some order. The sixth square can't be a 1, because box E already has a 1. And it can't be a 2, because a 2 already appears in the sixth column in box B. So the sixth square in the sixth row has to be a 9. Fill this in.

Now you're left with just 1 and 2 for the empty squares of this row. The fifth square can't be a 1, because box E already has a 1. So the fifth square must be a 2. The second square, by elimination, has a 1. Voilà! Your first complete row is filled in.

Box E now has only two empty squares, so this is a good spot to consider next. Only the 4 and 7 remain to be filled in. The leftmost square of the middle row can't be a 4, because a 4 already appears in this row in box F. So it must be 7. The remaining square must be 4. Your first complete box is done.

One more tip, and then you're on your own.

Consider 3's in the boxes A, B, and C. Only one 3 is filled in—in the third row, in box C. In box A you don't have enough information to fill in a 3 yet. However, you know the 3 can't appear in A's bottom row, because 3 appears in the bottom row of C. And it can't appear in the top row, because that row is already done. Therefore, it must appear in the middle row. Which square you don't know yet. But now, by elimination, you do know that in box B a 3 must appear in the top row. Specifically, it must appear in the fourth column, because 3's already appear in the fifth and sixth columns of E and H. Fill this in.

Following logic, using these and other techniques left for you to discover, you can work your way around the grid, filling in the rest of the missing numbers. The complete solution is shown below.

5	8	6	3	7	4	9	1	2
1	3	7	9	5	2	8	6	4
2	4	9	8	1	6	5	7	3
8	7	2	5	4	3	1	9	6
6	9	3	7	8	1	2	4	5
4	1	5	6	2	9	7	3	8
9	5	4	2	3	7	6	8	1
7	2	1	4	6	8	3	5	9
3	6	8	1	9	5	4	2	7

Remember, don't guess. Be careful not to repeat a number where you shouldn't, because a wrong answer may force you to start over. And don't give up. Soon you'll be a sudoku master!

1

Light and Easy

5	3			2		6	9	4
	2	4		5		3		7
6	1		3				8	5
		3			5			
2				7			5	
1		6		9		8	7	3
9	4				1	7		6
		1	4	3				
			7			1		

2

Light and Easy

5			2	6	8			4
			4				8	6
				1		9	3	
		1	3					7
8	2				6		5	
6			9		5	2	1	8
		4					2	
	6	5	7	2	9	8		1
2				5	4	7		

8	2		3					
	1	4			9			
			8			2	6	1
	6		2			4		
7	8							
			5	9				
				8			7	5
			4	3	6		2	
	3				7			

		6		5			9	
4		5	1		9			
					6	7	5	
7		1		6				8
	9	3			4		1	5
			2		5		7	
	4		3	9	7			
1	3	9	6	2				
	8							2

	5	3		2				4
			7	4	1	5	6	3
			9	3			7	
	7		2			4		
	6				4	7	5	
	8	4	5			3		6
8		9				6		7
6		1					3	5
5				1		8	4	2

	8	6				9	2	
		2						
		1	4	3	2			
1	6		5		4		9	
				9		8	7	1
2			8	1		5		
3		7				6	5	8
		1			7			
8		4	6		5			

7
Light and Easy

		6	8	3				
			1			8	5	
					9	6	1	2
	4							
			9			4	3	5
	3	5		8	1	2	9	6
3	6		2				7	4
9								
	1			6		3	2	

8
Light and Easy

8				7		1	5	
		9		1				7
	1			5				3
2			8		7			6
6		7	1		5		2	
3	5	8	2		4	9		
	3						4	
	7		3	2	6			
1			7		9		6	5

4								6
1			5			2		
6				3				9
	9	4	1	5	6	8		7
	5		3	7				1
				4		9	6	5
	4					6		
	6		4	2			5	
	2	1		9			7	

		8	2					
3		4			5	1	7	
7	2							
5			6			2		
				8				3
	3				4		8	
				5			2	
6			3	1				
2		7		9			5	

8	1					7		
			2			1	6	9
				9			4	3
		8		4				
1	4				3	9	7	
					6		1	5
6			8		9	5		1
	7							
				3				

4						9		
	5							
2	3	9	4			7		
			8	3			2	7
7					1			
	2	8			7	4		1
3			7		8	2		
	9	6		5	2		7	
8				9			5	3

13

Light and Easy

2	7		9		3			
				6	7		3	
3		6		8	5	9	1	
4		5	3	9			2	1
1		2				3		
9	3		6	2		4		
	5			3		8		
				4	9	1		6
6	9					5		

14

Light and Easy

3	4		5		2		1	6
5			6					
			1	4	3			2
8				3	6		4	9
	6	4					2	
2		3	4			6		1
4		7	8	6	1		9	3
		2	3		9			
1				2	4			5

15

Light and Easy

		8	2			5		
	9			6				
6	4		7	3				
4	5	6		9				
	7				4			
3	8		5			4		
			9	2				1
7		5		8		9		
	1					8	4	

16

Light and Easy

		3	5					
	9	2	3					
8			2			7		9
	1	5	6			3	8	
4								5
	2		8		7			
1	6	4					7	
						4		
					6	9	5	8

Puzzle 17:

		9			8		6	
								3
		5			9			1
6		1			4		7	9
3			1	8		2		
4		6					5	2
2	1	3						
				4		7		

Puzzle 18:

							2	5
				1				6
	2					8	1	
		3		9	7	1		
	4			6				
		1				3	7	8
		7		8			4	2
9		4			6			
	3				1			

Light and Easy

4		9		7	3			
				4		2		3
			8					
		4						
	5		7					
8		2	5				9	
		5	6	8			1	
	1	6			2		7	
9		7	1			4		

20
Light and Easy

		9		1			4	
	1		4	9	3		8	2
4		8		7		1		9
		5	9				7	
6				2			1	8
2							5	3
1						4		
9		2		3		8		
				8		3	9	5

			2		9		8	
				5	4			
6	7						2	9
	8	9		4			3	
		4			3	9		2
3		1					7	
		7	9					
	4		3		8	5		
5		2		7				

5		9		2	4			
	4				1			2
	6	8		3				
8		2	6		7	4		3
6	3	4			9	2	1	
			3	4	2		9	
4	7							
		5	2					
		1	4	7	8	3		5

23
Light and Easy

	6	9		1	2	3		
	5	3		8		1		
1		8		7		6	2	
8				6			1	
		6		2		9		8
				9	8			
3					1	2		
9		4	2		6		7	
			7	3				

24
Light and Easy

5		1	2	4				
		4		7				
			5	3				
	5		7		2	9		8
	7		8	6		3		
6	2				4			
9			1		6	4	8	2
		5				6		
		6	9	8	3	7		1

	7	2	1	3	4			
		4					1	
3				6		5		
		7		8				9
	2	3	9	1		8		
9				4	2		5	3
					3	7	6	5
					1			
8					7	9		

	9				3			
2						4		9
8	4	6			9	5		3
9				5				2
	8			6	4	3		7
	1		7			8		
					8	2		
1			4	2	5			

27
Light and Easy

	2	6		9			1	3
	8		1		7		6	
		1	2	6	3			
		9			1	7		8
					6			1
					2		5	
	7	4	8	3	5		9	6
2		8			4			7
3		5						

28
Light and Easy

7			3		1	4	2	
	1			7				8
	2		5				6	1
9	3		7				4	
	7				3	9	8	
4	5				6	1		3
5	4			9		2		
			2					
		2	6			8		

29

			2	9				8
		9		7		6		
	7		4		6	2		
	3			2		9		7
			1	3			4	
4	1	7			9		8	2
1				4			5	
2		5			8			
			3					

30

4	9	7						
					2			8
				6	1			7
	2				4	6	8	5
1	4						7	
6		3			8	9		
8	3			1		7	2	
		5		8		3		1
		4			7	8		6

						1	6	
1	7					9		
	6							4
	1			3		7		
9	4		6		2	3		
		3	9		1	8		6
	8			5			7	
	2	5	4					3
				1		2		

	9			2		4	6	
			3	9		2		7
	7		6		8		5	
	3		8			7	4	5
		8	9	4				
		1						
		7				1		4
	6	9						
1				3				8

33
Light and Easy

8	1			5			9	
2						7		
4		3			1		2	
	3		1			6		2
		2				4		
6	4			8	2		7	9
	2	1				5		
5	6		8	1	7			
				2	3			1

34
Light and Easy

3					5			
				3			8	
	2							1
		9			6			
		1	4	7	8			3
5		7			3			
		8			4		1	9
		3	5	6		2		
				9	7	6		5

	6	5	8				9	4
		2				8	3	
8			7	4	2		1	
3	7		9		4			
	4	9	2		3	7		
1				5			4	
	3	7	1				2	5
				7	6		8	9
9				2		6	7	

9	7			8				
				4		5	2	
2	1						7	
7	9				1			
	6	1			5		4	
							8	
				3				6
					4		3	1
8			9					

3		6	2	1				4
		1		6			7	
8				9	3			
		2				9	1	
5			1	4				6
		8					5	
			7					
6	8		4	3		2		1

5	1					3		2
		9	2				6	
	7							8
1		2	4					
3			9		2		1	
			8	5		6		
4		8	6					
		7		8	9			
			3		7			

39
Light and Easy

7			5	2		8		
3	2				7		6	
	6			4		5	2	
			7	8			9	6
6			9	3				
5	7	9			2		3	
9		3		7				
2	8						7	9
	1	7	2					

40
Light and Easy

6	5	8			7	2		
		9		5	6		7	1
	7							
		5	3		4		6	
	3	6						
		1	2			7	3	
			1	2		3		4
					9			
					8			

		2	5			3		
	4	5						7
7				6	1			4
9	1		4	8	2			
4	5		3	1				
3	2				5			6
2	8		1			7		
						3	2	
		1	8		9			

		6	7		8			2
1	4	7					6	5
		2	5			3	1	
6	2			7	1			
4	7			5				6
3					9	1		
		5		4				3
	1	4				6	2	
	6	3	2		7	4	5	1

43
Light and Easy

	6	3			9		1	
			1	5	3	8	7	6
1		5					4	9
		9	2				8	
		1		3	4			
3	2		7			1		
	3							1
4			3	9	8	5		
9				1				

44
Light and Easy

8	7		1	9	5			3
		4			3	6	8	
	3	5	6					1
		2						9
						2	5	
1			9			8		
	6			2			7	
		3	4	5	9			8
	9	1		6			3	

45

1	7	4			9			6
	2					5		
	9		8	4		3		
9								
			7					8
		7		8		1		
8			1	2	6			3
7	5			9		4		
	1				7		8	

46

		7			5		4	
5			4					
	1				2			
3				9		8		
9		6	8		4		5	2
						1		
1			9			7		3
		8			7	2		9

47
Light and Easy

6				7				1
		9			1			
3	5		8	4		6	2	
2							8	
	8					5	4	2
	1					7		9
4		8		1	5			
1		7	4				5	
	2							

48
Light and Easy

				4				
					8	4		2
	2	4		6	9	8		3
7					2			
	1		6			2	8	
		3					7	
	9		8		1			7
	8		3	7	6	9		
5						1		

	3		6	7	2		9	8
7			4		3		1	
					9		6	
2					5		4	9
	5	7	8				2	
		6	2					
		4	3					1
6	9	1	5	2	8		3	
5		3						

		2	6	5	7		8	
	6	1	8			7		9
7	5					2		
2				1			6	
5		6		8			9	2
	4	9	5	6			1	
					5			
		5	9	4		1		
			1		8		4	5

51
Light and Easy

				7			8	
	6						9	
5						4	7	3
			3	1				7
3		1	7	4	8		2	5
		7			6			
4			9		1	2	5	
2	8			3		7		
		9		8		3		4

52
Light and Easy

	2	7	4			5		3
				9				
	1	6			3	4		
4				6		8		
	9						3	6
		8					7	
						1		
				4				
8				1	2	3	6	9

53

Light and Easy

7	6						1	
			3			8		7
3	1	8	4					
	8		5				9	1
1				6	7		3	
			2			7		6
	3		1	8	5			
9				3		6	4	8

54

Light and Easy

9		7	2	5				
6		5	3	4		9	1	
					1		8	5
			7		5		6	4
	6					5	9	
5				6	4			3
								1
	3		4	1		6	5	7
					2	3		9

55
Light and Easy

4	7		1		9			
		5	7			4		
1	9			4				
2	3			5	1	7		6
		7			8		2	5
5		1	6					
3		4	8		6		1	
	1		9	3			6	
	6	8		1	4	3		7

56
Light and Easy

9				7		2		
	5		8		3			
4		8	9	6			1	
1	4		3	5				2
5							9	
	8	3	1		9	4	5	
			2	3		8		7
							3	9
			9					

57
Light and Easy

					9	1	4	
9	4	8				6	3	
	6		8					9
	7					8		5
8		4	7		5	3		2
					8			
2		9		6		7		
		7	9		2			
	3	1		8	7	9		

58
Light and Easy

	6		2					9
8				5				2
4			6	7	1			3
	5							
	8	9		2				
7			9		4		6	5
	1		8	9		4		
	7		1		3		9	6
	4			6	2	5	8	

59
Light and Easy

			3		4	6	5	2
9				6				7
				2			1	3
	7	5			3	1		8
	2			8			3	
			5		7			
	6					5		
					6		2	
	1			7		8		9

60
Light and Easy

7	6	8		1		2	3	
		2				1		9
9					3	7		
5	7	1				8		2
3			9	8			1	
	2			5	1		4	
	5		1		7	9		8
	9	7	6	4	8		2	
6				9				

61
Light and Easy

9								6
		5					2	
2	3	4					5	
	5				8		6	7
	1			9		8		
				1				
					4	7	3	
	9							
3			7			6	8	

62
Light and Easy

8				4		7	3	
			5				9	
		6	7				8	
6		3		9			5	7
				7	1	9	2	
2		9	8			1	4	
		2	3	8			1	9
		7		1	4			
	3	4		6		2		

	4			3			8	
8		6						
2		1	8					
4						5		
5	2		6	9		8		
6		8	7	5				4
	9			8			6	
			1		3	9		
3			2				4	

6		5	4			2		
			1	8	5		7	
					3	4	5	8
3	2	6	8		4			
	4	8		7		3	6	1
	7			5				
		1			8			
	6		7	3			4	
	5	3	6			1	8	7

5			6			9		
		6		8	9			
1							8	
	6			1		8		
	7			2				9
	8			9	3		1	
3		1		4				
			7				3	4
	7		3					

	1		9	3				
	7	6		5	2			
							8	1
		9	5					
4					1		6	
	3					2	9	
	9			4			7	
			7				3	
2				6				

			3	5		2		8
				1	2			
2			8		6	9		3
9	8							6
	6		2		5			
6	3					8		7
8		5	9				3	
			1			4		

	1	7		6	2		3	5
		3	8			9		
		4		7		1		
5		8			3	7		4
	7		1		6	3	8	
			7		8			6
		1			7		9	8
				9	1		5	
3	9	5		8			7	

	4			8		7		
9							8	
3							5	4
	9		5	4	1		7	
	1				6	3		
5		4	8			9		
			9			6		
		8	1					
2			7	5				

5	7			1				
		1		6	7			
8				3	9	5	1	
	5			8				1
				5		2		4
	3	9			6		7	
	8			9				
	2	4	3		8			
6								9

				2	7	4		9
							8	1
9					1			2
		2		7				
5	8		2	9			1	
7	4			8	5		9	
8			3				6	7
	9			1				4

				2	1			3
	3			8		2		7
2			3	6	4		5	
5	4	6			9			8
3					2		9	6
		2		5				4
			8	9	7	4		2
		9			6		7	5
4	2	7						

		3	8					
	5	9		4		7	8	
			6			9	4	
		6	4	8	7			9
	7				6	8	2	
8				2	1		3	
1	4				8	3	7	2
2			7		4		9	6
9		7		5				8

		2	5				3	
4				1				
	5		2			4		
		4	3			5	8	
				8		6	1	
8				9				
	7			6				
9		3					2	
5			9	3	8			7

75
Light and Easy

				4	9	2		
				2				
	9	8	1	6				
		3	5	9			1	6
1	7		2				4	
					8			3
3						4	7	
7		5					6	
		2				3		8

76
Light and Easy

				2	4			
	3						7	
4			3			1	2	5
		4		1				6
	2	7	9			4	5	
6							1	2
3		9	7			8	6	
2		1					3	
	5			3	9			

Puzzle 77:

2	3		7	1	9		8	
	5						9	
8		9		6	4			2
5		1		7		8	6	
	4	3	8				2	
	7				2	3		4
7			2			9	4	
			9			5	1	8
	9		6	8		2	7	

Puzzle 78:

4							2	
	3		5		9			
9			1					
			4					
	4				5	7	8	1
			7		3		9	
		9		7		6	3	
6		7		8		4		
						2		

79
Light and Easy

						6		8
4			7		8			1
7		8					9	
			5	4				
		4	6		3			
3	5	1	9				6	
9	8			3		7		5
5		6		7	2			9
			8					

80
Light and Easy

	6	5		8		2		
2	3		9		5			1
	4			7	2			6
		3	7	4		8		
		7		3				
8		4	2	5	9		6	7
9	5			2	8		7	
					3		5	
		6			7		9	2

81
Light and Easy

				4		5	9	
5		7	8				4	3
	8			5	3	7		
1	7					9	8	4
			9	7			1	
		2	3		1			5
8	9	5	4					7
3		4					5	
	2	1		9		4		6

82
Light and Easy

		5		2	6	8		
9				1	4	2	5	6
		8	5		7			
3				9				
7	1		4	6				8
	9	6		7	3			1
5		7	6				8	9
					9		2	3
				8	1	7	6	5

1								
	9		2	8		5		
	5		7					
6		5	3			9		
		1	9	7		2		
	2			4			1	3
5			8		4		6	
	4							
2		3	6		5	4		7

	3				1	6		
7		2				4		5
6	1	8						
3	2	7	6	9				
1				8			6	7
	5						4	3
			3	2			7	
					8	5		4
	6	1	9		7			

				3			1	
	4	3			2			9
				5	4	6		
		7	4					8
4					9	1	2	6
6				8	1	3	7	
		6		4		9		7
9			2					3
	5			9			4	

	1	7	3					
	6		5		9	2		
2								5
						1		
			4				9	6
	4				1	7		
1	9			2	3		6	
				4			5	
4				6	5	3	1	

		4		6				
1				2	9		4	
		8	4	5				
2				9				
			8		7			6
6		7	1	4	2			9
		3	5		4			
			2	7	6	9	3	
	7	2					5	4

				9	5			
	3	5		7		2		
		2			4			
		1					9	3
8	7		6	3		1		4
	4	3	7		9		8	2
7			5		3	8	2	
1					7			
3		4	8		1		6	

89 — Light and Easy

	5		7				1	4
	1	9		8				
	7	2						3
1					7	5	2	
2	3	5	6				9	7
8			1			3	4	
7				5			3	
9	2	6	8					1
5			2	7		6		

90 — Light and Easy

							7	9
2					7	6		8
	9	1	8			2		
9				8				
	4			5	6			
	3	5	1					
			9					
1		6		7	4			
					5		2	

91
Light and Easy

6		7			8			
					5	7	3	8
	9			2				
		4				3	8	7
8		1		7			5	
	3						6	2
	8		6			4		9
		9	3		7	5		6
5			1		4			

92
Light and Easy

	7			8			2	
8				7	2	3		9
	4	6				1	8	
	9			3			1	4
	3	1				9	6	5
6	2		9		1			
3	8	9		6				
						3	6	9	2
	6	2		1			7	

	2		8				4	
			5				6	9
4					9	5		
2			9		4	8		
3	4				1			
	1					2		
			6	1				3
8	3							
			2		3		5	8

4		3	7			1	6	
7			6			5		8
		2	1		5			
6			8	9				7
	8	9	2			6		4
1		7				3		9
2					6	4	3	5
	1		3		8			
					7	8	9	1

5	4				7	8	2	3
		3						4
				8				
9			2					
			6		5			7
	5	2		1			9	8
				7			3	
2		4	1					9
7					2		1	

2		3				6		
	9	8	5				4	7
6				3	4		9	1
	6	7			1			2
					3			9
						4	3	
7	5		3		8			
	3			5			2	8
8		6	4	2			7	3

6	2			4		1	3	
7	3					9	5	4
		9	5			7		
5						4	2	
3			2	5		6		
	7	4						3
			7	3			1	5
9				8				
			6	2	5			

				2				
9			6		1		4	3
		6		7	5			
2	4		8	5				1
3	1	5			6			
		8					5	2
5	9		7			2	1	4
		4		9		3		
1	6	2	5			7	8	

Puzzle 99:

			1					
						2	5	
					4	7		
	8						2	9
				1	6			4
	6	4						
9			5	6				
5		1		9	7		8	
3	7		2				9	

Puzzle 100:

			8		5	6		
			4		3			8
		9				1		
			9			6		1
		2	1	5			4	
				2		7		
8	9							6
5						4		
		3	2					

9	8					2		7
		3			9		6	
			2				8	9
5		7			3			6
	9	8	4		6			
		2	9		7		4	1
	7	9	1					3
	5			9				2
3	2	6		7		1		8

				3		1	4	
	1	4				6	5	
		3		1			2	7
3			4	5			6	
	4	9				5		1
			3	9				
		8					9	
5		7		4				6
6				8	3		7	2

103
Light and Easy

		5	3	2	1		8	4
		1	4	5		3		
4					9			
								3
5			2				4	
	4	3		7		2		6
3				8	2	6	1	
	5	6		9	7	4	3	
		7		4			2	

104
Light and Easy

5				6	7			
	4	1	2	9			8	7
9				4				
			8	1	4	3		9
						7	1	
1		3		5				4
		4						1
		7	4	8				6
		5			2	4	3	8

	6		7			4	8	5
		7	9			6	3	
	5	3	8	6				
6							7	4
				5	6			3
8		5	3			1		
				9	4		1	
					7			6
1	9				8	7		2

	7						2	4
	3	6						
	1	4	7			9		
8	4			9		6		
		1	4			8		2
6				1		5		7
			6	2			7	
	6			8	7			
7		5	9			2		1

	1			9				6
9		7	8			1	2	
	3			1	7			
7			6		3			5
2			4					8
		3	9	2		7	6	
		8	2		6			9
	4		7		9		3	
3		9						7

							8	7
	6							3
			9	8			5	
	1		7	5	9		4	
2				1	6			
	9		8		2	5		
	5			6	1			
4		7	2	9				
					4		9	

2		7	1				3	6
			3		6	2		5
6			5					9
			9			7		8
		2	8	6	7		4	
				5		6		
4				1			8	
3				4		9	2	7
	2	8		3	5	1		4

2	1				7			
	8	2	1				3	
9		7					6	1
8		1	4		5			
						5		3
7				8				9
1			2	4				
4		9	3	1	8			2
6		8	5		9			4

111

Light and Easy

	1							4
						1	7	9
2			7		1	8	5	
	8		9		4	2		1
4		3		1			9	
	2			5	3	7		
8					9			
7	6		3			4	1	2
	4	5		6		9		

112

Light and Easy

		3	1		9	8		2
7			6			9		3
				3	2			5
5		4	8			1		
2					1	5		
1		7		9	6	3		
3	7		2	1			6	
	5			6	8			
	1		4	7		2	5	

113
Light and Easy

3			8	4				9
	1				3	2	6	
		8			9	7		
7	4			1			2	
2			3			4		1
5		1		6				
4	3					8		
			5			3	4	6
8	6			3	2			

114
Light and Easy

6						5		
4	5		9				8	3
7			4	5	6			1
			3	1	9	7		6
	3		7					
	7	6			2			
			6	8	3	9		5
		5			4		3	
	4	8						

			5		7	3	1	
	1		9					
			6			4		8
		5			9	2		1
		8				7		6
1	9	7	4			8		5
7	5	3	2	9		1		
	6	1	3				7	
9		2		1	4	6		

						7		5
			2			4		
				8	5		6	
			3			5		
5				9				
4	6		7					2
	4			1			7	9
7	2		6					
	3				4		8	

Light and Easy

		3	2			5	9	4
				3			1	
			9		7		6	
8	7	4					2	6
		2	4					5
		5	7		3			
	9							8
	3			8		7	4	
	4		6		2			9

Light and Easy

	4						5	
3			7		5		4	
		2	9					1
		6	2	7				
7	1							
8					3	9		
					4	5		2
1				3				
2	9		5	6		3	1	

						5	7	1
8				6			2	
5	7		4	1				
		1			7	2		
2	9			3		6		
	8		6		9			5
1	6		2	8		9		
9			3			4		
		2		5	1		6	8

	6					2	9	
		8			6			
2						1		
			8		7	6		
	9		2					3
8		7			9		1	
	3			1				
7	2	6			5			
			3		4	5		

Puzzle 121:

	1	7		2	8	5		
	5		4	9		1	3	6
9		4	1	5		7		8
	7	1	8		2		6	
4		9		1		8		5
8			5	7	9			
7	8	2	9		1			4
	9				4	2		1
1	4	3		8	5			

Puzzle 122:

2			6		1	3		
9	1	3	7					8
						1		9
	3					8	1	
					9	4		
1			3					7
				2				4
4	5			7			6	
	6	8					3	

		2	6	8				
8			2		4			
			7	3			8	1
							9	
5				7			4	6
		6	5		3		2	8
		5		9		4		
	2	1			5			9
		3					1	

4		2	8				5	9
7		6	9	3		4		
9				4	2			
	7	3	2		9		4	
		1		6			3	7
2	6				7			8
3	5							
	4			2		5		1
	2	9		8	4	7		

Puzzle 125:

5			3			2		
	3	4	7					
7				4	1			
						1	6	
							9	8
8		3	6			7		
	5	7				4		
1		6					5	
	9			4			1	6

Puzzle 126:

6		1	9	3				
4	2	5		1				3
3			4	5				
8	6	4		7	9		1	5
2				4	6		9	
9		7			1		2	
	4		1	9				
	8			2				6
		2			5	7		

	8	7		1				
		9						4
3								
			6			4	9	2
	6	4			5			
				2	3			
9					1	5		
							6	
1	4		5		7		8	3

	2			4		7	3	
	6							8
9	5					6	4	
1					3	2		
		8		9			7	4
			8			9	2	
		9	2		5	8	6	3
2		5						

				9	8		7	6
3	8				6	4	5	
			2	4				
		7					3	5
5	6			3			4	2
		3			9	6	1	
	9				3		2	
		5	4		2	7		
			9		7	1		8

8		7	2	9		6		
			3				2	
					4	5	1	
3	1	9	6	7		2		
2			5	4				
	6		9	1	2	7		
1	4	2				9		
				2	6	3	7	
	3		1			9	4	

				1		9		4
			9		4	5	1	3
9	4	1	5			8	6	
	6		8	5	1	3		
	5	2		9	6			1
1		8	3		2		5	
	2		1	3				5
6		5			7	2		9
		9				1	4	8

8	2	6	4	1			7	9
7		5	9	3	8			4
9				2				1
1			7	8	6	9		
6		7						
			1				2	
2		8				1		
	4						3	7
				6		4		

133
Light and Easy

8	9			6				3
6	5			2	7		4	
1			4				5	
3	1					4		9
		2		1		5	8	
4							1	6
2				7	8		3	
			6	4	3			
			2		1			4

134
Light and Easy

		9			2		4	
	2	7					6	
6	8	1			4	2	3	
7	1		8	3	6	9		
	4			2	5	3		
	6			4	7			
	9	4	6			7	5	
8		3					9	2
	7					4	8	

135
Light and Easy

				6		2		3
			4					8
	4	2	9		8			
		8	5			1	6	7
5				1	4			
	1			7				
3		5						
	9	1	3					4
8		4			9	6		2

136
Light and Easy

	5		4				8	
8					6			
	1		7	8				6
			8		5	9	6	2
6								
5		8			3	7		
1						6		9
2		4		3		8		
		3		1	7			

137
Light and Easy

		9	1	3				
6				9			5	
		8			2		4	
		5		2		9		
		7						
3	6	4					7	5
					1			
			2	5	7		8	
	1		3		4			6

138
Light and Easy

		9			4			
	6	1			7	4	8	
	3		2				7	
	4			1	5	7		3
	5						4	6
		6	5			8		
7					2		3	9
		3	9	8		6		

4		7						6
	8	1						
							9	
2			7			1	6	
9				8		2		
8			1		4			
7	4	5		6	3			
6					5	9		
	3				2			

	3		7	4				
				6				7
	6		8		9	1	3	5
7	5	1		3		2		6
6	4		5	7		9	1	
		3		1				
	9	2	4					
8	1					3	5	
				8			9	

Puzzle 141:

		2	9					
6	7	9			8		4	
					1			3
9		5				3		2
	2							7
				3			6	4
7	5						8	
8								
				6		5		

Puzzle 142:

	8	4	5					
	7			4		8		
9	1						4	2
7		6	9	1		3	8	
	4	3					7	
	9		7		3	2	6	4
	3	1		2		7		6
4	6			3		5		
					9		1	

143
Light and Easy

5		1		6		2		4
	4	7	3					
	6	3	1		4			7
7		6	4	5			2	9
			7		6	4		
4		8		9	3		7	6
8	7							3
6				7				
	2	4	6	3	9	7	5	

144
Light and Easy

2	1		3				4	6
	8		9					1
5		6				8		
3			6		9		7	
8	6							
		1				6		5
	2		1				8	
		4		7			6	3
7	9	8	4	6			1	2

							3	
9	8		6	7				
		3				7	2	
	3				9			
	1			5				
						5	7	4
8			7					
3	6		8	2				
		7		1	5	4		

	5		3			1		6
	6		2		9	8	4	
						9		
6		7			5			
	4			3	2	6		7
9			1					4
		6	7		1	3		2
8	1	3					6	
				6			1	8

						1	7	8
	8	1			2	6		3
	5		8		3			
				6		5	4	
			2					1
9		4						7
2				4	8			
								2
	9				7			5

6	5	4	1				9	
	2						1	6
		8	3	2				
		7		3	9			
	6		2			3	4	8
	4	1		6	8	9		
9			7			6		
8	1			9			7	2
4	7	6		5				

8	6	1	5	2	3			
		2	4					
				9	8			
2	8				9	7		
				7		2		
7	5		6			3		
			2	3	7	9		4
					5	1		2
	2		8	6		5		3

2		8			4			3
	7			9			4	2
	1						8	
7	6	5	4	3				
		3		5			7	6
					9		3	
6	2	4	5		7			9
	9		6	1	3	2		4
						8		

	1	2					9	8
	5			9	7	6		
9	6				8		5	4
	7	1		8			6	3
		9					4	7
4			7	3	6			9
5							3	
	2	6		1		4		
	4	7						

5		7		3	8	2		6
				4	7		8	
	3	2			9	1		
3	7			1			2	9
4				5				
		5					1	
	8			9	5	7	3	
	6			2		8		
		4		8	1		6	

		3						
6						8		
1								2
			7					9
3		4		5	8			1
		2	1		3			4
	8	5	4					
						6	7	
				9	7	4		8

5	3			2		7		
			8		5	4	3	1
				9				2
4		7				2		
	5	3			4	6		
	8		3	7	9			4
7			5					
							7	
	6			1				

	4					6		
7		3		1				
9		1		8			2	
			7	3				2
4	8	2		6	9	5		
			5		2			6
				9	1		3	5
	3	5						8
8		4		5		7	6	

2				3		1		
	9	5						
		4		7	6	9	5	8
				1		6	8	9
4				9				7
		2			5		1	
			8	2				3
		3		4	7		9	5

9		2			7	8		
	8		4		2	9		7
	7			5				
7		1	3		9		8	4
3	4		7	2		1		9
5							7	
8		7	5		6			1
	5	4			3	6		
	6		2			7		

5				7			9	4
4	2		5		1			3
	1	9	3		4		5	2
	5		1				4	9
	4	1	8					5
8		2	4	5	9			
	6	8						
7		4	2	1				
		5		6	8		3	

5	6				4			3
	3	1	9			8		
	7	2			8	6	5	4
		9			2			8
6	2				9	1	3	
	5	4		3	1	2		
		5	8	9	6	3	2	
2	8							9
			2					

			8			7	1	
	1			2				
			3	9				4
			1	5				
					9		5	
	8	6		3			7	
			9		2	8		
	9					3		
1	5					4		

2		8					1	
	9	3	5		4	8		2
	4	5	8	2			7	3
6			3		9			8
8	5	1					2	
4	3			8			5	
3	8			7				5
		2	9					
9			2			7		

6							3	
9	3	5				6		
	1						5	4
			8	3				
	8	1	7					3
		6			9			2
	2			7			9	6
	5				1		7	
7			3			4	2	

163
Light and Easy

		1						
	4	2		3		1		
	3	8	2					6
		9		5	7			
8								5
	7				9			
						8		
			1		6	7		9
	6	7	9		8		2	

164
Light and Easy

5	3	9	7	4	6	2		
			8			5	4	
8	7			5		9	3	
		8					9	2
						7	1	
			4		7	8	5	3
9	6	1	3	7				
	2	7						5
	8		1					9

Puzzle 165:

8	9	6		1	2	3		
			4			8		
7	4	3	8					6
3		4	2		9		1	
9	1			4		5		
6	5			8			3	
		7					8	
					8	2		
	8		6	3				9

Puzzle 166:

			9				6	
			7		5		9	8
		5						3
		7			8	2		
9	4		6					
			3				7	6
5			8	4				
4	3						2	9
			1			4		

9		6		3				
2			1	8	9		5	
	1		5	2				
		9		6		8		
						5		
8		1	9		2			6
6			2	7		1	8	
4	7	2					3	
			3	9			6	2

		1			4			
			9				3	
9			1	2				
1	5		7			2		
				4		8		
4			2		6			3
	9				3			4
			8		9			2
	8	7		5				6

Puzzle 169

	3	1	2	5		4	7	
	5		8				6	9
	2			6				
	4	8	9	7	6	1		
	6		5		8			3
		5	3		4		8	
				4	2		9	
2	1			9		8		4
4	9	6		8	5			

Puzzle 170

			8				7	
	6	8		7		9	5	
	4					6		
4				6				
			9		2			
	5		4					3
		3				8		7
2			1		8		4	9
			2					

1			4		6			
3		5						4
		2		7		1		
		3						
9				8			1	6
	8		9	3	1	7		
		6						
			2					
4	3		7			8		

2						6	5	
		7		1				
				3	6	9	8	
3		6		2	7	1		
	7					5		
					1			
	4	2		8				5
5	6			4	9			
		8	1				3	

				7		3		
	7	4	5		3			6
					2	5		
				5	4			
7	6						9	
2							1	
	3			9		8		
			2		1			
			6	8	5	1		4

7			2	9				5
9		8	1					4
5	4	1		6				7
	1	7		4	2	5	3	
				8			4	9
		4			3		7	
	7			2				
				1		6	8	
6					9	7		1

175

Light and Easy

							9	
	7		2	5				
6		3			9	2		7
	8	7	9				4	
9		2	1			7		
5					6		3	
			4					
			6		1			8
8				7				

176

Light and Easy

3						6	2	
							5	8
	8	6					4	
			4	3			9	
		3	1	6	9	4		
		2			8		1	
	2				4			5
4		5	8	2				
6				5	7			

	3			8	7		9	
			3		6	7		1
	6			9			2	8
			2	3		8		9
8						2	4	
	2				8		1	
	1	5			2			
		9				1	8	2
		7			9	6	3	

			6		7		3	
				4	3	8		
	3		5			2	6	
7			9	3			1	
	1				2			8
6	5	2	8		1			
		7	3					
5	4							3
		3	2	1			7	

179
Light and Easy

180
Light and Easy

181
Light and Easy

			8	4	5		2	
3	4							
		6					4	
6	8	3				5	7	2
	9				3		1	
							3	6
	2			8	6	1	5	7
		1	7		4			9
5		7	2		9			

182
Light and Easy

9				4			7	
1	6	4	2				8	
					6		9	
4					2			9
7				8			1	4
	1			7	9	2	5	
2	7					8		
					8	3		
3	8			6	4			

2		5	6	3	9		8	
		8			7			3
	4			1	5			9
	7	1				6		
5	2	9		6	4	7		8
	3		7	2		1	9	
9								
7		4	9	8				1
1				7	2			

	3	6			7			
		1		4	2	7		
		8	5				2	
		7		3		2		
	2	9	8				3	4
	5		6			8		
9			4		3		6	8
	6			1		4	5	
4		5	2	6		9		3

185
Light and Easy

2	1	6	7		9		5	
7	5			4				
			4	2			9	7
4		7	5	9		6	3	
6	9	5				4	1	2
		4		1	8			5
		1					7	
9			6					

186
Light and Easy

	3				1	4		
	2				3	6		
	1	9	6					
	7	3		6			5	4
1			2				9	
		4	8				2	6
		6		1	2	3	7	8
					4			5
			5		6			1

187

Light and Easy

	1			5	6			3
	2				8		9	
	3	8	2	9			5	
	9			8			7	
6	8	2	4					9
1								
9	6	1		3			2	5
			1			9		7
					5		3	

188

Light and Easy

	3	8			1		9	2
		4			8	1		
		2			9	8	5	
6	8		7		3	5	2	
		3		6	5	7	8	
	7	5		9				
			9			2		5
1		7		5		9	4	
		9					1	7

189

Light and Easy

8			5		6	7	9	
			8					
	2	9				3		5
							3	
9								1
		7	9	6				8
3	1				2	7		
				1	4			
2	4	8						

190

Light and Easy

9			4					5
	7		9	8				2
3					6	7		
	8		1		4			
6			8					3
5				7				3
	5				9		3	
	3		7			2		1
4		1					5	

191
Light and Easy

2				1				
4				3		2		6
	6	3				8	1	7
7	5		4		1		3	
1					5			
	2					1		8
8		6	3	4			2	
	4					6		
3		2	8					9

192
Light and Easy

5	8		7		4		6	
3	7	6					4	8
9	1		6				7	2
8		7			6		9	
6	9	1		3	2	7		
	5	3	9		8		1	6
						8	5	
		8		7			3	4

Puzzle 193:

			1		8			5
5		6		4	7			
		8	5				4	
			4			8	1	9
				5		7		
	7				2	5		
		9				6	3	
2	3			1	4			
	6		9					

Puzzle 194:

		6	7	5				
7						3		9
		8			6	2		
							4	1
1	5	3			4			
	4	2			8	5		6
			9	4	7		5	
			5			6		
	2							

		7		2	3			6
			1	4	8	9	3	
	3		5					2
2	8				9	3	6	
	7			3				1
			4		2	7	5	
7	4			5			2	3
8	2	6					4	5
1	5		2		4		7	

9								5
		1		2	3		7	
	2						3	4
	6		9	8				
		2					4	
	5	8	4					6
			6	9				2
2				4		1		
5		6		7			8	9

Puzzle 197:

		2						
					3	8		
5	6		2					9
		4		5	7			
9					6		1	
				8				
	3		7			1		4
	7				1	3		
6	1		4			7	2	5

Puzzle 198:

				8		3		
	3		4		5		2	
6	9	1					5	4
4				8				
8	1					6	3	
			5	7		4		
			7	4		1		
		7	6					
				1	3		6	5

199
Light and Easy

9			7		1			
4							1	
				6	8			9
	6	3	9				5	
							7	4
1		7			5		3	2
			2		6			3
	5	1			7			
		9	1		3			

200
Light and Easy

			4	6				
	2							6
		8		7	9	1		
3						8		2
7	9			4				
	4					6		
	8	9				4		3
6						3		9
		4				6	2	5

		5		4				6
					9		3	7
4			8	6	3		9	5
6	7		4					9
	8	2		5			6	
				3				
	5	9			1			
7	6						5	2

								2
			6	2	7	4		
			1	8				
6	9	4	8			7	5	
3								
	1	8	5				3	
4			9	5		8		
	6		7					
1	8	5			6		9	

		1				8		
	3		5	9		2		
				2				7
9				6		5		1
			7		2		9	
1				4				
7	8		3					6
4		9	8	7		3		

6			3		1		5	8
				9		1	6	
				5		4		7
9	4		1		5		7	2
7	6			2		5		1
2			8	3				
		7	5		6		8	
5	3	6			9	7		
	8		7	4	3			

205
Light and Easy

6	7			1			3	
3					7	6	5	9
9	8				4	7		2
	9	6					7	
8		7		9	6	1		3
		3			2			
			4			5	2	
	6	4	8			3		
5			7					1

206
Light and Easy

1		2	4	5		3		8
						1		
				3		2		
	1		6		5		3	
	6	8	9		3		1	
		7	8			9		2
		4		9		5	8	
		5			4			7

207
Light and Easy

				3	5			
9	6					2		
3					2	8	4	
			8			5		4
	7							6
				7			9	
7	5			4		6	1	9
	9		7		1		8	
	8	1		6	9	7		5

208
Light and Easy

6			7					5
5	7				3	2		
	2		5	9	8			3
1		2	8			9		7
				5	1			
			9				3	
	4	5		2				
9		3	6	4		5		
		6			5			9

209 — Light and Easy

	4	8			3	5		
9				6				
6		5		1	8		2	
			6	4	5	3	9	8
		3	9			1	4	
	5		8					6
			7	8				
5					4	6	8	
						9	1	7

210 — Light and Easy

		1	3			2		9
		4	9	5	8	1	7	3
		9		4			5	
6	9	3	5			4		2
1	8	7	4			6	9	
		2		6				
	1		8					
9	3	8	6					7
						9		

211
Light and Easy

	6		3	1		2		
2				4	5			
3	9							
6	3			9	4			
1	5	8				9		
	2		1			8	7	3
					3	7		2
	8		2				5	6
	4		5			3	8	

212
Light and Easy

6		5	2				7	
	4					2	8	1
				1	4			
	9	8						
		3		5			6	
7	5			8	9	1		
	6						3	
	7	2	1	6				9
			8		7	5	1	

Puzzle 213:

						4		
	7		3		8	1		
6				9	2	8		
		1			6			
		3						2
5			9					
	2		1					3
	3	5	8		4		6	
1				2			4	

Puzzle 214:

	8	6			9		7	4
			7	6				
			4	8	3	5		
		8			5	6		1
2		9					5	
7							8	3
6				4	7			2
	7			9		1	6	
3	5						4	8

			4	7	8		1	9
7	9		2				3	8
8			7			9		
9			6			7		2
5		2	8					3
	8			5		3		7
2		3	9			1		
	5	7		4				

	9					8		5
1	5			8				
2		4			9			3
	3				1		9	2
4	7		9	3				
6		9	5					4
			8		2	9		
	2	8		4		5		1
7							3	8

7	6		5	3		9		1
		9	4	2		7	8	6
8					9			
			3	5	4	2		
				9	7			8
9			8	1		6	3	
	3				6			7
			1			8		
1	2							5

	7	4						6
1				2			5	
		9				1	2	
9				8		5	6	
	4			6	5			2
		1		9	7	8		
8	9			4	6	2		
	3	2		5	9	4	7	1
					2			

219
Light and Easy

			4	5			7	
		4		3	2		1	
5	2				1		9	3
7				6		2		5
8				7	4		3	
	9	7		4				
	3		1					6
2			3					7

220
Light and Easy

								6
		1	6		9			5
			8	7	2			
4		7						
5							7	
8	3	6	2			4	9	
7		4	5					2
				1	6	9	3	
	6					8		4

7		9	8		6	2		1
1			5	9	4			
		3		2	1	9	8	
5	2	1					9	4
6	4		9					
							2	8
	9		4			5	3	2
	7				9			6
				5			7	9

			4	3			9	
4				7	8	5		
			6	5		7		
	3			6		8		1
2		5	7		9			
	4	6			5			9
5		4			3		8	
	6	1		9	7		4	
3								

3		6	2			8	9	
		7	1					2
	4	2	5					7
	1		8		5			4
7		5	6					
4				2	1		8	
9		1	4	5	8			
							3	
	2	8						5

2	4						1	
					4	9	2	
	7			9		8		
					3	2		
9							5	1
				8		6	7	
		6	1					
4			8		2			
	3			5	9			6

		1				6	5	
3				6				8
8	6				9			
					1		2	
1		9	5	2		3		
			7		6			4
4		6		7			1	
		7	6		5	4	8	2
			4		3		7	6

1	9			2				
7	8			6	1		5	
9	4				2			5
3	1		4		7		6	
			5				9	7
4		9			6			8
8				4			3	
6	2		1		8		4	

227
Light and Easy

			1	8			3	9
2	7							
							1	
9	1			5				2
			8					
	5			4	3		9	
7						1		6
		4						5
6	9							8

228
Light and Easy

	2							
	1				7	3		9
4	3			2				6
	6						7	
		3	7	4	9			
			1		6	5		
	4	2	3		5	6		
			6			7	8	
			1	4				

229 Light and Easy

						1		
6					4		2	5
4		7	3		5		8	
		1		3		4		
2				5	9			
3		4	7				6	2
7	8			4		5		
	4		5	7		2		6
5	9			6			7	4

230 Light and Easy

		4	8		7	1	6	
		9		6		7		
		6	5			4		
				7	5			
8	6		1		2			
2	4				8		5	
		8					4	
4			2	7	3	6	5	
	1		2				7	

							8	
6				1				
5	3	7	6	4			1	2
				2	5			
8	9	5						
7							6	
					1	6	9	
	7				4	5		8
	5		9			7	1	

4	8		2	5		7		
	6	9	4		3			
	5			8	7	9		3
		8	1					2
		6		3				
9			5	4			3	
					1			
	9		3	6		1	7	4
			7			3	2	

				7			3	
		8				7		
7	6					4	2	8
2			1		7			
8		1	6			2		
	9	4		3	8		1	
	8		3	6	5	1	7	2
					9			
5			7	8				

3				2		4		6
			4				8	1
					6			9
								5
	8		7	6				
9		2		1	4	8		
	5							7
7	2		6			5	9	3
4		3			9			8

7								
8		6		7	3			1
	9	1	4	2		7		
	4			9		3		8
			5	3	4	6		
2				8		1		9
	7			6				4
			1		9	2		7
9					7	8	6	

			9			2	1	3
2		7			1			
	3	4		5				7
9	4	5	8					2
				3	9	4		
6		3				1		
		9	6		3	5	8	
	5					3		4
						9	2	

	9			1	2	4		3
1	2	3		8			6	
5		8	3	9			1	
3		4	9		5			
		2	1	4				
		5			8	6		7
	3						9	4
	8			5		2	3	
			6			1		8

			6		7	2		9
2					8	1	6	
	3	4		2	9		7	
		6	5		2			3
	8	5	4	9	6			
9	4	2			3		8	6
4	9							
8		1		3		9		
		3					1	

239
Light and Easy

	7	1		8			4	
	4	3			9	1		
	9						5	
		7	8			3		
		9		3	1	2		
3			4					2
	8		2	6				
	5				7			

240
Light and Easy

		7						
				2			4	
2		5				9	7	3
				3		1	5	
	1	6			2	8		
			7		6			
1	9							
6	5	2					3	
		8	5					2

241

			3				5	4
	1			5		6	2	8
2					8			1
	6							
4			1				8	3
	2	9		8	3		7	6
5		2	6		7			
8			2	1				7
						3	6	

242

2			9	1		8		
					3	4	1	2
1	6		2	8	7		5	
				2		6	3	4
7					6			1
6			8		1	7		9
4	8			7		3		
5					8		4	
	2		6		5	1	9	

4		8				7	9	
5	7			1		6		
				2		3		5
2				3		4		6
	3		5				1	2
8	1		7	6		5	3	
9			2	4	5			
		2		7	6		4	
		1	3			2		7

4		3	2	7		8		
5					9			3
	8	9		6		1		5
	5			4		2		
		1		5	3		8	
			6		2			
	3		9				4	
1			2	4		6		
7			4	5	2		3	

	4			7			8	
3					6			4
9			1	5	4			6
		9	5			6		8
7	2		6	3	8		4	
	6	4		9				3
2	9	3						
	1		2		7		5	
5	8		3		9		1	

	2							1
	9	7		8				2
1							7	
	7	6			9	3		8
5			3					
3	1				2		4	
	8		9	5	7			
9	5						8	
7			4	6				

4		8		7		1		
6	3			5				
5		1	8			6		
1					4		3	7
				1			8	
	8	4	7		3			6
9			5	3	8	4		
	4	5		6	7	3	2	
	1			2		8	7	

				2	9		6	
2			8	3		7		
	4		6			8	1	
7	2							6
8				6				
		6	7				3	
			1					
	8		5	9	6	2		1
4					3	6		8

249

1	2					7		
		8				9		
4						6	5	3
	1	4		2				
6		2	3		9			4
9					1		7	
		7			2			
	5			3				6

250

	5		8					
				9	6	7	1	4
		4	7	1				
6	4				3			7
		5						3
7		3		8				9
5	1		2		7			
							6	
		2						

7	3					6		
	2		4			8		
	8			3	6	2	5	9
	7				2		3	
	6			5		4		
		1					2	
		7	6		9	1		
9								
		8		4	5			

5	7	8	9	2			1	3
3				1				7
9				3		4		8
		9	5	4		8	7	
				9		3		
4					1	2		9
2	6	5	1					4
				5			8	
	8	3		6		7		

253

	3	1			9			
5		7				8		
		2		7	3	5	6	
1	6			8			7	
				1				6
7	2	9				1	8	
	1				5	6	4	3
		5			6		1	
3	9	6		4			5	2

254

					5	1		4
		4			6	8	9	2
	9	3						
				5				
		9	8	3	4			
	5	7	6			9		
1			7			2		8
		8			1			5

						3		
				7				4
1		5			9			
2		3	5	8		7		
						8		5
4				9	1		3	
	6	9			5			2
		2		1				
	1		3			9		

7			9			3		
9		8					5	2
		1	7	2	5	8		
3			1	9		2		
8								
	4				6		3	
	9					4	7	
	8		4	1	7		6	
6					9			1

	6	3						8
4	8						5	3
7	1		3	9		4	6	
3					7	5	2	
				3	5	7		1
					4		3	9
2	4	6			9	3		
	7			4				
						6		

	2				9	3		
9			8	3	7		5	
	3	8			4	7		6
			9	5		2	6	7
		3			2		8	
2			4					
3		6	7	9		5		
	1	9		6			7	3
	5				8		1	

259
Light and Easy

	7	5				2	4	
4		1	7		6	5	3	
		8		4				9
	9	3	1	6			8	7
					7			5
	8				4	9	6	
7		4		3	8	6		
	6	9	4	2			5	3
3						8		

260
Light and Easy

	9	2		5	7			
	8			1				
				9	6	7		
			9				3	2
	4		6	8	1			
9	6					4		
1						5		
	3				2		4	
		7						

	8	7		5		9	4	2
		4						
	6	3		9		7	8	
		6			1			
4			5					
	3	8		7	2	1		
6							9	4
		2		4		5		6
		9	2	6	5		7	1

	5	1	6				4	9
6	3			7	1			
2		7				6	3	
					5	8	7	
				8				
3	8		7	4	2			5
7	1				6			8
						9	5	6
5		8		9	4		1	

263
Light and Easy

	8		6		1			
	7	1	5	9				8
	2				4	5	1	3
		8			9	4	6	
	1	3		6				5
	6	7		4		3	8	
7		6	1	2			5	9
			9			7	2	
		2		5		1		

264
Light and Easy

1						7		
5		2	4		7		6	
8			2		1			
	1	8	5		2		7	
2						4	1	
4	3		8			5		
		1						
9		4		3	6			
	8		1					

Puzzle 265:

			7	6				
					8	6	7	1
7		9	2	1			5	
2		8	1	7				9
			8		9			5
9		1		5		7		6
4			5					
3	8	5	6				4	2
1		2			4			7

Puzzle 266:

	7					1		
4		1				3		
2	3	5			1	7	9	
		7	9					
			1	7			2	8
	5			8	2			3
				6		2	1	7
							3	
	1	2	3		4			

267
Light and Easy

				2	5		9	
5					8	2		
9			7					8
3		7						
	8	6		9	7	3		1
			1	6				2
				7	1	9		
				5				
	3			8	6		2	7

268
Light and Easy

	6		2	7				
	7						6	
								5
3							1	
			1		9			
		1		8	5	2		3
2	1							
	8	5	6					2
					8	4	3	

Puzzle 269:

	8	2	3			4		5
			6			9		7
3								8
			7		6			
4	7	1	5					2
	3	6				5		9
		7	8			3	9	
				5		8		
1			2		3			

Puzzle 270:

						4	5	2
		4	5		3		7	
9								
	8	3		1		2		
6			7					
		7			2		8	
4	6	8	1	7		5		
								8
	3	1		8			4	6

271
Light and Easy

6		3	7	5		4		
	9				6		5	
	5	4	3			8		1
	3	2			5	6		8
	7		2					
8			6				9	2
	4	7	5	3			8	6
			9	6	7	5		
5		9	8			2		

272
Light and Easy

			5					
								8
	8			2				3
8	4			5			2	
	5		1	4				
	9	2				6		
					5		8	7
7		4		3	8			5
			7	6			9	

2					6	1	5	
			9	2				
						6		9
5				4				
	7	1		8				
3		8		7	9	2		5
	6	5						1
	9	7	1			5	8	
			8				9	

		7			4		8	6
9			6		5	4		
				2	1	9		3
7							6	
	8				6	7	5	1
	1			4			9	
8		2	3	6		1	4	7
6		9	7			8		5
			4	5				

8			3					2
		2				5		
3		4	2	5		7		
	7	3						1
	2		1	6	3			
9		6	4	7	2		3	
				3	1	2	7	4
2				8	4		5	
			5	2	6			8

				4				2
	8			9		6		3
			3		6	9	8	
							1	2
1				8			7	6
		3			1			
	4		7	6			3	
		1			9			
		6			5	7		4

277
Light and Easy

				9	8	7		
	2				3			1
1				2	7	6		
5	1	6				2		8
				5				
4			9			1	3	
			7					
2						8		6
	3	4				9		

278
Light and Easy

		9	3	7			6	
8			9			1		
							9	4
3			2	5			1	8
		5		4				
7			8	1	9		4	
6	5		1					
	2	7	5			6		

		3	8		9	1	5	
2				1	6	7	9	
						3		
	4		5					
				3		8	1	
7			9			5	6	4
5					2			
							8	
			6					9

8	1		3	5			4	9
7	9		8			1		
			1			5		
				4		8	2	7
9	8						1	
	7	9			6			
1	3			2		7	6	
4					3	9		

		5		6	8			
			5	7	4		6	
		6		3	9	8		
	6			5	2	4	7	
			4	1			2	3
	5			9			1	8
	1	3		2		7		6
	7		6			9	3	
6	9				3	1	5	2

				9			4	2
5		9			4	1		7
				5				
	2		3		1	9		
	7		4	8	2		3	
		6				8		
4	5	2		1		7		
	1	8		2	6			
	9		8				1	

283

Light and Easy

3						6	8	7
			6	8	9	5		4
					7	9		
	4		9			8	6	3
8	2	9	3			7	1	
	3		1					9
	7			6	3			
1	5	6	2					
2							9	6

284

Light and Easy

3								8
		8					6	
7					9	5		3
					2		3	6
		9			4			
2	6							1
6		4			3	8		2
		1		8				9
			1			4		

285
Light and Easy

8	4		3	6				1
6	3							5
7	1		2					4
					4	8	1	
					9			3
	8			5				
5			9	4	7	3	6	
3	9		5		6			
	7			1		9		

286
Light and Easy

8		4	9		1	5		
	9			4		6	8	
				3				
	2	1	3		9		6	
7	3			2		4		
		8		7	4		9	
	4		6			8		7
		7		9	2			
6					5	3		

287
Light and Easy

1	3		8		2	7		4
7		9						
		5	6					1
			9	2	4	8		
		2		7			6	
8	7		5			2		
				5	9			
4			2		3	5		
3			4		1			8

288
Light and Easy

		8				6		
	6		7					3
	3				6			
8			2	4				7
		3				8		5
	1	6			5		4	
		2		9	1			
		4		3	7			6
	9			2				

289
Light and Easy

9	8	4	1			7		
2	7		4					
6	5						8	4
		5		2		9	4	
1	9	8	5			3	7	2
7				1	9			
		9	7					8
		6				4	9	7
				9	8	2	1	

290
Light and Easy

9			3		8	1	7	
			5					
7	5			4	1			6
		8			2			
2	6			1	5	9		3
1		9	8	3			2	4
			9					1
		7				2	3	9
					3		6	

291
Light and Easy

9	2		5				1	
			1	3	9	2		
1	5	3	6		4		9	
3			8			9	2	
8		2			6			7
5	6			4				
7								4
	3	6			5	8		9
						1	3	2

292
Light and Easy

9			6	5	8			
	1	2	7	9				
		8		3				
1	4		5		9			
2			4	7		6		5
	3				2	9	7	4
8	2		3		7	1		9
3		4		8		7		
	5					8		

293
Light and Easy

```
. 3 . | . . . | . . .
. 2 4 | . 3 9 | 5 . .
. 7 1 | . . 8 | 3 . .
------+-------+------
7 4 6 | . . . | 1 . .
3 . . | . 2 . | . . .
. 5 . | 7 . . | . 8 6
------+-------+------
. 1 . | . . . | . 9 7
. . . | . 6 . | . . .
. 6 . | . 1 . | 4 . 2
```

294
Light and Easy

```
2 . 3 | 5 . . | . . .
. . . | . 4 . | . 3 9
. 8 . | . . . | . . 5
------+-------+------
. . . | . . 6 | 5 . 8
. . . | 7 3 9 | . . .
1 9 . | . 8 . | . . .
------+-------+------
8 . . | 9 . . | . 7 6
6 . . | . 1 . | . . 4
4 7 9 | . . 8 | . . .
```

295
Light and Easy

					3		7	8
	3	7		9			6	
	9		1					
				4		8		5
3					8		4	1
			2					
5								
	6		4				5	9
			8			3		6

296
Light and Easy

9			6			5	3	
							4	2
4	3		1		7		6	
	9	6				2	7	
						8		
2	1				6			9
		3			8	7		
			3	4	2	6		5
5	2		7				9	

	4						3	
	1				3	8		4
3								
6		7	1	5				
			6				9	
1			9	4	2			
	8		2	9				
4		6		8			2	9
	2							

3	6						8	
		1			7		6	
8		9			6		5	
		3			9	5		
9			8	3		7	1	6
4		6	7		5	3		8
2	5	4					3	
		8	9	5		1	7	
	9			6			2	

299

Light and Easy

4			7	2	3	6	5	
7	6	5	8					
	8			4				
1	4	2				9		
	7					5		3
			7	4		1	2	6
3				1		2		
	2					9		1
8	9				7			

300

Light and Easy

					6			5
	5		8	2		1		
							9	8
				6		4		
	6	2	3	4	8	5		1
	3	7	9			8		
1			2	9		3		
6		3			7	2	5	
5			6					7

Puzzle 301:

			7	2		3	4	5
	4		6	5			8	
7					8			6
	3		9					
		5	1				9	7
					5	8	3	
2	9		3		1			
		8			2			
			8	9			7	

Puzzle 302:

				4			9	8
	6		5	8	1		2	
4	2			9				1
5		6		2		7		
8				3			4	6
			9		8			
	7				9			5
1			4			9		7
		4	3					2

303
Light and Easy

4				9		7		3
7	6			5				
3		1	2		7			6
					6			
	7		4					2
		5	7	1	8	4		9
				6	5		7	8
	1							
	2	8	9	7			1	4

304
Light and Easy

7					2		5	1
1	3			7	8	2		
		4				9		
2		7	5					9
	1	8	2		6			
		9			7	5	2	6
		1			4	3		2
	5		7		9			
6							9	5

305

Light and Easy

	8					3		
	9		2			4		
			4			1	7	
8	7		1			9	3	
4	5	1		7				6
				4	2			
3	4	9			5			
			3		4			5
		5	6		9	2	4	

306

Light and Easy

	9		8		6		5	
8	3			2	7			
1		4		9				
		8	5		9			
					4	5	9	
7		9	2		8		4	3
	8	1	9			7		6
9		3				8		5
		6	7		1	9		4

307
Light and Easy

	7	2			9			6
1				6			7	2
	4		2			3	5	
3	8	7		9	4			1
	2	5	8					
		1			2		8	3
				2			9	8
9				7	8	2	6	
2		8	9			7		

308
Light and Easy

4	3			7		1		
1		6		8				
				1		3		9
	9		7		2			6
					8	5	7	
	7	1			3			
	4					7		8
		3					9	1
						2	3	

309
Light and Easy

6		9				3	7	
		1	8	4		9		
3	4				6		5	
7	1		3	5	2	6		
			4	6	8	7		
		5		7		8	2	3
1	3	4						6
				1	9			7
2	9		6	3		5		

310
Light and Easy

2								
4	6	1				2	5	7
			5	4				6
8		2	4	6	1			
6	9				7	8	4	
1	4	5	3	9				2
9	8						1	3
				1		9	7	8
3	1		9		5			4

311
Light and Easy

		8				5		
				7	8			1
					3			4
4							3	
2			5				1	
		7	6					2
8		6	2		9		7	
5		4		6			8	
		9		1		6		

312
Light and Easy

		8					3	
	6		4				5	
9	2	7			1	4		
			2			6		8
	9				4	3		
	8	1	7	3				5
	7		9			1	2	
6							9	3
8			1			5	6	

313
Light and Easy

			9			8		
			5		6			9
8				3			2	1
6		5	8					
		3			5	4		
	8		4			5	7	2
	7				1			
4							6	
	3							5

314
Light and Easy

5		9		1				
	4	6			7	2	9	
								5
	6		9		1		2	
		2	8	6				7
7							4	
6	7				8	1	5	
					2	7		6
2				3				4

8			1	6		5		
		5	8			7		6
	6	3			5			4
3	8						5	
4			9		1	3	7	2
9			5					1
						9		
7		8	6					
6	2	9			7		1	8

	4			3		5	2	6
2					5			
			1				3	
	9		2	8			7	
		7					1	2
	5						9	3
4				7	6			
			9	4		3		
		9		1	8		5	

317 — Light and Easy

			3	8	1	4		
				5			6	
			4	2		5	3	1
							8	6
6	2		8			1		
3	7		1	6				4
7					2		1	5
					7	6	2	
	5		9		8	7		

318 — Light and Easy

				1	3		8	
	3	5				6		
8	2		9			1		
7	5	4	1			3		6
3		9	5				7	
		8				9	1	
	8		7			2	3	
		3	4	2	1			
6	4		8	3				

319
Light and Easy

				7		6	5	
		2	6					4
1				9			3	8
		4	9		5			
9	6	8	7					
							4	
	5	7					2	
				8		7		
6				5		1	8	

320
Light and Easy

	1		3		7			
					6	4	1	8
		8		4	1			
3		1	4			6		2
	2	6	1	5	8			
		4				1		5
7					4	5	2	
2				9				1
	4		8	3	2	7		9

		2		4	6		5	
4	7			9				
	1		3	2				
	3				9			5
8				5		4		7
	5	9	2	1		8		6
			4	6		3	7	
2	4		9					
3			5		2	1		

								2
	1		3		4		9	
6	8					4		5
		5		2				6
					6		4	7
3	4				7		5	
	6						8	4
1		7			2	5		
	5	8	6		3	7		1

							2	
9					7	4		
		4	5	2			6	7
	8	6	9			3		2
		7		4	8			6
2			3					4
6	4		7		2	5		
	2	5		1	3	6	7	
7		3		8	5		4	

4	3			6	9		8	7
6	8		3	2				5
2			8	7				
9	4				3		2	6
1					2			
		8		1			9	
	9			3	8			
			1	9				2
7		4		5				

325 — Light and Easy

7	6	3	1	2	5			
	1		4	9	7		2	3
4		2		3				
9	4		2		3	5		8
		6		8	1	4		
		8		6	4	7		1
1		7		4				
	3							
6	2				5	9	8	

326 — Light and Easy

5		1	8	9			2	
			6		5		3	
		8	3					
6						9		
						5		
4	8	7		2				
	2					7		
8							6	5
		9				8		3

3								9
				4		5		
		2		6		1		
		3	9	2			4	6
			6	5	8			1
	9			7				
	6	4		8			7	5
5							9	
			4		5			2

			5	8				6
			4	6			1	
	8	9		1				
2	4	5		7		1	9	
9				2		4	6	8
1					7	6		5
		2				3		
	9		3	4				

329

4		2					9	8
						1	4	
								3
				9			2	
	9	1		3				6
			1				8	
	3		6		8			
	8		7	9	2			
2		9	3				5	

330

	8		2		1		9	
		7		3		8		
5		9		7		4	2	
9		4	8				7	
7		8		6	2			3
3	1	2	5		7	6		
6	9						3	
			3	2	9		4	
2	4					7		

			4					2
			5	7				3
	3	1				9		
		6						
	2	4	7		6		8	
5			8					
9	4	3					7	
		2						6
	6	7	2		5			

1					2		3	
2	9	8	3			1		
7	4			1			2	8
3		1	4				9	
9		5		2	1	3	4	7
				9	3	6		
6	3	7			9		8	1
8	1					9		3
	2	9		3			6	

333
Light and Easy

					2	7		6
		7					5	
		8		3			4	
7				5		9		
1				4				
9			7		8	3		
	9	5			3	1	8	
				6				2
	4			7				3

334
Light and Easy

		8						
1		2			3		6	
	4		6		8			
	7		2				8	
6		4		5			3	
			8			9		7
						4	2	
	5		4			3		8
		1	3			5	9	

	9							7
3		7			6	9		
				2				3
	6		1		9	4		
9	5							6
2			4			3	7	
							8	5
	8	5		7				
1								

	4		9			7	2	
7	5				8			3
			4				9	
	7	5	6					4
	9	1				8	3	
	1	7	2				6	
	3				9			
	2		3			5	7	

3					4	5		
2				5		6		7
4	7					3	1	
				8	9	7	3	4
	4			7	6			
	8			4	3			1
	6				2		7	5
				1	5		9	
	5	4					8	3

8			3		1			
	9			4				3
				7				
	8				5	3		
	1		4					
4	6		2					
	2	7		6				
5				2				4
		6	7		3	5		1

8		7		6			2	
4		1			7			
					9			
1				9	5	6	3	4
		8	1	3				5
				5		8		
5						2	4	6
9	8						1	

	2			3			9	8
		1			8		2	
	3		2	5	6	1	7	
6						8	1	
4	1		5	8		6		7
	8	2	6		7			
			1			9		
					4	2		
	5			9	3	7	6	

341
Light and Easy

		6			4			9
9						7	5	
	5	3					8	
			8					
	3			7	1		6	
	7	9	2		6	5	4	
	1			4			9	
		7			3			2
3		5		8		4		

342
Light and Easy

4		9	7	5				
	3	5	8					
			6					1
	8				5			
2				4				3
		3		8		7		4
		8						
							2	7
	6	7			2	8	1	

	8		6	9	7			2
		5	4					1
	2					9	4	6
1		4	5		9	2	8	3
							1	
5	7	8		2	1		6	9
3	1	7	2	4		6		
8	4	2	9	1		7		
9			7	8		1	2	

9			4		2	3	6	
	6	2						
3				7			1	2
4		6		8		7	3	5
		7					9	6
								8
	7			6		9	5	3
6		3	7		1	2		4
2		8	5		4			

345

Light and Easy

1		4	7	2		6		3
3				9	6		7	
				3	4	2		
2					8		4	
	1	8			3			
			2	6			8	7
9	4	6	5			7		
		7			9			8
8		1	6		7		5	2

346

Light and Easy

	4	1	2				3	
	2			4	7		9	6
			5	1	3			8
		4	3			6	2	9
	8					4	1	7
	6		4	7				
5				2			7	
			7	3	4		8	
4	7	2					6	

347
Light and Easy

						5		9
		9	7			1	4	
		6	9					
				7	3	8	1	
		8	5	9			6	
	4			2				
	8	4						
		2				9		1
	9	7	2	6		3	8	

348
Light and Easy

				9			4	1
9		4	7		5			
			4		3	2		
8	9		2			3		
3			1	6		9		
7		1	3	5			2	8
	8	7		4			3	9
	2	5						
		9		8	1	7		

349
Light and Easy

3	5	7		1				6
	4							
	8	6			4			9
	3	1	7				8	
					3	5		
				8	1			2
			8	9				
4	6					2		
8	7						6	1

350
Light and Easy

	5			7				4
9		3	5	1	4			
8	4		6		9	3	7	
	3		4					6
4	1	7		6	3	5		9
		2	9		1			
1	6		8	9		7		
					5		9	
	9		1		6	8	5	2

351
Light and Easy

			5				1	
					6		5	4
	3	1		2	4		6	7
1		6			5	8		
		2					4	6
7		3			2			
2			6	9				
					3	1	7	
							8	

352
Light and Easy

	8				1			
	6	4		7			8	2
7				4				
	5	7	3	6				4
	3	8	1		9	5		
4					2	9		
			2					3
						4	9	
		3		9		2		5

Puzzle 353:

	7	1		4			5	9
4				5	1	2	3	
		8		6	2			
3	5					4	2	6
1	4						9	
	6	9	4	2	5	3		
				7	4	5		
					8			2
				1	6	9		

Puzzle 354:

					4		2	7
		2	9		7	8		
		6					1	5
7	3			1	5	4		
5			2		8			3
		1				8		
8			5	2		3		
			4	3				
	1							

355
Light and Easy

5	8	3		7		4		
	1		4	2			7	
				8	6	5		9
	4		6			7		5
	7	2		4	8		9	3
				1	9			4
	9	4	2					
2	5	8			3		4	7
			8					2

356
Light and Easy

4			5		3		9	
5				4			7	6
		9	7			8	5	
	5	6		2	1			
				9				
7		3	8			6	1	
8	9	5		1		4		7
	3	1						2
			9		8			

Light and Easy

	7	5				4	6	9
4	1					3		
2		6		4		8	5	
6			1			9	3	
3				6		2		
5				7				
	8	2						
			2	3	1			6
				5	8			

Light and Easy

		8	1	6				
			7	8		5	9	6
	6			9	2	8	1	7
			2				3	4
8	4			5		6		
4		5	9	2		7		
	8	6		1	4		2	3
					7			

		7	3	5				1
	9	4						
3					8			
9	6	1	8	4			5	
4		2						
					7	9		2
					4		1	7
					1	6		9
			7		5	8		

3	2		9		7		4	
4	5		2			7		9
			3		4		8	
1							2	
	6	7		3	8			
	8		4	2		1		
				9		4	1	8
	3		8	7			9	
		1	5		2		6	

361
Light and Easy

6				7	3			
		7	1					
9			5	2				
				6			1	9
	4				7		5	8
2	9		8					
		2		3			4	
1				4			6	
	5	3		9			8	

362
Light and Easy

	8			6			7	5
		7		3	5			4
3					2			
	5				9			7
9			1	2		5		
						2	3	
6		1					4	
				7			8	3
	2				3			

363
Light and Easy

8			7	4			9	
		5					3	8
	6						1	4
1	9			7	4	3		2
3	4		9	5				
			2	1				
	8	4			2		7	1
5			4	6	7			3
2	7		1	8		4		5

364
Light and Easy

4			8			3	7	6
3	6				7		2	
	7			3	1			
9		3		4	8	5		
	5	8						7
6	4		5		2		9	
	9						3	
		1			6	4		
	8	4	3	5	9	6	1	

Puzzle 365:

1		6			4			7
2							5	
8			6	5		9		
				9				
		8				2	1	
		5	1	2	8			9
		1		6				
3	9	7	8		1			
								3

Puzzle 366:

4				7	5	2	6	
2		8						
7		6			1	8		
9	8		6					2
5	4	7		8	9	3		6
3				5	4	7		
			5	4	2			3
6	2	4		9	8		7	
	3					4	2	

2	4				8	9		
			1	9			8	3
		1	3	4		6	2	
7		5	8	1				
		4			6			
			7					
3			4			5	1	6
	7		5	6	1	8		2
	1	6			3		9	

7		1	4			5		
3	2	8		9		4		
	5	4		1	3	9		2
5	3			7		6	1	
9			1		4	2		
			2	5		8		
8		5			7	1	4	
4	7			6				5
2	1		5					

Puzzle 369:

6	8	3	7	4		1	5	
1		4				8		
7		2	8		5	3		
		8			4	2		
9		6			7		8	
		1				9	4	
	6			2				
8				7	1			9
	1	7	9	5	3	6		

Puzzle 370:

7		6	8					3
5	8					2	7	
3			7		1	8		
	2	9	5	7				8
6		8		1			9	
	3		4				5	
8			2	6				
2		5	9	3				6
9	6	4	1			3	2	5

371
Light and Easy

4	6						8	2
			6	4	5	1		
								5
		9		5				
8		6			1		9	
					8			3
1					3	7		6
		7	2					
			7	8		3	5	

372
Light and Easy

	6			4				
		9						
8			3	6	7			4
			5		6	3	1	7
				2		8	4	
	9			7		2		
4	3				1			2
	5	6		8	2			
		2				7		

373
Light and Easy

3	9	6						5
	1	2			5	4		9
4					9		7	3
		3		1	8			6
	6				7	5		
8	7	4					9	1
2			7	9	3	6	5	
						4	1	2
	8	7	5			9		

374
Light and Easy

9		8			1	5	6	
3		1	9				2	
7						9	1	
2	9	5	6					
8				9				
			1			2	7	9
	7				6	8	9	
5				8		3		1
	8			1	9		5	

9	8				5		7	
		4	9		7	8		
	2					9		
5		3		6	8		2	
1	4	8	7		2	5		
7		2		1			4	
			2		4	6	1	3
4	3	6		5			9	
	1			7			8	

9	3				2			7
			9	7				
	7	1		3	5	4	2	
3				4	9	8		
	6				7			
	1	5	3					
1				5	4	6		2
2	5	6	1			7		
7			2	9			3	5

Puzzle 377:

9					4			
2								
3	6		5			7		8
				5		3	1	
					3			2
		6	2	4			9	
	4					1		7
	5	3	7	8		2		4
8								

Puzzle 378:

8			9					2
6							3	9
		4	6		7		5	
5		6		1		2	4	
		8			4			
4	9				3			
			3		1	7	6	5
							1	3

5			1	6	4	7	2	
		3				9	1	
1	7	6			3		5	
6	9					8		4
4	5		3			1		
		1	6		8	5		
7					6	2	4	1
	6	4		2				
8	1	2			5		9	

7			8	5		4	9	2
	9							5
5		4						
8	2	3		7				
			9				1	
	4		3	8	6	2		
3			2		9			
	6	7				5		
			7	6	5		3	1

381
Light and Easy

1		9				6		
			6			8		7
					1			5
		2	4			3		
9			1	2				
5		8	9			2		
	2			7	5		8	
7	8	1		6				4

382
Light and Easy

	9				6			8
3			5		1			9
					7			
	4	7						3
8		1		3		5		7
						6	8	
7	8					9	5	
	2				5			4
6			9					1

383
Light and Easy

4	8	7		6	5			
9					8	2	5	
1		5		3	9	4		
7							8	
		8		4		3		
							1	9
			6				4	
6			5			7		3
8		4		9				

384
Light and Easy

8	1		4	3				
9			1					6
			8		9		4	
2				7		3		8
	3			8			9	
							5	2
	8	9	6		2	1	7	
					8		6	
	7		3		4			

5	7		9		8		1	
			6			7		
	6			2			5	
			4		5	1		
1				9	7	6		4
9	3	4						
4		6						1
		8			9	5		
3		5			4			

	3	2			9			7
	1		3				5	8
5	8	7				6		
8	2			6		1	4	
7	4	6						2
1	5		4			9		6
					8	7	6	4
		5		9		8		
4		8	1				2	

	3	5	7		4			
	6				3			7
4			9	1			8	
			5			9	1	
			1				3	
		8			2			
		6				3	9	
				6		7		
			8	2		6		1

	7	1		8			6	
4			1				8	
			5	2	7			
2				9		5	1	8
8		7				9	2	
	4							
7		6		1				
1	5			4		2	7	3

7								
				3		7	4	1
3	8			1			9	
		8	7	6				9
	2			8	1	3	6	
6			5	9				2
5	4			7		6		8
	6					1		

	9					3	4	
6	1							
8		4				7	1	
				8		2		9
5					3	6		
	3			1				
	2	5		3	8			4
				5				3
			7		6	9		

6					4			5
			5		6		3	9
	5		2			4		1
2		1		9	8		5	
	6		7				4	
	4	7		5	3		8	2
3						5		
		4		6	5	3	2	
5	9	8	3		7	6		

			3	2	6	4		
	6	4	5					8
1				4			3	6
6	7	5		3		1		9
4	1		6		8		7	
				9				
9		3		6		8	2	
5	8						4	3
	2		4			9	5	

3	9	6						
5		2	9				8	
7							2	
		7	6	3	1	5		4
		1	5	9				8
9		3	7				1	
	8				6		7	
		4			9	2		
				7		8	4	

		1	9			3	6	
		3	7				4	9
	2	9			3	8		
			8					
				5		6	7	
	6					9	2	1
						1		
				9	8			
	9	4	6		7			2

2	8		3	5			9	
7					2	8		
3								1
			1	2	6			8
				3	5	4		
6				4	9	1		3
	3		2			1	9	
1		9	4			3		5
								6

	3			9	6		2	
4	8	1	5		3		7	
		2						8
	4	3		7	2	1		
						8		3
6			3		1			2
2	9			5				4
	1			4	9	2		
	7	4			8	6		9

397
Light and Easy

2				4	6		3	
			7				6	
	9	3	2			4		
	3				1	5		
	5	6				8	2	1
	8						9	
5			4				8	9
		7	8		9			
	2		1	6	5			

398
Light and Easy

1	2		3		5		8	4
	9		4		6	5		
		8		7				
8	7		1		2		3	
9				4		1		5
6		1	7					9
	4					8	6	
		5	9	6				1

399
Light and Easy

1		2	5					
8	9			7				1
							4	
2	7	5				8		4
6			4				9	
9					8		5	
				4			6	
5	6		7					
		8	6			3	2	7

400
Light and Easy

6			2		1			
					4		1	
			6		3	9	7	2
	5	3		1		4		7
7		2	4					
								5
		9			5			4
			9					3
4	1		3	6				

401
Light and Easy

7					2			8
		9	6	4	8			
6			3		1			5
					5		8	
		6			9	1	7	4
8			2			5	6	
	3				6		5	
	1	7		5				6
9	6					4		3

402
Light and Easy

	6		4		8		1	
			5	3	1		4	
9		4			2	5	3	8
1	3	6	9					5
		2			3	4		
		9		5	7	3		6
2	4			1	5		6	
	7	3					5	4
								3

6					4	1		
					7	2		
2		3				5		6
		7	8			9		1
	6				9	7		
		5		1			6	
	1	9	3	7				
								7
	2		4		5			9

		8	4				1	7
9		1	5		7	2		
7	4			3	1			
4		2	8					1
		9	1	5	2	6		4
	1			4	3			2
6	8			2			9	
			3	6	8		2	
	2	3	9					

405
Light and Easy

5	6		8	2	1	9		
	9					8	2	5
	7	2	9	5			4	
	8			4				
6		3		9		4		
9		5		3	7	6		8
	1	6						9
			5		6		8	4
4		8			9			

406
Light and Easy

8				4	5			
		5		9				7
	2	7		3			5	
					9			
5	6		8			2	4	1
		8					3	
1	8		9			5	2	
		2	1	5				8
9			6	3			7	

8			7	9	4	3	5	
7	5							
		9	1				7	
			8		3			
6	7	3	5		2			
						5		3
5	8				9	1		
			2	3		8		
4					8			7

	2			6	4			8
4		3			7		6	
8		6	2	9			7	3
6			7			8	4	
7	5	1	8	4		3	2	
2			5	3	6	7		
	6		4	7	3			9
	4							
3	7			5		6	8	

409
Light and Easy

6		9		4				
		3	8			2		4
8		2	5		7			3
7			6			8		
9		1			3		5	
		8				6		
			7			1		5
	1			9				
								7

410
Light and Easy

		4		7	2	6	5	9
	9			6	5			
		6	1		9	4		
	1	5			3			6
3		2		9	4		8	
7				5				
8		1		3		2	9	
6		3	9	4			1	5
	5		2					

411
Light and Easy

				8	7			2
5	3	4						
7	2			1	3			
							8	5
6	5		2		8		9	
				9		6		
		6	7			3		
	9	1		6		8	5	
							6	

412
Light and Easy

	4		1				5	2
			3		2			1
	1		6		9	4		8
	2	3		8		5	1	
		1			3	8	9	
8	9					3		7
1	8	9		3		7		
		2	4	9		1	8	3
4		5	8				6	

Puzzle 413

	3						6	
	8		3	4				7
	2	9	8					
2			6			7		3
		6	4				9	
							2	5
			2		1			6
		1		7		4	8	
8	9							

Puzzle 414

		1			9	5	6	
	7				6			
					4			
			2	1		7		
		3	4			9		
6		8						1
	5	7				9		
		4	9	3		1		7
	9		8			6		

415
Light and Easy

		9	1			2		
5	2		8		9		3	
1	3		7		2	6		
		5	2				4	3
	8		3	7		9	6	
					4	1	8	
6		1	4				2	
		3		2		8	1	
8				1			9	

416
Light and Easy

9	6				8	1	7	
	1			3				
		1						2
	3		7		4			6
6			2	5	9		4	
		6		4			3	9
3	8	7	5			2		4
5						8		

Light and Easy

		1	2		5		3	
5			4	9		6		
		8	1				7	5
	9		6					
1	5			7		9	2	4
8		4						7
3		7			9	5		
	8				1	7		3
	1			2				

Light and Easy

	7		6	1	8			4
		5						
8	2		5	4		7	3	6
1	5	2						9
	3	4			1	5	6	2
9	6					1	7	3
				6	5			
					4		1	
2	8	6		7		9		

4	3		5			1	8	
5	8	2				9		7
				9				5
	4							
3						7	4	8
1		8		7	4	5		6
7				4	6	8	9	1
9		6			8		5	
			9		1	6		3

		4	6			9		7
1					2			8
		9	7	3				
		1	8	5	6		7	
		3	4				6	
	5				7	8		
4	1		2		9	6		3
	3							
			1				8	

1	2				3	7		5
7	3	6	5					2
5						3	6	9
3		4	2		1	5		6
				4			1	3
	8	1		3	5		7	
9					2		5	
	5	2			4		3	1
		3			9	6	2	

			8	7				
		9			3			
			2			4	9	5
	5		1		8			
9		7					8	6
6								2
	8	1						5
					2	7	3	
5			9			1	4	

Puzzle 423:

	7		9				8	
3	8	5		4	6		2	
2		4		8			1	
		2	4		1			
8			2			3		6
4	6		8			1		
5		1		7			6	
7					4			

Puzzle 424:

7			8		9	4		
					4	3	7	2
			6		2		1	
								3
1				9		7		
			2	8	3	1	5	9
6	4							
3				6			8	
9					1			

			7					4
3			5	6	4			
		9	1		8			
4	7	5	2	8				
	3						4	
9	8				3		7	
		3				9	5	8
7			8		9		6	
5			3	2		4	1	

	2						8	1
3			1	4				
7	1	5	6	8				
8		3				9		6
	4					7		
		2	7		6			
	3	8			9	1		4
	9	1		3		6		
2				1	4			5

	3	8						2
9	4		2		7			6
		5	4		1		7	8
3				4		5		
1			3		6			4
6			9	5	8		3	1
	1			6			2	9
4	2		5	1		6		
	9	6		2		4	1	

4			9			3	5	
8	1	5						
	2	9		5				
5	3		1	7	2	9		
					8		2	3
	4			5			1	6
1			2		7	6		
7	5	2	8	9	6			
	9			1		2	7	

429
Light and Easy

9				8	4			
3	4		9	6		8		5
5						1		
8	7	5	1					6
	3	4		7	9			1
				4		3	7	8
					2	4		7
7		3			6			2
4	5		7	1		6		

430
Light and Easy

			8					
		6	2			8		5
8	1			7				
5		4			6	9		
		9						3
1	8	3	5	9			7	
3	9	1		8		2	5	6
	2	7	6	5				
6	5				9	1		

	4	9		2	1	7	5	3
		8	9					2
1	8	7		6	4	2	3	
				7	8	4		
		3					7	
9	1					3		
			6				1	7
7		5		9				

	1		2		9		6	5
		9	7			1		
	7			1	4	3	9	8
		7	6	2				4
5						6	7	
6						2	5	3
	8	1						
	4		8	9		5		
3	6	5		7		8	1	

Puzzle 433:

	7		5			4		
3	4	6	7		8	5		9
8			4					
			8				6	
	3	8	6	5		9		
2				9				3
6	5				4	3		
7								
4			3			6	9	2

Puzzle 434:

	1			5			6	3
	6		2					8
9								
		4						
	9	6	8			3		
	8	7		6	9			
8					2		3	1
		1	7	9		2		
4	7	2	1				9	

1			7					
8				3				
2			4		5			
	1		8	2		5		4
6				5				2
5	4							6
7	5	9		6		2		3
				4			9	
			2				1	

	8	9			7	5	6	1
	5				9			8
				8		4		
8		4			3		7	
		6		9				3
					4		8	5
6	9			7				4
2	1	7			6			
		5			8			

437

3				5	1	9		
		8		9			3	7
	4				3		7	
	3		6	1	5	4	2	
2		6					1	
		5			4	3		8
		4			6		5	
1								4

438

		2	7					5
		8				3		
	1	5		4	9			
8			1	2	6		7	
							5	
		7			3	6		
	2	9	7					1
		1	9	5			3	2
	8	3			2			9

439
Light and Easy

8		9		1		2		
5	7		4	2	9			1
			6	8				
	4		3					9
9			2	6	5			3
6	5			4	1		2	8
	6				4	1		
		4			2	5		
7	2	5	1				3	

440
Light and Easy

3		2	1	7				5
		6	2					
4		7	8		3	2		
	4		7		5			1
7				6				8
	1		3		8			
9						6		
		5	6					
								4

441
Light and Easy

2	7		1				8	6
		8	3		9			7
	9		8			3	2	1
	2			8	1		9	3
5			7	9				8
		1	4				7	
1	5	7			8			
3	4		5					
			2	3		7		5

442
Light and Easy

	2				3			7
7		8	4			6	5	
					7	4		
	6			3			8	5
1	8							9
3	5	2				6		
				2	6	8		
	4							
		5	3	8	4		7	

	1	5		2				
	7				8	4	5	9
8		4	7	9	5			6
				5		6		
3	2			6			9	
	6	1			3			2
		3	2	4	6		1	
1					9	2	3	4
	4	9			1		6	

5	4			1	9		3	
		1	8	6	2			
							1	2
	7		9		4	3		
		9	1			7		4
	8		3		6			
	1	6	2			5		
	2	3		8		6		
7				3			4	

				9		6	3	
		5			1		8	9
	7	8	5		3			
					4			
3		9				2		
		1	3		2			7
		7				9	1	
			2	8				
8		6	4					3

		3				6	4	2
		9		4	2	1		
	4		1	7		5		
		4		9	1			
	3				7		8	1
7		8						6
	2	6				3	1	
						8		4
	8		5				2	7

447
Light and Easy

5					2		8	
				1				2
	2		5		9			
					8		3	
4		7	3				5	
6		5			7	2	4	8
	1	2		8			7	
3								
	5					6		

448
Light and Easy

9				7		5	8	1
							2	
			2					3
		5	6		2	3		
3	9			8				
	4	8	7	9				2
	7						1	
	3	4	8		7			
		6			1			7

449 Light and Easy

							2	
						4		8
	2	1	7	4		6		3
8			1		6	9	3	
								4
	5	7			3		6	
			5	6				
1	3						5	
4	9		3		2		1	6

450 Light and Easy

9	4	7			5		2	1
8				4	9	6		5
6			1				8	9
		2		9				8
	1		7				9	3
7	8							
				2				
5	7		9	3		8	4	2
2			4	6	5		1	3

451
Moderate

6							7	
	8					2		
		2	5		4			1
	2				1		4	
	7			8				
						9		5
		6		9				
9	3						8	
4			6					

452
Moderate

						3		4
						9	5	
				9				
5		9					6	
		8			7			
	6				4	8		2
		3		1				5
	8				9		3	
			4		5			6

453

	5							
			7		5			
9		6		8	4			
		9	5	7		8		1
5					9	6		3
1	3			2				4
	7	1	6	5				8
4					8	7	6	
		8	4				3	5

454

5				8				
		8		1	7			4
1			6				7	
			2		4			
							5	
	4	9		6				
	1				5			6
						8		
7	3							

455
Moderate

				7				6
	6		9					
8					5		9	
				4				9
		3	7		6	2		
1						8		
			8	1		6		5
	8						7	4
	3			2				

456
Moderate

1						9		8
					1			
6				4		5		
					7		3	
	5							
		6	2		3			
							2	
	9				6		8	
	2	4	8	5				3

				4	8	9		
	2			7				
	8	4	3				1	7
	4	3				5	6	2
	5			3			4	
7	6	9				3		
4				6	5			
8	7		2		3		5	
5		6		1				

			1	5	7			
						9	6	
7								
	8	6			1			
					4			
	5		3			6		4
		4	6		8	5		1
		7						9
	3					2		

459
Moderate

			1	7	5	6		
	6	5		4		1		8
3	2				9		5	
			3			5	4	9
	7				8			
			6	1	4	2		
1			4					5
	8	2		3				
9				8	2		1	

460
Moderate

8			6	3	2	4		
				9	4		6	
						5		
5		1						4
			2	1				
	8				7			3
		6			3			
	1			6				
	4						1	2

		3		8	6			
8				1		3		
					7	4	2	
		5		4				
6					9	5	7	3
					8			
						7		
4		2				1		
			6		2		4	

5	7			1				
2		8	7		6		9	3
4	9			2			7	
7	5				2		8	9
8	6	4		7	5			1
		5						2
1		7	2		4	5		
	4					3		

463
Moderate

					4	2		
	8		2	9	3			
4					6			
9		6						
	3	1			5			9
	2					8	7	
	4					6		
				1			2	7
							9	

464
Moderate

6		7			2			
					4	1		
						6		3
	9		3		1			
		5	8				7	
		8	6				1	2
							6	
		2				7		
8	3		5	1				

465 — Moderate

9	4	7	2		5			
					4		8	7
		6						
	9							
			9		6			3
8					1		5	
2	3		6				4	
	1			3				
				5		6		

466 — Moderate

7	6				4			
8						5	3	
			2	9			1	
						8		
	5	8			9			6
		4						
4			7					
		2		8		9		
				3		1		

467
Moderate

			1	8				
	4	9						
			9	5				
1	5		6	2		9		
				9		5	2	
					8			
							9	8
7		4						3
			4	6	7			

468
Moderate

					4	6		
		2			7	3		
		9	6	8		7	1	
2	9			1				4
		3	2	9			8	
	5		4				9	3
	3	4		6				2
		6			8	9	5	
5	8					4		

Puzzle 469:

				6				
1	4	7	5					
					9	5		8
	3			4				
2						1	9	
9						6		
		9		8				
	6		3					7
	8					4		3

Puzzle 470:

					5			8
6			4				5	
9				8	1	3		
	1						8	
4				7			1	
		9						
	5					6	7	
		8		9	2			
				3				

471
Moderate

5								1
	4	6		1				9
3				7		6	5	
		8	7				2	
4		3			6	5		
2			1	5		8	4	3
1		4		3				
		5	6				3	8
		9			2	7		

472
Moderate

2		6		7				
7	9							
					8			9
							7	3
	8				6			
	5				4	9	2	
				8			4	
	2							
3	4			6			1	

473
Moderate

		1		2				
	5	6			7	9		
7						1		
		7		1			8	
					8	3	5	4
					6			
8				4			7	
6							4	
	9							

474
Moderate

	4	1					2	9
				5				
		9			3		6	
		4		2				7
7	8							
3								
			6			1		4
		2		9				8
			4				3	

475
Moderate

		3					6	
	2				5			1
		5			9	7		
	6	2					7	
					3	8		
4		9	1					
1	8						9	
			3					8
	9				8	2		

476
Moderate

5	2				6		7	
	4				2			9
				8	4		2	
7							9	
6								3
						1		
			4			3		8
		4						
			7	3	5	6		

477
Moderate

2			5					3
	3			1			2	
			8					
7	1	9						
						1		
		8		4	5	2		
	4						1	7
	2						6	
		3	9	8				

478
Moderate

			8		4			
		9					4	7
8			9					
2				3		7		
	4			5				6
			1					5
7	5			1			9	
	2		3	4				1
	6							

5		4			7	3		
			8					2
		2		3	5			
		5		2			1	
	1							
	6				3		9	
1	7						8	3
			6					

	5	6				2		
	9	1						
	4			6	7			
						1	5	4
								3
		4		2	5		7	
			1					
1				5				
8	2		4			9		

481
Moderate

	8			4	2		5	6
		2	5	3	9			
		7				3		9
			3					5
			9	2	4	7		
7			8			4	1	
		5	4		1		3	2
		8			5			
	1	4		9	3			

482
Moderate

	3			5				
		4				2		7
6							8	
					9	7		
		5						
8	6						3	
		8	5	1		3	4	
		9				1		
			8					

483
Moderate

				6		9		
1			9	3		2		
					5		4	1
5			4	9			6	2
4		6			1	7		
3					2		5	8
	3	4	7			5		
			2		6		7	9
	7				9		1	

484
Moderate

	3		9	2				
				6				
			1	5	8	4	6	
	6	9					5	
7								
1		8		9				
							1	8
	5				8			
						3		2

		3		5				
8				7	2	9	3	6
	2					4		8
	7	8		2				5
			4		8	6		
			7	3		8	4	
	5				9	7		4
2						5		
7	6	4		8	1			

	8		6			3		7
3	6	5	2			1		4
4			5			6		
		3	1		8			
		2			7	8		3
			9				1	
	2	7			5		3	
				9				8
	9			2	1	4	7	

Puzzle 487:

						5		
				8		9		
9		7						
	9				2			4
1						6	7	
8				4				3
						4		1
7		1	3		6			
	2		1	9				

Puzzle 488:

		6			4	2		8
		7		9				
	3							
				5				
		5	8				4	
7		1	6				9	
6			9					
8								5
						1	7	2

489 Moderate

		6				1		
5		8	4					
			9	1			7	
			7		8		2	
					6			
	5	1						3
8								
	2	7						5
		3				9	6	

490 Moderate

						4		5
	9	5		8		6		
2								
		1			2		8	
3					4	7		
				3	5			
7	8							
							7	6
			6	9			2	

491
Moderate

			3		1	6		
9	2					1		7
	1	6	7					4
					9			
6		7	2					
	5							
7							1	
		1	6	5	2		8	
8				7		9		5

492
Moderate

5	3			4	8		9	
7								
1			2					
	1				6			
4	9		8	3			1	2
2			4			7		3
	2					1		
6				9			8	
	4	1			2		3	6

493
Moderate

	4	8	5				7	
			8	9	2	3		4
					8			5
	3	1	7					
				3	1			7
		6						
	8	5			3			2
1	7			5			9	

494
Moderate

	5		8					
4			7				6	3
7	8	1			3	5	2	
6						4		
			4	9		7		
9	3				5			
					2	6		
2			5	6				4

495
Moderate

						1		
				2		5	8	9
2			1	3			4	
				1			3	2
3				9	4			
						6		
	8			4			1	
		9	5			3		
	3	4	2		7			

496
Moderate

	6	1	4		3			
		4				3		5
				9				
4	8	3						
1	2	7	8	3	4		5	
		9			7			
	3		5	1	6			
			9					6
							9	

497 Moderate

		8						
	7		1		4			
			5	3				
	5						4	3
		3						9
		7		9		6		
9			2	7		4		
	6			8				
3		2		4		1		

498 Moderate

			5	6				
		1	9			4		8
	5		7					
3	2	6	4			5		1
				8				4
						6		
1					4			3
	3	5					7	
	9		3	1		2		

4		3	8			9		
				5	4			
				9		7		
8				2	5			
			1	8		6		
		5	3				7	1
		4	5					2
					1	5		
6							9	

	3	2						9
		8	2			4		
1		6	7		9			
	8		4			7		1
		7	1		3		9	2
			8		2			
		3						
6			9				5	
				8		9	2	6

501
Moderate

2				1	4			9
							1	
	7				3	6		
					5			
5				2		3		
6		9						8
		2		3	9			
		3	2			4		
1		8		6				

502
Moderate

			3		1		8	4
4	1	9						
				8			2	3
6								
	7	4	1		6			
						1	5	7
8			4	5			6	
		2						

503
Moderate

3	8			6				
2		9			8			
							8	3
			7		4		2	
						7		
		6	5					8
		7	1	2			9	4
6		3						7
	1		6	9				

504
Moderate

3	5			1	6		2	
		1		9				8
			6		5		9	
						8		6
7	8		9		1		3	
			4	7				3
						2	7	
2	1						8	

3					5			
	6							
			2		3		5	
			3	2		8		
		1			4	6	2	
	7		5			9		1
		9	4			2		
	8						9	
7	2			3	8	1		

			3				5	
			4			7		6
	1			2				
		4						
5				7		8		
		8		1		9	2	
					7	4		
2	6							5
3		7						2

		5	4	3				8
7				1	9	4		5
4				5		2		
1			3	7				
		2					4	
					6			2
6		7	8	9				
						1	7	
	5	3						

7								9
2		6				8		7
5	9		3			1		
		7		3				
8			5		9			
1						2		
				6	4		3	
				5				8
		2		1			6	

509
Moderate

							9	7
	8	4				1	3	
	7			8				
			9	4	7			5
		3	1					8
			2			7	1	
								6
		1				4		
2	9	7			4			

510
Moderate

				4	3	7	5	
								4
	7	8			6	3		9
		3		1	4	2	7	
			8	2				6
	2		1		8			
		9			7	4		
6							8	

511
Moderate

			2					
		2		8	1	6	5	
	5			3			7	
3		4					6	
				4	3			2
5	2						4	
	4	5	8					3
1		9				4		
	8			6				1

512
Moderate

		9				2		
6					7	4		
8	4	3				5		
	8	7		3		6	9	
			4				7	8
				5				
	3							2
9			8	1				
				4			3	

513
Moderate

4		3	6			9	5	
9								
5		2				1		
				1		4		
6			9	2	3			1
		7	8			3		
					2		9	
	9		1	8				7
				4				

514
Moderate

2	9							
4			9			7		3
					5		1	
	2	1			3			
		8	7					5
						6	2	
		2			6	5		4
			3				9	
		4			1			

515 — Moderate

					1		5	
9	5	6	8	7				
						3		
		9	1	5	6		4	
1	2			8	9	5		
								7
2				1			8	
3								
	4	8					9	

516 — Moderate

			3				2	
		8	7				4	
								6
	5	1						
2	6				3	5		4
9		3				6		
		9						2
	4		6	9			7	
3			8					5

517
Moderate

4				3	2			
2					9		7	
				5				
		2	4			8	5	
5	8		7			9		
	9			6			1	
	3	1			4	2		
9								8
				7				

518
Moderate

			6			1	5	
	2				8		6	
	7			9				
		7		8				
	1				2			3
		5	3	6				
	3					8	1	5
6		2					9	
		4	8				2	

519
Moderate

				8		3		2
						7		
	5						4	6
						4		
8					3			
3			8	2	7	9		
7			1	4	6		9	
4		3			8			
	1		9					4

520
Moderate

				1	2			
	5				9	1		7
	8	9	3					
					8		6	
	4					5		
		7	1	5		3		
	7	5	2				4	
								5
	3	4		9		2		1

521

Moderate

		5	3	2				6
	4	8	5		6	3		
						2	8	5
3			8					2
	2							
				9				
4				5	1			
						7	6	
	9			7	2	4		

522

Moderate

3			1	4		6	2	
4						8		7
9		2						
					9			
2				3	8	5	1	
			7	4				
	6			1			9	
7		8						
	4				6	3		5

523
Moderate

					6	8		
8	1		5				7	
4		7			8	6		2
3				4				8
2				3			4	
	8						9	1
							8	9
					5			
6			1	8		7	5	

524
Moderate

		9						
		5			3			
		8		9		2	4	
6			5		1	4		
			3		2	7		
								6
1						3	5	
			6					8
			7					1

	3	2						8
					7			
		6		8		3		
3			5		4	6		
	7	4						
		1			6		9	2
1	6							
						5		4
4				9	8	7		1

5		3	1					2
4				5		6	1	
1				2		4		8
		2			6			9
			5					
					7	1		
			6					5
		4			2			6
						3	9	

7		1		2			9	
9		3	4					
					8	1	5	
								6
		8					7	
	4			3	6	5		
	2			5			6	9
	1		6		9	2		
3				4				

			7			1	4	
		7	8		2			
					4		3	
			5	2				4
		5		8	9			
9						5		3
3							2	
	1			7		4	8	9
			4		1		6	

529
Moderate

				6				7
5			4		8		3	6
	9	8			1			
1	2	9			7	8		
						6		1
8			9					
	5		8				2	
	6			9				
						3	6	5

530
Moderate

	3					9		2
6								
	4	8						1
1				2	8		7	
				5			8	3
			9					
			5		1	4		
						3	9	
5		3			7			

531
Moderate

7		1	9					
	2	9	1		3			
	6							7
8		7		9		6		5
3		2					1	8
2			5					
	1			6			8	
		8				4		

532
Moderate

			5		6			8
	8							
	9					7	1	5
			6		2			
	7	8				3		
	2			7				4
						5		3
	3	4	7	1		2		
				5	4			9

533 — Moderate

	9		7	8			3	
	7					2	5	
8					9			
		2						4
			5				8	
		6				5		7
9		7			8	3		1
3				9	5		2	
					1		4	

534 — Moderate

	3			6			1	
8						3		
2			7				8	
			8			2		5
3	4							7
		9		8				
	7	4	9		1			
6				7		5		

535
Moderate

6				9			4	
3	2	7				9		
			1					3
		5	4		2			
			9					6
4				1	3	5	7	
	9				1			
1	3			4		6		2
								4

536
Moderate

			4				3	
6					5	2	8	7
								9
			2					3
	5		6		8			
7				9				
	2			7				
						9	5	
		3	1				4	

Puzzle 537:

4			3				8	
			1				6	
	2			9	4			
	6		9			3		
		3			6	8		
7					2			
9	5	4						
		8		6		9		3
			2				4	

Puzzle 538:

						6		
							7	1
	7	1	3				8	
9	5				4	2		
								6
			8	6				4
		9		6	1			
1		2		4				
	4	7						5

539
Moderate

		5	4			1	7	
4						9		
			9	8				
			6	7				9
3							1	
		2		5			6	
8				4				
	7	9						4
5	1		7	6	3			

540
Moderate

	9		1		3			
		5			6			2
	7		4	5			6	
			2			1		
		7	9					
	8			1			5	
		2					4	
			3		8			1
								7

541
Moderate

	8							7
6							9	
		1	2	9				
			7					9
9				6				5
5					3		6	2
		2		7				1
3	6							
7			6				3	

542
Moderate

	2		7	6				3
			1			9		
8	5				3			
	3				7	1		
6			8	3				
5	7	2	9					
			6	2				9
	9							1
4				5				6

2				5	7			
			8				5	2
1					9	6		
					3		4	1
		4		8		9		3
7					2			6
6					4			
		9	6	3				
		5		2		3		

5							2	6
				6		8		
		9				5		
4			6				7	5
	7	6				3		9
	8			1	2	4		
	3				8	9	5	
		1		9				

			9		1	8	2	
2		6						
4				5		1		
					3			
1					2		5	
	3	2					7	
		8		7		5	4	
	6	7		1	9			2

						2		
							6	7
5			4	3				
		2	1					3
	1		5			4		
9	3	4			2			
2	6					1		
4			8				9	
						3		8

547
Moderate

3		7	2	5		1		
				8				
		8			7			
	3				8		1	
	8	2			4		7	
9				2	1			
4						3	5	
		9			3			
2				1		7	9	

548
Moderate

9								
	1				8			
5				9	8			
			8				2	9
	4		1					
3			6			4		
								7
		7			6	9		5
6		5			7			8

549
Moderate

				8		4	2	
4				3				9
	7			9	2	8		
				6				8
		8						7
3	1						4	
2		9				7		
			8					3
		3		4	5	9		

550
Moderate

				3	2		8	
			5			7		
	5	8		1			3	
	3	5		4				
4				5	7			
							9	
1			9	2	6		5	
	6					3	4	
								2

551
Moderate

	8				4	6		5
5				7				
	1					3	7	2
			2					
	6	4						8
		3	9	8				
	2		8		7		3	
		5			2			
3			1	5				

552
Moderate

	3							
5	8			7		1	9	
		4		5				2
		8		1				6
	7	2	6					
	1				9			
			7				1	
				8		6		
4	2	9					8	5

553
Moderate

7			8				2	9
		9	1					
	8					7		1
			2	3		9		
		5	9					
	4		6	8	5			
		3			6			
				2				
8		1	7				3	5

554
Moderate

		6	1	2				3
7			8					
			6				1	
6		4	3				2	
5					8		3	4
				6		7	5	
	2				1			
	7		9			1		
				3		9		5

3				7		9		4
						5	6	
		8			1			
			2	4				
	6			1	9	8		
		4					7	
1	7	9	4			3		
		6						
	5		1	6	8	7		

			2				3	
				9			7	4
		4			7	9		
			4	5		2		
	7				6		8	5
		8						
			1	6	4			
	4		9			5		8
1			8	7			4	

557
Moderate

2	4							
								6
6			5	8				
	9				1	6	2	3
								4
	5			2	9		1	
		8		1		5		
4						3		9
5	7			3		2		

558
Moderate

	3					4		
2		5	4				3	8
	4	1		2	9			
			2	5				6
		7						5
		4		9	1		8	
								1
1	5				6			
				4		2		

559
Moderate

9						6		
7		1						9
	8			5				
	9		5		2		7	8
	6			1		9		
3	5	2		7	8			
		3			4			
	4		3			5		7
				9			1	

560
Moderate

6				8		4		
				5		2		9
	3	4						
5	9							
	7					3	1	
					1			8
	2	3		4	5			
			9					2
		5	3		8			1

Puzzle 561:

	7	8	2			1		
	9					4		
	1							
		5	8		1			
2				6	9	7		
				7		3	1	
9				3		8		
			6	4			5	9

Puzzle 562:

7		3				8		6
					8			
2	4			6		7		
3		7		1				
	9			3				
				2	5	3	6	
		9			2			
					4		9	1
1			3					8

563
Moderate

2		8	9	6				
7							2	
		3			1			
	1			2		8		
9								
8		2				3		4
1		6	5			9		
	4			1			8	
			3			7	6	

564
Moderate

	4		2		8	9		7
5								
	6							8
		1	9		6	8		
9	2					6		
						3		1
	3		5					
		4		3				
	7		6		4		3	

565 — Moderate

			6			7	1	
8		1		5		9		
	7					5		
9		7			3			
						2		9
	4				8			5
		9			2			3
	6			7		1		
	1		3					

566 — Moderate

3	6		4					
				9	2			
					7		1	8
2	8		7		9	3		
	3		2					4
		4						
4			1			9		
9								5
	1			5		8	4	7

567
Moderate

9						1	8	6
	3		7		5	2		
						7		
		6						
	5	4	1					
1			8	4	3			
				8		9		3
			2			8	7	
	9	1	3		7			

568
Moderate

9	5					2		
8	4	7						
	3						6	
			2	8		5		
4			1					
			7	4	3			8
		3			7			6
	2		8	3				4
				2		3		9

Puzzle 569:

	4	5				9		6
1	6						8	
		2	8					
				5		8		7
	5		1	3				
9	7	3				6	5	
		6	2					3
							9	8
4	9							

Puzzle 570:

	9				3	4	7	
				2	1			9
		6				2		
9		1						
				9	2			
7	8							6
		2			9	8		
	6			1				3
	3	8		5		1		

571
Moderate

			5		7	6		3
8			5		7	6		3
2	3	9			1			
	6							1
				5				
	4	1				7		9
7		6	9		5	4		8
		8			4	5	3	6

572
Moderate

	1			6				
				9			5	8
4		8		2				
	6				4		7	
7		3						
	9	1	7		3			6
	2	6				3		
		7			2			4
			8		1	2		

573
Moderate

					4	6	7	2
9	1							
2	4			5	6			
	5			7		4		6
8	6			2				
				9				
							5	
							3	9
4	3		5				6	1

574
Moderate

4				8				
2				1			4	6
			5	6			8	
3	1					6		
		2	4					5
				9		3		
		9	3	7	5			
1	3		6					
			2	4		9		

				6		3		7
					8	5		
8	1			5			4	
	3		9			8		
				8				
4						2		
5			2					
9			3					1
						9	3	

8		1						
		7	8	3			6	
4		9	2	6				
		3						1
				9		5		
	5					6	4	
					7			
			9				1	8
	7	8		1		2		

Puzzle 577:

							1	
				4	3	9		
	9		1				3	2
3	7	8		9				
	6			1				
	2				4			5
						1	4	7
	3				7	5	2	
		9						

Puzzle 578:

9			2				7	
		5			7			
			4				3	8
2			1		5		9	4
6			7	9		1	8	
					8			
	8		5			4		
					1			
7	1					2		

579

Moderate

2				1				6
	6	4						
		5						8
	3			6	8			4
		9	5			2	7	
7								
	9	8						1
					4		2	
			3					

580

Moderate

9			3				6	
		6	1			2		
7								
5			7					
4	2			9	3		8	
	1			4		3		
			8			1		
		8		7			9	
								3

581 Moderate

	4							6
			6		9			
1					8			3
4		2					5	
	9		7			3	1	
7			8	9				
2				6				1
		6	9		2		8	4

582 Moderate

		7	6					1
								2
		9		4		8		
7		6		1		4	5	
3		4			8	2	6	
		8	1					
4	6		8	5	2			
5								

583
Moderate

		2						7
	8		1		4			6
						9	5	
		5		4	6			
3							7	
		7	2					9
7			8					3
		6			5			
			6			4	2	

584
Moderate

1		3			2		9	
				5		3		8
						7		
8		4	5	3				
		1			4			9
								1
	4		7			9		3
		2					6	
			9		6	4		

Puzzle 585:

5								
	6	3						
			8					5
				6	9			
	7					1		
4	8				1	6		9
2				5		4		
	5		7			2	1	
		9	4		6			3

Puzzle 586:

			2		9			7
6	1		3	5				4
						2		
			4				9	
3	5	7						
2								
	4					2	7	
		8						
		5			4	1	3	

587
Moderate

								5
				2		7	8	
3		6	4					
6					7			4
		9	3					2
5					4			8
						5	3	1
	2				1		9	7

588
Moderate

8	7							5
				9	5			
1		3	4		7	6		
			3					
			5	6			3	
4		7						
		5		1	9		4	
			2			3		
		1		4			8	

589 — Moderate

	4	6						1
1		5			9		3	
							6	
7	8					3		
				3	4		8	
		2		1				9
8	9		6					2
6					1			
	5							

590 — Moderate

	8		2					
5	6							9
	7	9		6				
8				7		3		
6	9		3				2	
		3	9		1		4	
								8
	5				4		3	

591
Moderate

			8		9		7	
				5	2	8		
	8	7						6
	4							5
			3		1			
		9				3	8	
2		8	1		6			
	5						4	8
4	3							

592
Moderate

		3	9				8	
	6							9
7			1				4	
	3	5			6			
		7					5	
2								7
1						7		
					2			6
	4			5	3			

593 — Moderate

	4			9			2	1
6			7			4		8
	2			4	1		9	
								6
	9				6		5	3
	3				8	5		
		4		5			1	
		5	9					4

594 — Moderate

				2		1		
		2					8	9
		6			4			
		9	2			5		
6		5		8			4	
								8
1			4		5	3		
	4					2	6	
				1				

1								
			3	7	5	2		
	6		4					
		7	9		6			
5	3					7		
				4				
8	4	5						7
			2	1			6	5
								4

3			5					
4							8	1
	9			4				
				9	3	4		
		2				1		
	3			6			5	
			8	5			4	3
		6	7					
	7					5		

	4					5		
	9							
				6	8		1	
9		7			1			
	6		4					
		5			9	8		
		2		3			7	4
			9				5	6
1						3		

5								
		9	2		6		3	
2		8		9	7			
7			1			5		
				6				
	9			3				
6	7				3		5	
					2			3
				8			7	6

599
Moderate

							1	9
	7		5		8	4		
	4					7	3	
	5			2				
6							2	8
	8	4			1			
3			6		4		8	
			7			9		
						6	7	

600
Moderate

		5					4	
						1		
		8		6	2			
		4			3			
1				5		7	3	
	9							
		6		7				4
					4	9		
	3				5		6	8

601
Moderate

7			8				3	
	5			2		1		
		6				7		
				5				
3	7		4					6
2		4						3
8						6	7	
	4	1	3	9				5
	2		1		8			

602
Moderate

	3	1						
	7			9				
5				7	2			
4	6		1				5	
		3		5		4		8
9								2
			9				3	
3						8		1
2	1				4	9		

603
Moderate

	2		7					
5			2		4			
				9	3			2
6	3				1			9
7								8
	9						2	
						4		6
1				3		5		
	7			1				

604
Moderate

								7
	6		3		7			1
	7	9	1	8			4	
6				9			7	8
		8				3		
		1				5	6	
5	1							2
8		6						
					8		9	

	5							
6	4		2				3	
				6				
				4			7	
7	3	1	9				4	
				8	6	5		
								9
4				7				
		8	3		9	1		

								5
					7			
		3		8			6	
				1				3
		4	5	6			2	8
2								1
					9			
5		6	4				7	
1					8	9		6

607
Moderate

		5				4		
7			6			9		
4		3		2		1		
		1	2	4				
					6			
					7		9	8
9							5	
8			7				6	
	5				1			

608
Moderate

	8				4			
1						3	9	6
			9		2		1	8
5						6		
			1	8			2	
	7							
					3			7
	1							9
		2	6	5				

		1					3	5
2				3				
			6		7			
	1	9			2			7
6					1			
	5		9	8				1
7		2			6			
8							9	2
1		6		5				

	6			8		3		
5	8	4						
						9	5	
				5		2	3	
			2	3				4
	7							
8		2	1					
	1			2		5		
			5			4		

611
Moderate

		7						
6			5			9		
5	3				8	6		
3			1	6			9	
							3	2
		2			3	1		
	7			1				
		1		7		2		
2	9			5				8

612
Moderate

	7	9	6					
	4						9	1
			5		3			
3	5		2	4				
	2	8	7					
	6				5	4		
							5	4
				3		6		8
2								3

Puzzle 613:

1						3		
9	2					4		
	4			3			6	
	6		2		1		5	
				4	5		7	
								9
				7		2	9	
		1		5				3

Puzzle 614:

	5		1			2		6
7				9				
		3				4		
	2		3			7	6	
			2		5			
	9	4	6			8	2	
3		8					4	
			5		4			
						1		

615

Moderate

3	2				6			
			3					5
		6		4	5	8		
5					3			7
			6		8		4	
4	9			1				
	4							
			1					
		3		2	4	1		6

616

Moderate

		4	2					9
3					5	7		
7			4	6		3		
			1		8	2	9	
8	9					4	6	
		1						5
						8		
	4		3		7			2

617
Moderate

	4	8						1
			9			4		
5		6						
	3		1	5			7	
			6			3	9	
	1	2	4		6		5	9
			3	2				
9							3	

618
Moderate

	8	4	9		5			
7				3	6			
5	6			8				
		1				5		
3			5					9
			8	7				
8	2			1		7		
							1	5
		9	4			2		

619
Moderate

		4		7		3		
								6
6							1	9
1		9	2					
				6			8	3
				3				
4	7						6	5
8			1					
				2		7	9	

620
Moderate

			6	5			4	9
5	6		9					
		8						
2	5		7				6	
	7			9	4			
4				3		5		8
		1						2
			8		9		1	5
			3	7				

5	7	3		4	2			
		2			6			
								7
4	9		1				7	
			9			5		
				7		8		6
3				5				
					3	7	8	
		4				6		3

		1			9	3		2
					6			7
2			1			6		
5								8
				3	4	9	5	
6								
8								
	2		6					1
	3			5		4		

623
Moderate

6				7				
	4					6	5	
		9	8					
			1		7			9
	1			2		3		
8						4	7	
		2	3			6		
					8			
4			5			9		

624
Moderate

		7		6	5			1
		9		7			5	
								4
		3					1	6
		8	4		6		3	
	9	4	7				8	
	2	6						
	7							
		5				8	7	2

625
Moderate

			9	7				5
	6			5		3		
	7			2				
		5					2	
6				4	5			3
1		4					6	8
		7			9		1	
			4				3	
2	9				7			

626
Moderate

6		7			1			9
				2	8		4	
		8						3
3	6					9	8	
			6					1
		4	3				5	
				6		7		
			4	7				
7		5	1					2

627
Moderate

9		6	7		8			4
5	1	4					3	
2	7							
		9		7		1		
		1	9			6	4	
1	5						2	
			5					
		2		6				1

628
Moderate

		1					2	
			5			8		9
7	6	8		4				3
9								7
			2	6		9		
	2				8		1	
4					6		7	
8		7			5			
	5							

629

Moderate

	6						8	
2						3		1
				5				4
	3				5			
		8	9		1	7		
4						1	2	
1	8							
								2
7		4	5				6	

630

Moderate

		7		6				8
	8			4	5			
								1
	9		2			6	3	
			4					
3			1	7		5		
	6		8				9	
7		8						
	5						1	

631
Moderate

	1				9			
							8	7
		4	3				6	
		6		7				
		5	4	3	9			
		1			5			
					8		1	
				9		6	4	
8		2			6			

632
Moderate

	7		6		1			8
	1			5			9	
		3				7		
						6		9
6		7		1	9		3	
			3			5		
		1	4		3			
4		8						5
					2			

633

Moderate

9							6	
			7	2				8
	5		6					
		4						
3		8		6				
		9	3			6	5	
			4	7				6
	3	7					8	
	2			1			3	

634

Moderate

	4							
	3		1				2	
1	9	5	8				4	
					4	1		
5		2						
	7	9	5			2	3	
		1					9	7
				1				
			7	8	2	6		4

			4					
3			2		9	1		5
		1		5			9	2
	3				7		8	
		8		6		4		
2	5					3		
					1			
7	9	5			8			
				4			7	

2	1		7	6	4	9		
	3							
		4			1			
	2			1	3			8
		3		4			6	
					5	7	9	
			4	2	9		5	1
3			5				8	

Puzzle 637:

		3						
	2		8		1			
	1							4
				8	6			
		9			2		1	
	5				9	8	4	6
				4		7	8	
		2	5			9		
		1	6		8			

Puzzle 638:

						7		6
				6	1			
						8	9	
		7						
					6			
		2		7				4
1	8					3		2
	4			8			6	
2		9	5					1

639
Moderate

						7	4	
	5	8	4			3		6
6						5		
			5					
7				8				
				4	7		3	9
		4			6			
	3		1			8		
	9			2				5

640
Moderate

	1		7	2		5		6
		9		1			2	
					3			
						1	3	
8	4					7		
				8				
			4	9			7	
					2		8	3
		5		3	7			9

641

Moderate

						5		7
2		8		6				
6			5				2	
	9		4	5	6			
	4					3		
					2			
					4	1		6
			9			4		
	7						5	

642

Moderate

4	7	5	3	9				2
		6					5	
							9	
					1	6		
2				6	5	4	1	
				2	7			
6	3		2					
							8	
5	8	2			6		7	

			6		8	1		7
		3		7	9		2	
5								
		4			3	5		
			9				6	
		1					7	
	4			8				
	6					7		
			3	1	2			

					6		8	
	4		9	1			5	
2								9
8		3					7	
				4				
7						8	2	
	3	7		8	5			
	5		1		7	6		
			6	9				

645
Moderate

9				8		1		
		6				7		
		4						8
			3				7	9
7	8			6				1
			2			5		4
		5				8	6	
				5				
			4					2

646
Moderate

				8				
	6			5	7	1		
	2		3			6		
				6		3	7	
		5						
		1						4
		4			8		3	2
					5	4	8	
3		8		2		9		5

647

Moderate

4		5		3		6	1	
		9	6		5			7
8			4				5	
				4	2		6	
9			8					4
		2				3		
	2							
	1					8		
3		6			1	5		

648

Moderate

	9		7		5	4		
		4			6		7	
7		5					9	
			3				8	9
							3	6
2		6		8				5
6					2			
1							2	4
		7				3		

Puzzle 649:

		3						1
		5	3		4			6
		6		5			9	
			7		8		3	9
2	4		1					
		7		4		6		
				7				
9			4	6			5	
1				9			2	

Puzzle 650:

	8				4			
1	4	5						
			9	6				5
	6	1	8			2	9	
7					3	4		2
				7			5	
	3					2		
		4		8			9	
					7	1		

651
Demanding

		4	3	5				9
					2	5		
1	6						3	
		7			6			1
	1			2	4	7	6	
				6	1			8
						9		
9							2	5

652
Demanding

	5							4
	6				9			
		8		6			5	
			3					
		1						
					5	4	8	3
1	4			9				
9			2		7			
6				4		7		1

653
Demanding

		3			2			
4	7				9	5		
		5	8					
		6			1		2	
		7		5		3	4	
2			4		3			
							1	
				8				2
			1		7		9	

654
Demanding

3			9	7				8
		6	5		2		4	
					3			
9				6		5		
1	7							
			9					
						2	8	
		3			5			9
	4						1	3

655
Demanding

		9			2			
	5	8			1		7	
	7					5		6
4			6	2			1	
				9				
		6						4
3			1	8				
	8	5			3			
						9		

656
Demanding

				7				3
8								9
9				8	6		2	
		3		9			6	
						7		
4						1		
		8	1					
	4	7	8			3		
	1			2				5

Puzzle 657:

5				6				
		8	2					
4			3					
		3			9			8
6			7					9
	8			4				
	6							1
	9	4		1		7		
		2				6	5	3

Puzzle 658:

					2	1		7
	1			6				4
	5				7			6
	6	7		4				
				3			9	2
5								
2	3				8		5	
4								
			5					

1					7		2	
6	4					7		3
	7	5			1	8		
		3	9					
	1		2			6		
	3		6		8		5	
						4		
		2						

		2						
	9						4	
7	5				2	8	9	
5	2	1						8
				9				
3					5			
			6	3	7			4
		5		8				
	6		9			7		

661 — Demanding

	3		5	6				7
4	5							
	8	2				4		
		5	4			9		1
3	6		1					
7								2
				8				9
9					3	2		
							3	

662 — Demanding

7			3	8				
1			5					
6		2						
5		4		6		2		
		3				4		1
							8	9
	5					3		
	7			3			1	4
			7		8			

		5				6		
		4						
6			2					4
					1			
	1	7			6			2
			2	5	3			
4	8		7					
		3	4					7
				8			2	

9								
			3				7	
6				8			4	
				1				
	2			4				8
1		3				2		
	5					9	2	
		2					6	7
			4	5				

```
. . . | . . 1 | . . 3
. 1 4 | 9 . . | 8 . .
9 . . | 2 . . | . . .
------+-------+------
8 6 . | . . . | 5 . 7
4 9 . | . 2 . | . . .
. . . | 3 . . | 9 . .
------+-------+------
. 2 . | . . . | 3 . .
. . . | 6 . . | 1 . .
. . . | 7 . 8 | . . 2
```

```
7 . . | . . . | . . .
. 9 . | . . 3 | . . .
6 . . | . 4 7 | . 2 .
------+-------+------
. 5 . | . . . | . 4 .
. . 7 | . . 6 | . 1 .
. 6 . | . . 8 | 5 . 9
------+-------+------
. . . | . . . | . 5 1
9 . . | 2 . . | 3 . .
. . 3 | . 1 9 | . . .
```

667
Demanding

5							2	
9	6							5
			7	3				
				2				1
		3			7			
1				8			6	
		8			6			3
	9			5		7		
7						1		8

668
Demanding

6			1					4
						2		
	2	8			7			9
						8		1
7	1	2		5				
	9						6	
		4				1		8
				1	9			
			8		3			

669
Demanding

		1			9	5		
4				2	5	9		
6				3			7	
7		8	6				9	
		9	5				2	
	4							
5						7	6	
	3							4
							8	

670
Demanding

3	6							9
	9							5
	4	8				6		
	7	9		2	3			
							9	
8				7	5		1	
		4		9			8	
	8	2			4			
7			6	3				

671
Demanding

		2	5		6			4
						7		
			9	4	8			
		6						
		7		5		1		
2			7	6				
	4		2			5	1	
8	6						9	2

672
Demanding

	9	4		2			6	
						7		
3				1	5			
1			8			3		
6	5				9			4
				4		1		
	2	7		8			9	
			2					
					4			5

			5	8				
9			6		7			
1	4							8
2			1					
					9		3	5
7		8						
		7		4		6		
						9		
			3		1	2	4	

		6	1		8			
						1	4	
	7				5	2		3
		9						8
3				7	6			
						3	1	5
			7	3				4
2	4						3	
						5		

675
Demanding

7								
			2					5
3	8					2		4
1			7		6	3		
					4		9	
		6			2			1
					3			
8							7	9
9		5	1				3	

676
Demanding

					1	4		
6	8	9						
3				2	7			
							5	
			2					8
		8	4	7	9	1		
			6	1			4	
7				3				
		6					3	5

Puzzle 677:

	2	3		5				
6			4					
	1					7		4
			5		3			
	8				2		9	
		9					2	6
			7	4				
			8			1		3
				2	5			

Puzzle 678:

		2		6				
6		8		7				
	1	7		3				5
		5		4			8	
					2			9
				5			3	6
			9					2
	8	6	3	1	4			
4								

679
Demanding

7						6		
	3						2	
2			9					7
			4	9	3			5
			7				8	
4					2			
8					5			2
	6						3	
			3		1	7		8

680
Demanding

1								
	8				7			5
					5	2		9
2	7	6		3				
							1	
	5		9		2		6	
						3	8	
		2				9		
8				1	3			

Sudoku grid 681:

				4				
7		9			8			
5							2	
	3		9	7				
2					5			4
								9
	1			6		8		
	4						3	
9				5	4	6		

Sudoku grid 682:

					9	6		
5								
		8		3	7			4
				6	3	7	4	
	8		9			5		
				2				
6				7				3
	1							
9	2	7		1	4			

683
Demanding

			8					
		4						8
	5	2					4	6
	1			2				3
		5			9			
3						9	6	7
			4					
				3		6		
	3		7	5	2		9	

684
Demanding

8	5			1	6	9	4	
							5	
	4		2			3		
2						8		
		3	5	8				1
		2		6		1		
9								
7			9		3		6	

685
Demanding

7			4					
	1	8						7
	9			1				
8		5		9		3		
		3	2			4		6
9		6						5
3								1
	8						2	
					7	5		

686
Demanding

4				3	6			
			5			2		
6	1				2			7
		3						
	2	9				3		4
1	6			7				
8			2					
		1	6					
3				1		7	8	

687
Demanding

5			6		1		3	4
	9		7		4			2
			3				5	8
	7			1	9			
		9	4			3		
	5		9	3				
	4						2	
							1	

688
Demanding

3			5			1		
		9				3		8
				6			2	
	2		3		1		9	
4								
		1						3
7				5				
	8				2	4		7
			7		8	9		2

				9	2		7	1
			1					9
5			8		7		6	
		1			4			3
	7				5			
2		3				1		
				6	9	2	8	
	8							
	6		7					

7							5	3
		3	2				4	
	9				6	2		
9				8		7	3	
			1					8
					7		6	
		4			5			1
	7							
			6	9	1			

691
Demanding

		4		7			5	9
		9		2	6			
3	6		4					8
	3		2		8			
	4	1					3	
								6
						7	1	
	5			3				2
		8						

692
Demanding

7			5		8			2
	2			3				
		8	4		9	1		
8	3							
			2			9	1	
	6				3			5
3		9					2	
					5			
								4

693
Demanding

		8	4			9		
				7	6	8		
6		7		3	5		2	
	2	4	5				1	
		3				4		
7				9				
						6		
								7
	4	5					3	

694
Demanding

4	3			2		9		
			6		8			1
		6	7		9			
6		3					5	
					6		9	
8			9					
			4		2	1		8
7						6		5
	2							

	9			1		5		6
	3		7					
7		2		9			1	
		7	9					1
		3	2			6	8	
				8				
1						2		
5								
	7	4				8		

2								
				5	6		8	
								7
			6	3	5			
9	1	7				8		
		4	1			2		
							9	
5		8	9	2		7		

Puzzle 697:

	4				2	5		
	6						3	
		2	6		9			
	9	1	4					
8	2		5					
	3			6			8	1
			2	3				4
					6		7	8

Puzzle 698:

							2	
4						8		
9		5	6	3				
3	2				8			7
								5
5				7				4
			3			1		
		8		2				
	3			9	1		4	2

699
Demanding

	3					2		
			4	7				
5			6			8		
				9				
9		6						3
3		8			1		2	
	1				2			4
					5		7	
	7						9	

700
Demanding

6		1			5			
			2					
			8			4	5	
		9	3			5		4
						1	8	
		3		7				2
7			9	3				
4		5		6				
1						2		

701
Demanding

			5				1	6
5							3	
					7	8		
				6				8
	9		8	1				
6			9				5	7
	4					3		
1		8	6					
		9				2		

702
Demanding

			3	6			5	
5							1	
	6	3		4				
			9		1	2		
	7							3
							4	1
			8				3	
1		8			9			
6					7	9	2	

3							4	
	5	9		4	8	3	1	
		6						9
7	9			8				5
			9					4
8								
	1	8			5			6
				2			8	
6					1			

					5			
			3				6	
2	1	9		4				3
8					4			
		1			3		8	
						4	9	6
7	4	3	2			1		
						9		
			8					

3								8
	5				4		6	
				5	7			
				7				6
			4					
9		4			6		5	7
1	3					2		
					9			
7	2				8	9		

			6					
9					1			5
	7				2			4
		2			7	9	4	
		6		8		7		
								8
	9		5			6		2
8				1				
			9		4		1	

		7				4	5	
8					4			
			2		7			
	6	9	4					8
2		8					1	9
					3			
	2	4						6
	9	3				8		
				6				

							8	
8			1		4		5	
		5						
1	8			4				
		9			3		1	8
	6		5				7	
	4	7		6		2		
					9	7		
	2							9

709
Demanding

			7			5	4	8
							9	2
6		2		8		3		
5					3		7	
		7		2				
		1			8			
	3				7			
							2	4
	9	5			1			

710
Demanding

				3		1		
	2	8						6
6	4							
			6			9		
						2		7
			2	8		3	4	
				7	4			
		6			1		8	
7			9					1

				3		5		
8			2		6	3		4
					1	6		
		2	9			8	7	
1			4				6	5
					3			
	3	1			9			
	7					4		
	9			6				

7		8			6			
1			5			3		
			1			6		
5						8	7	
6			8			2		
			2					5
		6						
8		1			4			
	5		3		2		4	

713
Demanding

		2		4		1		
			7					
				6	8	7		4
5					7			6
							3	
	9			8		5		
2			6		3		1	
	4			1		9		
6					9			

714
Demanding

			7			2		6
		8						
		7	9	5				1
5	7			1			9	
					2			
						3	4	
	3		8					
				6			1	
4						6		9

	8							
					3			2
3		2		8		9		1
	5							
			1					
	1	6		7	8			3
			4				5	7
				2		4	1	
	7				5		2	6

9	4							8
2					1			
7	1				5		2	
							7	
		7	2	3				
			4				5	
		6				8		3
	2		5		9		1	

Puzzle 717:

	5		7					4
			8	6			3	2
		3	1			6	9	7
							2	
				7				1
3		5	6					
2	1		9		4			
	8							

Puzzle 718:

	7		2				5	
4					6	9		7
	5						4	
6	1	3	8	2				
9								
			3	8				
5			1			9	6	
8				5			2	

	8			5		1		
		6				7		
		2	4					
8							5	
5			3					4
	9		1				7	
	4		2	6		9		
6					3			1
								2

			1		6			
	1				9	8		
	6	9					5	
		5	6				4	8
					1			
		4	7	8		9		
	2					4		
		8		9		7		2
								3

7				3		2	5	4
				6				
	3	1						
			5				8	
6							9	
4		9						5
2		5	8			3	4	
	6							
			1		2	5		6

			7		6			
2				9				
						9	1	
						1		
		9	4			6	2	
4	5				7			
	4							
5	1	6		2	9	8		
		8	5					

					7			
	3				5			
	8	5	6			2		
1	6	8	2				5	
9								8
			3			4		
		6	4		8		9	
7	9							1

			7	1			3	
	3	5						
	4				9		7	
8				9				
1		7		6				4
					5		9	
			5				4	
6	2							
					3	1	2	

Puzzle 725:

.	7	.	9	.	.	6	.	.
.	.	.	1	.	2	7	.	.
5	4	.	.	.	.	.	1	.
4	.	7	2	.	.	.	9	8
.	.	.	.	.	.	.	.	7
.	.	.	.	3	4	.	.	.
7	.	.	.	.	.	1	.	.
6	.	.	.	.	.	2	.	.
.	3	2	8	.	5	.	.	.

Puzzle 726:

4	8	.	6	5	.	.	1	.
.	.	7	.	.	.	.	.	.
.	.	.	8	.	3	.	.	.
.	.	3	.	.	.	.	.	.
8	4	.	.	.	.	2	.	5
.	.	.	2	7	.	.	.	.
3	.	.	.	.	4	.	.	.
.	.	.	.	.	.	5	6	.
5	.	.	.	2	.	.	9	1

727
Demanding

				7		8		
	4			9	3			7
		2		1				
3			9	2		4	6	
							1	
					4		2	5
	7	8						
4	1				5			9
9								2

728
Demanding

					5			
	6		7	3				8
4				8	1			
		1	2					
		8			6		5	2
	5					6	9	7
						8	1	6
			9		4			
2								

Puzzle 729:

	4					6		
				7	5		3	
1	5	3						
4			9		3			
6			1			4	2	
9								
			3		9	1		8
		9			4	5		
					2			

Puzzle 730:

7			4	3			8	
						9	5	
1								
		1	6					
	4	9				7	6	
2					4			3
			5		7			
				1	3		7	
5		4		2				

731
Demanding

	4	6						5
				5	3		7	2
	3	5						
4		8			9			
6				7				
						4		
	2			8	1			
	5			3		8		9

732
Demanding

					1		6	
	6		8		7			1
3	7		5			9		
4			9				5	
		6				4		8
			2			7	9	
			8					
5	9	2						
						1		

733
Demanding

9			4	2				
6						7		
		1	5				4	
	8			7				
		7		3				
			1			4		7
			2	1		9	6	
			3					
		3			5	8		

734
Demanding

			4		9			8
	3							
	1		7					4
		8	6					
	5				3			
	4	9		2	8	3		
		5		4			7	
		6			7	9		
			5					

735
Demanding

5		2			4			7
			8				4	
				5	3			
	8	1		9				
			7			4		5
				6		1		
	1	3					9	2
4								
				3				

736
Demanding

			4		1			
2	1		5		8			
				3				2
		5				6	7	1
		9					3	
					2		5	
		6			4			
1		3						
8	9		1	6		5		

5						2	8	
			4		3	5		
9								
	4		3		6			5
				8	4			2
			7			8		3
	7	1						
		9	8					
6		3	2			4		

		9	4		7			
2		7	5			4		
	5			8				6
3					6			8
	7					2		
	9		7	1	3			
					5		3	
	6		9					5
						1		

739
Demanding

		7		4				
			1					8
						3		
		9		2				
		1				6	8	5
		4	8			7		
3					7		5	
				8				4
1	7				5	8		9

740
Demanding

7	6	9			2	8		
		5		3				
			1			2	6	
		3	9					
				8			9	5
	8	2						1
			8		4	7		
		6						3

Puzzle 741:

4	7			5	9			
8	9							1
	6	1					5	
3		9	4			6		
			9			8		
			2	8		9		
					6		4	3
								5

Puzzle 742:

	8	6					1	
7		5			8			
		2						4
		4				3	6	
		8	5					
			1					
							8	1
8					4	2		
	2		6		3			

743
Demanding

		9	1				2	
		7						
		8	7		6	5		
4	2	1	6				7	
		5						1
								8
6					5	1		
			4				5	7
					2	3		

744
Demanding

	1							9
	2	9	3			4		
3								8
					5			1
9			4		1		3	
7					8			
	3		5					4
				2			6	
		2	9				5	3

745
Demanding

			6					
	7		5		3		4	1
	8		1	9	7			
6								
5	3	1	7					
2					4		5	3
	1	3	9	7				
							1	8
						5		

746
Demanding

					7		9	
		2						
7	5		8					3
							6	8
			5		4			
			9	2			3	1
9	2							5
8								
	1			4	3			7

					7		9	
			4					
		6	5				3	
		2	6		1			
	8				9		5	7
1			7			4		
9	7							8
4								
2				6		3		

	5			4				8
		1		6	8	9		
2					7			6
3							2	7
	9						5	
				8	1			
4		3						
8			9			5	4	

Puzzle 749:

			4		6	7		
	2	6				1		
1			8				9	
					3	8		
			5					
9	1			4			2	
8			7	5				
2			9					8
						6	7	

Puzzle 750:

				1	6			9
	8							
3					5	2		
		3					7	
		2					4	6
			7					1
7		9			1			
	2			5				8
6					4			2

751
Demanding

					5	9		
					4			2
4	1		3		8	5		
		7					9	
	4	6					3	
3	9		5			4		
			7					
		8						
2	5		9				4	

752
Demanding

		9		4				
				9	8	7		
2	1			3				
	3	5						6
	2						3	
8	6					9	5	
					5			
	4					2		
		7	8	6		1		

```
9 . . | . 2 . | 3 . .
. 1 . | 7 . . | . . .
. . . | . 8 . | 5 . 4
------+-------+------
. . . | . . . | 1 . .
3 . . | . . 2 | 9 . .
. . 5 | . 4 8 | . . .
------+-------+------
. . 1 | 6 . . | . . .
2 . . | . 9 . | . . .
. . 8 | . 5 . | 6 . 9
```

```
. . 8 | . . . | . 4 .
. . . | 6 2 . | . . .
. . 5 | 8 . . | . . .
------+-------+------
. . . | 5 . 6 | . . 8
1 2 . | . . . | . . 9
5 . 3 | . . . | 7 . .
------+-------+------
9 . . | . 8 . | 1 . .
. . . | . . 1 | . . .
3 . 7 | . 4 9 | . . 5
```

755
Demanding

		8	5		3			
4			7					9
6	2						4	
	4						7	
		9				3		
	3						1	2
1			4					
	8			6	2		3	
						8	2	

756
Demanding

			5		8			
3			9			6		
	1						5	
		3		4			1	9
	9				5		3	
	4							
		7	6					
		1	4	2			9	7
	3	8						

2				9				
				6				1
					5	7		6
9	1					2		4
				6				
								9
		8			7	9		
5		9				1		8
3			5				6	7

	6		7				5	9
5						4		
			4		3		8	
		8						
			3				4	
	5	9	2	8				
		6						2
	2		5			8	6	
4			9			1	3	

759
Demanding

6		5	3	7				
	9							5
			6				7	9
				5		1	2	
	8				6			
		4			8			
3	4							
			5		7		9	1
			9	8				3

760
Demanding

				6			9	
				1				
3						7	4	
7	2							6
1			7	9		2		
				3				
		7	4		9			8
	8	6						
							3	4

761
Demanding

		1						
6			3		4			5
7	8		9					1
9	2	3	1	6				
				8		5		
	3			7	1			2
				3				6
5						9		

762
Demanding

9				7	3			
	7	4						
3							8	
1	5			3		7		2
2			5				1	
				6		9		
							5	
		6	7		1	4		
			2	8				

763
Demanding

4	1			5	6		2	
					4	1		
		8		3				5
			2				5	
		9					8	
3		1			9			
				1		4		
							7	
8	5		3	4				

764
Demanding

9			4	3				
				9	1			
						7		6
			5					
3	6	5						
8		1		2			3	
				7				5
				8	9		2	
	4	2						

			3	7				5
4	5							8
			6					
				3				7
		3				1		
9	2	4			1			
						9		
2		6					5	
	1				9	8		3

	6							
		5	3	2				4
	8				4			
	9							1
5			2			8	6	
			7			3		9
						4		
7				5				3
2			8	1			9	

		5						9
6		2		3	8			1
			1					2
	9		5					
	7					3		
				7			1	
8		1					6	
			3		7	8		
				4				

9					4			
				8				1
3						7	9	8
		8	6					
						5	6	
1		6			9		4	
					7			
8	4			3	1		2	
	3			4				

769
Demanding

1					8	7		5
					5	4		3
		3			4			
4	1		2				5	
								2
	9			3	7			
					2	5		
		2			1		6	8
		9	4					

770
Demanding

6	9					7		1
								3
		8	9		4	5		
	2			1	8			9
3		6	4					
		7	6	2				
								5
	5			8			3	2
		4						

Demanding

					1		8	3
		4					7	6
		1		2				
						9		
	7			6		3		1
1		9		8				
2			9					
		6		4			5	
	8							

Demanding

		5	9				7	
							8	
					3			9
		7		4				
		1			6			
6	2	3						5
3		2				4		7
		4			8		9	
				1		6		

Puzzle 773:

		5						1
			9		4			
7	6						3	8
5	8							4
							7	5
9			6					
6	7			8		4		
		8			7		5	
			1	9				

Puzzle 774:

1				7		9		
			1		6	7		
3	8		9					
			5	4				
		2						
7	5	1				8		
					3	6		7
		6			5	2	8	
2						5	1	

Puzzle 775:

9								3
			4	1		7		
	3			7				
		6		4				5
		5	7					9
				2	1		4	
8							3	6
4	2			3				
				8	4			

Puzzle 776:

						3		8
		3				2	1	
7	5							9
	7		9	3				2
	9			2	7			
		6		1				
	1					9		
2					5		8	
4			6			1		

		1		9			3	
8			5			6		
	6	7			3			
								3
6		2			8			
						4	1	
2			9					1
		5	6	2				
			1			9		5

			3			4		
		5					1	6
				6	4		3	2
3		4			6	8		
				7				
9				5		4		
	5		9		3			
	6		2					
				8				

Puzzle 779:

		4						
	5		2					6
		2	3	6				
								3
							1	2
2	1		7					9
			9		3		8	
	9	3	8			7		
	8				4			

Puzzle 780:

				9		8	5	3
		2						
6					3			2
4				1				9
		7	9	2		3		
	5				7			
				4			7	
					2			
	9		8				6	

		3				6		
1		8		6	3			
2						7		
	1			7				3
	4	6		3				1
8			1					6
3					2	8		9
				4	1			

	2							
			4					
4		3	9			1	7	
9		5	1			8		
								2
				6	5			4
	8	9	3		4			
		1	2					
	3					6		9

3					5	1	2	4
8	9			1				
			2					
7				8		9	5	
	4			6	3	8		
				5			1	
5				7			8	
						5		
		3						7

		2	8				9	6
	8				1			
				3				
	6				9		5	
		7	3					2
					7		4	
	3					7		
	5			7		9	6	4
	2				8			

```
. 8 . | . 5 . | . 6 7
. . . | 3 . . | . . 4
. 6 . | . 7 . | . 9 .
------+-------+------
. . 4 | . . . | 1 . .
. 9 . | 6 . . | 1 . 3
8 3 . | . . . | 2 . .
------+-------+------
. . . | . . 5 | . . .
. . . | . . . | . 1 3
. . 9 | 7 . . | 2 . .
```

```
. . . | . 1 . | . . 6
8 . . | . . 4 | 3 . .
5 . . | . 8 . | 2 . .
------+-------+------
. 3 . | . . . | . . 2
. . 9 | . . . | . . 4
. . 8 | 1 2 . | 6 . .
------+-------+------
7 8 . | 6 . . | 4 . .
. . 5 | . . 9 | . . .
. . . | . 3 . | . . .
```

787
Demanding

			8	9	5		1	
		9		3		6		4
3			1			5		
		4			8		6	
					4			
1	3	8						2
	2			7				

788
Demanding

							6	2
		5		6				
7	4		2		5			
2								9
	5	4			9			6
					3			
		3	6		8			7
9				5				
				3			1	4

789
Demanding

8			5		6			
6			8				4	5
			1					
2	6				8			
5	7			2				3
				4		9		
	3							
							9	4
7				5		8		

790
Demanding

	3	2					5	
					8			
			5	6	4			
4	5	6				2		
					7	8		
								9
5		9	4			6		
			2	7				
		3	8				1	

791
Demanding

			3			9	7	
					6		8	2
						3		1
	9		2	3				
				7				8
			4					
4		5	9			8		
	7		6				5	
2			5			4		3

792
Demanding

	2				3		6	
7			2			1		8
	6		8				1	7
	3	9			6			
8	1					9		
2				8	7		9	
			4	2			7	
								3

793

Demanding

		9				2		
		2	7	5				
	8				2		9	1
						1	2	
3					8		6	4
5	6		4					
2						8		
		5		3			4	
			8					

794

Demanding

								1
	6					9		
	1			2	8		4	
3		2	5	1				
			9			8		7
					3			
				7				5
	5		1			3		
7							8	9

				1				
				5	2		3	4
				4		5	2	7
2			9			6	8	
6	9	4						
	1	3		8			9	
				9	3			
		8					1	5

		1				6		
	4		6			3		
5				8				9
4		7		2				
			1			4		
	2		3					1
					3			
7							4	
9	6				7	5		

1		7				9		5
				8				
	6		2				8	
	5			2				9
7		4			9			
3		9				6	4	
			7		3			4
		8	5				1	
								6

	5			8				
	6		9				7	
					3			8
			7				9	
7		4	3			2		5
			2		4			
5	3						8	4
6	8							
1		2						

	5	6			2		4	3
	9			7	3	8		
8		5						
			3		4			5
				2		9		7
				3	1	6		8
					7		5	
	2						1	

	1		9			8		
		5					3	4
				6				5
		4				2		3
3							4	7
5								
8						4		
6				8	7			
9					5			6

Puzzle 801:

		7					9	
4				1		8		
			8			3		
			9		3		5	6
2								
		3	5		4		7	
9			2			1		
8			7					
					5			

Puzzle 802:

						9		
4		1				6		
							5	
				7		3		2
5		8			1			
6	7			8				
2	5							3
	8			6	7			
				1		2		

803

Demanding

	6	9				8	7	5
7	4				3	9		
				6		2		
	3		1					4
8		1			9			
			8		4			3
		5						
	1			5			2	

804

Demanding

		5						
4					5		7	8
6				1				4
9	2	3		8				
		7						
					1			5
			6	3				
	9					3		
	8				4	9		1

		2					3	5
	7				9		4	
			6				9	
				3	5			8
3	5		9		2			
2					1			
	1	5						
	6						1	
			7					3

	2	6					3	
			1	4	9		2	
	1							
6					7			
	3	9		1		6	8	
		3		8			4	
	6					5		
			3	2				1

807
Demanding

		9					5	
6								9
	3		7	6				
	1							
5					2		4	
3		7	8			2		
8								
4			2				3	
				3		6	7	5

808
Demanding

	4			5				
1			3				4	
		3				2		9
						8		
	9	2		4		1		3
				6				
8							6	
			2				3	8
	6		1			5		

Puzzle 809:

							3	
4	7							
9				1				
		8	1				2	
2			5					7
		3		6			1	
		5		7				2
					5			9
		7	2		8			1

Puzzle 810:

		1			9	8	6	
	4	9	3					
				6				
	6	3		7				
			1			5		
						9	2	
2		5			4			
							1	2
	3							8

Puzzle 811:

			8					9
			4		7			
6							5	2
8						1		
			5		4	3	2	
					6			4
2	3							
	4		1			7		
		7						

Puzzle 812:

5								7
				6			1	
9					1	6		
	2				9	8		
		7	8			9	3	4
		3						
8				1		2	7	
		9		3		1	5	

813
Demanding

2					9			1
9							3	4
				4				
1		7			8	2		
	2	8	1		5			9
	5		6		1			
			8				6	
			4	7		8		

814
Demanding

	6							
8	7		9			1		
						7	9	4
		4				9	7	
5				8				
		2		9				1
			1		5		4	
			2	7				
					6			

8			7	4	1	3		
		2						
			3	9				
					9		5	
						4		9
				5		7		6
	3				8	1	4	
5		8						
2			1	7			8	

	8				2			
					1			4
5	1	9						
1	9		6					
				9	4	6		1
		4	7				5	
				4			3	
						8		9
	2				5			6

817
Demanding

3			9			2		
9							3	7
4		1	8					
	9	5						
				2		9		
				6		8		
	6		3					5
2		3			1			
			7	9			6	

818
Demanding

	5							
		7					6	3
				1	7			
1								9
4		2	5			6		
3			2				4	
	1				8			
		4		6	3		8	7
							9	

						2	5	
	8	3		4	1			
	1					3		
		5						4
	7		4		9			3
			7	6		8		
1				2	8			
						1		
	9	4		3			6	

		5			9			2
	1	7		8			6	
			7					
		8			3			
2					1	3		
				6				
4				2		1		3
	8			4				
				1			5	9

					4			
		6						
	5		6	8			3	
	4			9		5		
	3			1				4
8	2			5				7
			5		8		9	
		7						
5	8	2				7	6	

			9	3				4
					2		5	6
							3	
	7		2			9		
		4		6				
	9			4	1		8	
		7			3	1		
			5					
2	8	1						

			4					1
				9				6
	3		2				4	
		9		5	8			
		3		6		2		
					4	7		
	5		6	7				
8								
		6			5		3	9

		9	4	5	7			
2		7		8			3	
				6		8		
1	2	6					5	
						1		6
					9	7		8
9		8		4				
		1	6					9

825
Demanding

9			2	6			5	
			8		7		3	
8					5			
								2
5							8	
		3				9		7
		5		7		1	6	8
7								
6	8		4	1			7	

826
Demanding

					4	3		8
	2					6		
			6					7
		8					7	2
		1	3			9		
				9				
		6	4				8	
	4	2			3			
3			8	1	7			

827
Demanding

A 9×9 Sudoku puzzle with the following given numbers:

- Row 1: 3 (column 4), 1 (column 7)
- Row 2: 3 (column 1), 4 (column 2), 1 (column 6), 2 (column 7), 7 (column 9)
- Row 3: (empty)
- Row 4: 1 (column 2), 2 (column 6), 4 (column 7)
- Row 5: 7 (column 3), 8 (column 6)
- Row 6: 6 (column 3), 8 (column 8)
- Row 7: 5 (column 5)
- Row 8: 3 (column 2), 9 (column 3), 4 (column 8), 8 (column 9)
- Row 9: 7 (column 1), 6 (column 4), 3 (column 7), 5 (column 8)

828
Demanding

A 9×9 Sudoku puzzle with the following given numbers:

- Row 1: 4 (column 1), 3 (column 2), 9 (column 5)
- Row 2: 6 (column 3), 2 (column 8)
- Row 3: 1 (column 1), 3 (column 6), 5 (column 7)
- Row 4: 9 (column 2), 6 (column 4), 8 (column 7)
- Row 5: 3 (column 1), 7 (column 5), 5 (column 6)
- Row 6: 7 (column 3), 8 (column 6)
- Row 7: 8 (column 2), 6 (column 7), 9 (column 9)
- Row 8: 1 (column 8)
- Row 9: 2 (column 2), 4 (column 4), 5 (column 5)

		3	7	1				
						1		4
		7	9			8		
	5							
	6			4	9	5	3	
		2				9		
		9						8
		4		5	6			
2							5	

						9	7	
			6					8
4				8	3		5	
		3		9				2
5			7		4		6	
1	3		9					
		8				5		
	9	4	2			6		

831

Beware!
Very Challenging

		1						
3	5							
9		4	7			5	2	
4	1			2			7	
	6		8			9		
	2	8						
		5	1		9	7		
					6			9
				3		8		

832

Beware!
Very Challenging

							9	6
	7	5		3				
9		2						
					8	3	7	
		3		4			5	
		6			1			
		4	2	8			1	
					4			2
	1		5			9		

Beware!
Very Challenging

					9	8	4	2
	9		1					
4		8						7
5		4					6	
6								5
	8			7				
	1	6				9		
					2	3	8	
			8		1			

Beware!
Very Challenging

	8		6			1		
								8
				3		5		
2		8	6					9
	7							
	1			5	3	6		
4	6		5	7		8		
								1
			1		9			

**Beware!
Very Challenging**

	7			4			5	
				2			1	
3		1			9	8		
	2	9	8			6		
	4			6				8
		4		1				
1			9		2		4	
								3

**Beware!
Very Challenging**

		5		9		6		
	4		2				8	
	7				6			
				2				
		2						3
9			4	7	8		5	
	9							6
							4	7
8					1	9		

837

		9	7					
	2							1
8	7						6	
7		4		5		3		
	9			1				
				4		2		
		2				4		5
					9	1		
	6				8			

838

	4			3	5		1	
					6	7	3	
				9			8	
		3						
9	1			2				5
	2			5		1		
8		1			9			
								8
7			2			4	9	

**Beware!
Very Challenging**

	1					7		
					2		3	
7	3	8	6					5
		5		9	7			8
		6						
	7		3			9		
				1				4
5				8				1
					6		2	

**Beware!
Very Challenging**

					5			
2	8			7			6	
	6	7				1		3
6	5					9		
		9	5		1			
					7		8	
	3							
1					2		5	
	9				3		7	

**Beware!
Very Challenging**

			1		5	3		
	3				8			
5	6	7				9		
							9	
8		6	3	7		4	1	
		5			4	7		
			4					
							2	
4	2	3			7			

**Beware!
Very Challenging**

				2		9		
3		4	9	1		7		
					4		1	5
								6
	1	6	5	4	7			9
			1	6			4	
		3	8					
	4						8	7
		5						

	1			3		7	6	
9							5	
	5			7	9	4	3	
5		8						
					3		9	
				4		6	7	
			8	5		1		
2			4		6			

	8				7			2
	7		5	4		3	9	
								6
2		9						
			3		2			
	4					8		
		6						
			9	5		7		
4		1				5		

**Beware!
Very Challenging**

1		7						6
5								9
2	6							
	1			3				
					2			1
			8	7		5	4	
9				1		8		
			7		3			
8				4	5		7	

**Beware!
Very Challenging**

1							4	
	2		8		9			
				4				2
				7	5	9		
	8						2	
2	5	9				7	6	
	7	6		9		5		
				1		8		

**Beware!
Very Challenging**

3		7				6		
		5				2		
					8	9		
	6			5	3			4
					6			
			7					
7		2		4				
9			8			5	1	
				6	7			8

**Beware!
Very Challenging**

				7	9			1
			6	1			7	
7						4		8
			9	2		3	8	
	9		5		7			
	1			8				6
4							5	
	2	5	4				3	

849

	4							
7			6					
8		9		2		3		4
5				8				1
					3			
		6		4		7		
	8	2	1			6		
						4		
		3			5			

850

	3		7		2	8	6	
1					5	9		
	8				4			
	6					5		1
2				5		7		9
		8						
	7		4	3				
		3	9					8

851

Beware! Very Challenging

		9	8					4
	2			1				
			3	5				
	3	4					2	9
		7			6		1	
5							6	
	7			4		1	9	
8								
					7		3	8

852

Beware! Very Challenging

		9			5			
2		4		7			1	
							9	6
			7	5	1			
		5						2
8	3		4					
						8	6	7
	1				8	3		
	4				9			

853

**Beware!
Very Challenging**

		3		4			9	6
9		8		6				7
						5		8
2	5		8					
	1	6						
		9						
								4
			6	9			3	
1	3	4		5				

854

**Beware!
Very Challenging**

	4							7
		3				2		
	5	8	9	4				
		2	8					
					9	1	7	
			5	3	4			
		4						
	1				8		9	
	9		3	2	6			1

7				3				
	3		1			2	5	
			5					4
		6	2			9	8	1
								6
	1			8				
			6	5				
			9		4	3		
		5		2		6		

4		2		5				6
		8			7	4		
	2	6	4					
		5						
8			9				7	5
								9
	6		2	4				3
2				7			5	

		3	7	4				
	8				1		6	
					9			4
			2					7
							4	8
2					6		3	
4			6					
				7				
9	3	8				1		

								4
6		4					5	7
				8			9	
		6			3	7		
			2					
		7		1			8	
	1						2	9
				7				
	5	8	6	9				

859

3		5						8
			4	6				
	7			9				1
			6	8				
	9			1		8		
						7		2
		7				1	5	
8	2						6	
		9		7				

860

			7				6	
						3		
5		6	4					
				6		1		
	3			7	8			9
8		7			2	6		
3								2
				9				
7	2			8	1		5	

				9		5		6
	8		6				7	
			2			3		
		4						
		3	5	1		6		
	1				4		3	
		6			9	2		
7					8			5

	5			4			7	
7		8	9			6		
		6						
9	7				5			
5				1			2	
	6					3		
6		4				1	9	
	2		8					
		5						3

863

Beware!
Very Challenging

8		5		6				
						1		
3						8	5	4
		8			2		3	
			1			2		5
7			8	9				
		3	4					
6		9	5	3				
								9

864

Beware!
Very Challenging

4		9					1	
	5		6		7			8
2						8		7
			1	4				
8						5	4	
		8	7					2
				6		1		
3			8	9				

**Beware!
Very Challenging**

1							6	
		6	4		3			
							4	
2				7				8
	3		6		5		9	
	7		3			2		
		3				1		
		5		8				9
4		2				5		

**Beware!
Very Challenging**

		1						9
	4		5					
		7			8		6	
					5			4
3					6		2	5
	8		7			6		
1		6		4	9			
	2			6	8		1	

867

Beware!
Very Challenging

		7			6			8
3					1			
1		8					5	
		4						9
6		5			9	4		
			3			7		
	5	9	8				6	3
7			2					

868

Beware!
Very Challenging

				3			6	
9			7		5			
		2				3	4	
					7			8
	3		1					
		4				9		
		5			9			
						7		2
1		9	2	7		8		

Puzzle 869:

				5	2			
	7	8				4		
9			4		8			
	3			7			6	
		1			4	2		
		2	9		1	8		
1		3		2				
								3

Puzzle 870:

7	4						2	
	5			6	7			8
9		8		5				
8					9			7
		9						
						3		
				1	6	5		
		6		4				
		2			5	1	9	

**Beware!
Very Challenging**

**Beware!
Very Challenging**

873

		4	5				3	
9				6				
	8	7			4			
				7		9		
	4		6				1	
3								
				5			6	3
	2	1	8		6			5
				9				

874

	5	4		2			6	
2	1							
3					8	5		
5		9		7				
			9				2	
4					6			
			3					4
		6	8			9		7

875

**Beware!
Very Challenging**

	7							
9			7		1		4	
	8				3			
		5			4	8		
		4						2
3		2			8	6		
			6		7		3	
			3			4		5
								9

876

**Beware!
Very Challenging**

					1			
3	1					9		2
		9	3	6		1		
				8			5	7
6		7						
	2		1			6		
			5		4			3
		8	9				4	
2	7							

877

Beware!
Very Challenging

2			4			9		6
								5
			6		2		1	
9		4			5		3	
	7		9					2
			1	7				4
3					6	7		
	1	5		8		3		

878

Beware!
Very Challenging

			3			5	6	
	9	1						
		8					4	
			8		7			3
		9	5			2	8	
	4							5
							9	6
5					8			2
		4			1			

879

Beware!
Very Challenging

							2	9
1						6		
7			5		6			4
				8				
6		7			9			3
						4		
8	4			2	1		3	
					7		8	
		3				2		

880

Beware!
Very Challenging

	3	1	9	8				7
							1	
	6			7	1	3		
	8	9					2	4
			7			8		
5							3	
6	1							8
		8	3		9	2		5

		6		1	3	9		
	5					2		
	4	8		2		1		
				8				4
			1					5
	2			4		3		
	3		9					7
						8		
	8		6					

			4		8		1	
	7						8	
			9	1				2
						5		
6					3		2	1
1				9				
	3		5					
5	8						9	
			3		7	4		

Beware!
Very Challenging

				9	4			
		7						4
2			3					
					5			
		3	1		9			7
	8		2				3	
		5	7			9		2
6	1			2				
	7		6				8	

Beware!
Very Challenging

	8		1			9		
		4			5	1		
5					6			3
2			3					
	4							
		3	8				7	9
	5		9	1				
	1				3		2	
				7				

885

Beware!
Very Challenging

			5		2		9	
						3		6
		9						
6								2
1	3		6		7			
2							5	
	1			8				
						8	7	
	6		3	9		1		

886

Beware!
Very Challenging

			4		3			5
		5			8		6	
					5	2	1	
	5			6			7	4
6		4		9				
						5	9	
	8	9				3		
	7						2	

887

		8					2	6
4			3				5	
				1				8
	9						1	
		7						
		3		9				5
5		2		6	8	7		
	4				5			
	6			7				3

888

		7						8
	1		3		9		7	
3			2					
7							2	
2		6		8		4		5
								1
9			6					
		5			4			
	7		5			6		

Beware!
Very Challenging

```
. . . | . 6 9 | 4 . 7
2 . . | . . . | . . .
. . . | . . 8 | 1 . .
------+-------+------
. 2 . | . . . | . . 6
. 9 6 | . . . | 3 . .
. . . | 5 . . | . 1 .
------+-------+------
8 6 . | 9 . 4 | 2 . .
. . . | . 1 . | . . 3
9 7 . | 5 . . | . . .
```

Beware!
Very Challenging

```
1 . 2 | . . . | . . .
. . 7 | 4 . . | . . 3
. . . | 6 . . | . 9 .
------+-------+------
. . . | . . 2 | 3 . .
. . . | . 1 . | . 4 .
. . . | 5 9 7 | . . 2
------+-------+------
. . . | . . . | 4 . .
8 . . | . . . | 5 . .
4 3 . | 9 8 . | 6 . .
```

891

Beware!
Very Challenging

	4		3			6		
						2	9	
		9	7					
		4						6
8				1				
			5			3		
			6					8
7		8				1		
			1		5		4	7

892

Beware!
Very Challenging

8				3	6	1		
3								
1	6		2			4		9
						8	4	2
9	8			1		5		
	3							7
		5			8	6		
				9	1			

893

Beware!
Very Challenging

7		4						
			3	7		9		
	9			6	4	8		
	5		8					
				2			6	5
			7					1
1						3		4
2			6	5				
		9						

894

Beware!
Very Challenging

	5			2		1		3
	6							
3	7		8		1		2	
8		9		5		4		
	2							
		5	2				3	
			7					1
					8	2	9	
			1	3				8

Beware!
Very Challenging

	1							7
3						8	1	
2					4			
				6		4		5
	7			3		6		
4				7				
5				8	2			
		9				2		
	8				5			6

Beware!
Very Challenging

			8			2		
7							8	
	4	1						7
						9	4	1
4					5			
		7	3		9		6	
					4			
	8		5	6	1			
		9		7				

897

Beware!
Very Challenging

					3		9	
	2		8	9	1		3	
		7				6		
1								
6	4							
8		2	6		7	4	1	
			2	3				
						8	7	
		8	1					

898

Beware!
Very Challenging

						2		
	5		8			6		9
6			9					
					9		1	
8		2		1		3		
				7				
					4	9		6
	7	8		3				
		3	2		1			

8					5			
								3
		9		6			7	5
6	3		7		4		9	
4	2			9	1			
								8
2		5						
						7	3	6
	6			4		1		

3						6		
1		8	4		9		3	
9					2	7		
	5					9		
			3		1			2
				2				
							9	7
				6	8	3		
2	8							

**Beware!
Very Challenging**

		7	8		9		3	1
	8				4			
	9	4					8	
	2							
6				3			4	2
		1		5		6		
		2						
				1		9		8
					3	5	7	

**Beware!
Very Challenging**

1							2	
			1					
4		9						8
		7			9		1	5
	2		6		1			
			4	5				2
			6					
		8	3			6	7	
	9		7				4	

903

Beware!
Very Challenging

9			4				7	
	7	1						8
					6		1	
				5		8	6	
		2	9	1				
	3					7	2	
						3		5
4				6				
		3						

904

Beware!
Very Challenging

						7	6	
8			7		6			
		7	9					
	4	2	1	3				
					4		5	
				5				9
						4		1
	3	8						
	6				5		9	3

905

Beware!
Very Challenging

4					6			
	9					1		
	5			7	8		9	
	8		9					
	6					5		3
		3			1			2
5	7							
			3				5	4
			4			6		

906

Beware!
Very Challenging

3	9						8	
6				1			5	2
	4							3
		4						
					3	8		6
			2		6			5
		5						
	1				9	6		4
			7					1

Beware!
Very Challenging

			3				5	
	2	9						
	4				9			
				1			8	3
			4		6	5	1	
	5							
1	9							
		4			8			2
	8		6		2		3	

908

Beware!
Very Challenging

3				7	5			
1				9			3	7
2			4					
6					4		5	
		4		2	1			3
	7			6				
								4
		6	2				7	9
4	8					3		6

909

Beware!
Very Challenging

9					3			6
	1		5	4	6			9
		8				3		
	3			7	2			
		4		1				
	5		4				8	
	2		6					
						5		
4							7	

910

Beware!
Very Challenging

							5	
			1		7	9	8	
8		9				6	7	2
7								4
	3				1			
9	5			7			2	
		5	2					
4				6				
			1		4		9	

911

Beware!
Very Challenging

	8		9		1			5
						6		4
				2			8	
							7	
	7	3				8		
		6		5	8			
		8	5				6	
		5			4			
		4		7	2		9	

912

Beware!
Very Challenging

					2		9	
		5		1	4	7		
	7							8
	4	3				5		
			4					
			7	6	8	3		
	1					9	2	3
				9				
8					5			1

				3	6			
4	2						8	
		3				4		
				7				
5		6				3		
		7		1				9
				9	2			5
	7				3		4	6
		9						8

9								
		8				7		3
				9	4		5	
	1				6	2	3	4
		3		4		9		
		7		2				
	7	1						
					9	8	2	
			7					

Beware!
Very Challenging

	2		7			9	5	
	3		5					
						4		6
	5							
					8	7		
1						8		
9			8				1	
4			3	5			7	
		1	4	6		3		

Beware!
Very Challenging

9				7				
		2		1		5		
	9	5	3				7	
	4		7			1		
	2		4				6	
	5			8	9		1	6
	3						4	
		6		3			5	

917
Beware! Very Challenging

	6	7			9		2	
2							5	
				1	6		3	8
		3		2				
			9		4			
	2		6			4	9	
6	1				2			
	9	4						
7							4	3

918
Beware! Very Challenging

9				1	4	8		
				8		5		
	2		6			9		
					7	4		
		9	3	2				
	3						1	
	1							4
					1	7		2
6				5				

919

	2		1					
			9				6	7
	4	8	3			9		
			7			8	9	6
							3	
								2
7				8			5	
	3			5				4
		4			9			

920

						8	7	
7	8		9	4				
				5			2	
			3					
	5	6						
8		9			2		1	
				9			8	
						4		7
		1	7		6			

Puzzle 921:

	3				1		2	
			2				4	
1			3					5
3	8				7	6		
9				1			8	
8						2		6
	9							
	2		9		3	8	5	7

Puzzle 922:

		5						2
							1	4
2	3						6	
6	1			3	7			
8	7		4					
								8
1	5	7					9	
	9		1	2			8	

Beware!
Very Challenging

3					7	8		
	4			2				
5		9		7				8
							5	7
7					6			4
	2			3				
6	1							
			1	9	4	3		

Beware!
Very Challenging

				8	9	6	5	2
			6					
				7				1
9			5	1			3	
		8						
6						2		4
			4					
	3	4			8			6
5	9							7

**Beware!
Very Challenging**

8			6	2				
	3							
		1	5			9	7	
			2				4	
5			9		8			
				1				6
	2		7			6		5
	9	5						3
1				3				

**Beware!
Very Challenging**

				2				
2	8	6	4					
	1	4		3			9	7
					1		6	
	2					4		1
			7				5	8
8					7	3		
	3							6
	7			9				

927

Beware!
Very Challenging

6	7	5			2			
				6			8	
			7		1	9		2
3		4				8		
		6	1					
5	9			2				3
1	6							
								9
			9	4			7	

928

Beware!
Very Challenging

4			2				7	
	1							
5		6				3	1	
				3		6		
6		7						
				4	9			
		3			1			4
	9					2		
		1	3	9				

929

Beware!
Very Challenging

5	1				2		9	8
8			7				2	
4					9		3	
3	2				5			
	8		6		7			9
				6				3
	3			2				4
						8	5	

930

Beware!
Very Challenging

2	1							
					3	1		
		9	4					7
8	2	5			4			
			6					
1					8	2		
	7			9				
				3	1		4	
						3	8	

931

**Beware!
Very Challenging**

	5		4			1		2
	9						6	
			8	7				
		6			5			1
				1				
		4	9	8				
2		5				8		
		8	7		4		3	
			5			4		9

932

**Beware!
Very Challenging**

1			3			6		
		7	4					2
	6				1			
3	7							
			2				8	
9		2	7		8			
							9	8
								6
8		4		3		5		

933

Beware!
Very Challenging

9	1		4	8				
			3					1
								9
						3	6	
2		4	9					
	6			3				7
7					4			
		2				6		
		9			5	8	7	

934

Beware!
Very Challenging

	9		4		2			
4					5		3	
8	1							
				3		9		6
	4	7	1					
	8		5			1		
					6	5		4
								8
5	7		8					

Beware!
Very Challenging

Beware!
Very Challenging

937

Beware!
Very Challenging

		8		3	2	1		
		4				3	8	
	6			4	9			
		3						
8			1				6	
				6	5			2
2	7					8	1	
					8			9

938

Beware!
Very Challenging

			6					
		1					9	
5	3				4	2		
9	8		2			3	5	
	4						2	8
						9		
6			7	8				
			9				6	
	7						4	5

Beware!
Very Challenging

2							4	6
8	9				2			
			8	4	3			
		3	5					
	4				9	6	8	
							9	
			1	3				
5	6					7		
				2		5		

Beware!
Very Challenging

6					2		1	3
	4	2						
		1	3			5		
8				1			5	
			4					7
	7				8	4		
	6		9	2				
		5						
	2				6	8		

941

Beware!
Very Challenging

2						5		8
3	5					6		1
		9					7	
				3	4			
5			2					
8	1				5			9
				2				7
						1	8	
1		6	3	9				

942

Beware!
Very Challenging

	6							
			3				6	
3				9			4	1
9		8	5					7
			4	2		5		
					7			
5			7		4			
	3	1						
6					8	4	2	

943

**Beware!
Very Challenging**

1					2		8	
				5	7	6		
	4					1	2	8
				6				9
			3		8			4
			4	2				
		1						
9		8			6	7		

944

**Beware!
Very Challenging**

8				2				
				9	8	2		
				7				3
	6		1					
9	2		3	5				
		1						7
					5		7	6
		3	8					
		9					1	5

			5			7		8
		3		4				
						6		
	4			6			5	
			7	2				
5		8	3				1	
3			9		8		7	
		2		5				
4	8				2			

2			1					
			9				5	3
	4			5	6			2
4	2		3					
	8				5			4
		6		1			3	
			2				1	
		7				9		
8	3							

947

Beware!
Very Challenging

	8			5	9		4	
	1			4				
9				7	6		5	
1								
	9					1	2	8
	3					6		
			6	2				
		5			4	2	6	
					8			

948

Beware!
Very Challenging

2					5			3
		7				6		
				8		9		
	3	9		1		5		
7		6						9
	8				2	7		
	6					2		
			5					
3			2		7			8

949

4					3			
6					7		9	
5				6		3	1	
		5						
			6					
8			4	7				5
			8	1			2	
	3					9		
	1		7				8	

950

|
		5				4		
2	8						7	3
	6							
				1	7	8	6	
		3	2					
4			9					2
			4	8		9		
						2		
7		2					3	

3	6	9	1				8	
						2		
		2				1		4
7			5			3	2	
4	2						1	
					6		5	
					1			
	7		8	5				
	5	8		9				

1				8			7	5
	5			3	7			8
						2		
8						9	1	
			3	1				
		6						
				2	4	5		
9	7					1	8	
				9		6		

953

Beware!
Very Challenging

	4							
				7	8		2	
					9	4		3
8					7		3	1
			9					7
2	3						5	
	6					7		
3				8		1		2
		9		5				

954

Beware!
Very Challenging

	4		8					
			1	7				3
		6	3		4			
7	2							
	5				6		3	8
4				1				
6	3						4	
		1					9	
2				8				

955

Beware!
Very Challenging

		3		7			1	
	6				8		5	
7			2		3			
	3	1				9		8
					9			
			1				4	2
								4
				6	5		7	
	7		8			6		

956

Beware!
Very Challenging

		4	2		1			8
	8			5	4		7	
					7			
	5		1	7	2			
3			4			6	9	
			3					
1						7		
	4							2
	7						8	

957

**Beware!
Very Challenging**

			2				9	5
			5	1		2		
		6				8	7	
	1	9						
5				4	8		6	
			7			6		
	8						5	4
		4					3	7

958

**Beware!
Very Challenging**

	6			4				5
	8						9	
				1	5	3	8	
7	4							
			9	2				
						6		
		9				5		1
3	5		2					8
		8						4

**Beware!
Very Challenging**

	9					8	6	
2			3					4
1	8			5				
				8				
5					7	1		
		6		9				3
	7		2					
9	3					1	2	7

**Beware!
Very Challenging**

			3	2		4	9	1
			1				3	
					5			
1	5				4			
								9
	7					2		
		8		4				
3			5		6		2	
2		4			3		8	

961

```
. . . | . . . | . . .
3 . 8 | . . . | . . 2
. . . | 6 7 4 | 5 . .
------+-------+------
. . . | 7 . . | 8 . .
9 . . | . . . | . 6 .
5 . . | . . 2 | 3 . .
------+-------+------
. . . | . . . | . . 1
. 4 . | . . 5 | . . 3
1 . . | . 2 3 | . 4 .
```

962

```
. . . | 3 . . | . . .
. . 1 | . . 9 | . 7 6
5 . . | 4 . . | 9 . 8
------+-------+------
. . . | . . . | 6 . 7
. . 5 | . . . | . . .
2 8 . | . . . | . . .
------+-------+------
. . . | 9 . . | 8 . 2
7 3 . | 5 1 . | . . .
. 6 . | . 3 . | . . .
```

963

Beware! Very Challenging

					9			
	2					8		
		6				2		5
3			6					
	8				7	1		
2	1	7			3			6
			5	4			7	8
		5			2			
					8		9	

964

Beware! Very Challenging

		3	2	8	4			
					6			
		2	7				9	
3								
5	6	7				9		
	1		8	2				
						6		5
	7		1	6		8		
			9			1		

4				5				
		3				7		8
		9	6				3	4
			2		4		8	
								7
7			3					
5			9		8			
3	7	4			5			
		8					4	6

			2	1				
		3	4	9				1
9					5			
		8		6		5		
1								7
		6	8					
5				2		7	8	3
		4	1	3	8			
								4

Beware!
Very Challenging

		2			5		6	
	1	9	2			4		
			9				2	
								3
	9	5				1		
2				6			7	
3	6			4				5
				1				
	8							

Beware!
Very Challenging

	1		6				9	
	2		8		5			
				7	9	2		
7			5				3	
8		6				1		
								2
	3			8				9
							7	6
			3	6				5

969

	1		5					6
			4	7				8
		5						
8	6						9	
1							4	
		2	3					
4			6	5	3		1	
2		7		9			6	
				4	2			

970

								7
			6	7			1	8
		1	9		5			2
3								5
5	7		3				2	1
6						7		
	4	2	5					
			1					9
9				4				

**Beware!
Very Challenging**

	7							2
		5				4	1	
6	3		4					
1								3
					7			
5		8			4	2		
				7	8		9	
				5	2			6
			6					7

**Beware!
Very Challenging**

					4			7
2						9	8	
	3	6		2				
	7							1
		4	3		5			
9								
	2			7				
1		8		4			5	
			1	9				

973 — Beware! Very Challenging

						3		
7			5		9			
	3	5						
		6		1		2	8	9
		4		9			1	7
		1			3			
			8	7			2	4
	6			2			7	

974 — Beware! Very Challenging

8						2		
		7		9		3	8	
6			1					
2		1		6				
	3						4	5
4							2	
		8				7		
				2	6			
3	5		4					

975
Beware! Very Challenging

	2					1		6
9	3	4	7					
6	9			3				
		8						5
	1		4				8	2
7						5		
			1				9	
4				5	9			

976
Beware! Very Challenging

1		3						
4			1			7	2	5
							1	
						2	8	
		4	3					6
2	5	1						
7	9			8			4	3
				6				
					2			

977

**Beware!
Very Challenging**

	7							3
	2					8		
	8		9	3	6			4
			7	2			1	5
		8				6		
					4		3	
6				7	3			
				1		2		
							9	

978

**Beware!
Very Challenging**

	6		1		3			
4								5
2	8							
		8				1		
	9			6		3		7
			2					
5							3	
		7		3	2			
6			7		8		9	

Beware!
Very Challenging

			4	6		2	7	
				3				4
		1						
9		4		1				
2		8					3	
	6				3			
5							2	
			2		8	9		
		7		5	6	8		

Beware!
Very Challenging

		1		9		2	6	
				4				
7						9		
		3			8		2	
			1		5			
	6			7				
5	2		8				4	
	9							8
4							5	

981

Beware!
Very Challenging

			5					
	7	9					6	
				6	7	8		
1				8		7		
	6	5	3	4				
	4							
9							3	
2				3	5			1
			4	7				

982

Beware!
Very Challenging

3	5				4			
	4	9				8	2	
			1					
2			3			1		
		6				5	3	
		3		8	6	2	4	
			2					
8			7		5			
6								5

Beware!
Very Challenging

							4	
		9					1	
1			5	2		3		
	6							
8			4			5		
	7		3			8	9	
				3				
	4		1	5				
	2		9			7		4

Beware!
Very Challenging

2				5		6		
8	5		4		1			
		7				9	5	
5					6	3		
			3					
				1	8			4
		4	7	3		8		
	9							
6		8						9

985

**Beware!
Very Challenging**

				5	2			
							8	1
	6		7					3
6					9			2
	1							
				2		9	5	
3								
		5			7	2		
			6		1		7	8

986

**Beware!
Very Challenging**

	6							
		1	5	6	3			2
				4				9
		9						
				2	8			
2	8		4		1			5
4			6				7	
8	9	5					3	4

987

Beware!
Very Challenging

		5		8				
	7			4		3	5	2
	3				1			
					9	4		
	2	3	7					1
	5				8	6	2	
	8	6					7	
								5
		4		1				

988

Beware!
Very Challenging

8	7			2				1
		5						
9					5			4
	3	9						6
		2	9					
			4		1			
				8	3	7		
	2			5				
				4		5		3

989

Beware!
Very Challenging

2								
	7				8		4	
	6				9	7		8
			9		4	5		
5							6	3
			1					
		7	8					9
	3	6						7
				4		3	1	

990

Beware!
Very Challenging

			5					2
8		3	2				5	
		1			9			7
	7					1		
		8						
			4		5		8	
			3	4	2			
						9	4	
7				8		5		

**Beware!
Very Challenging**

	8	4	9				2	
		7		3		5		9
		3	8					
				6		2		
9			3					4
		8	4					
	4		7		6			5
						8		6
					5	3		

**Beware!
Very Challenging**

8		5						
1	7						9	
6			2	1				
					4			
3							8	
		6	3			1		
	2		1		9			7
								8
7			6	8		5	3	

**Beware!
Very Challenging**

	6		1		9		4	
		7				8	6	
						5		
1		2		3				
						4		
		8	5			6		3
2			8					
9			4	7				
				1			2	

**Beware!
Very Challenging**

4				9				
2							4	8
			8					
		1			4		6	
		3	7	8			5	
				3				9
3		6	9					4
7					3		1	
		4		1				2

Beware!
Very Challenging

6		9			7	5	3	
	3		6				8	4
		1						
	6		7		1	9		
4					6	7		2
								9
7		8						
			8	2				

Beware!
Very Challenging

	1			7		4		
	7		3		8			
				5		8		
			2				3	8
		9	4					
	8		5	6				
9								2
						1	6	4
		5	8					9

	5			4	6			
8			1	9				
7								3
			7	9			1	
6	1		2	8			5	
								2
1	3							
4						1		
		7					8	9

7		9			3	4		2
			6				1	
		6					8	
4								6
9	5	7		1				
						1	2	
			5	7				
		5		4		3		
	4							

999

Beware!
Very Challenging

6	2				7			
			9	4		1		
								7
		2		1	3	7	4	
		9	7		8		2	
		6		5			9	
3					1	6		
						8		

1000

Beware!
Very Challenging

				3				6
	8				6			
1	2		9	7			5	
	3					7		
			2		4			
	6	2					9	
	7	3	1	6		8		
						9		
		8					3	2

ANSWERS

1

5	3	7	1	2	8	6	9	4
8	2	4	9	5	6	3	1	7
6	1	9	3	4	7	2	8	5
4	7	3	8	1	5	9	6	2
2	9	8	6	7	3	4	5	1
1	5	6	2	9	4	8	7	3
9	4	2	5	8	1	7	3	6
7	6	1	4	3	9	5	2	8
3	8	5	7	6	2	1	4	9

2

5	3	9	2	6	8	1	7	4
1	7	2	4	9	3	5	8	6
4	8	6	5	1	7	9	3	2
9	5	1	3	8	2	4	6	7
8	2	7	1	4	6	3	5	9
6	4	3	9	7	5	2	1	8
7	9	4	8	3	1	6	2	5
3	6	5	7	2	9	8	4	1
2	1	8	6	5	4	7	9	3

3

8	2	5	3	6	1	7	9	4
6	1	4	7	2	9	8	5	3
9	7	3	8	4	5	2	6	1
5	6	1	2	7	3	4	8	9
7	8	9	6	1	4	5	3	2
3	4	2	5	9	8	6	1	7
4	9	6	1	8	2	3	7	5
1	5	7	4	3	6	9	2	8
2	3	8	9	5	7	1	4	6

4

3	1	6	7	5	2	8	9	4
4	7	5	1	8	9	2	6	3
9	2	8	4	3	6	7	5	1
7	5	1	9	6	3	4	2	8
2	9	3	8	7	4	6	1	5
8	6	4	2	1	5	3	7	9
5	4	2	3	9	7	1	8	6
1	3	9	6	2	8	5	4	7
6	8	7	5	4	1	9	3	2

5

7	5	3	8	2	6	1	9	4
2	9	8	7	4	1	5	6	3
4	1	6	9	3	5	2	7	8
9	7	5	2	6	3	4	8	1
3	6	2	1	8	4	7	5	9
1	8	4	5	9	7	3	2	6
8	4	9	3	5	2	6	1	7
6	2	1	4	7	8	9	3	5
5	3	7	6	1	9	8	4	2

6

4	8	6	7	5	1	9	2	3
7	3	2	9	6	8	4	1	5
9	1	5	4	3	2	7	8	6
1	6	8	5	7	4	3	9	2
5	4	3	2	9	6	8	7	1
2	7	9	8	1	3	5	6	4
3	2	7	1	4	9	6	5	8
6	5	1	3	8	7	2	4	9
8	9	4	6	2	5	1	3	7

7

1	5	6	8	3	2	9	4	7
4	9	2	1	7	6	8	5	3
8	7	3	5	4	9	6	1	2
2	4	9	6	5	3	7	8	1
6	8	1	9	2	7	4	3	5
7	3	5	4	8	1	2	9	6
3	6	8	2	9	5	1	7	4
9	2	7	3	1	4	5	6	8
5	1	4	7	6	8	3	2	9

8

8	6	3	9	7	2	1	5	4
5	2	9	4	1	3	6	8	7
7	1	4	6	5	8	2	9	3
2	4	1	8	9	7	5	3	6
6	9	7	1	3	5	4	2	8
3	5	8	2	6	4	9	7	1
9	3	6	5	8	1	7	4	2
4	7	5	3	2	6	8	1	9
1	8	2	7	4	9	3	6	5

9

4	3	2	9	8	7	5	1	6
1	7	9	5	6	4	2	8	3
6	8	5	2	3	1	7	4	9
2	9	4	1	5	6	8	3	7
8	5	6	3	7	9	4	2	1
7	1	3	8	4	2	9	6	5
3	4	8	7	1	5	6	9	2
9	6	7	4	2	3	1	5	8
5	2	1	6	9	8	3	7	4

10

1	6	8	2	4	7	5	3	9
3	9	4	8	6	5	1	7	2
7	2	5	9	3	1	4	6	8
5	8	1	6	7	3	2	9	4
4	7	2	5	8	9	6	1	3
9	3	6	1	2	4	7	8	5
8	4	3	7	5	6	9	2	1
6	5	9	3	1	2	8	4	7
2	1	7	4	9	8	3	5	6

11

8	1	9	3	6	4	7	5	2
4	3	7	2	5	8	1	6	9
2	6	5	1	9	7	8	4	3
7	5	8	9	4	1	3	2	6
1	4	6	5	2	3	9	7	8
3	9	2	7	8	6	4	1	5
6	2	4	8	7	9	5	3	1
9	7	3	6	1	5	2	8	4
5	8	1	4	3	2	6	9	7

12

4	8	1	5	7	3	9	6	2
6	5	7	1	2	9	3	4	8
2	3	9	4	8	6	7	1	5
9	1	4	8	3	5	6	2	7
7	6	3	2	4	1	5	8	9
5	2	8	9	6	7	4	3	1
3	4	5	7	1	8	2	9	6
1	9	6	3	5	2	8	7	4
8	7	2	6	9	4	1	5	3

13

2	7	8	9	1	3	6	5	4
5	1	9	4	6	7	2	3	8
3	4	6	2	8	5	9	1	7
4	6	5	3	9	8	7	2	1
1	8	2	7	5	4	3	6	9
9	3	7	6	2	1	4	8	5
7	5	4	1	3	6	8	9	2
8	2	3	5	4	9	1	7	6
6	9	1	8	7	2	5	4	3

14

3	4	8	5	7	2	9	1	6
5	2	1	6	9	8	4	3	7
9	7	6	1	4	3	5	8	2
8	1	5	2	3	6	7	4	9
7	6	4	9	1	5	3	2	8
2	9	3	4	8	7	6	5	1
4	5	7	8	6	1	2	9	3
6	8	2	3	5	9	1	7	4
1	3	9	7	2	4	8	6	5

15

1	3	8	2	4	9	5	7	6
5	9	7	1	6	8	2	3	4
6	4	2	7	3	5	1	9	8
4	5	6	8	9	2	3	1	7
2	7	9	3	1	4	6	8	5
3	8	1	5	7	6	4	2	9
8	6	4	9	2	3	7	5	1
7	2	5	4	8	1	9	6	3
9	1	3	6	5	7	8	4	2

16

7	4	3	5	9	1	8	6	2
6	9	2	3	7	8	5	4	1
8	5	1	2	6	4	7	3	9
9	1	5	6	4	2	3	8	7
4	7	8	1	3	9	6	2	5
3	2	6	8	5	7	1	9	4
1	6	4	9	8	5	2	7	3
5	8	9	7	2	3	4	1	6
2	3	7	4	1	6	9	5	8

17

1	2	9	3	5	8	4	6	7
8	6	4	7	1	2	5	9	3
7	3	5	4	6	9	8	2	1
6	8	1	5	2	4	3	7	9
5	4	2	9	3	7	6	1	8
3	9	7	1	8	6	2	4	5
4	7	6	8	9	3	1	5	2
2	1	3	6	7	5	9	8	4
9	5	8	2	4	1	7	3	6

18

8	1	9	6	3	4	7	2	5
3	7	5	2	1	8	4	9	6
4	2	6	5	7	9	8	1	3
2	5	3	8	9	7	1	6	4
7	4	8	1	6	3	2	5	9
6	9	1	4	5	2	3	7	8
1	6	7	3	8	5	9	4	2
9	8	4	7	2	6	5	3	1
5	3	2	9	4	1	6	8	7

19

4	6	9	2	7	3	1	8	5
5	7	8	9	4	1	2	6	3
1	2	3	8	5	6	9	4	7
7	9	4	3	1	8	6	5	2
6	5	1	7	2	9	8	3	4
8	3	2	5	6	4	7	9	1
2	4	5	6	8	7	3	1	9
3	1	6	4	9	2	5	7	8
9	8	7	1	3	5	4	2	6

20

3	7	9	2	1	8	5	4	6
5	1	6	4	9	3	7	8	2
4	2	8	5	7	6	1	3	9
8	3	5	9	6	1	2	7	4
6	4	7	3	2	5	9	1	8
2	9	1	8	4	7	6	5	3
1	8	3	6	5	9	4	2	7
9	5	2	7	3	4	8	6	1
7	6	4	1	8	2	3	9	5

21

4	1	3	2	6	9	7	8	5
9	2	8	7	5	4	1	6	3
6	7	5	8	3	1	4	2	9
2	8	9	5	4	7	6	3	1
7	6	4	1	8	3	9	5	2
3	5	1	6	9	2	8	7	4
8	3	7	9	1	5	2	4	6
1	4	6	3	2	8	5	9	7
5	9	2	4	7	6	3	1	8

22

5	1	9	8	2	4	7	3	6
7	4	3	9	6	1	5	8	2
2	6	8	7	3	5	9	4	1
8	9	2	6	1	7	4	5	3
6	3	4	5	8	9	2	1	7
1	5	7	3	4	2	6	9	8
4	7	6	1	5	3	8	2	9
3	8	5	2	9	6	1	7	4
9	2	1	4	7	8	3	6	5

23

7	6	9	5	1	2	3	8	4
2	5	3	6	8	4	1	9	7
1	4	8	9	7	3	6	2	5
8	9	7	3	6	5	4	1	2
4	3	6	1	2	7	9	5	8
5	2	1	4	9	8	7	3	6
3	7	5	8	4	1	2	6	9
9	1	4	2	5	6	8	7	3
6	8	2	7	3	9	5	4	1

24

5	6	1	2	4	9	8	7	3
3	8	4	6	7	1	2	9	5
7	9	2	5	3	8	1	4	6
4	5	3	7	1	2	9	6	8
1	7	9	8	6	5	3	2	4
6	2	8	3	9	4	5	1	7
9	3	7	1	5	6	4	8	2
8	1	5	4	2	7	6	3	9
2	4	6	9	8	3	7	5	1

25

5	7	2	1	3	4	6	9	8
6	9	4	5	7	8	3	1	2
3	1	8	2	6	9	5	4	7
1	5	7	3	8	6	4	2	9
4	2	3	9	1	5	8	7	6
9	8	6	7	4	2	1	5	3
2	4	1	8	9	3	7	6	5
7	3	9	6	5	1	2	8	4
8	6	5	4	2	7	9	3	1

26

7	9	5	2	4	3	1	8	6
2	3	1	5	8	6	4	7	9
8	4	6	1	7	9	5	2	3
9	7	3	8	5	1	6	4	2
5	8	2	9	6	4	3	1	7
6	1	4	7	3	2	8	9	5
4	5	7	3	9	8	2	6	1
1	6	9	4	2	5	7	3	8
3	2	8	6	1	7	9	5	4

27

7	2	6	5	9	8	4	1	3
5	8	3	1	4	7	9	6	2
9	4	1	2	6	3	8	7	5
6	3	9	4	5	1	7	2	8
8	5	2	9	7	6	3	4	1
4	1	7	3	8	2	6	5	9
1	7	4	8	3	5	2	9	6
2	9	8	6	1	4	5	3	7
3	6	5	7	2	9	1	8	4

28

7	8	5	3	6	1	4	2	9
6	1	9	4	7	2	5	3	8
3	2	4	5	8	9	7	6	1
9	3	1	7	5	8	6	4	2
2	7	6	1	4	3	9	8	5
4	5	8	9	2	6	1	7	3
5	4	3	8	9	7	2	1	6
8	6	7	2	1	5	3	9	4
1	9	2	6	3	4	8	5	7

29

6	5	4	2	9	3	1	7	8
8	2	9	5	7	1	6	3	4
3	7	1	4	8	6	2	9	5
5	3	6	8	2	4	9	1	7
9	8	2	1	3	7	5	4	6
4	1	7	6	5	9	3	8	2
1	6	3	7	4	2	8	5	9
2	4	5	9	1	8	7	6	3
7	9	8	3	6	5	4	2	1

30

4	9	7	8	5	3	1	6	2
3	6	1	7	4	2	5	9	8
5	8	2	9	6	1	4	3	7
7	2	9	1	3	4	6	8	5
1	4	8	5	9	6	2	7	3
6	5	3	2	7	8	9	1	4
8	3	6	4	1	5	7	2	9
2	7	5	6	8	9	3	4	1
9	1	4	3	2	7	8	5	6

31

5	3	2	8	4	9	1	6	7
1	7	4	3	6	5	9	2	8
8	6	9	1	2	7	5	3	4
6	1	8	5	3	4	7	9	2
9	4	7	6	8	2	3	5	1
2	5	3	9	7	1	8	4	6
3	8	1	2	5	6	4	7	9
7	2	5	4	9	8	6	1	3
4	9	6	7	1	3	2	8	5

32

8	9	3	7	2	5	4	6	1
5	1	6	3	9	4	2	8	7
2	7	4	6	1	8	9	5	3
9	3	2	8	6	1	7	4	5
7	5	8	9	4	2	3	1	6
6	4	1	5	7	3	8	2	9
3	8	7	2	5	6	1	9	4
4	6	9	1	8	7	5	3	2
1	2	5	4	3	9	6	7	8

33

8	1	7	2	5	6	3	9	4
2	9	6	4	3	8	7	1	5
4	5	3	7	9	1	8	2	6
9	3	8	1	7	4	6	5	2
1	7	2	9	6	5	4	3	8
6	4	5	3	8	2	1	7	9
3	2	1	6	4	9	5	8	7
5	6	9	8	1	7	2	4	3
7	8	4	5	2	3	9	6	1

34

3	8	6	1	4	5	9	2	7
1	9	5	7	3	2	4	8	6
7	2	4	6	8	9	3	5	1
8	3	9	2	5	6	1	7	4
2	6	1	4	7	8	5	9	3
5	4	7	9	1	3	8	6	2
6	5	8	3	2	4	7	1	9
9	7	3	5	6	1	2	4	8
4	1	2	8	9	7	6	3	5

35

7	6	5	8	3	1	2	9	4
4	1	2	5	6	9	8	3	7
8	9	3	7	4	2	5	1	6
3	7	6	9	8	4	1	5	2
5	4	9	2	1	3	7	6	8
1	2	8	6	5	7	9	4	3
6	3	7	1	9	8	4	2	5
2	5	1	4	7	6	3	8	9
9	8	4	3	2	5	6	7	1

36

9	7	5	2	8	6	4	1	3
6	8	3	1	4	7	5	2	9
2	1	4	3	5	9	6	7	8
7	9	8	4	2	1	3	6	5
3	6	1	8	7	5	9	4	2
4	5	2	6	9	3	1	8	7
1	4	7	5	3	8	2	9	6
5	2	9	7	6	4	8	3	1
8	3	6	9	1	2	7	5	4

37

3	9	6	2	1	7	5	8	4
2	5	1	8	6	4	3	7	9
8	7	4	5	9	3	1	6	2
7	4	2	3	5	6	9	1	8
5	3	9	1	4	8	7	2	6
1	6	8	9	7	2	4	5	3
4	1	5	6	2	9	8	3	7
9	2	3	7	8	1	6	4	5
6	8	7	4	3	5	2	9	1

38

5	1	6	7	9	8	3	4	2
8	4	9	2	1	3	5	6	7
2	7	3	5	6	4	1	9	8
1	8	2	4	3	6	7	5	9
3	6	5	9	7	2	8	1	4
7	9	4	8	5	1	6	2	3
4	3	8	6	2	5	9	7	1
6	2	7	1	8	9	4	3	5
9	5	1	3	4	7	2	8	6

39

7	9	4	5	2	6	8	1	3
3	2	5	8	1	7	9	6	4
8	6	1	3	4	9	5	2	7
1	3	2	7	8	5	4	9	6
6	4	8	9	3	1	7	5	2
5	7	9	4	6	2	1	3	8
9	5	3	6	7	8	2	4	1
2	8	6	1	5	4	3	7	9
4	1	7	2	9	3	6	8	5

40

6	5	8	4	1	7	2	9	3
3	2	9	8	5	6	4	7	1
1	7	4	9	3	2	5	8	6
7	8	5	3	9	4	1	6	2
2	3	6	7	8	1	9	4	5
4	9	1	2	6	5	7	3	8
9	6	7	1	2	8	3	5	4
8	1	3	5	4	9	6	2	7
5	4	2	6	7	3	8	1	9

41

```
8 6 2 5 4 7 3 9 1
1 4 5 9 3 8 6 2 7
7 3 9 2 6 1 8 5 4
9 1 6 4 8 2 5 7 3
4 5 7 3 1 6 9 8 2
3 2 8 7 9 5 1 4 6
2 8 3 1 5 4 7 6 9
5 9 4 6 7 3 2 1 8
6 7 1 8 2 9 4 3 5
```

42

```
5 3 6 7 1 8 9 4 2
1 4 7 9 3 2 8 6 5
9 8 2 5 6 4 3 1 7
6 2 9 4 7 1 5 3 8
4 7 1 8 5 3 2 9 6
3 5 8 6 2 9 1 7 4
2 9 5 1 4 6 7 8 3
7 1 4 3 8 5 6 2 9
8 6 3 2 9 7 4 5 1
```

43

```
8 6 3 4 7 9 2 1 5
2 9 4 1 5 3 8 7 6
1 7 5 8 2 6 3 4 9
5 4 9 2 6 1 7 8 3
7 8 1 9 3 4 6 5 2
3 2 6 7 8 5 1 9 4
6 3 8 5 4 7 9 2 1
4 1 2 3 9 8 5 6 7
9 5 7 6 1 2 4 3 8
```

44

```
8 7 6 1 9 5 4 2 3
9 1 4 2 7 3 6 8 5
2 3 5 6 8 4 7 9 1
6 8 2 5 4 7 3 1 9
3 4 9 8 1 6 2 5 7
1 5 7 9 3 2 8 4 6
5 6 8 3 2 1 9 7 4
7 2 3 4 5 9 1 6 8
4 9 1 7 6 8 5 3 2
```

45

```
1 7 4 5 3 9 8 2 6
3 2 8 6 7 1 5 4 9
5 9 6 8 4 2 3 1 7
9 8 5 2 1 3 6 7 4
4 3 1 7 6 5 2 9 8
2 6 7 9 8 4 1 3 5
8 4 9 1 2 6 7 5 3
7 5 2 3 9 8 4 6 1
6 1 3 4 5 7 9 8 2
```

46

```
2 6 7 1 3 5 9 4 8
5 8 3 4 7 9 6 2 1
4 1 9 6 8 2 5 3 7
3 5 1 2 9 6 8 7 4
9 7 6 8 1 4 3 5 2
8 2 4 7 5 3 1 9 6
1 4 5 9 2 8 7 6 3
6 3 8 5 4 7 2 1 9
7 9 2 3 6 1 4 8 5
```

47

```
6 4 2 5 7 3 8 9 1
8 7 9 2 6 1 4 3 5
3 5 1 8 4 9 6 2 7
2 9 6 7 5 4 1 8 3
7 8 3 1 9 6 5 4 2
5 1 4 3 2 8 7 6 9
4 3 8 9 1 5 2 7 6
1 6 7 4 3 2 9 5 8
9 2 5 6 8 7 3 1 4
```

48

```
8 5 9 2 4 3 7 1 6
3 7 6 5 1 8 4 9 2
1 2 4 7 6 9 8 5 3
7 6 8 4 9 2 5 3 1
9 1 5 6 3 7 2 8 4
2 4 3 1 8 5 6 7 9
6 9 2 8 5 1 3 4 7
4 8 1 3 7 6 9 2 5
5 3 7 9 2 4 1 6 8
```

49

```
1 3 5 6 7 2 4 9 8
7 6 9 4 8 3 5 1 2
4 8 2 1 5 9 3 6 7
2 1 8 7 3 5 6 4 9
9 5 7 8 4 6 1 2 3
3 4 6 2 9 1 8 7 5
8 2 4 3 6 7 9 5 1
6 9 1 5 2 8 7 3 4
5 7 3 9 1 4 2 8 6
```

50

```
9 3 2 6 5 7 4 8 1
4 6 1 8 2 3 7 5 9
7 5 8 4 9 1 2 3 6
2 8 7 3 1 9 5 6 4
5 1 6 7 8 4 3 9 2
3 4 9 5 6 2 8 1 7
1 9 4 2 3 5 6 7 8
8 7 5 9 4 6 1 2 3
6 2 3 1 7 8 9 4 5
```

51

```
9 3 2 1 7 4 5 8 6
7 6 4 8 5 3 1 9 2
5 1 8 6 9 2 4 7 3
6 2 5 3 1 9 8 4 7
3 9 1 7 4 8 6 2 5
8 4 7 5 2 6 9 3 1
4 7 3 9 6 1 2 5 8
2 8 6 4 3 5 7 1 9
1 5 9 2 8 7 3 6 4
```

52

```
9 2 7 4 8 6 5 1 3
3 8 4 1 9 5 6 2 7
5 1 6 2 7 3 4 9 8
4 3 2 9 6 7 8 5 1
7 9 1 8 5 4 2 3 6
6 5 8 3 2 1 9 7 4
2 7 9 6 3 8 1 4 5
1 6 3 5 4 9 7 8 2
8 4 5 7 1 2 3 6 9
```

53

```
7 6 5 9 2 8 3 1 4
2 9 4 3 5 1 8 6 7
3 1 8 4 7 6 5 2 9
6 8 7 5 4 3 2 9 1
1 2 9 8 6 7 4 3 5
5 4 3 2 1 9 7 8 6
4 3 6 1 8 5 9 7 2
8 7 2 6 9 4 1 5 3
9 5 1 7 3 2 6 4 8
```

54

```
9 1 7 2 5 8 4 3 6
6 8 5 3 4 7 9 1 2
2 4 3 6 9 1 7 8 5
3 9 1 7 8 5 2 6 4
7 6 4 1 2 3 5 9 8
5 2 8 9 6 4 1 7 3
4 7 9 5 3 6 8 2 1
8 3 2 4 1 9 6 5 7
1 5 6 8 7 2 3 4 9
```

55

```
4 7 6 1 8 9 5 3 2
8 2 5 7 6 3 4 9 1
1 9 3 5 4 2 6 7 8
2 3 9 4 5 1 7 8 6
6 4 7 3 9 8 1 2 5
5 8 1 6 2 7 9 4 3
3 5 4 8 7 6 2 1 9
7 1 2 9 3 5 8 6 4
9 6 8 2 1 4 3 5 7
```

56

```
9 3 1 5 7 4 2 6 8
2 5 6 8 1 3 9 7 4
4 7 8 9 6 2 5 1 3
1 4 9 3 5 6 7 8 2
5 6 2 4 8 7 3 9 1
7 8 3 1 2 9 4 5 6
6 9 5 2 3 1 8 4 7
8 2 7 6 4 5 1 3 9
3 1 4 7 9 8 6 2 5
```

57

```
7 2 5 6 3 9 1 4 8
9 4 8 2 5 1 6 3 7
1 6 3 8 7 4 2 5 9
3 7 2 4 1 6 8 9 5
8 1 4 7 9 5 3 6 2
5 9 6 3 2 8 4 7 1
2 5 9 1 6 3 7 8 4
6 8 7 9 4 2 5 1 3
4 3 1 5 8 7 9 2 6
```

58

```
1 6 5 2 3 8 7 4 9
8 3 7 4 5 9 6 1 2
4 9 2 6 7 1 8 5 3
6 5 4 3 1 7 9 2 8
3 8 9 5 2 6 1 7 4
7 2 1 9 8 4 3 6 5
2 1 6 8 9 5 4 3 7
5 7 8 1 4 3 2 9 6
9 4 3 7 6 2 5 8 1
```

59

```
7 8 1 3 9 4 6 5 2
9 3 2 1 6 5 4 8 7
4 5 6 7 2 8 9 1 3
6 7 5 2 4 3 1 9 8
1 2 4 6 8 9 7 3 5
3 9 8 5 1 7 2 4 6
2 6 9 8 3 1 5 7 4
8 4 7 9 5 6 3 2 1
5 1 3 4 7 2 8 6 9
```

60

```
7 6 8 5 1 9 2 3 4
4 3 2 8 7 6 1 5 9
9 1 5 4 2 3 7 8 6
5 7 1 3 6 4 8 9 2
3 4 6 9 8 2 5 1 7
8 2 9 7 5 1 6 4 3
2 5 4 1 3 7 9 6 8
1 9 7 6 4 8 3 2 5
6 8 3 2 9 5 4 7 1
```

61

9	8	1	5	4	2	3	7	6
6	7	5	3	8	9	4	2	1
2	3	4	1	7	6	9	5	8
4	5	9	2	3	8	1	6	7
7	1	3	6	9	5	8	4	2
8	2	6	4	1	7	5	9	3
1	6	8	9	2	4	7	3	5
5	9	7	8	6	3	2	1	4
3	4	2	7	5	1	6	8	9

62

8	9	5	1	4	6	7	3	2
7	2	1	5	3	8	6	9	4
3	4	6	7	2	9	5	8	1
6	1	3	4	9	2	8	5	7
4	5	8	6	7	1	9	2	3
2	7	9	8	5	3	1	4	6
5	6	2	3	8	7	4	1	9
9	8	7	2	1	4	3	6	5
1	3	4	9	6	5	2	7	8

63

9	4	7	5	3	6	2	8	1
8	3	6	9	2	1	4	7	5
2	5	1	8	4	7	6	3	9
4	7	9	3	1	8	5	2	6
5	2	3	6	9	4	8	1	7
6	1	8	7	5	2	3	9	4
1	9	2	4	8	5	7	6	3
7	8	4	1	6	3	9	5	2
3	6	5	2	7	9	1	4	8

64

6	8	5	4	9	7	2	1	3
2	3	4	1	8	5	9	7	6
9	1	7	2	6	3	4	5	8
3	2	6	8	1	4	7	9	5
5	4	8	9	7	2	3	6	1
1	7	9	3	5	6	8	2	4
7	9	1	5	4	8	6	3	2
8	6	2	7	3	1	5	4	9
4	5	3	6	2	9	1	8	7

65

5	2	8	6	3	4	9	7	1
7	3	6	1	8	9	4	2	5
1	4	9	2	7	5	6	8	3
9	6	3	5	1	7	8	4	2
4	1	7	8	6	2	3	5	9
2	8	5	4	9	3	7	1	6
3	5	1	9	4	8	2	6	7
8	9	2	7	5	6	1	3	4
6	7	4	3	2	1	5	9	8

66

5	1	4	9	3	8	6	2	7
8	7	6	1	5	2	9	4	3
9	2	3	4	7	6	5	8	1
7	6	9	5	2	4	3	1	8
4	8	2	3	9	1	7	6	5
1	3	5	6	8	7	2	9	4
3	9	1	2	4	5	8	7	6
6	5	8	7	1	9	4	3	2
2	4	7	8	6	3	1	5	9

67

4	1	6	3	5	9	2	7	8
3	9	8	7	1	2	6	5	4
2	5	7	8	4	6	9	1	3
9	8	3	4	7	1	5	2	6
5	7	2	6	9	8	3	4	1
1	6	4	2	3	5	7	8	9
6	3	1	5	2	4	8	9	7
8	4	5	9	6	7	1	3	2
7	2	9	1	8	3	4	6	5

68

9	1	7	4	6	2	8	3	5
6	2	3	8	1	5	9	4	7
8	5	4	3	7	9	1	6	2
5	6	8	9	2	3	7	1	4
4	7	2	1	5	6	3	8	9
1	3	9	7	4	8	5	2	6
2	4	1	5	3	7	6	9	8
7	8	6	2	9	1	4	5	3
3	9	5	6	8	4	2	7	1

69

1	4	5	3	8	2	7	9	6
9	7	6	4	1	5	2	8	3
3	8	2	6	7	9	1	5	4
6	9	3	5	4	1	8	7	2
8	1	7	2	9	6	3	4	5
5	2	4	8	3	7	9	6	1
4	5	1	9	2	8	6	3	7
7	3	8	1	6	4	5	2	9
2	6	9	7	5	3	4	1	8

70

5	7	2	8	1	4	9	6	3
3	9	1	5	6	7	4	2	8
8	4	6	2	3	9	5	1	7
4	5	7	9	8	2	6	3	1
1	6	8	7	5	3	2	9	4
2	3	9	1	4	6	8	7	5
7	8	5	6	9	1	3	4	2
9	2	4	3	7	8	1	5	6
6	1	3	4	2	5	7	8	9

71

6	5	8	1	2	7	4	3	9
2	7	9	4	5	3	6	8	1
4	1	3	9	6	8	7	2	5
9	6	4	8	3	1	5	7	2
1	3	2	5	7	6	9	4	8
5	8	7	2	9	4	3	1	6
7	4	1	6	8	5	2	9	3
8	2	5	3	4	9	1	6	7
3	9	6	7	1	2	8	5	4

72

9	6	5	7	2	1	8	4	3
1	3	4	9	8	5	2	6	7
2	7	8	3	6	4	9	5	1
5	4	6	1	3	9	7	2	8
3	8	1	4	7	2	5	9	6
7	9	2	6	5	8	1	3	4
6	5	3	8	9	7	4	1	2
8	1	9	2	4	6	3	7	5
4	2	7	5	1	3	6	8	9

73

4	1	3	8	7	9	2	6	5
6	5	9	1	4	2	7	8	3
7	8	2	6	3	5	9	4	1
3	2	6	4	8	7	1	5	9
5	7	1	3	9	6	8	2	4
8	9	4	5	2	1	6	3	7
1	4	5	9	6	8	3	7	2
2	3	8	7	1	4	5	9	6
9	6	7	2	5	3	4	1	8

74

6	8	2	5	4	9	7	3	1
4	9	7	8	1	3	2	6	5
3	5	1	2	7	6	4	9	8
7	6	4	3	2	1	5	8	9
2	3	9	7	8	5	6	1	4
8	1	5	6	9	4	3	7	2
1	7	8	4	6	2	9	5	3
9	4	3	1	5	7	8	2	6
5	2	6	9	3	8	1	4	7

75

5	1	6	3	4	9	2	8	7
4	3	7	8	2	5	6	9	1
2	9	8	1	6	7	5	3	4
8	2	3	5	9	4	7	1	6
1	7	9	2	3	6	8	4	5
6	5	4	7	1	8	9	2	3
3	8	1	6	5	2	4	7	9
7	4	5	9	8	3	1	6	2
9	6	2	4	7	1	3	5	8

76

7	1	5	6	2	4	3	9	8
9	3	2	5	8	1	6	7	4
4	6	8	3	9	7	1	2	5
5	9	4	2	1	3	7	8	6
1	2	7	9	6	8	4	5	3
6	8	3	4	7	5	9	1	2
3	4	9	7	5	2	8	6	1
2	7	1	8	4	6	5	3	9
8	5	6	1	3	9	2	4	7

77

2	3	6	7	1	9	4	8	5
4	5	7	3	2	8	6	9	1
8	1	9	5	6	4	7	3	2
5	2	1	4	7	3	8	6	9
9	4	3	8	5	6	1	2	7
6	7	8	1	9	2	3	5	4
7	8	5	2	3	1	9	4	6
3	6	2	9	4	5	7	1	8
1	9	4	6	8	5	2	7	3

78

4	5	1	8	6	7	9	2	3
8	3	2	5	4	9	1	7	6
9	7	6	1	3	2	8	4	5
7	9	5	4	1	8	3	6	2
2	4	3	6	9	5	7	8	1
1	6	8	7	2	3	5	9	4
5	1	9	2	7	4	6	3	8
6	2	7	3	8	1	4	5	9
3	8	4	9	5	6	2	1	7

79

2	1	5	3	9	4	6	7	8
4	3	9	7	6	8	5	2	1
7	6	8	2	1	5	3	9	4
6	2	7	5	4	1	9	8	3
8	9	4	6	2	3	1	5	7
3	5	1	9	8	7	4	6	2
9	8	2	4	3	6	7	1	5
5	4	6	1	7	2	8	3	9
1	7	3	8	5	9	2	4	6

80

7	6	5	1	8	4	2	3	9
2	3	8	9	6	5	7	4	1
1	4	9	3	7	2	5	8	6
6	9	3	7	4	1	8	2	5
5	2	7	8	3	6	9	1	4
8	1	4	2	5	9	3	6	7
9	5	1	4	2	8	6	7	3
4	7	2	6	9	3	1	5	8
3	8	6	5	1	7	4	9	2

81

```
2 3 6 1 4 7 5 9 8
5 1 7 8 6 9 2 4 3
4 8 9 2 5 3 7 6 1
1 7 3 6 2 5 9 8 4
6 5 8 9 7 4 3 1 2
9 4 2 3 8 1 6 7 5
8 9 5 4 3 6 1 2 7
3 6 4 7 1 2 8 5 9
7 2 1 5 9 8 4 3 6
```

82

```
1 4 5 9 2 6 8 3 7
9 7 3 8 1 4 2 5 6
2 6 8 5 3 7 9 1 4
3 5 4 1 9 8 6 7 2
7 1 2 4 6 5 3 9 8
8 9 6 2 7 3 5 4 1
5 3 7 6 4 2 1 8 9
6 8 1 7 5 9 4 2 3
4 2 9 3 8 1 7 6 5
```

83

```
1 6 8 4 5 3 7 2 9
7 9 4 2 8 1 5 3 6
3 5 2 7 6 9 8 4 1
6 8 5 3 1 2 9 7 4
4 3 1 9 7 6 2 5 8
9 2 7 5 4 8 6 1 3
5 7 9 8 3 4 1 6 2
8 4 6 1 2 7 3 9 5
2 1 3 6 9 5 4 8 7
```

84

```
4 3 5 2 7 1 6 8 9
7 9 2 8 3 6 4 1 5
6 1 8 4 5 9 7 3 2
3 2 7 6 9 4 8 5 1
1 4 9 5 8 3 2 6 7
8 5 6 7 1 2 9 4 3
9 8 4 3 2 5 1 7 6
2 7 3 1 6 8 5 9 4
5 6 1 9 4 7 3 2 8
```

85

```
7 6 2 9 3 8 4 1 5
5 4 3 1 6 2 7 8 9
8 9 1 7 5 4 6 3 2
1 3 7 4 2 6 5 9 8
4 8 5 3 7 9 1 2 6
6 2 9 5 8 1 3 7 4
2 1 6 8 4 3 9 5 7
9 7 4 2 1 5 8 6 3
3 5 8 6 9 7 2 4 1
```

86

```
5 1 7 3 8 2 6 4 9
8 6 4 5 7 9 2 3 1
2 3 9 6 1 4 8 7 5
3 5 8 7 9 6 1 2 4
7 2 1 4 3 8 5 9 6
9 4 6 2 5 1 7 8 3
1 9 5 8 2 3 4 6 7
6 8 3 1 4 7 9 5 2
4 7 2 9 6 5 3 1 8
```

87

```
3 2 4 7 6 8 1 9 5
1 5 6 3 2 9 8 4 7
7 9 8 4 5 1 3 6 2
2 8 1 6 9 5 4 7 3
5 4 9 8 3 7 2 1 6
6 3 7 1 4 2 5 8 9
9 6 3 5 8 4 7 2 1
4 1 5 2 7 6 9 3 8
8 7 2 9 1 3 6 5 4
```

88

```
4 8 7 2 9 5 3 1 6
9 3 5 1 7 6 2 4 8
6 1 2 3 8 4 5 7 9
2 6 1 4 5 8 7 9 3
8 7 9 6 3 2 1 5 4
5 4 3 7 1 9 6 8 2
7 9 6 5 4 3 8 2 1
1 2 8 9 6 7 4 3 5
3 5 4 8 2 1 9 6 7
```

89

```
3 5 8 7 6 2 9 1 4
6 1 9 4 8 3 2 7 5
4 7 2 5 1 9 8 6 3
1 6 4 3 9 7 5 2 8
2 3 5 6 4 8 1 9 7
8 9 7 1 2 5 3 4 6
7 8 1 9 5 6 4 3 2
9 2 6 8 3 4 7 5 1
5 4 3 2 7 1 6 8 9
```

90

```
4 6 8 5 2 1 3 7 9
2 5 3 4 9 7 6 1 8
7 9 1 8 6 3 2 4 5
9 1 7 3 8 2 4 5 6
8 4 2 7 5 6 9 3 1
6 3 5 1 4 9 7 8 2
5 2 4 9 3 8 1 6 7
1 8 6 2 7 4 5 9 3
3 7 9 6 1 5 8 2 4
```

91

```
6 5 7 4 3 8 2 9 1
4 1 2 9 6 5 7 3 8
3 9 8 7 2 1 6 4 5
9 2 4 5 1 6 3 8 7
8 6 1 2 7 3 9 5 4
7 3 5 8 4 9 1 6 2
1 8 3 6 5 2 4 7 9
2 4 9 3 8 7 5 1 6
5 7 6 1 9 4 8 2 3
```

92

```
9 7 3 1 8 4 5 2 6
8 1 5 6 7 2 3 4 9
2 4 6 3 9 5 1 8 7
5 9 8 7 3 6 2 1 4
7 3 1 4 2 8 9 6 5
6 2 4 9 5 1 7 3 8
3 8 9 2 6 7 4 5 1
1 5 7 8 4 3 6 9 2
4 6 2 5 1 9 8 7 3
```

93

```
9 2 5 8 3 6 1 4 7
7 8 1 5 4 2 3 6 9
4 6 3 1 7 9 5 8 2
2 5 7 9 6 4 8 3 1
3 4 8 7 2 1 6 9 5
6 1 9 3 8 5 2 7 4
5 9 4 6 1 8 7 2 3
8 3 2 4 5 7 9 1 6
1 7 6 2 9 3 4 5 8
```

94

```
4 5 3 7 8 9 1 6 2
7 9 1 6 3 2 5 4 8
8 6 2 1 4 5 9 7 3
6 4 5 8 9 3 2 1 7
3 8 9 2 7 1 6 5 4
1 2 7 5 6 4 3 8 9
2 7 8 9 1 6 4 3 5
9 1 4 3 5 8 7 2 6
5 3 6 4 2 7 8 9 1
```

95

```
5 4 1 9 6 7 8 2 3
8 7 3 5 2 1 9 6 4
6 2 9 3 8 4 1 7 5
9 6 7 2 4 8 3 5 1
3 1 8 6 9 5 2 4 7
4 5 2 7 1 3 6 9 8
1 8 6 4 7 9 5 3 2
2 3 4 1 5 6 7 8 9
7 9 5 8 3 2 4 1 6
```

96

```
2 4 3 1 9 7 6 8 5
1 9 8 5 6 2 3 4 7
6 7 5 8 3 4 2 9 1
3 6 7 9 4 1 8 5 2
5 2 4 6 8 3 7 1 9
9 8 1 2 7 5 4 3 6
7 5 2 3 1 8 9 6 4
4 3 9 7 5 6 1 2 8
8 1 6 4 2 9 5 7 3
```

97

```
6 2 5 9 4 7 1 3 8
7 3 1 8 6 2 9 5 4
8 4 9 5 1 3 7 6 2
5 9 6 3 7 8 4 2 1
3 1 8 2 5 4 6 9 7
2 7 4 1 9 6 5 8 3
4 6 2 7 3 9 8 1 5
9 5 3 4 8 1 2 7 6
1 8 7 6 2 5 3 4 9
```

98

```
8 5 1 4 2 3 9 7 6
9 2 7 6 8 1 5 4 3
4 3 6 9 7 5 1 2 8
2 4 9 8 5 7 6 3 1
3 1 5 2 4 6 8 9 7
6 7 8 3 1 9 4 5 2
5 9 3 7 6 8 2 1 4
7 8 4 1 9 2 3 6 5
1 6 2 5 3 4 7 8 9
```

99

```
6 3 5 1 7 2 9 4 8
4 1 7 6 8 9 2 5 3
8 9 2 3 5 4 7 6 1
1 8 3 7 4 6 5 2 9
7 5 9 8 2 1 6 3 4
2 6 4 9 3 5 8 1 7
9 4 8 5 6 3 1 7 2
5 2 1 4 9 7 3 8 6
3 7 6 2 1 8 4 9 5
```

100

```
3 1 4 7 8 9 5 6 2
2 6 5 4 1 3 9 7 8
7 8 9 5 6 2 1 3 4
4 5 8 9 3 7 6 2 1
6 7 2 1 5 8 3 4 9
9 3 1 6 2 4 7 8 5
8 9 7 3 4 5 2 1 6
5 2 6 8 7 1 4 9 3
1 4 3 2 9 6 8 5 7
```

101

```
9 8 4 6 3 5 2 1 7
2 1 3 7 8 9 5 6 4
7 6 5 2 4 1 3 8 9
5 4 7 8 1 3 9 2 6
1 9 8 4 2 6 7 3 5
6 3 2 9 5 7 8 4 1
8 7 9 1 6 2 4 5 3
4 5 1 3 9 8 6 7 2
3 2 6 5 7 4 1 9 8
```

102

```
2 7 6 9 3 5 1 4 8
9 1 4 7 2 8 6 5 3
8 5 3 6 1 4 9 2 7
3 8 2 4 5 1 7 6 9
7 4 9 8 6 2 5 3 1
1 6 5 3 9 7 2 8 4
4 2 8 1 7 6 3 9 5
5 3 7 2 4 9 8 1 6
6 9 1 5 8 3 4 7 2
```

103

```
9 6 5 3 2 1 7 8 4
7 2 1 4 5 8 3 6 9
4 3 8 7 6 9 1 5 2
6 8 2 9 1 4 5 7 3
5 7 9 2 3 6 8 4 1
1 4 3 8 7 5 2 9 6
3 9 4 5 8 2 6 1 7
2 5 6 1 9 7 4 3 8
8 1 7 6 4 3 9 2 5
```

104

```
5 2 8 1 6 7 9 4 3
3 4 1 2 9 5 6 8 7
9 7 6 3 4 8 1 5 2
7 5 2 8 1 4 3 6 9
4 8 9 6 2 3 7 1 5
1 6 3 7 5 9 8 2 4
8 9 4 5 3 6 2 7 1
2 3 7 4 8 1 5 9 6
6 1 5 9 7 2 4 3 8
```

105

```
9 6 1 7 2 3 4 8 5
2 8 7 9 4 5 6 3 1
4 5 3 8 6 1 2 9 7
6 3 2 1 8 9 5 7 4
7 1 9 4 5 6 8 2 3
8 4 5 3 7 2 1 6 9
5 7 6 2 9 4 3 1 8
3 2 8 5 1 7 9 4 6
1 9 4 6 3 8 7 5 2
```

106

```
5 7 8 3 6 9 1 2 4
9 3 6 2 4 1 7 8 5
2 1 4 7 5 8 9 3 6
8 4 7 5 9 2 6 1 3
3 5 1 4 7 6 8 9 2
6 2 9 8 1 3 5 4 7
1 9 3 6 2 5 4 7 8
4 6 2 1 8 7 3 5 9
7 8 5 9 3 4 2 6 1
```

107

```
8 1 4 3 9 2 5 7 6
9 5 7 8 6 4 1 2 3
6 3 2 5 1 7 9 8 4
7 9 1 6 8 3 2 4 5
2 6 5 4 7 1 3 9 8
4 8 3 9 2 5 7 6 1
5 7 8 2 3 6 4 1 9
1 4 6 7 5 9 8 3 2
3 2 9 1 4 8 6 5 7
```

108

```
9 4 3 6 2 5 1 8 7
5 6 8 1 4 7 9 2 3
1 7 2 9 8 3 4 5 6
3 1 6 7 5 9 8 4 2
2 8 5 4 1 6 7 3 9
7 9 4 8 3 2 5 6 1
8 5 9 3 6 1 2 7 4
4 3 7 2 9 8 6 1 5
6 2 1 5 7 4 3 9 8
```

109

```
2 5 7 1 9 4 8 3 6
8 4 9 3 7 6 2 1 5
6 3 1 5 8 2 4 7 9
1 6 4 9 2 3 7 5 8
5 9 2 8 6 7 3 4 1
7 8 3 4 5 1 6 9 2
4 7 6 2 1 9 5 8 3
3 1 5 6 4 8 9 2 7
9 2 8 7 3 5 1 6 4
```

110

```
3 1 6 9 2 7 4 5 8
5 8 2 1 6 4 9 3 7
9 4 7 8 5 3 2 6 1
8 9 1 4 3 5 7 2 6
2 6 4 7 9 1 5 8 3
7 3 5 6 8 2 1 4 9
1 7 3 2 4 6 8 9 5
4 5 9 3 1 8 6 7 2
6 2 8 5 7 9 3 1 4
```

111

```
6 1 7 5 9 8 3 2 4
3 5 8 4 2 6 1 7 9
2 9 4 7 3 1 8 5 6
5 8 6 9 7 4 2 3 1
4 7 3 8 1 2 6 9 5
9 2 1 6 5 3 7 4 8
8 3 2 1 4 9 5 6 7
7 6 9 3 8 5 4 1 2
1 4 5 2 6 7 9 8 3
```

112

```
6 4 3 1 5 9 8 7 2
7 2 5 6 8 4 9 1 3
8 9 1 7 3 2 6 4 5
5 3 4 8 2 7 1 9 6
2 6 9 3 4 1 5 8 7
1 8 7 5 9 6 3 2 4
3 7 8 2 1 5 4 6 9
4 5 2 9 6 8 7 3 1
9 1 6 4 7 3 2 5 8
```

113

```
3 7 2 8 4 6 5 1 9
9 1 4 7 5 3 2 6 8
6 5 8 1 2 9 7 3 4
7 4 3 9 1 8 6 2 5
2 9 6 3 7 5 4 8 1
5 8 1 2 6 4 9 7 3
4 3 7 6 9 1 8 5 2
1 2 9 5 8 7 3 4 6
8 6 5 4 3 2 1 9 7
```

114

```
6 9 1 2 3 8 5 7 4
4 5 2 9 7 1 6 8 3
7 8 3 4 5 6 2 9 1
8 2 4 3 1 9 7 5 6
1 3 9 7 6 5 4 2 8
5 7 6 8 4 2 3 1 9
2 1 7 6 8 3 9 4 5
9 6 5 1 2 4 8 3 7
3 4 8 5 9 7 1 6 2
```

115

```
8 2 6 5 4 7 3 1 9
3 1 4 9 2 8 5 6 7
5 7 9 6 3 1 4 2 8
6 3 5 8 7 9 2 4 1
2 4 8 1 5 3 7 9 6
1 9 7 4 6 2 8 3 5
7 5 3 2 9 6 1 8 4
4 6 1 3 8 5 9 7 2
9 8 2 7 1 4 6 5 3
```

116

```
1 8 6 9 4 3 7 2 5
3 5 9 2 6 7 4 1 8
2 7 4 1 8 5 9 6 3
8 9 7 3 2 6 5 4 1
5 1 2 4 9 8 6 3 7
4 6 3 7 5 1 8 9 2
6 4 5 8 1 2 3 7 9
7 2 8 6 3 9 1 5 4
9 3 1 5 7 4 2 8 6
```

117

```
7 8 3 2 1 6 5 9 4
6 5 9 8 3 4 2 1 7
4 2 1 9 5 7 8 6 3
8 7 4 1 9 5 3 2 6
3 1 2 4 6 8 9 7 5
9 6 5 7 2 3 4 8 1
2 9 7 3 4 1 6 5 8
1 3 6 5 8 9 7 4 2
5 4 8 6 7 2 1 3 9
```

118

```
9 4 8 3 2 1 7 5 6
3 6 1 7 8 5 2 4 9
5 7 2 9 4 6 8 3 1
4 3 6 2 7 9 1 8 5
7 1 9 6 5 8 4 2 3
8 2 5 4 1 3 9 6 7
6 8 3 1 9 4 5 7 2
1 5 7 8 3 2 6 9 4
2 9 4 5 6 7 3 1 8
```

119

```
4 2 6 8 9 3 5 7 1
8 1 9 7 6 5 3 2 4
5 7 3 4 1 2 8 9 6
6 3 1 5 4 7 2 8 9
2 9 5 1 3 8 6 4 7
7 8 4 6 2 9 1 3 5
1 6 7 2 8 4 9 5 3
9 5 8 3 7 6 4 1 2
3 4 2 9 5 1 7 6 8
```

120

```
5 6 1 4 7 3 2 9 8
9 4 8 1 2 6 7 3 5
2 7 3 5 9 8 1 6 4
3 1 2 8 4 7 6 5 9
6 9 4 2 5 1 8 7 3
8 5 7 6 3 9 4 1 2
4 3 5 7 1 2 9 8 6
7 2 6 9 8 5 3 4 1
1 8 9 3 6 4 5 2 7
```

121

```
3 1 7 6 2 8 5 4 9
2 5 8 4 9 7 1 3 6
9 6 4 1 5 3 7 2 8
5 7 1 8 4 2 9 6 3
4 2 9 3 1 6 8 7 5
8 3 6 5 7 9 4 1 2
7 8 2 9 6 1 3 5 4
6 9 5 7 3 4 2 8 1
1 4 3 2 8 5 6 9 7
```

122

```
2 8 4 6 9 1 3 7 5
9 1 3 7 5 2 6 4 8
6 7 5 4 3 8 1 2 9
5 3 9 2 4 7 8 1 6
8 2 7 1 6 9 4 5 3
1 4 6 3 8 5 2 9 7
3 9 1 5 2 6 7 8 4
4 5 2 8 7 3 9 6 1
7 6 8 9 1 4 5 3 2
```

123

```
3 7 2 6 8 1 9 5 4
8 1 9 2 5 4 3 6 7
6 5 4 7 3 9 2 8 1
2 4 7 8 1 6 5 9 3
5 3 8 9 7 2 1 4 6
1 9 6 5 4 3 7 2 8
7 6 5 1 9 8 4 3 2
4 2 1 3 6 5 8 7 9
9 8 3 4 2 7 6 1 5
```

124

```
4 3 2 8 7 6 1 5 9
7 1 6 9 3 5 4 8 2
9 8 5 1 4 2 3 7 6
8 7 3 2 1 9 6 4 5
5 9 1 4 6 8 2 3 7
2 6 4 3 5 7 9 1 8
3 5 7 6 9 1 8 2 4
6 4 8 7 2 3 5 9 1
1 2 9 5 8 4 7 6 3
```

125

```
5 8 1 3 9 6 2 7 4
6 3 4 7 2 5 9 8 1
7 2 9 4 1 8 6 3 5
9 7 5 2 8 4 1 6 3
4 6 2 1 7 3 5 9 8
8 1 3 6 5 9 7 4 2
3 5 7 8 6 1 4 2 9
1 4 6 9 3 2 8 5 7
2 9 8 5 4 7 3 1 6
```

126

```
6 7 1 9 3 2 4 5 8
4 2 5 6 1 8 9 7 3
3 9 8 4 5 7 2 6 1
8 6 4 2 7 9 3 1 5
2 1 3 5 4 6 8 9 7
9 5 7 3 8 1 6 2 4
7 4 6 1 9 3 5 8 2
5 8 9 7 2 4 1 3 6
1 3 2 8 6 5 7 4 9
```

127

```
4 8 7 9 1 6 3 2 5
6 5 9 7 3 2 8 1 4
3 2 1 8 5 4 6 7 9
5 1 3 6 7 8 4 9 2
2 6 4 1 9 5 7 3 8
7 9 8 4 2 3 1 5 6
9 3 6 2 8 1 5 4 7
8 7 5 3 4 9 2 6 1
1 4 2 5 6 7 9 8 3
```

128

```
8 2 1 5 4 6 7 3 9
4 6 3 9 2 7 1 5 8
9 5 7 3 8 1 6 4 2
1 9 4 7 5 3 2 8 6
5 7 2 4 6 8 3 9 1
6 3 8 1 9 2 5 7 4
3 1 6 8 7 4 9 2 5
7 4 9 2 1 5 8 6 3
2 8 5 6 3 9 4 1 7
```

129

```
4 5 1 3 9 8 2 7 6
3 8 2 1 7 6 4 5 9
9 7 6 2 4 5 3 8 1
1 2 7 8 6 4 9 3 5
5 6 9 7 3 1 8 4 2
8 4 3 5 2 9 6 1 7
7 9 8 6 1 3 5 2 4
6 1 5 4 8 2 7 9 3
2 3 4 9 5 7 1 6 8
```

130

```
8 5 7 2 9 1 6 4 3
4 9 1 3 6 5 8 2 7
6 2 3 7 8 4 5 1 9
3 1 9 6 7 8 2 5 4
2 7 8 5 4 3 1 9 6
5 6 4 9 1 2 7 3 8
1 4 2 8 3 7 9 6 5
9 8 5 4 2 6 3 7 1
7 3 6 1 5 9 4 8 2
```

131

```
5 7 3 6 1 8 9 2 4
2 8 6 9 7 4 5 1 3
9 4 1 5 2 3 8 6 7
4 6 7 8 5 1 3 9 2
3 5 2 7 9 6 4 8 1
1 9 8 3 4 2 7 5 6
8 2 4 1 3 9 6 7 5
6 1 5 4 8 7 2 3 9
7 3 9 2 6 5 1 4 8
```

132

```
8 2 6 4 1 5 3 7 9
7 1 5 9 3 8 2 6 4
9 3 4 6 2 7 8 5 1
1 5 2 7 8 6 9 4 3
6 9 7 2 4 3 5 1 8
4 8 3 1 5 9 7 2 6
2 6 8 3 7 4 1 9 5
5 4 1 8 9 2 6 3 7
3 7 9 5 6 1 4 8 2
```

133

```
8 9 4 1 6 5 2 7 3
6 5 3 8 2 7 9 4 1
1 2 7 4 3 9 6 5 8
3 1 5 7 8 6 4 2 9
9 6 2 3 1 4 5 8 7
4 7 8 5 9 2 3 1 6
2 4 6 9 7 8 1 3 5
5 8 1 6 4 3 7 9 2
7 3 9 2 5 1 8 6 4
```

134

```
5 3 9 7 6 2 1 4 8
4 2 7 3 1 8 5 6 9
6 8 1 5 9 4 2 3 7
7 1 5 8 3 6 9 2 4
9 4 8 1 2 5 3 7 6
3 6 2 9 4 7 8 1 5
2 9 4 6 8 3 7 5 1
8 5 3 4 7 1 6 9 2
1 7 6 2 5 9 4 8 3
```

135

```
1 8 9 7 6 5 2 4 3
6 5 3 4 2 1 9 7 8
7 4 2 9 3 8 5 1 6
4 3 8 5 9 2 1 6 7
5 2 7 6 1 4 3 8 9
9 1 6 8 7 3 4 2 5
3 6 5 2 4 7 8 9 1
2 9 1 3 8 6 7 5 4
8 7 4 1 5 9 6 3 2
```

136

```
7 5 6 4 9 1 2 8 3
8 4 2 3 5 6 1 9 7
3 1 9 7 8 2 5 4 6
4 3 1 8 7 5 9 6 2
6 9 7 1 2 4 3 5 8
5 2 8 9 6 3 7 1 4
1 7 5 2 4 8 6 3 9
2 6 4 5 3 9 8 7 1
9 8 3 6 1 7 4 2 5
```

137

```
4 7 9 1 3 5 8 6 2
6 2 1 4 9 8 7 5 3
5 3 8 6 7 2 1 4 9
1 8 5 7 2 6 9 3 4
2 9 7 5 4 3 6 1 8
3 6 4 8 1 9 2 7 5
8 5 3 9 6 1 4 2 7
9 4 6 2 5 7 3 8 1
7 1 2 3 8 4 5 9 6
```

138

```
8 7 9 1 5 4 3 6 2
2 6 1 3 9 7 4 8 5
5 3 4 2 6 8 9 7 1
6 4 2 8 1 5 7 9 3
3 9 7 4 2 6 5 1 8
1 5 8 7 3 9 2 4 6
9 1 6 5 7 3 8 2 4
7 8 5 6 4 2 1 3 9
4 2 3 9 8 1 6 5 7
```

139

```
4 9 7 2 5 1 3 8 6
3 8 1 6 9 7 4 2 5
5 6 2 3 4 8 7 9 1
2 5 4 7 3 9 1 6 8
9 1 3 5 8 6 2 4 7
8 7 6 1 2 4 5 3 9
7 4 5 9 6 3 8 1 2
6 2 8 4 1 5 9 7 3
1 3 9 8 7 2 6 5 4
```

140

```
2 3 5 7 4 1 8 6 9
1 8 9 3 6 5 4 2 7
4 6 7 8 2 9 1 3 5
7 5 1 9 3 8 2 4 6
6 4 8 5 7 2 9 1 3
9 2 3 6 1 4 5 7 8
3 9 2 4 5 6 7 8 1
8 1 6 2 9 7 3 5 4
5 7 4 1 8 3 6 9 2
```

141

```
3 1 2 9 4 5 6 7 8
6 7 9 3 2 8 1 4 5
5 4 8 6 7 1 2 9 3
9 6 5 7 8 4 3 1 2
4 2 3 1 9 6 8 5 7
1 8 7 5 3 2 9 6 4
7 5 6 2 1 3 4 8 9
8 3 1 4 5 9 7 2 6
2 9 4 8 6 7 5 3 1
```

142

```
6 8 4 5 9 2 1 3 7
3 7 2 6 4 1 8 5 9
9 1 5 3 7 8 6 4 2
7 2 6 9 1 4 3 8 5
5 4 3 2 8 6 9 7 1
1 9 8 7 5 3 2 6 4
8 3 1 4 2 5 7 9 6
4 6 9 1 3 7 5 2 8
2 5 7 8 6 9 4 1 3
```

143

```
5 8 1 9 6 7 2 3 4
9 4 7 3 2 5 8 6 1
2 6 3 1 8 4 5 9 7
7 1 6 4 5 8 3 2 9
3 9 2 7 1 6 4 8 5
4 5 8 2 9 3 1 7 6
8 7 9 5 4 2 6 1 3
6 3 5 8 7 1 9 4 2
1 2 4 6 3 9 7 5 8
```

144

```
2 1 9 3 5 8 7 4 6
4 8 7 9 2 6 3 5 1
5 3 6 7 4 1 8 2 9
3 4 5 6 1 9 2 7 8
8 6 2 5 3 7 1 9 4
9 7 1 2 8 4 6 3 5
6 2 3 1 9 5 4 8 7
1 5 4 8 7 2 9 6 3
7 9 8 4 6 3 5 1 2
```

145

```
1 7 6 5 4 2 8 3 9
9 8 2 6 7 3 1 4 5
5 4 3 9 8 1 7 2 6
7 3 5 4 6 9 2 8 1
4 1 8 2 5 7 6 9 3
6 2 9 1 3 8 5 7 4
8 5 4 7 9 6 3 1 2
3 6 1 8 2 4 9 5 7
2 9 7 3 1 5 4 6 8
```

146

```
2 5 9 3 4 8 1 7 6
7 6 1 2 5 9 8 4 3
3 8 4 6 1 7 9 2 5
6 3 7 4 9 5 2 8 1
1 4 5 8 3 2 6 9 7
9 2 8 1 7 6 5 3 4
4 9 6 7 8 1 3 5 2
8 1 3 5 2 4 7 6 9
5 7 2 9 6 3 4 1 8
```

147

```
3 2 9 4 5 6 1 7 8
4 8 1 9 7 2 6 5 3
7 5 6 8 1 3 9 2 4
8 3 2 7 6 1 5 4 9
5 6 7 2 9 4 8 3 1
9 1 4 3 8 5 2 6 7
2 7 5 1 4 8 3 9 6
6 4 8 5 3 9 7 1 2
1 9 3 6 2 7 4 8 5
```

148

```
6 5 4 1 8 7 2 9 3
7 2 3 9 4 5 8 1 6
1 9 8 3 2 6 7 5 4
2 8 7 4 3 9 5 6 1
5 6 9 2 7 1 3 4 8
3 4 1 5 6 8 9 2 7
9 3 2 7 1 4 6 8 5
8 1 5 6 9 3 4 7 2
4 7 6 8 5 2 1 3 9
```

149

```
8 6 1 5 2 3 4 9 7
9 7 2 4 1 6 8 3 5
3 4 5 7 9 8 6 2 1
2 8 3 1 5 9 7 4 6
1 9 6 3 7 4 2 5 8
7 5 4 6 8 2 3 1 9
5 1 8 2 3 7 9 6 4
6 3 7 9 4 5 1 8 2
4 2 9 8 6 1 5 7 3
```

150

```
2 5 8 1 7 4 6 9 3
3 7 6 8 9 5 1 4 2
4 1 9 3 2 6 7 8 5
7 6 5 4 3 8 9 2 1
9 8 3 2 5 1 4 7 6
1 4 2 7 6 9 5 3 8
6 2 4 5 8 7 3 1 9
8 9 7 6 1 3 2 5 4
5 3 1 9 4 2 8 6 7
```

151

```
7 1 2 6 4 5 3 9 8
8 5 4 3 9 7 6 2 1
9 6 3 1 2 8 7 5 4
2 7 1 9 8 4 5 6 3
6 3 9 2 5 1 8 4 7
4 8 5 7 3 6 2 1 9
5 9 8 4 7 2 1 3 6
3 2 6 8 1 9 4 7 5
1 4 7 5 6 3 9 8 2
```

152

```
5 4 7 1 3 8 2 9 6
1 9 6 2 4 7 3 8 5
8 3 2 5 6 9 1 4 7
3 7 8 4 1 6 5 2 9
4 1 9 8 5 2 6 7 3
6 2 5 9 7 3 4 1 8
2 8 1 6 9 5 7 3 4
9 6 3 7 2 4 8 5 1
7 5 4 3 8 1 9 6 2
```

153

```
8 5 3 2 7 9 1 4 6
6 2 9 3 4 1 8 5 7
1 4 7 6 8 5 9 3 2
5 1 8 7 2 4 3 6 9
3 6 4 9 5 8 7 2 1
9 7 2 1 6 3 5 8 4
7 8 5 4 1 6 2 9 3
4 9 1 8 3 2 6 7 5
2 3 6 5 9 7 4 1 8
```

154

```
5 3 8 4 2 1 7 6 9
9 7 2 8 6 5 4 3 1
6 4 1 7 9 3 8 5 2
4 9 7 1 5 6 2 8 3
1 5 3 2 8 4 6 9 7
2 8 6 3 7 9 5 1 4
7 2 9 5 3 8 1 4 6
3 1 5 6 4 2 9 7 8
8 6 4 9 1 7 3 2 5
```

155

```
5 4 8 3 2 7 6 1 9
7 2 3 9 1 6 8 5 4
9 6 1 4 8 5 3 2 7
6 5 9 7 3 8 1 4 2
4 8 2 1 6 9 5 7 3
3 1 7 5 4 2 9 8 6
2 7 6 8 9 1 4 3 5
1 3 5 6 7 4 2 9 8
8 9 4 2 5 3 7 6 1
```

156

```
2 7 8 5 3 9 1 4 6
6 9 5 1 8 4 7 3 2
3 1 4 2 7 6 9 5 8
5 3 7 4 1 2 6 8 9
4 6 1 3 9 8 5 2 7
9 8 2 7 6 5 3 1 4
8 4 6 9 5 3 2 7 1
7 5 9 8 2 1 4 6 3
1 2 3 6 4 7 8 9 5
```

157

```
9 1 2 6 3 7 8 4 5
6 8 5 4 1 2 9 3 7
4 7 3 9 5 8 2 1 6
7 2 1 3 6 9 5 8 4
3 4 8 7 2 5 1 6 9
5 9 6 8 4 1 3 7 2
8 3 7 5 9 6 4 2 1
2 5 4 1 7 3 6 9 8
1 6 9 2 8 4 7 5 3
```

158

```
5 8 3 6 7 2 1 9 4
4 2 7 5 9 1 6 8 3
6 1 9 3 8 4 7 5 2
3 5 6 1 2 7 8 4 9
9 4 1 8 3 6 2 7 5
8 7 2 4 5 9 3 1 6
1 6 8 9 4 3 5 2 7
7 3 4 2 1 5 9 6 8
2 9 5 7 6 8 4 3 1
```

159

```
5 6 8 7 2 4 9 1 3
4 3 1 9 6 5 8 7 2
9 7 2 3 1 8 6 5 4
3 1 9 5 7 2 4 6 8
6 2 7 4 8 9 1 3 5
8 5 4 6 3 1 2 9 7
7 4 5 8 9 6 3 2 1
2 8 6 1 5 3 7 4 9
1 9 3 2 4 7 5 8 6
```

160

```
9 3 5 8 4 6 7 1 2
8 1 4 5 2 7 9 3 6
2 6 7 3 9 1 5 8 4
7 2 9 1 5 8 6 4 3
3 4 1 7 6 9 2 5 8
5 8 6 2 3 4 1 7 9
4 7 3 9 1 2 8 6 5
6 9 8 4 7 5 3 2 1
1 5 2 6 8 3 4 9 7
```

161

```
2 6 8 | 7 9 3 | 5 1 4
7 9 3 | 5 1 4 | 8 6 2
1 4 5 | 8 2 6 | 9 7 3
------+-------+------
6 2 7 | 3 5 9 | 1 4 8
8 5 1 | 6 4 7 | 3 2 9
4 3 9 | 1 8 2 | 6 5 7
------+-------+------
3 8 6 | 4 7 1 | 2 9 5
5 7 2 | 9 6 8 | 4 3 1
9 1 4 | 2 3 5 | 7 8 6
```

162

```
6 4 2 | 5 8 7 | 1 3 9
9 3 5 | 2 1 4 | 6 8 7
8 1 7 | 9 6 3 | 2 5 4
------+-------+------
2 9 4 | 8 3 6 | 7 1 5
5 8 1 | 7 4 2 | 9 6 3
3 7 6 | 1 5 9 | 8 4 2
------+-------+------
1 2 3 | 4 7 8 | 5 9 6
4 5 9 | 6 2 1 | 3 7 8
7 6 8 | 3 9 5 | 4 2 1
```

163

```
6 5 1 | 7 8 4 | 3 9 2
9 4 2 | 6 3 5 | 1 8 7
7 3 8 | 2 9 1 | 4 5 6
------+-------+------
4 2 9 | 3 5 7 | 6 1 8
8 1 3 | 4 6 2 | 9 7 5
5 7 6 | 8 1 9 | 2 3 4
------+-------+------
2 9 4 | 5 7 3 | 8 6 1
3 8 5 | 1 2 6 | 7 4 9
1 6 7 | 9 4 8 | 5 2 3
```

164

```
5 3 9 | 7 4 6 | 2 8 1
6 1 2 | 8 3 9 | 5 4 7
8 7 4 | 2 5 1 | 9 3 6
------+-------+------
7 4 8 | 5 1 3 | 6 9 2
2 5 3 | 6 9 8 | 7 1 4
1 9 6 | 4 2 7 | 8 5 3
------+-------+------
9 6 1 | 3 7 5 | 4 2 8
3 2 7 | 9 8 4 | 1 6 5
4 8 5 | 1 6 2 | 3 7 9
```

165

```
8 9 6 | 7 1 2 | 3 4 5
1 2 5 | 4 6 3 | 8 9 7
7 4 3 | 8 9 5 | 1 2 6
------+-------+------
3 7 4 | 2 5 9 | 6 1 8
9 1 8 | 3 4 6 | 5 7 2
6 5 2 | 1 8 7 | 9 3 4
------+-------+------
5 6 7 | 9 2 1 | 4 8 3
4 3 9 | 5 7 8 | 2 6 1
2 8 1 | 6 3 4 | 7 5 9
```

166

```
7 8 4 | 9 3 1 | 5 6 2
3 2 6 | 7 4 5 | 1 9 8
1 9 5 | 2 8 6 | 7 4 3
------+-------+------
6 1 7 | 5 9 8 | 2 3 4
9 4 3 | 6 7 2 | 8 5 1
8 5 2 | 3 1 4 | 9 7 6
------+-------+------
5 6 8 | 4 2 9 | 3 1 7
4 3 1 | 8 5 7 | 6 2 9
2 7 9 | 1 6 3 | 4 8 5
```

167

```
9 5 6 | 4 3 7 | 2 1 8
2 3 4 | 1 8 9 | 6 5 7
7 1 8 | 5 2 6 | 4 9 3
------+-------+------
5 2 9 | 7 6 3 | 8 4 1
3 6 7 | 8 4 1 | 5 2 9
8 4 1 | 9 5 2 | 3 7 6
------+-------+------
6 9 3 | 2 7 5 | 1 8 4
4 7 2 | 6 1 8 | 9 3 5
1 8 5 | 3 9 4 | 7 6 2
```

168

```
7 6 1 | 3 8 4 | 9 2 5
8 2 5 | 9 6 7 | 4 3 1
9 4 3 | 1 2 5 | 6 7 8
------+-------+------
1 5 6 | 7 3 8 | 2 4 9
2 3 9 | 5 4 1 | 8 6 7
4 7 8 | 2 9 6 | 5 1 3
------+-------+------
5 9 2 | 6 1 3 | 7 8 4
6 1 4 | 8 7 9 | 3 5 2
3 8 7 | 4 5 2 | 1 9 6
```

169

```
6 3 1 | 2 5 9 | 4 7 8
7 5 4 | 8 3 1 | 2 6 9
8 2 9 | 4 6 7 | 5 3 1
------+-------+------
3 4 8 | 9 7 6 | 1 2 5
9 6 2 | 5 1 8 | 7 4 3
1 7 5 | 3 2 4 | 9 8 6
------+-------+------
5 8 3 | 1 4 2 | 6 9 7
2 1 7 | 6 9 3 | 8 5 4
4 9 6 | 7 8 5 | 3 1 2
```

170

```
3 9 5 | 8 2 6 | 4 7 1
1 6 8 | 3 7 4 | 9 5 2
7 4 2 | 5 1 9 | 6 3 8
------+-------+------
4 2 9 | 7 6 3 | 1 8 5
8 3 1 | 9 5 2 | 7 6 4
6 5 7 | 4 8 1 | 2 9 3
------+-------+------
9 1 3 | 6 4 5 | 8 2 7
2 7 6 | 1 3 8 | 5 4 9
5 8 4 | 2 9 7 | 3 1 6
```

171

```
1 7 9 | 4 5 6 | 2 8 3
3 6 5 | 8 1 2 | 9 7 4
8 4 2 | 3 7 9 | 1 6 5
------+-------+------
5 1 3 | 6 2 7 | 4 9 8
9 2 7 | 5 8 4 | 3 1 6
6 8 4 | 9 3 1 | 7 5 2
------+-------+------
2 9 6 | 1 4 8 | 5 3 7
7 5 8 | 2 9 3 | 6 4 1
4 3 1 | 7 6 5 | 8 2 9
```

172

```
2 3 9 | 4 7 8 | 6 5 1
6 8 7 | 9 1 5 | 3 2 4
4 1 5 | 2 3 6 | 9 8 7
------+-------+------
3 5 6 | 8 2 7 | 1 4 9
8 7 1 | 3 9 4 | 5 6 2
9 2 4 | 5 6 1 | 8 7 3
------+-------+------
1 4 2 | 6 8 3 | 7 9 5
5 6 3 | 7 4 9 | 2 1 8
7 9 8 | 1 5 2 | 4 3 6
```

173

```
5 9 2 | 8 7 6 | 3 4 1
8 7 4 | 5 1 3 | 9 2 6
3 1 6 | 9 4 2 | 5 8 7
------+-------+------
1 8 9 | 7 5 4 | 2 6 3
7 6 3 | 1 2 8 | 4 9 5
2 4 5 | 3 6 9 | 7 1 8
------+-------+------
6 3 1 | 4 9 7 | 8 5 2
4 5 8 | 2 3 1 | 6 7 9
9 2 7 | 6 8 5 | 1 3 4
```

174

```
7 6 3 | 2 9 4 | 8 1 5
9 2 8 | 1 7 5 | 3 6 4
5 4 1 | 3 6 8 | 9 2 7
------+-------+------
8 1 7 | 9 4 2 | 5 3 6
3 5 6 | 7 8 1 | 2 4 9
2 9 4 | 6 5 3 | 1 7 8
------+-------+------
1 7 5 | 8 2 6 | 4 9 3
4 3 9 | 5 1 7 | 6 8 2
6 8 2 | 4 3 9 | 7 5 1
```

175

```
2 5 8 | 3 6 7 | 1 9 4
1 7 9 | 2 5 4 | 8 6 3
6 4 3 | 8 1 9 | 2 5 7
------+-------+------
3 8 7 | 9 2 5 | 6 4 1
9 6 2 | 1 4 3 | 7 8 5
5 1 4 | 7 8 6 | 9 3 2
------+-------+------
7 9 1 | 4 3 8 | 5 2 6
4 2 5 | 6 9 1 | 3 7 8
8 3 6 | 5 7 2 | 4 1 9
```

176

```
3 5 4 | 7 8 1 | 6 2 9
2 9 7 | 6 4 3 | 1 5 8
1 8 6 | 2 9 5 | 7 4 3
------+-------+------
8 6 1 | 4 3 2 | 5 9 7
5 7 3 | 1 6 9 | 4 8 2
9 4 2 | 5 7 8 | 3 1 6
------+-------+------
7 2 9 | 3 1 4 | 8 6 5
4 3 5 | 8 2 6 | 9 7 1
6 1 8 | 9 5 7 | 2 3 4
```

177

```
5 3 2 | 1 8 7 | 4 9 6
4 9 8 | 3 2 6 | 7 5 1
7 6 1 | 5 9 4 | 3 2 8
------+-------+------
1 7 4 | 2 3 5 | 8 6 9
8 5 6 | 9 7 1 | 2 4 3
9 2 3 | 6 4 8 | 5 1 7
------+-------+------
3 1 5 | 8 6 2 | 9 7 4
6 4 9 | 7 5 3 | 1 8 2
2 8 7 | 4 1 9 | 6 3 5
```

178

```
8 9 5 | 6 2 7 | 4 3 1
2 7 6 | 1 4 3 | 8 9 5
4 3 1 | 5 8 9 | 2 6 7
------+-------+------
7 8 4 | 9 3 5 | 6 1 2
3 1 9 | 4 6 2 | 7 5 8
6 5 2 | 8 7 1 | 3 4 9
------+-------+------
1 2 7 | 3 5 4 | 9 8 6
5 4 8 | 7 9 6 | 1 2 3
9 6 3 | 2 1 8 | 5 7 4
```

179

```
2 3 6 | 4 7 1 | 9 8 5
1 5 8 | 9 2 3 | 6 7 4
4 7 9 | 8 6 5 | 3 2 1
------+-------+------
9 8 5 | 6 3 7 | 4 1 2
7 4 1 | 5 9 2 | 8 6 3
6 2 3 | 1 8 4 | 5 9 7
------+-------+------
8 1 7 | 3 4 9 | 2 5 6
3 6 2 | 7 5 8 | 1 4 9
5 9 4 | 2 1 6 | 7 3 8
```

180

```
3 9 4 | 2 8 6 | 1 5 7
8 5 2 | 7 9 1 | 6 4 3
7 1 6 | 5 3 4 | 8 2 9
------+-------+------
4 2 1 | 9 6 3 | 5 7 8
6 8 5 | 4 1 7 | 9 3 2
9 3 7 | 8 2 5 | 4 1 6
------+-------+------
2 4 9 | 1 7 8 | 3 6 5
5 7 3 | 6 4 9 | 2 8 1
1 6 8 | 3 5 2 | 7 9 4
```

181

1	7	9	8	4	5	6	2	3
3	4	8	1	6	2	7	9	5
2	5	6	9	3	7	8	4	1
6	8	3	4	9	1	5	7	2
7	9	5	6	2	3	4	1	8
4	1	2	5	7	8	9	3	6
9	2	4	3	8	6	1	5	7
8	3	1	7	5	4	2	6	9
5	6	7	2	1	9	3	8	4

182

9	2	5	8	4	3	1	7	6
1	6	4	2	9	7	5	8	3
8	3	7	1	5	6	4	9	2
4	5	8	6	1	2	7	3	9
7	9	2	3	8	5	6	1	4
6	1	3	4	7	9	2	5	8
2	7	6	9	3	1	8	4	5
5	4	9	7	2	8	3	6	1
3	8	1	5	6	4	9	2	7

183

2	1	5	6	3	9	4	8	7
6	9	8	2	4	7	5	1	3
3	4	7	8	1	5	2	6	9
8	7	1	5	9	3	6	4	2
5	2	9	1	6	4	7	3	8
4	3	6	7	2	8	1	9	5
9	6	2	3	5	1	8	7	4
7	5	4	9	8	6	3	2	1
1	8	3	4	7	2	9	5	6

184

2	3	6	1	8	7	5	4	9
5	9	1	3	4	2	7	8	6
7	4	8	5	9	6	3	2	1
6	8	7	9	3	4	2	1	5
1	2	9	8	7	5	6	3	4
3	5	4	6	2	1	8	9	7
9	7	2	4	5	3	1	6	8
8	6	3	7	1	9	4	5	2
4	1	5	2	6	8	9	7	3

185

2	1	6	7	8	9	3	5	4
7	5	3	1	4	2	9	8	6
8	4	9	3	6	5	7	2	1
1	3	8	4	2	6	5	9	7
4	2	7	5	9	1	6	3	8
6	9	5	8	7	3	4	1	2
3	7	4	9	1	8	2	6	5
5	6	1	2	3	4	8	7	9
9	8	2	6	5	7	1	4	3

186

6	3	5	7	9	1	4	8	2
8	2	7	4	5	3	6	1	9
4	1	9	6	2	8	5	3	7
2	7	3	1	6	9	8	5	4
1	6	8	2	4	5	7	9	3
9	5	4	8	3	7	1	2	6
5	4	6	9	1	2	3	7	8
7	9	1	3	8	4	2	6	5
3	8	2	5	7	6	9	4	1

187

4	1	9	7	5	6	2	8	3
5	2	6	3	1	8	7	9	4
7	3	8	2	9	4	1	5	6
3	9	4	5	8	1	6	7	2
6	8	2	4	7	3	5	1	9
1	7	5	6	2	9	3	4	8
9	6	1	8	3	7	4	2	5
8	5	3	1	4	2	9	6	7
2	4	7	9	6	5	8	3	1

188

5	3	8	6	7	1	4	9	2
9	6	4	5	2	8	1	7	3
7	1	2	4	3	9	8	5	6
6	8	1	7	4	3	5	2	9
2	9	3	1	6	5	7	8	4
4	7	5	8	9	2	3	6	1
8	4	6	9	1	7	2	3	5
1	2	7	3	5	6	9	4	8
3	5	9	2	8	4	6	1	7

189

8	3	1	5	2	6	7	9	4
5	7	4	8	3	9	1	2	6
6	2	9	4	7	1	3	8	5
4	6	2	1	5	8	9	3	7
9	8	3	2	4	7	5	6	1
1	5	7	9	6	3	2	4	8
3	1	5	6	8	2	4	7	9
7	9	6	3	1	4	8	5	2
2	4	8	7	9	5	6	1	3

190

9	6	2	4	7	1	3	8	5
1	7	5	9	8	3	6	4	2
3	4	8	5	2	6	7	1	9
2	8	7	1	3	4	5	9	6
6	9	3	8	5	2	1	7	4
5	1	4	6	9	7	8	2	3
7	5	6	2	1	9	4	3	8
8	3	9	7	4	5	2	6	1
4	2	1	3	6	8	9	5	7

191

2	9	7	6	1	8	3	4	5
4	8	1	5	3	7	2	9	6
5	6	3	9	2	4	8	1	7
7	5	8	4	6	1	9	3	2
1	3	9	2	8	5	7	6	4
6	2	4	7	9	3	1	5	8
8	7	6	3	4	9	5	2	1
9	4	5	1	7	2	6	8	3
3	1	2	8	5	6	4	7	9

192

5	8	2	7	1	4	3	6	9
3	7	6	5	2	9	1	4	8
9	1	4	6	8	3	5	7	2
8	2	7	1	5	6	4	9	3
4	3	5	8	9	7	6	2	1
6	9	1	4	3	2	7	8	5
7	5	3	9	4	8	2	1	6
2	4	9	3	6	1	8	5	7
1	6	8	2	7	5	9	3	4

193

9	4	3	1	6	8	2	7	5
5	1	6	2	4	7	3	9	8
7	2	8	5	3	9	1	4	6
3	5	2	4	7	6	8	1	9
6	9	4	8	5	1	7	2	3
8	7	1	3	9	2	5	6	4
4	8	9	7	2	5	6	3	1
2	3	5	6	1	4	9	8	7
1	6	7	9	8	3	4	5	2

194

2	3	6	7	5	9	1	8	4
7	1	5	4	8	2	3	6	9
4	9	8	3	1	6	2	7	5
6	8	7	2	3	5	9	4	1
1	5	3	6	9	4	7	2	8
9	4	2	1	7	8	5	3	6
3	6	1	9	4	7	8	5	2
8	7	4	5	2	1	6	9	3
5	2	9	8	6	3	4	1	7

195

4	1	7	9	2	3	5	8	6
5	6	2	1	4	8	9	3	7
9	3	8	5	7	6	4	1	2
2	8	5	7	1	9	3	6	4
6	7	4	8	3	5	2	9	1
3	9	1	4	6	2	7	5	8
7	4	9	6	5	1	8	2	3
8	2	6	3	9	7	1	4	5
1	5	3	2	8	4	6	7	9

196

9	7	3	8	6	4	2	1	5
6	4	1	5	2	3	9	7	8
8	2	5	7	1	9	6	3	4
3	6	4	9	8	7	5	2	1
7	9	2	1	5	6	8	4	3
1	5	8	4	3	2	7	9	6
4	1	7	6	9	8	3	5	2
2	8	9	3	4	5	1	6	7
5	3	6	2	7	1	4	8	9

197

8	9	2	5	7	4	6	3	1
7	4	1	6	9	3	8	5	2
5	6	3	2	1	8	4	7	9
1	8	4	9	5	7	2	6	3
9	2	7	3	4	6	5	1	8
3	5	6	1	8	2	9	4	7
2	3	9	7	6	5	1	8	4
4	7	5	8	2	1	3	9	6
6	1	8	4	3	9	7	2	5

198

2	5	4	9	8	1	3	7	6
7	3	8	4	6	5	9	2	1
6	9	1	3	2	7	8	5	4
4	7	6	1	3	8	5	9	2
8	1	5	2	9	4	6	3	7
3	2	9	5	7	6	4	1	8
5	6	3	7	4	2	1	8	9
1	8	7	6	5	9	2	4	3
9	4	2	8	1	3	7	6	5

199

9	8	2	7	3	1	4	6	5
4	3	6	5	2	9	7	1	8
7	1	5	4	6	8	3	2	9
2	6	3	9	7	4	8	5	1
5	9	8	3	1	2	6	7	4
1	4	7	6	8	5	9	3	2
8	7	4	2	5	6	1	9	3
3	5	1	8	9	7	2	4	6
6	2	9	1	4	3	5	8	7

200

9	1	3	4	6	2	5	8	7
4	2	7	5	8	1	9	3	6
5	6	8	3	7	9	1	2	4
3	5	6	9	1	7	8	4	2
7	9	2	6	4	8	3	1	5
8	4	1	2	3	5	6	7	9
2	8	9	1	5	4	7	6	3
6	7	5	8	2	3	4	9	1
1	3	4	7	9	6	2	5	8

201

9	3	5	7	4	2	1	8	6
8	2	6	5	1	9	4	3	7
4	1	7	8	6	3	2	9	5
6	7	3	4	2	8	5	1	9
1	8	2	9	5	7	3	6	4
5	9	4	1	3	6	7	2	8
2	5	9	6	7	1	8	4	3
3	4	8	2	9	5	6	7	1
7	6	1	3	8	4	9	5	2

202

8	4	6	3	9	5	1	7	2
5	3	1	6	2	7	4	8	9
7	2	9	1	8	4	5	6	3
6	9	4	8	3	2	7	5	1
3	5	7	4	6	1	9	2	8
2	1	8	5	7	9	6	3	4
4	7	2	9	5	3	8	1	6
9	6	3	7	1	8	2	4	5
1	8	5	2	4	6	3	9	7

203

2	7	1	6	3	4	8	5	9
8	3	6	5	9	7	2	1	4
5	9	4	1	2	8	6	3	7
9	2	7	4	6	3	5	8	1
3	4	8	9	1	5	7	6	2
6	1	5	7	8	2	4	9	3
1	5	3	2	4	6	9	7	8
7	8	2	3	5	9	1	4	6
4	6	9	8	7	1	3	2	5

204

6	9	4	3	7	1	2	5	8
8	7	5	4	9	2	1	6	3
3	1	2	6	5	8	4	9	7
9	4	3	1	6	5	8	7	2
7	6	8	9	2	4	5	3	1
2	5	1	8	3	7	9	4	6
4	2	7	5	1	6	3	8	9
5	3	6	2	8	9	7	1	4
1	8	9	7	4	3	6	2	5

205

6	7	2	9	1	5	8	3	4
3	4	1	2	8	7	6	5	9
9	8	5	6	3	4	7	1	2
1	9	6	3	4	8	2	7	5
8	2	7	5	9	6	1	4	3
4	5	3	1	7	2	9	8	6
7	1	9	4	6	3	5	2	8
2	6	4	8	5	1	3	9	7
5	3	8	7	2	9	4	6	1

206

1	9	2	4	5	6	3	7	8
7	4	3	2	8	9	1	5	6
5	8	6	1	3	7	4	2	9
2	1	9	6	7	5	8	3	4
4	6	8	9	2	3	7	1	5
3	5	7	8	4	1	9	6	2
9	7	1	5	6	8	2	4	3
6	3	4	7	9	2	5	8	1
8	2	5	3	1	4	6	9	7

207

8	2	7	4	3	5	9	6	1
9	6	4	1	8	7	2	5	3
3	1	5	6	9	2	8	4	7
1	3	9	8	2	6	5	7	4
5	7	8	9	1	4	3	2	6
2	4	6	5	7	3	1	9	8
7	5	2	3	4	8	6	1	9
6	9	3	7	5	1	4	8	2
4	8	1	2	6	9	7	3	5

208

6	3	8	7	1	2	4	9	5
5	7	9	4	6	3	2	1	8
4	2	1	5	9	8	6	7	3
1	6	2	8	3	4	9	5	7
3	9	7	2	5	1	8	6	4
8	5	4	9	7	6	1	3	2
7	4	5	1	2	9	3	8	6
9	8	3	6	4	7	5	2	1
2	1	6	3	8	5	7	4	9

209

7	4	8	2	9	3	5	6	1
9	2	1	5	6	7	8	3	4
6	3	5	4	1	8	7	2	9
1	7	2	6	4	5	3	9	8
8	6	3	9	7	2	1	4	5
4	5	9	8	3	1	2	7	6
3	1	6	7	8	9	4	5	2
5	9	7	1	2	4	6	8	3
2	8	4	3	5	6	9	1	7

210

8	5	1	3	7	6	2	4	9
2	6	4	9	5	8	1	7	3
3	7	9	2	4	1	8	5	6
6	9	3	5	8	7	4	1	2
1	8	7	4	2	3	6	9	5
5	4	2	1	6	9	7	3	8
7	1	5	8	9	2	3	6	4
9	3	8	6	1	4	5	2	7
4	2	6	7	3	5	9	8	1

211

8	6	5	3	1	7	2	4	9
2	7	1	9	4	5	6	3	8
3	9	4	6	2	8	5	1	7
6	3	7	8	9	4	1	2	5
1	5	8	7	3	2	9	6	4
4	2	9	1	5	6	8	7	3
5	1	6	4	8	3	7	9	2
9	8	3	2	7	1	4	5	6
7	4	2	5	6	9	3	8	1

212

6	1	5	2	9	8	3	7	4
3	4	9	5	7	6	2	8	1
2	8	7	3	1	4	6	9	5
1	9	8	6	3	2	4	5	7
4	2	3	7	5	1	9	6	8
7	5	6	4	8	9	1	2	3
8	6	1	9	4	5	7	3	2
5	7	2	1	6	3	8	4	9
9	3	4	8	2	7	5	1	6

213

3	5	8	7	6	1	4	2	9
2	7	9	3	4	8	1	5	6
6	1	4	5	9	2	8	3	7
7	4	1	2	3	6	5	9	8
8	9	3	4	1	5	6	7	2
5	6	2	9	8	7	3	1	4
4	2	6	1	5	9	7	8	3
9	3	5	8	7	4	2	6	1
1	8	7	6	2	3	9	4	5

214

1	8	6	5	2	9	3	7	4
5	4	3	7	6	1	8	2	9
9	2	7	4	8	3	5	1	6
4	3	8	2	7	5	6	9	1
2	6	9	1	3	8	4	5	7
7	1	5	9	4	6	2	8	3
6	9	1	8	5	4	7	3	2
8	7	4	3	9	2	1	6	5
3	5	2	6	1	7	9	4	8

215

6	1	8	5	9	3	2	7	4
3	2	5	4	7	8	6	1	9
7	9	4	2	6	1	5	3	8
8	3	6	7	2	4	9	5	1
9	4	1	6	3	5	7	8	2
5	7	2	8	1	9	4	6	3
4	8	9	1	5	6	3	2	7
2	6	3	9	8	7	1	4	5
1	5	7	3	4	2	8	9	6

216

3	9	6	2	7	4	8	1	5
1	5	7	3	8	6	4	2	9
2	8	4	1	5	9	6	7	3
8	3	5	4	6	1	7	9	2
4	7	2	9	3	8	1	5	6
6	1	9	5	2	7	3	8	4
5	6	3	8	1	2	9	4	7
9	2	8	7	4	3	5	6	1
7	4	1	6	9	5	2	3	8

217

7	6	2	5	3	8	9	4	1
3	5	9	4	2	1	7	8	6
8	1	4	7	6	9	3	5	2
6	8	1	3	5	4	2	7	9
2	4	3	6	9	7	5	1	8
9	7	5	8	1	2	6	3	4
5	3	8	2	4	6	1	9	7
4	9	6	1	7	5	8	2	3
1	2	7	9	8	3	4	6	5

218

2	7	4	5	1	8	3	9	6
1	8	6	9	2	3	7	5	4
3	5	9	6	7	4	1	2	8
9	2	3	4	8	1	5	6	7
7	4	8	3	6	5	9	1	2
5	6	1	2	9	7	8	4	3
8	9	7	1	4	6	2	3	5
6	3	2	8	5	9	4	7	1
4	1	5	7	3	2	6	8	9

219

1	8	3	4	5	9	6	7	2
9	7	4	6	3	2	5	1	8
5	2	6	7	8	1	4	9	3
7	4	1	9	6	3	2	8	5
8	6	2	5	7	4	1	3	9
3	5	9	2	1	8	7	6	4
6	9	7	8	4	5	3	2	1
4	3	8	1	2	7	9	5	6
2	1	5	3	9	6	8	4	7

220

9	7	2	1	5	4	3	8	6
3	8	1	6	2	9	7	4	5
6	4	5	3	8	7	2	1	9
4	1	7	9	6	3	5	2	8
5	2	9	8	4	1	6	7	3
8	3	6	2	7	5	4	9	1
7	9	4	5	3	8	1	6	2
2	5	8	4	1	6	9	3	7
1	6	3	7	9	2	8	5	4

221

7	5	9	8	3	6	2	4	1
1	8	2	5	9	4	3	6	7
4	6	3	7	2	1	9	8	5
5	2	1	3	6	8	7	9	4
6	4	8	9	7	2	1	5	3
9	3	7	1	4	5	6	2	8
8	9	6	4	1	7	5	3	2
3	7	5	2	8	9	4	1	6
2	1	4	6	5	3	8	7	9

222

6	5	7	4	3	2	1	9	8
4	1	3	9	7	8	5	2	6
9	2	8	6	5	1	7	3	4
7	3	9	2	6	4	8	5	1
2	8	5	7	1	9	4	6	3
1	4	6	3	8	5	2	7	9
5	9	4	1	2	3	6	8	7
8	6	1	5	9	7	3	4	2
3	7	2	8	4	6	9	1	5

223

3	5	6	2	7	4	8	9	1
8	9	7	1	3	6	4	5	2
1	4	2	5	8	9	3	6	7
2	1	3	8	9	5	6	7	4
7	8	5	6	4	3	2	1	9
4	6	9	7	2	1	5	8	3
9	3	1	4	5	8	7	2	6
5	7	4	9	6	2	1	3	8
6	2	8	3	1	7	9	4	5

224

2	4	9	6	7	8	3	1	5
6	5	8	3	1	4	9	2	7
3	7	1	2	9	5	8	6	4
1	6	7	5	4	3	2	9	8
9	8	3	7	2	6	4	5	1
5	2	4	9	8	1	6	7	3
8	9	6	1	3	7	5	4	2
4	1	5	8	6	2	7	3	9
7	3	2	4	5	9	1	8	6

225

7	2	1	3	8	4	6	5	9
3	9	5	1	6	7	2	4	8
8	6	4	2	5	9	7	3	1
6	7	3	9	4	1	8	2	5
1	4	9	5	2	8	3	6	7
5	8	2	7	3	6	1	9	4
4	5	6	8	7	2	9	1	3
9	3	7	6	1	5	4	8	2
2	1	8	4	9	3	5	7	6

226

1	9	4	8	2	5	6	7	3
5	3	6	9	7	4	2	8	1
7	8	2	3	6	1	9	5	4
9	4	7	6	8	2	3	1	5
3	1	5	4	9	7	8	6	2
2	6	8	5	1	3	4	9	7
4	5	9	7	3	6	1	2	8
8	7	1	2	4	9	5	3	6
6	2	3	1	5	8	7	4	9

227

5	4	6	1	8	7	2	3	9
2	7	1	9	3	5	8	6	4
3	8	9	6	2	4	5	1	7
9	1	3	7	5	6	4	8	2
4	6	2	8	1	9	7	5	3
8	5	7	2	4	3	6	9	1
7	3	8	5	9	2	1	4	6
1	2	4	3	6	8	9	7	5
6	9	5	4	7	1	3	2	8

228

9	2	8	5	6	3	4	1	7
6	1	5	4	8	7	3	2	9
4	3	7	9	2	1	8	5	6
1	6	4	2	5	8	9	7	3
5	8	3	7	4	9	1	6	2
2	7	9	1	3	6	5	4	8
8	4	2	3	7	5	6	9	1
3	5	1	6	9	2	7	8	4
7	9	6	8	1	4	2	3	5

229

8	2	5	6	9	7	1	4	3
6	3	9	8	1	4	7	2	5
4	1	7	3	2	5	6	8	9
9	7	1	2	3	6	4	5	8
2	6	8	4	5	9	3	1	7
3	5	4	7	8	1	9	6	2
7	8	6	9	4	2	5	3	1
1	4	3	5	7	8	2	9	6
5	9	2	1	6	3	8	7	4

230

3	5	4	8	2	7	1	6	9
1	2	9	4	6	3	7	8	5
7	8	6	5	1	9	4	3	2
9	3	1	6	7	5	8	2	4
8	6	5	1	4	2	3	9	7
2	4	7	3	9	8	6	5	1
6	7	8	9	5	1	2	4	3
4	9	2	7	3	6	5	1	8
5	1	3	2	8	4	9	7	6

231

1	2	4	5	9	7	3	8	6
6	8	9	3	1	2	4	5	7
5	3	7	6	4	8	1	2	9
4	6	3	8	2	5	9	7	1
8	9	5	1	7	6	2	4	3
7	1	2	4	3	9	8	6	5
3	4	8	7	5	1	6	9	2
9	7	1	2	6	4	5	3	8
2	5	6	9	8	3	7	1	4

232

4	8	3	2	5	9	7	1	6
7	6	9	4	1	3	2	8	5
2	5	1	6	8	7	9	4	3
5	3	8	1	7	6	4	9	2
1	4	6	9	3	2	8	5	7
9	2	7	5	4	8	6	3	1
3	7	4	8	2	1	5	6	9
8	9	2	3	6	5	1	7	4
6	1	5	7	9	4	3	2	8

233

1	4	2	8	7	6	9	3	5
9	3	8	5	4	2	7	6	1
7	6	5	9	1	3	4	2	8
2	5	3	1	9	7	6	8	4
8	7	1	6	5	4	2	9	3
6	9	4	2	3	8	5	1	7
4	8	9	3	6	5	1	7	2
3	1	7	4	2	9	8	5	6
5	2	6	7	8	1	3	4	9

234

3	1	7	9	2	8	4	5	6
6	9	5	4	3	7	2	8	1
2	4	8	1	5	6	3	7	9
1	3	6	8	9	2	7	4	5
5	8	4	7	6	3	1	9	2
9	7	2	5	1	4	8	6	3
8	5	9	3	4	1	6	2	7
7	2	1	6	8	5	9	3	4
4	6	3	2	7	9	5	1	8

235

7	2	4	6	1	8	5	9	3
8	5	6	9	7	3	4	2	1
3	9	1	4	2	5	7	8	6
6	4	7	2	9	1	3	5	8
1	8	9	5	3	4	6	7	2
2	3	5	7	8	6	1	4	9
5	7	3	8	6	2	9	1	4
4	6	8	1	5	9	2	3	7
9	1	2	3	4	7	8	6	5

236

5	6	8	9	4	7	2	1	3
2	9	7	3	6	1	8	4	5
1	3	4	2	5	8	6	9	7
9	4	5	8	1	6	7	3	2
7	1	2	5	3	9	4	6	8
6	8	3	7	2	4	1	5	9
4	2	9	6	7	3	5	8	1
8	5	6	1	9	2	3	7	4
3	7	1	4	8	5	9	2	6

237

6	9	7	5	1	2	4	8	3
1	2	3	7	8	4	9	6	5
5	4	8	3	9	6	7	1	2
3	7	4	9	6	5	8	2	1
8	6	2	1	4	7	3	5	9
9	1	5	2	3	8	6	4	7
2	3	6	8	7	1	5	9	4
7	8	1	4	5	9	2	3	6
4	5	9	6	2	3	1	7	8

238

1	5	8	6	4	7	2	3	9
2	7	9	3	5	8	1	6	4
6	3	4	1	2	9	8	7	5
7	1	6	5	8	2	4	9	3
3	8	5	4	9	6	7	2	1
9	4	2	7	1	3	5	8	6
4	9	7	8	6	1	3	5	2
8	6	1	2	3	5	9	4	7
5	2	3	9	7	4	6	1	8

239

2	7	1	5	8	3	6	4	9
5	4	3	6	7	9	1	2	8
6	9	8	1	4	2	7	5	3
1	2	7	8	5	4	3	9	6
4	6	9	7	3	1	2	8	5
8	3	5	9	2	6	4	1	7
3	1	6	4	9	8	5	7	2
7	8	4	2	6	5	9	3	1
9	5	2	3	1	7	8	6	4

240

8	3	7	9	4	5	2	6	1
9	6	1	3	2	7	5	4	8
2	4	5	6	8	1	9	7	3
7	2	4	8	3	9	1	5	6
3	1	6	4	5	2	8	9	7
5	8	9	7	1	6	3	2	4
1	9	3	2	6	4	7	8	5
6	5	2	1	7	8	4	3	9
4	7	8	5	9	3	6	1	2

241

6	8	7	3	2	1	9	5	4
9	1	3	7	5	4	6	2	8
2	5	4	9	6	8	7	3	1
3	6	8	4	7	2	1	9	5
4	7	5	1	9	6	2	8	3
1	2	9	5	8	3	4	7	6
5	4	2	6	3	7	8	1	9
8	3	6	2	1	9	5	4	7
7	9	1	8	4	5	3	6	2

242

2	3	5	9	1	4	8	7	6
9	7	8	5	6	3	4	1	2
1	6	4	2	8	7	9	5	3
8	5	1	7	2	9	6	3	4
7	9	2	4	3	6	5	8	1
6	4	3	8	5	1	7	2	9
4	8	9	1	7	2	3	6	5
5	1	6	3	9	8	2	4	7
3	2	7	6	4	5	1	9	8

243

4	2	8	6	5	3	7	9	1
5	7	3	9	1	8	6	2	4
1	6	9	4	2	7	3	8	5
2	9	5	8	3	1	4	7	6
7	3	6	5	9	4	8	1	2
8	1	4	7	6	2	5	3	9
9	8	7	2	4	5	1	6	3
3	5	2	1	7	6	9	4	8
6	4	1	3	8	9	2	5	7

244

4	1	3	2	7	5	8	6	9
5	7	6	1	8	9	4	2	3
2	8	9	3	6	4	1	7	5
9	5	7	8	4	1	2	3	6
6	2	1	7	5	3	9	8	4
3	4	8	6	9	2	5	1	7
8	3	5	9	1	7	6	4	2
1	9	2	4	3	6	7	5	8
7	6	4	5	2	8	3	9	1

245

6	4	2	9	7	3	1	8	5
3	5	1	8	2	6	7	9	4
9	7	8	1	5	4	2	3	6
1	3	9	5	4	2	6	7	8
7	2	5	6	3	8	9	4	1
8	6	4	7	9	1	5	2	3
2	9	3	4	1	5	8	6	7
4	1	6	2	8	7	3	5	9
5	8	7	3	6	9	4	1	2

246

8	2	5	7	3	4	9	6	1
4	9	7	6	8	1	5	3	2
1	6	3	2	9	5	8	7	4
2	7	6	5	4	9	3	1	8
5	4	8	3	1	6	2	9	7
3	1	9	8	7	2	6	4	5
6	8	1	9	5	7	4	2	3
9	5	4	1	2	3	7	8	6
7	3	2	4	6	8	1	5	9

247

4	9	8	3	7	6	1	5	2
6	3	2	9	5	1	7	4	8
5	7	1	8	4	2	6	9	3
1	5	9	6	8	4	2	3	7
7	6	3	2	1	5	9	8	4
2	8	4	7	9	3	5	1	6
9	2	7	5	3	8	4	6	1
8	4	5	1	6	7	3	2	9
3	1	6	4	2	9	8	7	5

248

1	7	8	4	2	9	3	6	5
2	6	5	8	3	1	7	9	4
9	4	3	6	5	7	8	1	2
7	2	9	3	1	4	5	8	6
8	3	4	9	6	5	1	2	7
5	1	6	7	8	2	4	3	9
6	5	2	1	4	8	9	7	3
3	8	7	5	9	6	2	4	1
4	9	1	2	7	3	6	5	8

249

1	2	3	5	9	6	7	4	8
5	6	8	7	4	3	9	2	1
4	7	9	2	1	8	6	5	3
7	1	4	8	2	5	3	6	9
6	8	2	3	7	9	5	1	4
9	3	5	4	6	1	8	7	2
3	4	7	6	8	2	1	9	5
2	5	1	9	3	7	4	8	6
8	9	6	1	5	4	2	3	7

250

1	5	7	8	3	4	2	9	6
2	3	8	5	9	6	7	1	4
9	6	4	7	1	2	3	8	5
6	4	1	9	2	3	8	5	7
8	9	5	4	7	1	6	2	3
7	2	3	6	8	5	1	4	9
5	1	6	2	4	7	9	3	8
3	7	9	1	5	8	4	6	2
4	8	2	3	6	9	5	7	1

251

7	3	9	5	2	8	6	1	4
5	2	6	4	9	1	8	7	3
1	8	4	7	3	6	2	5	9
4	7	5	8	1	2	9	3	6
2	6	3	9	5	7	4	8	1
8	9	1	3	6	4	7	2	5
3	5	7	6	8	9	1	4	2
9	4	2	1	7	3	5	6	8
6	1	8	2	4	5	3	9	7

252

5	7	8	9	2	4	6	1	3
3	4	2	8	1	6	5	9	7
9	1	6	7	3	5	4	2	8
6	3	9	5	4	2	8	7	1
8	2	1	6	9	7	3	4	5
4	5	7	3	8	1	2	6	9
2	6	5	1	7	8	9	3	4
7	9	4	2	5	3	1	8	6
1	8	3	4	6	9	7	5	2

253

6	3	1	5	8	9	4	2	7
5	4	7	1	6	2	8	3	9
9	8	2	4	7	3	5	6	1
1	6	3	9	5	8	2	7	4
8	5	4	2	1	7	3	9	6
7	2	9	6	3	4	1	8	5
2	1	8	7	9	5	6	4	3
4	7	5	3	2	6	9	1	8
3	9	6	8	4	1	7	5	2

254

8	7	6	2	9	5	1	3	4
5	1	4	3	7	6	8	9	2
2	9	3	1	4	8	5	6	7
3	8	1	9	5	7	4	2	6
6	2	9	8	3	4	7	5	1
4	5	7	6	1	2	9	8	3
1	3	5	7	6	9	2	4	8
9	6	8	4	2	1	3	7	5
7	4	2	5	8	3	6	1	9

255

8	2	7	6	5	4	3	1	9
9	3	6	1	7	8	5	2	4
1	4	5	2	3	9	6	8	7
2	9	3	5	8	6	7	4	1
6	7	1	4	2	3	8	9	5
4	5	8	7	9	1	2	3	6
3	6	9	8	4	5	1	7	2
5	8	2	9	1	7	4	6	3
7	1	4	3	6	2	9	5	8

256

7	2	5	9	6	8	3	1	4
9	6	8	3	4	1	7	5	2
4	3	1	7	2	5	8	9	6
3	5	6	1	9	4	2	8	7
8	1	9	2	7	3	6	4	5
2	4	7	5	8	6	1	3	9
1	9	3	6	5	2	4	7	8
5	8	2	4	1	7	9	6	3
6	7	4	8	3	9	5	2	1

257

9	6	3	4	5	2	1	7	8
4	8	2	1	7	6	9	5	3
7	1	5	3	9	8	4	6	2
3	9	4	8	1	7	5	2	6
6	2	8	9	3	5	7	4	1
1	5	7	2	6	4	8	3	9
2	4	6	5	8	9	3	1	7
8	7	1	6	4	3	2	9	5
5	3	9	7	2	1	6	8	4

258

5	2	7	6	1	9	3	4	8
9	6	4	8	3	7	1	5	2
1	3	8	5	2	4	7	9	6
8	4	1	9	5	3	2	6	7
6	9	3	1	7	2	4	8	5
2	7	5	4	8	6	9	3	1
3	8	6	7	9	1	5	2	4
4	1	9	2	6	5	8	7	3
7	5	2	3	4	8	6	1	9

259

9	7	5	8	1	3	2	4	6
4	2	1	7	9	6	5	3	8
6	3	8	2	4	5	1	7	9
5	9	3	1	6	2	4	8	7
1	4	6	9	8	7	3	2	5
2	8	7	3	5	4	9	6	1
7	1	4	5	3	8	6	9	2
8	6	9	4	2	1	7	5	3
3	5	2	6	7	9	8	1	4

260

3	9	2	8	5	7	1	6	4
7	8	6	3	1	4	2	9	5
5	1	4	2	9	6	7	8	3
8	7	1	9	4	5	6	3	2
2	4	3	6	8	1	9	5	7
9	6	5	7	2	3	4	1	8
1	2	8	4	3	9	5	7	6
6	3	9	5	7	2	8	4	1
4	5	7	1	6	8	3	2	9

261

```
1 8 7 6 5 3 9 4 2
9 5 4 8 2 7 6 1 3
2 6 3 1 9 4 7 8 5
7 2 6 9 3 1 4 5 8
4 9 1 5 8 6 3 2 7
5 3 8 4 7 2 1 6 9
6 7 5 3 1 8 2 9 4
8 1 2 7 4 9 5 3 6
3 4 9 2 6 5 8 7 1
```

262

```
8 5 1 6 2 3 7 4 9
6 3 4 9 7 1 5 8 2
2 9 7 4 5 8 6 3 1
9 4 2 1 6 5 8 7 3
1 7 5 3 8 9 2 6 4
3 8 6 7 4 2 1 9 5
7 1 9 5 3 6 4 2 8
4 2 3 8 1 7 9 5 6
5 6 8 2 9 4 3 1 7
```

263

```
5 8 4 6 3 1 9 7 2
3 7 1 5 9 2 6 4 8
6 2 9 8 7 4 5 1 3
2 5 8 3 1 9 4 6 7
4 1 3 7 6 8 2 9 5
9 6 7 2 4 5 3 8 1
7 4 6 1 2 3 8 5 9
1 3 5 9 8 6 7 2 4
8 9 2 4 5 7 1 3 6
```

264

```
1 4 6 3 9 5 7 8 2
5 9 2 4 8 7 1 6 3
8 7 3 2 6 1 9 4 5
6 1 8 5 4 2 3 7 9
2 5 9 6 7 3 4 1 8
4 3 7 8 1 9 5 2 6
7 6 1 9 5 8 2 3 4
9 2 4 7 3 6 8 5 1
3 8 5 1 2 4 6 9 7
```

265

```
8 1 4 7 6 5 9 2 3
5 2 3 9 4 8 6 7 1
7 6 9 2 1 3 8 5 4
2 5 8 1 7 6 4 3 9
6 4 7 8 3 9 2 1 5
9 3 1 4 5 2 7 8 6
4 7 6 5 2 1 3 9 8
3 8 5 6 9 7 1 4 2
1 9 2 3 8 4 5 6 7
```

266

```
9 7 8 6 2 3 1 5 4
4 6 1 7 5 9 3 8 2
2 3 5 8 4 1 7 9 6
8 2 7 9 3 6 5 4 1
6 4 3 1 7 5 9 2 8
1 5 9 4 8 2 6 7 3
3 9 4 5 6 8 2 1 7
5 8 6 2 1 7 4 3 9
7 1 2 3 9 4 8 6 5
```

267

```
8 4 1 6 2 5 7 9 3
5 7 3 9 1 8 2 6 4
9 6 2 7 3 4 1 8 5
3 1 7 8 4 2 6 5 9
2 8 6 5 9 7 3 4 1
4 9 5 1 6 3 8 7 2
6 5 4 2 7 1 9 3 8
7 2 8 3 5 9 4 1 6
1 3 9 4 8 6 5 2 7
```

268

```
5 6 8 2 7 1 3 4 9
9 7 2 3 5 4 1 6 8
1 3 4 8 9 6 7 2 5
3 5 9 4 6 2 8 1 7
8 2 7 1 3 9 6 5 4
6 4 1 7 8 5 2 9 3
2 1 3 9 4 7 5 8 6
4 8 5 6 1 3 9 7 2
7 9 6 5 2 8 4 3 1
```

269

```
7 8 2 3 9 1 4 6 5
5 1 4 6 2 8 9 3 7
3 6 9 4 7 5 2 1 8
9 2 5 7 8 6 1 4 3
4 7 1 5 3 9 6 8 2
8 3 6 1 4 2 5 7 9
2 5 7 8 1 4 3 9 6
6 4 3 9 5 7 8 2 1
1 9 8 2 6 3 7 5 4
```

270

```
3 7 6 8 9 1 4 5 2
8 1 4 5 2 3 6 7 9
9 2 5 4 6 7 8 3 1
5 8 3 9 1 4 2 6 7
6 4 2 7 3 8 1 9 5
1 9 7 6 5 2 3 8 4
4 6 8 1 7 9 5 2 3
2 5 9 3 4 6 7 1 8
7 3 1 2 8 5 9 4 6
```

271

```
6 8 3 7 5 1 4 2 9
2 9 1 4 8 6 3 5 7
7 5 4 3 2 9 8 6 1
9 3 2 1 7 5 6 4 8
4 7 6 2 9 8 1 3 5
8 1 5 6 4 3 7 9 2
1 4 7 5 3 2 9 8 6
3 2 8 9 6 7 5 1 4
5 6 9 8 1 4 2 7 3
```

272

```
2 3 1 5 8 7 9 4 6
4 7 5 3 9 6 2 1 8
9 8 6 4 2 1 5 7 3
8 4 3 6 5 9 7 2 1
6 5 7 1 4 2 8 3 9
1 9 2 8 7 3 6 5 4
3 6 9 2 1 5 4 8 7
7 2 4 9 3 8 1 6 5
5 1 8 7 6 4 3 9 2
```

273

```
2 8 9 7 3 6 1 5 4
6 1 4 9 2 5 8 3 7
7 5 3 4 1 8 6 2 9
5 2 6 3 4 1 9 7 8
9 7 1 5 8 2 4 6 3
3 4 8 6 7 9 2 1 5
8 6 5 2 9 7 3 4 1
4 9 7 1 6 3 5 8 2
1 3 2 8 5 4 7 9 6
```

274

```
1 2 7 9 3 4 5 8 6
9 3 8 6 7 5 4 1 2
5 6 4 8 2 1 9 7 3
7 9 5 1 8 3 2 6 4
4 8 3 2 9 6 7 5 1
2 1 6 5 4 7 3 9 8
8 5 2 3 6 9 1 4 7
6 4 9 7 1 2 8 3 5
3 7 1 4 5 8 6 2 9
```

275

```
8 5 7 3 1 9 4 6 2
1 9 2 6 4 7 5 8 3
3 6 4 2 5 8 7 1 9
4 7 3 8 9 5 6 2 1
5 2 8 1 6 3 9 4 7
9 1 6 4 7 2 8 3 5
6 8 5 9 3 1 2 7 4
2 3 9 7 8 4 1 5 6
7 4 1 5 2 6 3 9 8
```

276

```
3 6 9 8 4 7 5 1 2
5 8 7 1 9 2 6 4 3
2 1 4 3 5 6 9 8 7
4 5 8 6 7 3 1 2 9
1 9 2 5 8 4 3 7 6
6 7 3 9 2 1 4 5 8
9 4 5 7 6 8 2 3 1
7 2 1 4 3 9 8 6 5
8 3 6 2 1 5 7 9 4
```

277

```
6 4 5 1 9 8 7 2 3
9 2 7 6 4 3 5 8 1
1 8 3 5 2 7 6 4 9
5 1 6 3 7 4 2 9 8
3 9 8 2 1 5 4 6 7
4 7 2 9 8 6 1 3 5
8 6 9 7 5 2 3 1 4
2 5 1 4 3 9 8 7 6
7 3 4 8 6 1 9 5 2
```

278

```
5 4 9 3 7 1 8 6 2
8 3 6 9 2 4 1 5 7
2 7 1 6 8 5 3 9 4
3 9 4 2 5 6 7 1 8
1 8 5 7 4 3 9 2 6
7 6 2 8 1 9 5 4 3
6 5 8 1 3 2 4 7 9
9 1 3 4 6 7 2 8 5
4 2 7 5 9 8 6 3 1
```

279

```
6 7 3 8 4 9 1 5 2
2 5 4 3 1 6 7 9 8
8 1 9 7 2 5 3 4 6
1 4 8 5 6 7 9 2 3
9 6 5 2 3 4 8 1 7
7 3 2 9 8 1 5 6 4
5 8 7 4 9 2 6 3 1
4 9 6 1 7 3 2 8 5
3 2 1 6 5 8 4 7 9
```

280

```
8 1 2 3 5 7 6 4 9
7 9 5 8 6 4 1 3 2
3 6 4 1 9 2 5 7 8
6 5 3 9 4 1 8 2 7
9 8 7 2 3 5 4 1 6
2 4 1 6 7 8 3 9 5
5 7 9 4 1 6 2 8 3
1 3 8 5 2 9 7 6 4
4 2 6 7 8 3 9 5 1
```

281

1	4	5	2	6	8	3	9	7
8	3	9	5	7	4	2	6	1
7	2	6	1	3	9	8	4	5
3	6	1	8	5	2	4	7	9
9	8	7	4	1	6	5	2	3
2	5	4	3	9	7	6	1	8
4	1	3	9	2	5	7	8	6
5	7	2	6	8	1	9	3	4
6	9	8	7	4	3	1	5	2

282

7	6	3	1	9	8	5	4	2
5	8	9	2	3	4	1	6	7
2	4	1	6	5	7	3	9	8
8	2	4	3	6	1	9	7	5
9	7	5	4	8	2	6	3	1
1	3	6	5	7	9	8	2	4
4	5	2	9	1	3	7	8	6
3	1	8	7	2	6	4	5	9
6	9	7	8	4	5	2	1	3

283

3	9	5	4	2	1	6	8	7
7	1	2	6	8	9	5	3	4
4	6	8	5	3	7	9	2	1
5	4	1	9	7	2	8	6	3
8	2	9	3	4	6	7	1	5
6	3	7	1	5	8	2	4	9
9	7	4	8	6	3	1	5	2
1	5	6	2	9	4	3	7	8
2	8	3	7	1	5	4	9	6

284

3	4	2	7	6	5	1	9	8
9	5	8	3	2	1	7	6	4
7	1	6	8	4	9	5	2	3
4	8	5	1	7	2	9	3	6
1	3	9	6	5	4	2	8	7
2	6	7	9	3	8	4	5	1
6	7	4	5	9	3	8	1	2
5	2	1	4	8	6	3	7	9
8	9	3	2	1	7	6	4	5

285

8	4	2	3	6	5	7	9	1
6	3	9	4	7	1	2	8	5
7	1	5	2	9	8	6	3	4
2	5	7	6	3	4	8	1	9
1	6	4	7	8	9	5	2	3
9	8	3	1	5	2	4	7	6
5	2	1	9	4	7	3	6	8
3	9	8	5	2	6	1	4	7
4	7	6	8	1	3	9	5	2

286

8	7	4	9	6	1	5	3	2
2	9	3	5	4	7	6	8	1
1	5	6	2	3	8	9	7	4
4	2	1	3	5	9	7	6	8
7	3	9	8	2	6	4	1	5
5	6	8	1	7	4	2	9	3
9	4	5	6	1	3	8	2	7
3	8	7	4	9	2	1	5	6
6	1	2	7	8	5	3	4	9

287

1	3	6	8	9	2	7	5	4
7	4	9	1	3	5	6	8	2
2	8	5	6	4	7	3	9	1
5	6	3	9	2	4	8	1	7
9	1	2	3	7	8	4	6	5
8	7	4	5	1	6	2	3	9
6	2	8	7	5	9	1	4	3
4	9	1	2	8	3	5	7	6
3	5	7	4	6	1	9	2	8

288

9	2	8	3	5	4	6	7	1
4	6	1	7	8	2	9	5	3
5	3	7	9	1	6	4	8	2
8	5	9	2	4	3	1	6	7
7	4	3	1	6	9	8	2	5
2	1	6	8	7	5	3	4	9
6	7	2	4	9	1	5	3	8
1	8	4	5	3	7	2	9	6
3	9	5	6	2	8	7	1	4

289

9	8	4	1	5	6	7	2	3
2	7	1	4	8	3	5	6	9
6	5	3	9	7	2	1	8	4
3	6	5	8	2	7	9	4	1
1	9	8	5	6	4	3	7	2
7	4	2	3	1	9	8	5	6
5	2	9	7	4	1	6	3	8
8	1	6	2	3	5	4	9	7
4	3	7	6	9	8	2	1	5

290

9	4	2	3	6	8	1	7	5
6	8	1	5	7	9	3	4	2
7	5	3	2	4	1	8	9	6
5	3	8	4	9	2	6	1	7
2	6	4	7	1	5	9	8	3
1	7	9	8	3	6	5	2	4
3	2	6	9	8	7	4	5	1
8	1	7	6	5	4	2	3	9
4	9	5	1	2	3	7	6	8

291

9	2	4	5	7	8	6	1	3
6	7	8	1	3	9	2	4	5
1	5	3	6	2	4	7	9	8
3	4	7	8	5	1	9	2	6
8	1	2	3	9	6	4	5	7
5	6	9	7	4	2	3	8	1
7	9	1	2	8	3	5	6	4
2	3	6	4	1	5	8	7	9
4	8	5	9	6	7	1	3	2

292

9	7	3	6	5	8	4	2	1
5	1	2	7	9	4	3	8	6
4	6	8	2	3	1	5	9	7
1	4	7	5	6	9	2	3	8
2	8	9	4	7	3	6	1	5
6	3	5	8	1	2	9	7	4
8	2	6	3	4	7	1	5	9
3	9	4	1	8	5	7	6	2
7	5	1	9	2	6	8	4	3

293

9	3	5	4	7	1	2	6	8
8	2	4	6	3	9	5	7	1
6	7	1	2	5	8	3	4	9
7	4	6	8	9	5	1	2	3
3	8	9	1	6	2	7	5	4
1	5	2	7	4	3	9	8	6
2	1	3	5	8	4	6	9	7
4	9	7	3	2	6	8	1	5
5	6	8	9	1	7	4	3	2

294

2	6	3	5	9	1	8	4	7
7	5	1	8	4	2	6	3	9
9	8	4	6	7	3	2	1	5
3	4	7	1	2	6	5	9	8
5	2	8	7	3	9	4	6	1
1	9	6	4	8	5	7	2	3
8	1	2	9	5	4	3	7	6
6	3	5	2	1	7	9	8	4
4	7	9	3	6	8	1	5	2

295

1	5	4	6	2	3	9	7	8
8	3	7	5	9	4	1	6	2
2	9	6	1	8	7	5	3	4
6	7	1	3	4	9	8	2	5
3	2	9	7	5	8	6	4	1
4	8	5	2	1	6	7	9	3
5	1	3	9	6	2	4	8	7
7	6	8	4	3	1	2	5	9
9	4	2	8	7	5	3	1	6

296

9	8	1	6	2	4	5	3	7
7	6	5	9	8	3	1	4	2
4	3	2	1	5	7	9	6	8
8	9	6	4	1	5	2	7	3
3	5	4	2	7	9	8	1	6
2	1	7	8	3	6	4	5	9
6	4	3	5	9	8	7	2	1
1	7	9	3	4	2	6	8	5
5	2	8	7	6	1	3	9	4

297

8	4	5	7	6	9	2	3	1
7	1	9	5	2	3	8	6	4
3	6	2	8	1	4	9	7	5
6	9	7	1	5	8	3	4	2
2	5	4	6	3	7	1	9	8
1	3	8	9	4	2	7	5	6
5	8	3	2	9	6	4	1	7
4	7	6	3	8	1	5	2	9
9	2	1	4	7	5	6	8	3

298

3	6	2	5	9	1	4	8	7
5	4	1	2	8	7	9	6	3
8	7	9	3	4	6	2	5	1
7	8	3	6	1	9	5	4	2
9	2	5	8	3	4	7	1	6
4	1	6	7	2	5	3	9	8
2	5	4	1	7	8	6	3	9
6	3	8	9	5	2	1	7	4
1	9	7	4	6	3	8	2	5

299

4	1	9	7	2	3	6	5	8
7	6	5	8	9	1	4	3	2
2	8	3	5	4	6	7	9	1
1	4	2	3	6	5	9	8	7
9	7	6	1	8	2	5	4	3
5	3	8	9	7	4	1	2	6
3	5	4	6	1	8	2	7	9
6	2	7	4	3	9	8	1	5
8	9	1	2	5	7	3	6	4

300

3	8	9	4	1	6	7	2	5
7	5	6	8	2	9	1	4	3
2	4	1	5	7	3	6	9	8
8	1	5	7	6	2	4	3	9
9	6	2	3	4	8	5	7	1
4	3	7	9	5	1	8	6	2
1	7	4	2	9	5	3	8	6
6	9	3	1	8	7	2	5	4
5	2	8	6	3	4	9	1	7

301

6	8	1	7	2	9	3	4	5
9	4	2	6	5	3	7	8	1
7	5	3	4	1	8	9	2	6
4	3	6	9	8	7	1	5	2
8	2	5	1	3	4	6	9	7
1	7	9	2	6	5	8	3	4
2	9	7	3	4	1	5	6	8
3	6	8	5	7	2	4	1	9
5	1	4	8	9	6	2	7	3

302

3	1	5	2	4	7	6	9	8
7	6	9	5	8	1	3	2	4
4	2	8	6	9	3	5	7	1
5	3	6	1	2	4	7	8	9
8	9	1	7	3	5	2	4	6
2	4	7	9	6	8	1	5	3
6	7	2	8	1	9	4	3	5
1	8	3	4	5	2	9	6	7
9	5	4	3	7	6	8	1	2

303

4	8	2	6	9	1	7	5	3
7	6	9	3	5	4	8	2	1
3	5	1	2	8	7	9	4	6
8	9	4	5	2	6	1	3	7
1	7	6	4	3	9	5	8	2
2	3	5	7	1	8	4	6	9
9	4	3	1	6	5	2	7	8
6	1	7	8	4	2	3	9	5
5	2	8	9	7	3	6	1	4

304

7	9	6	4	3	2	8	5	1
1	3	5	9	7	8	2	6	4
8	2	4	1	6	5	9	3	7
2	6	7	5	4	3	1	8	9
5	1	8	2	9	6	7	4	3
3	4	9	8	1	7	5	2	6
9	8	1	6	5	4	3	7	2
4	5	3	7	2	9	6	1	8
6	7	2	3	8	1	4	9	5

305

1	8	4	5	9	7	3	6	2
6	9	7	2	3	1	4	5	8
5	2	3	4	6	8	1	7	9
8	7	2	1	5	6	9	3	4
4	5	1	9	7	3	8	2	6
9	3	6	8	4	2	5	1	7
3	4	9	7	2	5	6	8	1
2	6	8	3	1	4	7	9	5
7	1	5	6	8	9	2	4	3

306

2	9	7	8	4	6	3	5	1
8	3	5	1	2	7	4	6	9
1	6	4	3	9	5	2	8	7
6	4	8	5	3	9	1	7	2
3	1	2	6	7	4	5	9	8
7	5	9	2	1	8	6	4	3
4	8	1	9	5	3	7	2	6
9	7	3	4	6	2	8	1	5
5	2	6	7	8	1	9	3	4

307

5	7	2	3	8	9	4	1	6
1	3	9	4	6	5	8	7	2
8	4	6	2	1	7	3	5	9
3	8	7	6	9	4	5	2	1
6	2	5	8	3	1	9	4	7
4	9	1	7	5	2	6	8	3
7	6	4	5	2	3	1	9	8
9	5	3	1	7	8	2	6	4
2	1	8	9	4	6	7	3	5

308

4	3	9	2	7	6	1	8	5
1	5	6	3	8	9	4	2	7
7	2	8	5	1	4	3	6	9
3	9	5	7	4	2	8	1	6
2	6	4	1	9	8	5	7	3
8	7	1	6	5	3	9	4	2
6	4	2	9	3	1	7	5	8
5	8	3	4	2	7	6	9	1
9	1	7	8	6	5	2	3	4

309

6	8	9	1	2	5	3	7	4
5	7	1	8	4	3	9	6	2
3	4	2	7	9	6	1	5	8
7	1	8	3	5	2	6	4	9
9	2	3	4	6	8	7	1	5
4	6	5	9	7	1	8	2	3
1	3	4	5	8	7	2	9	6
8	5	6	2	1	9	4	3	7
2	9	7	6	3	4	5	8	1

310

2	5	8	1	7	6	4	3	9
4	6	1	8	3	9	2	5	7
7	3	9	5	4	2	1	8	6
8	7	2	4	6	1	3	9	5
6	9	3	2	5	7	8	4	1
1	4	5	3	9	8	7	6	2
9	8	6	7	2	4	5	1	3
5	2	4	6	1	3	9	7	8
3	1	7	9	8	5	6	2	4

311

3	4	8	1	2	6	5	9	7
6	9	5	4	7	8	3	2	1
1	7	2	9	5	3	8	6	4
4	5	1	7	8	2	9	3	6
2	6	3	5	9	4	7	1	8
9	8	7	6	3	1	4	5	2
8	3	6	2	4	9	1	7	5
5	1	4	3	6	7	2	8	9
7	2	9	8	1	5	6	4	3

312

4	5	8	6	7	9	2	3	1
1	6	3	4	8	2	7	5	9
9	2	7	3	5	1	4	8	6
7	3	4	2	9	5	6	1	8
5	9	6	8	1	4	3	7	2
2	8	1	7	3	6	9	4	5
3	7	5	9	6	8	1	2	4
6	1	2	5	4	7	8	9	3
8	4	9	1	2	3	5	6	7

313

3	6	7	9	1	2	8	5	4
2	1	4	5	8	6	7	3	9
8	5	9	7	3	4	6	2	1
6	4	5	8	2	7	9	1	3
7	2	3	1	9	5	4	8	6
9	8	1	4	6	3	5	7	2
5	7	6	2	4	1	3	9	8
4	9	2	3	5	8	1	6	7
1	3	8	6	7	9	2	4	5

314

5	2	9	6	1	3	4	7	8
3	4	6	5	8	7	2	9	1
1	8	7	2	4	9	3	6	5
4	6	5	9	7	1	8	2	3
9	3	2	8	6	4	5	1	7
7	1	8	3	2	5	6	4	9
6	7	3	4	9	8	1	5	2
8	9	4	1	5	2	7	3	6
2	5	1	7	3	6	9	8	4

315

8	9	7	1	6	4	5	2	3
1	4	5	8	2	3	7	9	6
2	6	3	7	9	5	1	8	4
3	8	1	4	7	2	6	5	9
4	5	6	9	8	1	3	7	2
9	7	2	5	3	6	8	4	1
5	3	4	2	1	8	9	6	7
7	1	8	6	4	9	2	3	5
6	2	9	3	5	7	4	1	8

316

9	4	1	8	3	7	5	2	6
2	3	8	6	9	5	1	4	7
5	7	6	1	2	4	9	3	8
1	9	4	2	8	3	6	7	5
3	6	7	4	5	9	8	1	2
8	5	2	7	6	1	4	9	3
4	1	3	5	7	6	2	8	9
7	8	5	9	4	2	3	6	1
6	2	9	3	1	8	7	5	4

317

5	6	2	3	8	1	4	7	9
4	3	1	7	5	9	8	6	2
8	9	7	4	2	6	5	3	1
9	1	5	2	7	4	3	8	6
6	2	4	8	9	3	1	5	7
3	7	8	1	6	5	2	9	4
7	8	3	6	4	2	9	1	5
1	4	9	5	3	7	6	2	8
2	5	6	9	1	8	7	4	3

318

4	9	7	6	1	3	5	8	2
1	3	5	2	8	4	6	9	7
8	2	6	9	7	5	1	4	3
7	5	4	1	9	8	3	2	6
3	1	9	5	6	2	4	7	8
2	6	8	3	4	7	9	1	5
9	8	1	7	5	6	2	3	4
5	7	3	4	2	1	8	6	9
6	4	2	8	3	9	7	5	1

319

4	9	3	8	7	2	6	5	1
5	8	2	6	3	1	9	7	4
1	7	6	5	9	4	2	3	8
3	1	4	9	2	5	8	6	7
9	6	8	7	4	3	5	1	2
7	2	5	1	6	8	3	4	9
8	5	7	3	1	9	4	2	6
2	3	1	4	8	6	7	9	5
6	4	9	2	5	7	1	8	3

320

4	1	2	3	8	7	9	5	6
5	3	7	9	2	6	4	1	8
6	9	8	5	4	1	2	3	7
3	5	1	4	7	9	6	8	2
9	2	6	1	5	8	3	7	4
8	7	4	2	6	3	1	9	5
7	8	9	6	1	4	5	2	3
2	6	3	7	9	5	8	4	1
1	4	5	8	3	2	7	6	9

321

9	8	2	1	4	6	7	5	3
4	7	3	8	9	5	6	2	1
5	1	6	3	2	7	9	8	4
6	3	4	7	8	9	2	1	5
8	2	1	6	5	3	4	9	7
7	5	9	2	1	4	8	3	6
1	9	5	4	6	8	3	7	2
2	4	7	9	3	1	5	6	8
3	6	8	5	7	2	1	4	9

322

5	3	4	9	6	8	1	7	2
7	1	2	3	5	4	6	9	8
6	8	9	2	7	1	4	3	5
8	7	5	4	2	9	3	1	6
9	2	1	5	3	6	8	4	7
3	4	6	1	8	7	2	5	9
2	6	3	7	1	5	9	8	4
1	9	7	8	4	2	5	6	3
4	5	8	6	9	3	7	2	1

323

5	7	8	1	6	4	9	2	3
9	6	2	8	3	7	4	1	5
1	3	4	5	2	9	8	6	7
4	8	6	9	7	1	3	5	2
3	5	7	2	4	8	1	9	6
2	1	9	3	5	6	7	8	4
6	4	1	7	9	2	5	3	8
8	2	5	4	1	3	6	7	9
7	9	3	6	8	5	2	4	1

324

4	3	1	5	6	9	2	8	7
6	8	7	3	2	4	9	1	5
2	5	9	8	7	1	4	6	3
9	4	5	7	8	3	1	2	6
1	7	6	9	4	2	3	5	8
3	2	8	6	1	5	7	9	4
5	9	2	4	3	8	6	7	1
8	6	3	1	9	7	5	4	2
7	1	4	2	5	6	8	3	9

325

7	6	3	1	2	5	9	8	4
8	1	5	4	9	7	6	2	3
4	9	2	8	3	6	1	7	5
9	4	1	2	7	3	5	6	8
3	7	6	5	8	1	4	9	2
2	5	8	9	6	4	7	3	1
1	8	7	6	4	2	3	5	9
5	3	9	7	1	8	2	4	6
6	2	4	3	5	9	8	1	7

326

5	3	1	8	9	4	6	2	7
9	4	2	6	7	5	1	3	8
7	6	8	3	1	2	4	5	9
6	1	5	7	4	3	9	8	2
2	9	3	1	8	6	5	7	4
4	8	7	5	2	9	3	1	6
3	2	6	4	5	8	7	9	1
8	7	4	9	3	1	2	6	5
1	5	9	2	6	7	8	4	3

327

3	8	5	2	1	7	4	6	9
6	1	9	8	4	3	5	2	7
4	7	2	5	6	9	1	8	3
8	5	3	9	2	1	7	4	6
2	4	7	6	5	8	9	3	1
1	9	6	3	7	4	2	5	8
9	6	4	1	8	2	3	7	5
5	2	1	7	3	6	8	9	4
7	3	8	4	9	5	6	1	2

328

4	2	1	5	8	3	9	7	6
3	5	7	4	6	9	8	1	2
6	8	9	7	1	2	5	3	4
2	4	5	6	7	8	1	9	3
8	1	6	9	3	4	2	5	7
9	7	3	1	2	5	4	6	8
1	3	4	2	9	7	6	8	5
7	6	2	8	5	1	3	4	9
5	9	8	3	4	6	7	2	1

329

4	1	2	5	6	3	7	9	8
6	5	3	9	8	7	1	4	2
9	7	8	4	2	1	5	6	3
5	4	6	8	7	9	3	2	1
8	9	1	2	3	5	4	7	6
3	2	7	1	4	6	9	8	5
7	3	4	6	5	8	2	1	9
1	8	5	7	9	2	6	3	4
2	6	9	3	1	4	8	5	7

330

4	8	6	2	5	1	3	9	7
1	2	7	9	3	4	8	6	5
5	3	9	6	7	8	4	2	1
9	6	4	8	1	3	5	7	2
7	5	8	4	6	2	9	1	3
3	1	2	5	9	7	6	8	4
6	9	1	7	4	5	2	3	8
8	7	5	3	2	9	1	4	6
2	4	3	1	8	6	7	5	9

331

6	7	5	4	3	9	8	1	2
2	9	8	5	7	1	6	4	3
4	3	1	6	8	2	9	5	7
7	8	6	9	5	4	3	2	1
3	2	4	7	1	6	5	8	9
5	1	9	8	2	3	7	6	4
9	4	3	1	6	8	2	7	5
8	5	2	3	4	7	1	9	6
1	6	7	2	9	5	4	3	8

332

1	5	6	7	8	2	4	3	9
2	9	8	3	5	4	1	7	6
7	4	3	9	1	6	5	2	8
3	6	1	4	7	5	8	9	2
9	8	5	6	2	1	3	4	7
4	7	2	8	9	3	6	1	5
6	3	7	5	4	9	2	8	1
8	1	4	2	6	7	9	5	3
5	2	9	1	3	8	7	6	4

333

4	1	9	5	8	2	7	3	6
2	3	7	6	9	4	8	5	1
5	6	8	1	3	7	2	4	9
7	2	4	3	5	6	9	1	8
1	8	3	2	4	9	6	7	5
9	5	6	7	1	8	3	2	4
6	9	5	4	2	3	1	8	7
3	7	1	8	6	5	4	9	2
8	4	2	9	7	1	5	6	3

334

7	6	8	1	9	4	2	5	3
1	9	2	5	7	3	8	6	4
5	4	3	6	2	8	7	1	9
3	7	9	2	4	1	6	8	5
6	8	4	7	5	9	1	3	2
2	1	5	8	3	6	9	4	7
8	3	7	9	6	5	4	2	1
9	5	6	4	1	2	3	7	8
4	2	1	3	8	7	5	9	6

335

5	9	6	8	4	3	1	2	7
3	2	7	5	1	6	9	4	8
8	4	1	9	2	7	5	6	3
7	6	3	1	8	9	4	5	2
9	5	4	7	3	2	8	1	6
2	1	8	4	6	5	3	7	9
4	3	2	6	9	1	7	8	5
6	8	5	3	7	4	2	9	1
1	7	9	2	5	8	6	3	4

336

1	4	3	9	5	6	7	2	8
7	5	9	1	2	8	6	4	3
6	8	2	4	7	3	1	9	5
8	7	5	6	3	2	9	1	4
2	9	1	5	4	7	8	3	6
3	6	4	8	9	1	2	5	7
4	1	7	2	8	5	3	6	9
5	3	6	7	1	9	4	8	2
9	2	8	3	6	4	5	7	1

337

3	1	6	7	9	4	5	2	8
2	9	8	3	5	1	6	4	7
4	7	5	6	2	8	3	1	9
6	2	1	5	8	9	7	3	4
9	4	3	1	7	6	8	5	2
5	8	7	2	4	3	9	6	1
8	6	9	4	3	2	1	7	5
7	3	2	8	1	5	4	9	6
1	5	4	9	6	7	2	8	3

338

8	7	4	3	5	1	9	6	2
6	9	1	8	4	2	7	5	3
2	5	3	6	9	7	4	1	8
7	8	2	9	1	5	3	4	6
3	1	9	4	7	6	2	8	5
4	6	5	2	8	3	1	9	7
1	2	7	5	6	4	8	3	9
5	3	8	1	2	9	6	7	4
9	4	6	7	8	3	5	2	1

339

8	9	7	5	6	3	4	2	1
4	6	1	2	8	7	3	5	9
2	3	5	4	1	9	7	6	8
1	7	2	8	9	5	6	3	4
6	4	8	1	3	2	9	7	5
3	5	9	7	4	6	1	8	2
7	2	4	6	5	1	8	9	3
5	1	3	9	7	8	2	4	6
9	8	6	3	2	4	5	1	7

340

7	2	6	4	3	1	5	9	8
5	4	1	9	7	8	3	2	6
9	3	8	2	5	6	1	7	4
6	7	5	3	4	9	8	1	2
4	1	9	5	8	2	6	3	7
3	8	2	6	1	7	4	5	9
8	6	7	1	2	5	9	4	3
1	9	3	7	6	4	2	8	5
2	5	4	8	9	3	7	6	1

341

```
7 8 6 3 5 4 1 2 9
9 4 1 6 2 8 7 5 3
2 5 3 9 1 7 6 8 4
1 6 4 8 9 5 2 3 7
5 3 2 4 7 1 9 6 8
8 7 9 2 3 6 5 4 1
6 1 8 7 4 2 3 9 5
4 9 7 5 6 3 8 1 2
3 2 5 1 8 9 4 7 6
```

342

```
4 1 9 7 5 3 2 6 8
6 3 5 8 2 1 4 7 9
8 7 2 6 9 4 5 3 1
7 8 4 3 1 5 6 9 2
2 5 6 9 4 7 1 8 3
1 9 3 2 8 6 7 5 4
5 2 8 1 7 9 3 4 6
3 4 1 5 6 8 9 2 7
9 6 7 4 3 2 8 1 5
```

343

```
4 8 1 6 9 7 3 5 2
6 9 5 4 3 2 8 7 1
7 2 3 1 5 8 9 4 6
1 6 4 5 7 9 2 8 3
2 3 9 8 6 4 5 1 7
5 7 8 3 2 1 4 6 9
3 1 7 2 4 5 6 9 8
8 4 2 9 1 6 7 3 5
9 5 6 7 8 3 1 2 4
```

344

```
9 8 1 4 5 2 3 6 7
7 6 2 8 1 3 5 4 9
3 4 5 9 7 6 8 1 2
4 2 6 1 8 9 7 3 5
8 1 7 3 2 5 4 9 6
5 3 9 6 4 7 1 2 8
1 7 4 2 6 8 9 5 3
6 5 3 7 9 1 2 8 4
2 9 8 5 3 4 6 7 1
```

345

```
1 8 4 7 2 5 6 9 3
3 5 2 1 9 6 8 7 4
7 6 9 8 3 4 2 1 5
2 7 3 9 5 8 1 4 6
6 1 8 4 7 3 5 2 9
4 9 5 2 6 1 3 8 7
9 4 6 5 8 2 7 3 1
5 2 7 3 1 9 4 6 8
8 3 1 6 4 7 9 5 2
```

346

```
8 4 1 2 6 9 7 3 5
3 2 5 8 4 7 1 9 6
6 9 7 5 1 3 2 4 8
7 5 4 3 8 1 6 2 9
2 8 3 6 9 5 4 1 7
1 6 9 4 7 2 8 5 3
5 3 8 1 2 6 9 7 4
9 1 6 7 3 4 5 8 2
4 7 2 9 5 8 3 6 1
```

347

```
4 2 3 1 8 6 5 7 9
8 5 9 7 3 2 1 4 6
7 1 6 9 5 4 2 3 8
9 6 5 4 7 3 8 1 2
2 7 8 5 9 1 4 6 3
3 4 1 6 2 8 7 9 5
6 3 2 8 4 7 9 5 1
5 8 4 3 1 9 6 2 7
1 9 7 2 6 5 3 8 4
```

348

```
2 7 3 8 9 6 5 4 1
9 1 4 7 2 5 8 6 3
5 6 8 4 1 3 2 9 7
8 9 6 2 7 4 3 1 5
3 5 2 1 6 8 9 7 4
7 4 1 3 5 9 6 2 8
6 8 7 5 4 2 1 3 9
1 2 5 9 3 7 4 8 6
4 3 9 6 8 1 7 5 2
```

349

```
3 5 7 2 1 9 8 4 6
9 4 2 6 7 8 1 5 3
1 8 6 3 5 4 7 2 9
5 3 1 7 6 2 9 8 4
6 2 8 9 4 3 5 1 7
7 9 4 5 8 1 6 3 2
2 1 3 8 9 6 4 7 5
4 6 5 1 3 7 2 9 8
8 7 9 4 2 5 3 6 1
```

350

```
2 5 6 3 7 8 9 1 4
9 7 3 5 1 4 2 6 8
8 4 1 6 2 9 3 7 5
5 3 9 4 8 7 1 2 6
4 1 7 2 6 3 5 8 9
6 8 2 9 5 1 4 3 7
1 6 5 8 9 2 7 4 3
3 2 8 7 4 5 6 9 1
7 9 4 1 3 6 8 5 2
```

351

```
6 7 4 5 3 9 2 1 8
8 2 9 7 1 6 3 5 4
5 3 1 8 2 4 9 6 7
1 4 6 9 7 5 8 2 3
9 5 2 3 8 1 7 4 6
7 8 3 4 6 2 5 9 1
2 1 7 6 9 8 4 3 5
4 6 8 2 5 3 1 7 9
3 9 5 1 4 7 6 8 2
```

352

```
3 8 5 6 2 1 7 4 9
1 6 4 9 7 5 3 8 2
7 9 2 8 3 4 6 5 1
9 5 7 3 6 8 1 2 4
2 3 8 1 4 9 5 7 6
4 1 6 7 5 2 9 3 8
5 4 9 2 1 7 8 6 3
6 2 1 5 8 3 4 9 7
8 7 3 4 9 6 2 1 5
```

353

```
2 7 1 8 4 3 6 5 9
4 9 6 7 5 1 2 3 8
5 3 8 9 6 2 1 7 4
3 5 7 1 8 9 4 2 6
1 4 2 6 3 7 8 9 5
8 6 9 4 2 5 3 1 7
9 8 3 2 7 4 5 6 1
6 1 5 3 9 8 7 4 2
7 2 4 5 1 6 9 8 3
```

354

```
9 8 3 1 5 4 6 2 7
1 5 2 9 6 7 8 3 4
4 7 6 3 8 2 9 1 5
7 3 8 6 1 5 4 9 2
5 6 4 2 9 8 1 7 3
2 9 1 7 4 3 5 8 6
8 4 7 5 2 9 3 6 1
6 2 9 4 3 1 7 5 8
3 1 5 8 7 6 2 4 9
```

355

```
5 8 3 9 7 1 4 2 6
9 1 6 4 2 5 3 7 8
4 2 7 3 8 6 5 1 9
1 4 9 6 3 2 7 8 5
6 7 2 5 4 8 1 9 3
8 3 5 7 1 9 2 6 4
3 9 4 2 6 7 8 5 1
2 5 8 1 9 3 6 4 7
7 6 1 8 5 4 9 3 2
```

356

```
4 6 7 5 8 3 2 9 1
5 8 2 1 4 9 3 7 6
3 1 9 7 6 2 8 5 4
9 5 6 3 2 1 7 4 8
1 4 8 6 9 7 5 2 3
7 2 3 8 5 4 6 1 9
8 9 5 2 1 6 4 3 7
6 3 1 4 7 5 9 8 2
2 7 4 9 3 8 1 6 5
```

357

```
8 7 5 3 1 2 4 6 9
4 1 9 5 8 6 3 2 7
2 3 6 7 4 9 8 5 1
6 4 7 1 2 5 9 3 8
3 9 1 8 6 4 2 7 5
5 2 8 9 7 3 6 1 4
1 8 2 6 9 7 5 4 3
9 5 4 2 3 1 7 8 6
7 6 3 4 5 8 1 9 2
```

358

```
9 7 8 1 6 5 3 4 2
1 2 4 7 8 3 5 9 6
5 6 3 4 9 2 8 1 7
6 5 9 2 7 8 1 3 4
3 1 7 6 4 9 2 5 8
8 4 2 3 5 1 6 7 9
4 3 5 9 2 6 7 8 1
7 8 6 5 1 4 9 2 3
2 9 1 8 3 7 4 6 5
```

359

```
2 8 7 3 5 9 4 6 1
5 9 4 1 2 6 3 7 8
3 1 6 4 7 8 2 9 5
9 6 1 8 4 2 7 5 3
4 7 2 5 9 3 1 8 6
8 5 3 6 1 7 9 4 2
6 2 8 9 3 4 5 1 7
7 4 5 2 8 1 6 3 9
1 3 9 7 6 5 8 2 4
```

360

```
3 2 6 9 8 7 5 4 1
4 5 8 2 1 6 7 3 9
7 1 9 3 5 4 6 8 2
1 4 5 7 6 9 8 2 3
2 6 7 1 3 8 9 5 4
9 8 3 4 2 5 1 7 6
5 7 2 6 9 3 4 1 8
6 3 4 8 7 1 2 9 5
8 9 1 5 4 2 3 6 7
```

361

6	2	8	4	7	3	1	9	5
5	3	7	1	8	9	6	2	4
9	1	4	5	2	6	8	3	7
7	8	5	3	6	2	4	1	9
3	4	6	9	1	7	2	5	8
2	9	1	8	5	4	3	7	6
8	6	2	7	3	5	9	4	1
1	7	9	2	4	8	5	6	3
4	5	3	6	9	1	7	8	2

362

4	8	2	9	6	1	3	7	5
1	9	7	8	3	5	6	2	4
3	6	5	7	4	2	8	9	1
2	5	6	3	8	9	4	1	7
9	7	3	1	2	4	5	6	8
8	1	4	6	5	7	2	3	9
6	3	1	5	9	8	7	4	2
5	4	9	2	7	6	1	8	3
7	2	8	4	1	3	9	5	6

363

8	3	1	7	4	5	2	9	6
4	2	5	6	9	1	7	3	8
9	6	7	3	2	8	5	1	4
1	9	6	8	7	4	3	5	2
3	4	2	9	5	6	1	8	7
7	5	8	2	1	3	6	4	9
6	8	4	5	3	2	9	7	1
5	1	9	4	6	7	8	2	3
2	7	3	1	8	9	4	6	5

364

4	1	9	8	2	5	3	7	6
3	6	5	4	9	7	1	2	8
8	7	2	6	3	1	9	5	4
9	2	3	7	4	8	5	6	1
1	5	8	9	6	3	2	4	7
6	4	7	5	1	2	8	9	3
2	9	6	1	8	4	7	3	5
5	3	1	2	7	6	4	8	9
7	8	4	3	5	9	6	1	2

365

1	5	6	9	8	4	3	2	7
2	4	9	7	1	3	8	5	6
8	7	3	6	5	2	9	4	1
7	1	2	5	9	6	4	3	8
9	6	8	4	3	7	2	1	5
4	3	5	1	2	8	6	7	9
5	2	1	3	6	9	7	8	4
3	9	7	8	4	1	5	6	2
6	8	4	2	7	5	1	9	3

366

4	9	3	8	7	5	2	6	1
2	1	8	4	6	3	9	5	7
7	5	6	9	2	1	8	3	4
9	8	1	6	3	7	5	4	2
5	4	7	2	8	9	3	1	6
3	6	2	1	5	4	7	9	8
1	7	9	5	4	2	6	8	3
6	2	4	3	9	8	1	7	5
8	3	5	7	1	6	4	2	9

367

2	4	3	6	5	8	9	7	1
6	5	7	1	9	2	4	8	3
8	9	1	3	4	7	6	2	5
7	3	5	8	1	4	2	6	9
1	8	4	9	2	6	3	5	7
9	6	2	7	3	5	1	4	8
3	2	8	4	7	9	5	1	6
4	7	9	5	6	1	8	3	2
5	1	6	2	8	3	7	9	4

368

7	9	1	4	8	2	5	3	6
3	2	8	6	9	5	4	7	1
6	5	4	7	1	3	9	8	2
5	3	2	9	7	8	6	1	4
9	8	6	1	3	4	2	5	7
1	4	7	2	5	6	8	9	3
8	6	5	3	2	7	1	4	9
4	7	9	8	6	1	3	2	5
2	1	3	5	4	9	7	6	8

369

6	8	3	7	4	9	1	5	2
1	5	4	3	6	2	8	9	7
7	9	2	8	1	5	3	6	4
5	3	8	1	9	4	2	7	6
9	4	6	2	3	7	5	8	1
2	7	1	5	8	6	9	4	3
3	6	9	4	2	8	7	1	5
8	2	5	6	7	1	4	3	9
4	1	7	9	5	3	6	2	8

370

7	4	6	8	2	9	5	1	3
5	8	1	6	4	3	2	7	9
3	9	2	7	5	1	8	6	4
4	2	9	5	7	6	1	3	8
6	5	8	3	1	2	4	9	7
1	3	7	4	9	8	6	5	2
8	7	3	2	6	5	9	4	1
2	1	5	9	3	4	7	8	6
9	6	4	1	8	7	3	2	5

371

4	6	5	1	3	7	9	8	2
9	2	8	6	4	5	1	3	7
7	1	3	8	2	9	4	6	5
3	7	9	4	5	2	6	1	8
8	5	6	3	7	1	2	9	4
2	4	1	9	6	8	5	7	3
1	8	4	5	9	3	7	2	6
5	3	7	2	1	6	8	4	9
6	9	2	7	8	4	3	5	1

372

5	6	7	8	4	9	1	2	3
3	4	9	2	1	5	6	7	8
8	2	1	3	6	7	5	9	4
2	8	4	5	9	6	3	1	7
6	7	5	1	2	3	8	4	9
1	9	3	4	7	8	2	5	6
4	3	8	7	5	1	9	6	2
7	5	6	9	8	2	4	3	1
9	1	2	6	3	4	7	8	5

373

3	9	6	4	7	2	8	1	5
7	1	2	8	3	5	4	6	9
4	5	8	1	6	9	2	7	3
5	2	3	9	1	8	7	4	6
1	6	9	3	4	7	5	8	2
8	7	4	2	5	6	3	9	1
2	4	1	7	9	3	6	5	8
9	3	5	6	8	4	1	2	7
6	8	7	5	2	1	9	3	4

374

9	2	8	4	3	1	5	6	7
3	5	1	9	6	7	4	2	8
7	4	6	8	2	5	9	1	3
2	9	5	6	7	3	1	8	4
8	1	7	2	9	4	6	3	5
6	3	4	1	5	8	2	7	9
1	7	3	5	4	6	8	9	2
5	6	9	7	8	2	3	4	1
4	8	2	3	1	9	7	5	6

375

9	8	1	3	4	5	2	7	6
6	5	4	9	2	7	8	3	1
3	2	7	1	8	6	9	5	4
5	9	3	4	6	8	1	2	7
1	4	8	7	3	2	5	6	9
7	6	2	5	1	9	3	4	8
8	7	5	2	9	4	6	1	3
4	3	6	8	5	1	7	9	2
2	1	9	6	7	3	4	8	5

376

9	3	8	4	6	2	5	1	7
5	4	2	9	7	1	3	6	8
6	7	1	8	3	5	4	2	9
3	2	7	6	4	9	8	5	1
8	6	9	5	1	7	2	4	3
4	1	5	3	2	8	9	7	6
1	9	3	7	5	4	6	8	2
2	5	6	1	8	3	7	9	4
7	8	4	2	9	6	1	3	5

377

9	8	5	1	7	4	6	2	3
2	7	4	6	3	8	9	5	1
3	6	1	5	9	2	7	4	8
4	9	2	8	5	7	3	1	6
5	1	8	9	6	3	4	7	2
7	3	6	2	4	1	8	9	5
6	4	9	3	2	5	1	8	7
1	5	3	7	8	9	2	6	4
8	2	7	4	1	6	5	3	9

378

8	1	3	9	4	5	6	7	2
6	5	7	1	2	8	4	3	9
9	2	4	6	3	7	1	5	8
5	3	6	8	1	9	2	4	7
1	7	8	2	5	4	3	9	6
4	9	2	7	6	3	5	8	1
3	8	1	5	7	6	9	2	4
2	4	9	3	8	1	7	6	5
7	6	5	4	9	2	8	1	3

379

5	8	9	1	6	4	7	2	3
2	4	3	8	5	7	9	1	6
1	7	6	2	9	3	4	5	8
6	9	7	5	1	2	8	3	4
4	5	8	3	7	9	1	6	2
3	2	1	6	4	8	5	7	9
7	3	5	9	8	6	2	4	1
9	6	4	7	2	1	3	8	5
8	1	2	4	3	5	6	9	7

380

7	1	6	8	5	3	4	9	2
2	9	8	4	1	7	3	6	5
5	3	4	6	9	2	1	7	8
8	2	3	5	7	1	6	4	9
6	7	5	9	2	4	8	1	3
1	4	9	3	8	6	2	5	7
3	5	1	2	4	9	7	8	6
9	6	7	1	3	8	5	2	4
4	8	2	7	6	5	9	3	1

381

1	7	9	5	8	2	6	4	3
2	5	4	6	9	3	8	1	7
8	6	3	7	4	1	9	2	5
6	1	2	4	5	7	3	9	8
9	3	7	1	2	8	4	5	6
5	4	8	9	3	6	2	7	1
4	2	6	3	7	5	1	8	9
3	9	5	8	1	4	7	6	2
7	8	1	2	6	9	5	3	4

382

5	9	2	3	4	6	7	1	8
3	7	8	5	2	1	4	6	9
4	1	6	8	9	7	3	2	5
2	4	7	6	5	8	1	9	3
8	6	1	2	3	9	5	4	7
9	3	5	1	7	4	6	8	2
7	8	3	4	1	2	9	5	6
1	2	9	7	6	5	8	3	4
6	5	4	9	8	3	2	7	1

383

4	8	7	2	6	5	9	3	1
9	6	3	4	1	8	2	5	7
1	2	5	7	3	9	4	6	8
7	3	1	9	5	2	6	8	4
5	9	8	1	4	6	3	7	2
2	4	6	8	7	3	5	1	9
3	7	9	6	2	1	8	4	5
6	1	2	5	8	4	7	9	3
8	5	4	3	9	7	1	2	6

384

8	1	6	4	3	5	9	2	7
9	4	5	1	2	7	8	3	6
7	2	3	8	6	9	5	4	1
2	9	4	5	7	6	3	1	8
5	3	7	2	8	1	6	9	4
1	6	8	9	4	3	7	5	2
4	8	9	6	5	2	1	7	3
3	5	2	7	1	8	4	6	9
6	7	1	3	9	4	2	8	5

385

5	7	3	9	4	8	2	1	6
2	4	1	6	5	3	7	9	8
8	6	9	7	2	1	4	5	3
6	8	7	4	3	5	1	2	9
1	5	2	8	9	7	6	3	4
9	3	4	2	1	6	8	7	5
4	9	6	5	7	2	3	8	1
7	1	8	3	6	9	5	4	2
3	2	5	1	8	4	9	6	7

386

6	3	2	8	5	9	4	1	7
9	1	4	3	7	6	2	5	8
5	8	7	2	4	1	6	9	3
8	2	9	7	6	3	1	4	5
7	4	6	9	1	5	3	8	2
1	5	3	4	8	2	9	7	6
3	9	1	5	2	8	7	6	4
2	7	5	6	9	4	8	3	1
4	6	8	1	3	7	5	2	9

387

1	3	5	7	8	4	2	6	9
8	6	9	2	5	3	1	4	7
4	2	7	9	1	6	5	8	3
6	7	4	5	3	8	9	1	2
5	9	2	1	4	7	8	3	6
3	1	8	6	9	2	4	7	5
2	5	6	4	7	1	3	9	8
9	8	1	3	6	5	7	2	4
7	4	3	8	2	9	6	5	1

388

5	7	1	9	8	3	4	6	2
4	9	2	1	6	7	3	8	5
6	3	8	4	5	2	7	9	1
2	6	3	7	9	4	5	1	8
8	1	7	5	3	6	9	2	4
9	4	5	8	2	1	6	3	7
7	2	6	3	1	5	8	4	9
3	8	4	2	7	9	1	5	6
1	5	9	6	4	8	2	7	3

389

7	9	1	2	5	4	8	3	6
2	5	6	9	3	8	7	4	1
3	8	4	6	1	7	2	9	5
4	3	8	7	6	2	5	1	9
9	2	5	4	8	1	3	6	7
6	1	7	5	9	3	4	8	2
5	4	3	1	7	9	6	2	8
1	7	2	8	4	6	9	5	3
8	6	9	3	2	5	1	7	4

390

2	9	7	1	6	5	3	4	8
6	1	3	8	7	4	5	9	2
8	5	4	3	2	9	7	1	6
1	4	6	5	8	7	2	3	9
5	7	2	4	9	3	6	8	1
9	3	8	6	1	2	4	5	7
7	2	5	9	3	8	1	6	4
4	6	9	2	5	1	8	7	3
3	8	1	7	4	6	9	2	5

391

6	8	9	1	3	4	2	7	5
4	1	2	5	7	6	8	3	9
7	5	3	2	8	9	4	6	1
2	3	1	4	9	8	7	5	6
8	6	5	7	1	2	9	4	3
9	4	7	6	5	3	1	8	2
3	2	6	8	4	1	5	9	7
1	7	4	9	6	5	3	2	8
5	9	8	3	2	7	6	1	4

392

8	9	7	3	2	6	4	1	5
3	6	4	5	1	7	2	9	8
1	5	2	8	4	9	7	3	6
6	7	5	2	3	4	1	8	9
4	1	9	6	5	8	3	7	2
2	3	8	7	9	1	5	6	4
9	4	3	1	6	5	8	2	7
5	8	1	9	7	2	6	4	3
7	2	6	4	8	3	9	5	1

393

3	9	6	8	2	4	1	5	7
5	1	2	9	6	7	4	8	3
7	4	8	1	5	3	9	2	6
8	2	7	6	3	1	5	9	4
4	6	1	5	9	2	7	3	8
9	5	3	7	4	8	6	1	2
2	8	5	4	1	6	3	7	9
1	7	4	3	8	9	2	6	5
6	3	9	2	7	5	8	4	1

394

7	4	1	9	8	2	3	6	5
5	8	3	7	6	1	2	4	9
6	2	9	5	4	3	8	1	7
9	1	7	8	2	6	4	5	3
4	3	2	1	5	9	6	7	8
8	6	5	3	7	4	9	2	1
2	7	8	4	3	5	1	9	6
1	5	6	2	9	8	7	3	4
3	9	4	6	1	7	5	8	2

395

2	8	1	3	5	4	6	9	7
7	9	4	6	1	2	8	3	5
3	5	6	9	7	8	2	4	1
9	4	3	1	2	6	5	7	8
8	1	2	7	3	5	4	6	9
6	7	5	8	4	9	1	2	3
5	3	7	2	6	1	9	8	4
1	6	9	4	8	3	7	5	2
4	2	8	5	9	7	3	1	6

396

7	3	5	8	9	6	4	2	1
4	8	1	5	2	3	9	7	6
9	6	2	7	1	4	5	3	8
8	4	3	9	7	2	1	6	5
1	2	7	4	6	5	8	9	3
6	5	9	3	8	1	7	4	2
2	9	6	1	5	7	3	8	4
3	1	8	6	4	9	2	5	7
5	7	4	2	3	8	6	1	9

397

2	7	5	9	4	6	1	3	8
4	1	8	7	5	3	9	6	2
6	9	3	2	1	8	4	5	7
9	3	2	6	8	1	5	7	4
7	5	6	3	9	4	8	2	1
1	8	4	5	7	2	3	9	6
5	6	1	4	3	7	2	8	9
3	4	7	8	2	9	6	1	5
8	2	9	1	6	5	7	4	3

398

1	2	6	3	9	5	7	8	4
3	9	7	4	8	6	5	1	2
4	5	8	2	7	1	6	9	3
5	1	2	6	3	9	4	7	8
8	7	4	1	5	2	9	3	6
9	6	3	8	4	7	1	2	5
6	8	1	7	2	4	3	5	9
2	4	9	5	1	3	8	6	7
7	3	5	9	6	8	2	4	1

399

1	4	2	5	3	6	9	7	8
8	9	6	2	7	4	5	3	1
3	5	7	9	8	1	6	4	2
2	7	5	3	6	9	8	1	4
6	8	1	4	5	7	2	9	3
9	3	4	1	2	8	7	5	6
7	2	9	8	4	3	1	6	5
5	6	3	7	1	2	4	8	9
4	1	8	6	9	5	3	2	7

400

6	3	7	2	9	1	5	4	8
2	9	8	5	7	4	3	1	6
5	4	1	6	8	3	9	7	2
9	5	3	8	1	2	4	6	7
7	6	2	4	5	9	8	3	1
1	8	4	7	3	6	2	9	5
3	7	9	1	2	5	6	8	4
8	2	6	9	4	7	1	5	3
4	1	5	3	6	8	7	2	9

401

7	4	1	5	9	2	6	3	8
3	5	9	6	4	8	2	1	7
6	8	2	3	7	1	9	4	5
1	9	4	7	6	5	3	8	2
5	2	6	8	3	9	1	7	4
8	7	3	2	1	4	5	6	9
4	3	8	9	2	6	7	5	1
2	1	7	4	5	3	8	9	6
9	6	5	1	8	7	4	2	3

402

3	6	5	4	9	8	7	1	2
8	2	7	5	3	1	6	4	9
9	1	4	6	7	2	5	3	8
1	3	6	9	2	4	8	7	5
7	5	2	8	6	3	4	9	1
4	8	9	1	5	7	3	2	6
2	4	8	3	1	5	9	6	7
6	7	3	2	8	9	1	5	4
5	9	1	7	4	6	2	8	3

403

6	7	8	2	5	4	1	9	3
5	9	1	6	3	7	2	8	4
2	4	3	1	9	8	5	7	6
4	3	7	8	2	6	9	5	1
1	6	2	5	4	9	7	3	8
9	8	5	7	1	3	4	6	2
8	1	9	3	7	2	6	4	5
3	5	4	9	6	1	8	2	7
7	2	6	4	8	5	3	1	9

404

2	5	8	4	9	6	3	1	7
9	3	1	5	8	7	2	4	6
7	4	6	2	3	1	8	5	9
4	6	2	8	7	9	5	3	1
3	7	9	1	5	2	6	8	4
8	1	5	6	4	3	9	7	2
6	8	4	7	2	5	1	9	3
1	9	7	3	6	8	4	2	5
5	2	3	9	1	4	7	6	8

405

5	6	4	8	2	1	9	7	3
3	9	1	7	6	4	8	2	5
8	7	2	9	5	3	1	4	6
1	8	7	6	4	5	3	9	2
6	2	3	1	9	8	4	5	7
9	4	5	2	3	7	6	1	8
7	1	6	4	8	2	5	3	9
2	3	9	5	1	6	7	8	4
4	5	8	3	7	9	2	6	1

406

8	9	1	7	4	5	3	6	2
6	3	5	2	9	8	4	1	7
4	2	7	6	3	1	8	5	9
2	4	3	5	1	9	7	8	6
5	6	9	8	7	3	2	4	1
7	1	8	4	2	6	9	3	5
1	8	4	9	6	7	5	2	3
3	7	2	1	5	4	6	9	8
9	5	6	3	8	2	1	7	4

407

8	1	6	7	9	4	3	5	2
7	5	4	3	2	6	9	1	8
3	2	9	1	8	5	6	7	4
2	9	5	8	4	3	7	6	1
6	7	3	5	1	2	4	8	9
1	4	8	9	6	7	5	2	3
5	8	2	4	7	9	1	3	6
9	6	7	2	3	1	8	4	5
4	3	1	6	5	8	2	9	7

408

5	2	7	3	6	4	9	1	8
4	9	3	1	8	7	5	6	2
8	1	6	2	9	5	4	7	3
6	3	9	7	1	2	8	4	5
7	5	1	8	4	9	3	2	6
2	8	4	5	3	6	7	9	1
1	6	8	4	7	3	2	5	9
9	4	5	6	2	8	1	3	7
3	7	2	9	5	1	6	8	4

409

6	7	9	3	4	2	5	1	8
1	5	3	8	6	9	2	7	4
8	4	2	5	1	7	9	6	3
7	3	5	6	2	1	8	4	9
9	6	1	4	8	3	7	5	2
4	2	8	9	7	5	6	3	1
2	8	4	7	3	6	1	9	5
5	1	7	2	9	4	3	8	6
3	9	6	1	5	8	4	2	7

410

1	8	4	3	7	2	6	5	9
2	9	7	4	6	5	1	3	8
5	3	6	1	8	9	4	7	2
9	1	5	8	2	3	7	4	6
3	6	2	7	9	4	5	8	1
7	4	8	6	5	1	9	2	3
8	7	1	5	3	6	2	9	4
6	2	3	9	4	7	8	1	5
4	5	9	2	1	8	3	6	7

411

1	6	9	4	8	7	5	3	2
5	3	4	9	2	6	1	7	8
7	2	8	5	1	3	9	4	6
9	1	2	6	3	4	7	8	5
6	5	3	2	7	8	4	9	1
8	4	7	1	9	5	6	2	3
2	8	6	7	5	9	3	1	4
4	9	1	3	6	2	8	5	7
3	7	5	8	4	1	2	6	9

412

3	4	6	1	7	8	9	5	2
9	5	8	3	4	2	6	7	1
2	1	7	6	5	9	4	3	8
7	2	3	9	8	4	5	1	6
5	6	1	7	2	3	8	9	4
8	9	4	5	6	1	3	2	7
1	8	9	2	3	6	7	4	5
6	7	2	4	9	5	1	8	3
4	3	5	8	1	7	2	6	9

413

1	3	4	7	5	2	8	6	9
6	8	5	3	4	9	2	1	7
7	2	9	8	1	6	5	3	4
2	1	8	6	9	5	7	4	3
3	5	6	4	2	7	1	9	8
9	4	7	1	3	8	6	2	5
4	7	3	2	8	1	9	5	6
5	6	1	9	7	3	4	8	2
8	9	2	5	6	4	3	7	1

414

2	8	1	7	3	9	5	6	4
4	7	9	8	5	6	2	1	3
5	3	6	2	1	4	7	8	9
9	4	5	3	2	1	8	7	6
7	1	3	4	6	8	9	5	2
6	2	8	9	7	5	4	3	1
1	5	7	6	4	2	3	9	8
8	6	4	5	9	3	1	2	7
3	9	2	1	8	7	6	4	5

415

4	6	9	1	5	3	2	7	8
5	2	7	8	6	9	4	3	1
1	3	8	7	4	2	6	5	9
9	1	5	2	8	6	7	4	3
2	8	4	3	7	1	9	6	5
3	7	6	5	9	4	1	8	2
6	9	1	4	3	8	5	2	7
7	4	3	9	2	5	8	1	6
8	5	2	6	1	7	3	9	4

416

9	6	3	4	2	8	1	7	5
7	1	4	9	3	5	6	2	8
8	5	2	1	7	6	4	9	3
4	9	1	6	8	3	7	5	2
2	3	5	7	1	4	9	8	6
6	7	8	2	5	9	3	4	1
1	2	6	8	4	7	5	3	9
3	8	7	5	9	1	2	6	4
5	4	9	3	6	2	8	1	7

417

6	7	1	2	8	5	4	3	9
5	2	3	4	9	7	6	8	1
9	4	8	1	3	6	2	7	5
7	9	2	6	1	4	3	5	8
1	5	6	3	7	8	9	2	4
8	3	4	9	5	2	1	6	7
3	6	7	8	4	9	5	1	2
2	8	9	5	6	1	7	4	3
4	1	5	7	2	3	8	9	6

418

3	7	9	6	1	8	2	5	4
6	4	5	3	2	7	8	9	1
8	2	1	5	4	9	7	3	6
1	5	2	7	3	6	4	8	9
7	3	4	8	9	1	5	6	2
9	6	8	4	5	2	1	7	3
4	1	7	9	6	5	3	2	8
5	9	3	2	8	4	6	1	7
2	8	6	1	7	3	9	4	5

419

4	3	9	5	6	7	1	8	2
5	8	2	4	1	3	9	6	7
6	7	1	8	9	2	4	3	5
2	4	7	6	8	5	3	1	9
3	6	5	1	2	9	7	4	8
1	9	8	3	7	4	5	2	6
7	5	3	2	4	6	8	9	1
9	1	6	7	3	8	2	5	4
8	2	4	9	5	1	6	7	3

420

3	8	4	6	1	5	9	2	7
1	6	7	9	4	2	5	3	8
5	2	9	7	3	8	1	4	6
2	4	1	8	5	6	3	7	9
8	7	3	4	9	1	2	6	5
9	5	6	3	2	7	8	1	4
4	1	8	2	7	9	6	5	3
6	3	2	5	8	4	7	9	1
7	9	5	1	6	3	4	8	2

421

1	2	9	4	6	3	7	8	5
7	3	6	5	9	8	1	4	2
5	4	8	1	2	7	3	6	9
3	7	4	2	8	1	5	9	6
2	9	5	7	4	6	8	1	3
6	8	1	9	3	5	2	7	4
9	6	7	3	1	2	4	5	8
8	5	2	6	7	4	9	3	1
4	1	3	8	5	9	6	2	7

422

1	4	5	8	7	9	6	2	3
7	2	9	6	5	3	8	1	4
8	6	3	2	1	4	9	5	7
2	5	4	1	6	8	3	7	9
9	3	7	4	2	5	1	8	6
6	1	8	3	9	7	5	4	2
3	8	1	7	4	6	2	9	5
4	9	6	5	8	2	7	3	1
5	7	2	9	3	1	4	6	8

423

1	7	6	9	2	3	4	8	5
3	8	5	1	4	6	7	2	9
2	9	4	5	8	7	6	1	3
6	5	2	4	3	1	9	7	8
8	1	7	2	9	5	3	4	6
9	4	3	7	6	8	2	5	1
4	6	9	8	5	2	1	3	7
5	2	1	3	7	9	8	6	4
7	3	8	6	1	4	5	9	2

424

7	1	2	8	3	9	4	6	5
8	6	9	1	5	4	3	7	2
5	3	4	6	7	2	9	1	8
2	9	5	7	1	6	8	4	3
1	8	3	4	9	5	7	2	6
4	7	6	2	8	3	1	5	9
6	4	7	3	2	8	5	9	1
3	5	1	9	6	7	2	8	4
9	2	8	5	4	1	6	3	7

425

8	5	1	7	9	2	6	3	4
3	2	7	5	6	4	1	8	9
6	4	9	1	3	8	7	2	5
4	7	5	2	8	1	3	9	6
1	3	6	9	7	5	8	4	2
9	8	2	6	4	3	5	7	1
2	6	3	4	1	7	9	5	8
7	1	4	8	5	9	2	6	3
5	9	8	3	2	6	4	1	7

426

6	2	4	9	7	3	5	8	1
3	8	9	1	4	5	2	6	7
7	1	5	6	8	2	4	3	9
8	7	3	4	2	1	9	5	6
9	4	6	3	5	8	7	1	2
1	5	2	7	9	6	8	4	3
5	3	8	2	6	9	1	7	4
4	9	1	5	3	7	6	2	8
2	6	7	8	1	4	3	9	5

427

7	3	8	6	9	5	1	4	2
9	4	1	2	8	7	3	5	6
2	6	5	4	3	1	9	7	8
3	8	9	1	4	2	5	6	7
1	5	2	3	7	6	8	9	4
6	7	4	9	5	8	2	3	1
5	1	3	8	6	4	7	2	9
4	2	7	5	1	9	6	8	3
8	9	6	7	2	3	4	1	5

428

4	6	7	9	8	1	3	5	2
8	1	5	6	2	3	7	4	9
3	2	9	7	5	4	8	1	6
5	3	6	1	7	2	9	8	4
9	7	1	4	6	8	5	2	3
2	4	8	5	3	9	1	6	7
1	8	3	2	4	7	6	9	5
7	5	2	8	9	6	4	3	1
6	9	4	3	1	5	2	7	8

429

9	2	1	5	8	4	7	6	3
3	4	7	9	6	1	8	2	5
5	6	8	2	3	7	1	9	4
8	7	5	1	2	3	9	4	6
6	3	4	8	7	9	2	5	1
2	1	9	6	4	5	3	7	8
1	9	6	3	5	2	4	8	7
7	8	3	4	9	6	5	1	2
4	5	2	7	1	8	6	3	9

430

9	4	2	8	6	5	7	3	1
7	3	6	2	1	4	8	9	5
8	1	5	9	7	3	4	6	2
5	7	4	1	3	6	9	2	8
2	6	9	7	4	8	5	1	3
1	8	3	5	9	2	6	7	4
3	9	1	4	8	7	2	5	6
4	2	7	6	5	1	3	8	9
6	5	8	3	2	9	1	4	7

431

6	4	9	8	2	1	7	5	3
3	7	8	9	5	6	1	4	2
2	5	1	7	4	3	8	9	6
1	8	7	5	6	4	2	3	9
5	9	2	3	7	8	4	6	1
4	6	3	2	1	9	5	7	8
9	1	6	4	8	7	3	2	5
8	2	4	6	3	5	9	1	7
7	3	5	1	9	2	6	8	4

432

4	1	3	2	8	9	7	6	5
8	5	9	7	6	3	1	4	2
2	7	6	5	1	4	3	9	8
1	3	7	6	2	5	9	8	4
5	2	4	9	3	8	6	7	1
6	9	8	1	4	7	2	5	3
9	8	1	3	5	6	4	2	7
7	4	2	8	9	1	5	3	6
3	6	5	4	7	2	8	1	9

433

9	7	2	5	6	1	4	3	8
3	4	6	7	2	8	5	1	9
8	1	5	4	3	9	7	2	6
5	9	7	8	4	3	2	6	1
1	3	8	6	5	2	9	7	4
2	6	4	1	9	7	8	5	3
6	5	9	2	1	4	3	8	7
7	2	3	9	8	6	1	4	5
4	8	1	3	7	5	6	9	2

434

2	1	8	9	5	7	4	6	3
7	6	3	2	1	4	9	5	8
9	4	5	3	8	6	1	2	7
1	2	4	5	7	3	6	8	9
5	9	6	8	2	1	3	7	4
3	8	7	4	6	9	5	1	2
8	5	9	6	4	2	7	3	1
6	3	1	7	9	8	2	4	5
4	7	2	1	3	5	8	9	6

435

1	6	4	7	8	2	3	5	9
8	7	5	6	3	9	4	2	1
2	9	3	4	1	5	8	6	7
9	1	7	8	2	6	5	3	4
6	3	8	9	5	4	1	7	2
5	4	2	3	7	1	9	8	6
7	5	9	1	6	8	2	4	3
3	2	1	5	4	7	6	9	8
4	8	6	2	9	3	7	1	5

436

4	8	9	3	2	7	5	6	1
1	5	2	6	4	9	7	3	8
7	6	3	5	8	1	4	9	2
8	2	4	1	5	3	9	7	6
5	7	6	8	9	2	1	4	3
9	3	1	7	6	4	2	8	5
6	9	8	2	7	5	3	1	4
2	1	7	4	3	6	8	5	9
3	4	5	9	1	8	6	2	7

437

4	1	9	3	6	7	5	8	2
3	7	2	8	5	1	9	4	6
5	6	8	4	9	2	1	3	7
9	4	1	2	8	3	6	7	5
8	3	7	6	1	5	4	2	9
2	5	6	7	4	9	8	1	3
6	2	5	1	7	4	3	9	8
7	8	4	9	3	6	2	5	1
1	9	3	5	2	8	7	6	4

438

3	6	2	8	7	1	4	9	5
9	4	8	2	6	5	3	1	7
7	1	5	3	4	9	2	8	6
8	5	4	1	2	6	9	7	3
2	3	6	4	9	7	1	5	8
1	9	7	5	8	3	6	2	4
4	2	9	7	3	8	5	6	1
6	7	1	9	5	4	8	3	2
5	8	3	6	1	2	7	4	9

439

8	3	9	5	1	7	2	4	6
5	7	6	4	2	9	3	8	1
4	1	2	6	8	3	9	7	5
2	4	1	3	7	8	6	5	9
9	8	7	2	6	5	4	1	3
6	5	3	9	4	1	7	2	8
3	6	8	7	5	4	1	9	2
1	9	4	8	3	2	5	6	7
7	2	5	1	9	6	8	3	4

440

3	8	2	1	7	6	9	4	5
1	5	6	2	4	9	8	7	3
4	9	7	8	5	3	2	1	6
6	4	8	7	9	5	3	2	1
7	2	3	4	6	1	5	9	8
5	1	9	3	2	8	4	6	7
9	3	4	5	1	7	6	8	2
2	7	5	6	8	4	1	3	9
8	6	1	9	3	2	7	5	4

441

2	7	3	1	4	5	9	8	6
6	1	8	3	2	9	4	5	7
4	9	5	8	7	6	3	2	1
7	2	4	6	8	1	5	9	3
5	3	6	7	9	2	1	4	8
9	8	1	4	5	3	6	7	2
1	5	7	9	6	8	2	3	4
3	4	2	5	1	7	8	6	9
8	6	9	2	3	4	7	1	5

442

6	2	4	8	5	3	1	9	7
7	9	8	4	1	2	6	5	3
5	3	1	6	9	7	4	2	8
4	6	9	7	3	1	2	8	5
1	8	7	2	6	5	3	4	9
3	5	2	9	4	8	7	6	1
9	7	3	5	2	6	8	1	4
8	4	6	1	7	9	5	3	2
2	1	5	3	8	4	9	7	6

443

9	1	5	6	2	4	3	7	8
6	7	2	3	1	8	4	5	9
8	3	4	7	9	5	1	2	6
4	9	7	1	5	2	6	8	3
3	2	8	4	6	7	5	9	1
5	6	1	9	8	3	7	4	2
7	8	3	2	4	6	9	1	5
1	5	6	8	7	9	2	3	4
2	4	9	5	3	1	8	6	7

444

5	4	2	7	1	9	8	3	6
3	9	1	8	6	2	4	5	7
8	6	7	5	4	3	9	1	2
1	7	5	9	2	4	3	6	8
6	3	9	1	5	8	7	2	4
2	8	4	3	7	6	1	9	5
4	1	6	2	9	7	5	8	3
9	2	3	4	8	5	6	7	1
7	5	8	6	3	1	2	4	9

445

1	2	4	8	9	7	6	3	5
6	3	5	2	4	1	7	8	9
9	7	8	5	6	3	1	4	2
7	5	2	9	8	4	3	6	1
3	8	9	7	1	6	2	5	4
4	6	1	3	5	2	8	9	7
2	4	7	6	3	5	9	1	8
5	9	3	1	2	8	4	7	6
8	1	6	4	7	9	5	2	3

446

1	7	3	9	5	8	6	4	2
6	5	9	3	4	2	1	7	8
8	4	2	1	7	6	5	3	9
2	6	4	8	9	1	7	5	3
9	3	5	6	2	7	4	8	1
7	1	8	4	3	5	2	9	6
4	2	6	7	8	9	3	1	5
5	9	7	2	1	3	8	6	4
3	8	1	5	6	4	9	2	7

447

5	4	9	7	6	2	1	8	3
7	6	3	8	1	4	5	9	2
1	2	8	5	3	9	4	6	7
2	9	1	4	5	8	7	3	6
4	8	7	3	2	6	9	5	1
6	3	5	1	9	7	2	4	8
9	1	2	6	8	5	3	7	4
3	7	6	9	4	1	8	2	5
8	5	4	2	7	3	6	1	9

448

9	2	3	4	7	6	5	8	1
4	8	1	5	3	9	7	2	6
5	6	7	2	1	8	9	4	3
7	1	5	6	4	2	3	9	8
3	9	2	1	8	5	6	7	4
6	4	8	7	9	3	1	5	2
2	7	9	3	6	4	8	1	5
1	3	4	8	5	7	2	6	9
8	5	6	9	2	1	4	3	7

449

7	8	4	6	3	9	1	2	5
3	6	9	2	1	5	4	7	8
5	2	1	7	4	8	6	9	3
8	4	2	1	5	6	9	3	7
6	1	3	9	2	7	5	8	4
9	5	7	4	8	3	2	6	1
2	7	8	5	6	1	3	4	9
1	3	6	8	9	4	7	5	2
4	9	5	3	7	2	8	1	6

450

9	4	7	8	6	5	3	2	1
8	2	1	3	4	9	6	7	5
6	5	3	1	7	2	4	8	9
3	6	2	5	9	4	7	1	8
4	1	5	7	8	6	2	9	3
7	8	9	2	1	3	5	6	4
1	3	8	4	2	7	9	5	6
5	7	6	9	3	1	8	4	2
2	9	4	6	5	8	1	3	7

451

6	4	1	8	2	9	5	7	3
3	8	5	7	1	6	2	9	4
7	9	2	5	3	4	8	6	1
5	2	9	3	6	1	7	4	8
1	7	4	9	8	5	6	3	2
8	6	3	2	4	7	9	1	5
2	1	6	4	9	8	3	5	7
9	3	7	1	5	2	4	8	6
4	5	8	6	7	3	1	2	9

452

8	9	6	5	7	1	3	2	4
7	3	2	8	4	6	9	5	1
1	5	4	2	9	3	6	7	8
5	4	9	1	8	2	7	6	3
2	1	8	3	6	7	5	4	9
3	6	7	9	5	4	8	1	2
6	2	3	7	1	8	4	9	5
4	8	5	6	2	9	1	3	7
9	7	1	4	3	5	2	8	6

453

7	5	4	9	3	1	2	8	6
8	2	3	7	6	5	4	1	9
9	1	6	2	8	4	3	5	7
6	4	9	5	7	3	8	2	1
5	8	2	1	4	9	6	7	3
1	3	7	8	2	6	5	9	4
3	7	1	6	5	2	9	4	8
4	9	5	3	1	8	7	6	2
2	6	8	4	9	7	1	3	5

454

5	7	3	4	8	2	9	6	1
9	6	8	3	1	7	5	2	4
1	2	4	6	5	9	3	7	8
3	5	1	2	7	4	6	8	9
6	8	7	1	9	3	4	5	2
2	4	9	5	6	8	1	3	7
8	1	2	9	3	5	7	4	6
4	9	5	7	2	6	8	1	3
7	3	6	8	4	1	2	9	5

455

3	9	2	1	7	8	4	5	6
5	6	7	9	3	4	1	8	2
8	1	4	2	6	5	7	9	3
7	2	8	3	4	1	5	6	9
9	5	3	7	8	6	2	4	1
1	4	6	5	9	2	8	3	7
4	7	9	8	1	3	6	2	5
2	8	1	6	5	9	3	7	4
6	3	5	4	2	7	9	1	8

456

1	3	2	6	7	5	9	4	8
5	4	7	9	8	1	3	6	2
6	8	9	3	4	2	5	7	1
4	1	8	5	9	7	2	3	6
2	5	3	4	6	8	1	9	7
9	7	6	2	1	3	8	5	4
8	6	5	1	3	4	7	2	9
3	9	1	7	2	6	4	8	5
7	2	4	8	5	9	6	1	3

457

3	1	7	6	4	8	9	2	5
6	2	5	9	7	1	8	3	4
9	8	4	3	5	2	6	1	7
1	4	3	7	8	9	5	6	2
2	5	8	1	3	6	7	4	9
7	6	9	5	2	4	3	8	1
4	9	2	8	6	5	1	7	3
8	7	1	2	9	3	4	5	6
5	3	6	4	1	7	2	9	8

458

6	9	3	1	5	7	4	2	8
8	1	5	2	4	3	9	6	7
7	4	2	9	8	6	3	1	5
4	8	6	5	2	1	7	9	3
3	7	9	8	6	4	1	5	2
2	5	1	3	7	9	6	8	4
9	2	4	6	3	8	5	7	1
5	6	7	4	1	2	8	3	9
1	3	8	7	9	5	2	4	6

459

8	4	9	1	7	5	6	3	2
7	6	5	2	4	3	1	9	8
3	2	1	8	6	9	7	5	4
6	1	8	3	2	7	5	4	9
2	7	4	9	5	8	3	6	1
5	9	3	6	1	4	2	8	7
1	3	7	4	9	6	8	2	5
4	8	2	5	3	1	9	7	6
9	5	6	7	8	2	4	1	3

460

8	5	9	6	3	2	4	7	1
1	2	7	5	9	4	3	6	8
4	6	3	8	7	1	5	2	9
5	7	1	3	8	6	2	9	4
9	3	4	2	1	5	7	8	6
6	8	2	9	4	7	1	5	3
7	9	6	1	2	3	8	4	5
2	1	5	4	6	8	9	3	7
3	4	8	7	5	9	6	1	2

461

5	4	3	2	8	6	9	1	7
8	2	7	9	1	4	3	5	6
9	1	6	3	5	7	4	2	8
2	9	5	7	4	3	6	8	1
6	8	4	1	2	9	5	7	3
7	3	1	5	6	8	2	9	4
3	5	8	4	9	1	7	6	2
4	6	2	8	7	5	1	3	9
1	7	9	6	3	2	8	4	5

462

5	7	3	4	1	9	8	2	6
2	1	8	7	5	6	4	9	3
4	9	6	8	2	3	1	7	5
7	5	1	3	4	2	6	8	9
3	2	9	6	8	1	7	5	4
8	6	4	9	7	5	2	3	1
6	8	5	1	3	7	9	4	2
1	3	7	2	9	4	5	6	8
9	4	2	5	6	8	3	1	7

463

7	9	3	1	5	4	2	8	6
6	8	5	2	9	3	7	4	1
4	1	2	8	7	6	9	3	5
9	7	6	3	4	8	1	5	2
8	3	1	7	2	5	4	6	9
5	2	4	9	6	1	8	7	3
2	4	9	5	3	7	6	1	8
3	6	8	4	1	9	5	2	7
1	5	7	6	8	2	3	9	4

464

6	8	7	1	3	2	4	9	5
5	2	3	9	6	4	1	8	7
4	1	9	7	5	8	6	2	3
2	9	4	3	7	1	8	5	6
1	6	5	8	2	9	3	7	4
3	7	8	6	4	5	9	1	2
7	4	1	2	9	3	5	6	8
9	5	2	4	8	6	7	3	1
8	3	6	5	1	7	2	4	9

465

9	4	7	2	8	5	3	1	6
3	5	2	1	6	4	9	8	7
1	8	6	7	9	3	4	2	5
7	9	3	5	2	8	1	6	4
5	2	1	9	4	6	8	7	3
8	6	4	3	7	1	2	5	9
2	3	5	6	1	9	7	4	8
6	1	8	4	3	7	5	9	2
4	7	9	8	5	2	6	3	1

466

7	6	1	3	5	4	2	8	9
8	2	9	6	1	7	5	3	4
5	4	3	2	9	8	6	1	7
2	7	6	5	4	3	8	9	1
3	5	8	1	7	9	4	2	6
9	1	4	8	6	2	7	5	3
4	9	5	7	2	1	3	6	8
1	3	2	4	8	6	9	7	5
6	8	7	9	3	5	1	4	2

467

5	7	6	1	8	4	2	3	9
8	4	9	3	6	2	1	7	5
2	1	3	9	5	7	8	4	6
1	5	7	6	2	3	9	8	4
3	6	8	4	9	1	5	2	7
4	9	2	5	7	8	3	6	1
6	2	1	7	3	5	4	9	8
7	8	4	2	1	9	6	5	3
9	3	5	8	4	6	7	1	2

468

8	7	5	1	3	4	6	2	9
6	1	2	9	5	7	3	4	8
3	4	9	6	8	2	7	1	5
2	9	7	8	1	3	5	6	4
4	6	3	2	9	5	1	8	7
1	5	8	4	7	6	2	9	3
9	3	4	5	6	1	8	7	2
7	2	6	3	4	8	9	5	1
5	8	1	7	2	9	4	3	6

469

8	9	5	4	6	3	7	2	1
1	4	7	5	2	8	3	6	9
6	2	3	1	7	9	5	4	8
5	3	6	9	4	1	8	7	2
2	7	4	8	3	6	1	9	5
9	1	8	2	5	7	6	3	4
3	5	9	7	8	4	2	1	6
4	6	2	3	1	5	9	8	7
7	8	1	6	9	2	4	5	3

470

2	7	1	3	6	5	4	9	8
6	8	3	4	2	9	7	5	1
9	4	5	7	8	1	3	6	2
5	1	7	2	4	3	9	8	6
4	2	6	9	7	8	5	1	3
8	3	9	1	5	6	2	4	7
3	5	2	8	1	4	6	7	9
7	6	8	5	9	2	1	3	4
1	9	4	6	3	7	8	2	5

471

5	7	2	9	6	4	3	8	1
8	4	6	3	1	5	2	7	9
3	9	1	2	7	8	6	5	4
9	5	8	7	4	3	1	2	6
4	1	3	8	2	6	5	9	7
2	6	7	1	5	9	8	4	3
1	8	4	5	3	7	9	6	2
7	2	5	6	9	1	4	3	8
6	3	9	4	8	2	7	1	5

472

2	1	6	3	7	9	5	8	4
7	9	8	6	4	5	1	3	2
5	3	4	2	1	8	7	6	9
4	6	2	5	9	1	8	7	3
9	8	3	7	2	6	4	5	1
1	5	7	8	3	4	9	2	6
6	7	9	1	8	2	3	4	5
8	2	1	4	5	3	6	9	7
3	4	5	9	6	7	2	1	8

473

9	3	1	8	2	5	4	6	7
4	5	6	1	3	7	9	2	8
7	2	8	9	6	4	1	3	5
5	4	7	3	1	9	6	8	2
1	6	9	2	7	8	3	5	4
2	8	3	4	5	6	7	9	1
8	1	5	6	4	3	2	7	9
6	7	2	5	9	1	8	4	3
3	9	4	7	8	2	5	1	6

474

5	4	1	8	6	7	3	2	9
8	6	3	2	5	9	7	4	1
2	7	9	1	4	3	8	6	5
1	9	4	3	2	6	5	8	7
7	8	6	5	1	4	2	9	3
3	2	5	9	7	8	4	1	6
9	5	8	6	3	2	1	7	4
4	3	2	7	9	1	6	5	8
6	1	7	4	8	5	9	3	2

475

9	4	3	8	7	1	5	6	2
7	2	8	4	6	5	9	3	1
6	1	5	2	3	9	7	8	4
8	6	2	9	5	4	1	7	3
5	7	1	6	2	3	8	4	9
4	3	9	1	8	7	6	2	5
1	8	6	5	4	2	3	9	7
2	5	7	3	9	6	4	1	8
3	9	4	7	1	8	2	5	6

476

5	2	8	3	9	6	4	7	1
1	4	6	5	7	2	8	3	9
9	3	7	1	8	4	5	2	6
7	8	1	6	5	3	2	9	4
6	5	2	9	4	1	7	8	3
4	9	3	8	2	7	1	6	5
2	7	5	4	6	9	3	1	8
3	6	4	2	1	8	9	5	7
8	1	9	7	3	5	6	4	2

477

2	8	1	5	6	4	7	9	3
6	3	4	7	1	9	8	2	5
5	9	7	8	3	2	6	4	1
7	1	9	6	2	8	5	3	4
4	5	2	3	9	7	1	8	6
3	6	8	1	4	5	2	7	9
8	4	6	2	5	3	9	1	7
9	2	5	4	7	1	3	6	8
1	7	3	9	8	6	4	5	2

478

5	1	2	8	7	4	9	6	3
6	3	9	5	2	1	8	4	7
8	7	4	9	6	3	1	5	2
2	8	5	4	3	6	7	1	9
1	4	7	2	5	9	3	8	6
3	9	6	1	8	7	4	2	5
7	5	3	6	1	8	2	9	4
9	2	8	3	4	5	6	7	1
4	6	1	7	9	2	5	3	8

479

5	8	4	2	9	7	3	6	1
3	9	1	8	6	4	7	5	2
6	2	7	3	5	1	8	4	9
8	4	2	1	3	5	9	7	6
7	3	5	9	2	6	4	1	8
9	1	6	4	7	8	2	3	5
2	6	8	7	1	3	5	9	4
1	7	9	5	4	2	6	8	3
4	5	3	6	8	9	1	2	7

480

3	5	6	8	1	9	2	4	7
7	9	1	2	3	4	5	6	8
2	4	8	5	6	7	3	9	1
9	3	2	7	8	6	1	5	4
5	8	7	9	4	1	6	2	3
6	1	4	3	2	5	8	7	9
4	6	3	1	9	2	7	8	5
1	7	9	6	5	8	4	3	2
8	2	5	4	7	3	9	1	6

481

9	8	3	7	4	2	1	5	6
1	6	2	5	3	9	8	7	4
4	5	7	1	6	8	3	2	9
8	4	6	3	1	7	2	9	5
5	3	1	9	2	4	7	6	8
7	2	9	8	5	6	4	1	3
6	7	5	4	8	1	9	3	2
3	9	8	2	7	5	6	4	1
2	1	4	6	9	3	5	8	7

482

7	3	2	4	5	8	6	9	1
9	8	4	3	6	1	2	5	7
6	5	1	9	7	2	4	8	3
4	2	3	6	8	9	7	1	5
1	9	5	7	4	3	8	2	6
8	6	7	1	2	5	9	3	4
2	7	8	5	1	6	3	4	9
5	4	9	2	3	7	1	6	8
3	1	6	8	9	4	5	7	2

483

2	4	8	1	6	7	9	3	5
1	6	5	9	3	4	2	8	7
7	9	3	8	2	5	6	4	1
5	8	7	4	9	3	1	6	2
4	2	6	5	8	1	7	9	3
3	1	9	6	7	2	4	5	8
9	3	4	7	1	8	5	2	6
8	5	1	2	4	6	3	7	9
6	7	2	3	5	9	8	1	4

484

8	3	6	9	2	4	1	7	5
5	1	4	8	6	7	2	3	9
9	7	2	3	1	5	8	4	6
3	6	9	7	8	2	4	5	1
7	2	5	6	4	1	9	8	3
1	4	8	5	9	3	6	2	7
2	9	3	4	7	6	5	1	8
6	5	1	2	3	8	7	9	4
4	8	7	1	5	9	3	6	2

485

6	9	3	8	5	4	1	2	7
8	4	5	1	7	2	9	3	6
1	2	7	6	9	3	4	5	8
4	7	8	9	2	6	3	1	5
5	3	2	4	1	8	6	7	9
9	1	6	7	3	5	8	4	2
3	5	1	2	6	9	7	8	4
2	8	9	3	4	7	5	6	1
7	6	4	5	8	1	2	9	3

486

2	8	9	6	1	4	3	5	7
3	6	5	2	7	9	1	8	4
4	7	1	5	8	3	6	9	2
7	5	3	1	6	8	2	4	9
9	1	2	4	5	7	8	6	3
8	4	6	9	3	2	7	1	5
6	2	7	8	4	5	9	3	1
1	3	4	7	9	6	5	2	8
5	9	8	3	2	1	4	7	6

487

4	1	3	9	6	7	5	2	8
2	6	5	4	8	3	9	1	7
9	8	7	5	2	1	3	4	6
3	9	6	7	1	2	8	5	4
1	5	4	8	3	9	6	7	2
8	7	2	6	4	5	1	9	3
5	3	9	2	7	8	4	6	1
7	4	1	3	5	6	2	8	9
6	2	8	1	9	4	7	3	5

488

9	5	6	7	3	4	2	1	8
1	2	7	5	9	8	4	3	6
4	3	8	2	6	1	7	5	9
3	6	4	1	5	9	8	2	7
2	9	5	8	7	3	6	4	1
7	8	1	6	4	2	5	9	3
6	7	2	9	1	5	3	8	4
8	1	3	4	2	7	9	6	5
5	4	9	3	8	6	1	7	2

489

9	7	6	8	2	3	1	5	4
5	1	8	4	6	7	3	9	2
2	3	4	9	1	5	8	7	6
4	6	9	7	3	8	5	2	1
3	8	2	1	5	6	7	4	9
7	5	1	2	9	4	6	8	3
8	9	5	6	4	1	2	3	7
6	2	7	3	8	9	4	1	5
1	4	3	5	7	2	9	6	8

490

6	7	8	2	1	9	4	3	5
4	9	5	7	8	3	6	1	2
2	1	3	4	5	6	8	9	7
5	6	1	9	7	2	3	8	4
3	2	9	8	6	4	7	5	1
8	4	7	1	3	5	2	6	9
7	8	6	5	2	1	9	4	3
9	5	2	3	4	8	1	7	6
1	3	4	6	9	7	5	2	8

491

5	7	4	3	2	1	6	9	8
9	2	8	5	4	6	1	3	7
3	1	6	7	9	8	2	5	4
2	4	3	8	6	9	5	7	1
6	8	7	2	1	5	3	4	9
1	5	9	4	3	7	8	2	6
7	6	5	9	8	3	4	1	2
4	9	1	6	5	2	7	8	3
8	3	2	1	7	4	9	6	5

492

5	3	2	1	4	8	6	9	7
7	8	4	9	6	5	3	2	1
1	6	9	2	7	3	4	5	8
3	1	7	5	2	6	8	4	9
4	9	6	8	3	7	5	1	2
2	5	8	4	1	9	7	6	3
9	2	3	6	8	4	1	7	5
6	7	5	3	9	1	2	8	4
8	4	1	7	5	2	9	3	6

493

3	4	8	5	1	6	2	7	9
5	6	7	8	9	2	3	1	4
2	1	9	3	4	7	5	8	6
7	9	2	4	6	8	1	3	5
6	3	1	7	2	5	9	4	8
8	5	4	9	3	1	6	2	7
4	2	3	6	8	9	7	5	1
9	8	5	1	7	3	4	6	2
1	7	6	2	5	4	8	9	3

494

3	5	6	8	2	9	1	4	7
4	2	9	7	5	1	8	6	3
7	8	1	6	4	3	5	2	9
6	7	5	2	3	8	4	9	1
8	1	2	4	9	6	7	3	5
9	3	4	1	7	5	2	8	6
5	4	3	9	1	2	6	7	8
2	9	8	5	6	7	3	1	4
1	6	7	3	8	4	9	5	2

495

6	7	8	4	5	9	1	2	3
4	1	3	7	2	6	5	8	9
2	9	5	1	3	8	7	4	6
9	6	7	8	1	5	4	3	2
3	5	2	6	9	4	8	7	1
8	4	1	3	7	2	6	9	5
5	8	6	9	4	3	2	1	7
7	2	9	5	8	1	3	6	4
1	3	4	2	6	7	9	5	8

496

5	6	1	4	8	3	9	2	7
2	9	4	7	6	1	3	8	5
3	7	8	2	9	5	1	6	4
4	8	3	6	5	9	7	1	2
1	2	7	8	3	4	6	5	9
6	5	9	1	2	7	8	4	3
9	3	2	5	1	6	4	7	8
7	1	5	9	4	8	2	3	6
8	4	6	3	7	2	5	9	1

497

4	3	8	7	6	9	5	2	1
5	7	6	1	2	4	9	3	8
2	9	1	5	3	8	6	7	4
6	5	9	8	1	7	2	4	3
8	2	3	4	5	6	7	1	9
1	4	7	3	9	2	8	6	5
9	1	5	2	7	3	4	8	6
7	6	4	9	8	1	3	5	2
3	8	2	6	4	5	1	9	7

498

2	4	3	5	6	8	7	1	9
7	6	1	9	2	3	4	5	8
8	5	9	7	4	1	3	6	2
3	2	6	4	7	9	5	8	1
5	1	7	2	8	6	9	3	4
9	8	4	1	3	5	6	2	7
1	7	2	6	5	4	8	9	3
4	3	5	8	9	2	1	7	6
6	9	8	3	1	7	2	4	5

499

4	2	3	8	1	7	9	5	6
1	7	9	6	5	4	2	8	3
5	8	6	2	9	3	7	1	4
8	6	1	7	2	5	4	3	9
3	4	7	1	8	9	6	2	5
2	9	5	3	4	6	8	7	1
9	1	4	5	7	8	3	6	2
7	3	2	9	6	1	5	4	8
6	5	8	4	3	2	1	9	7

500

7	3	2	5	4	8	6	1	9
9	5	8	2	6	1	4	7	3
1	4	6	7	3	9	2	8	5
2	8	5	4	9	6	7	3	1
4	6	7	1	5	3	8	9	2
3	1	9	8	7	2	5	6	4
8	9	3	6	2	5	1	4	7
6	2	4	9	1	7	3	5	8
5	7	1	3	8	4	9	2	6

501

2	8	5	6	1	4	7	3	9
3	4	6	9	7	2	8	1	5
9	7	1	5	8	3	6	4	2
8	2	4	3	9	5	1	7	6
5	1	7	8	2	6	3	9	4
6	3	9	7	4	1	2	5	8
4	6	2	1	3	9	5	8	7
7	9	3	2	5	8	4	6	1
1	5	8	4	6	7	9	2	3

502

3	6	8	9	4	5	7	1	2
5	2	7	3	6	1	9	8	4
4	1	9	2	7	8	5	3	6
1	9	5	7	8	4	6	2	3
6	8	3	5	9	2	4	7	1
2	7	4	1	3	6	8	9	5
9	4	6	8	2	3	1	5	7
8	3	1	4	5	7	2	6	9
7	5	2	6	1	9	3	4	8

503

3	8	4	9	6	1	5	7	2
2	7	9	3	5	8	4	6	1
5	6	1	4	7	2	9	8	3
9	3	5	7	8	4	1	2	6
1	4	8	2	3	6	7	5	9
7	2	6	5	1	9	3	4	8
8	5	7	1	2	3	6	9	4
6	9	3	8	4	5	2	1	7
4	1	2	6	9	7	8	3	5

504

3	5	8	7	1	6	9	2	4
9	7	4	8	2	3	6	5	1
6	2	1	5	9	4	3	7	8
4	3	2	6	8	5	1	9	7
1	9	5	2	3	7	8	4	6
7	8	6	9	4	1	5	3	2
5	6	9	4	7	8	2	1	3
8	4	3	1	5	2	7	6	9
2	1	7	3	6	9	4	8	5

505

3	9	2	1	7	5	4	6	8
5	6	7	8	4	9	3	1	2
1	4	8	2	6	3	7	5	9
9	5	6	3	2	1	8	7	4
8	3	1	7	9	4	6	2	5
2	7	4	5	8	6	9	3	1
6	1	9	4	5	7	2	8	3
4	8	3	6	1	2	5	9	7
7	2	5	9	3	8	1	4	6

506

7	8	6	3	9	1	2	5	4
9	3	2	4	8	5	7	1	6
4	1	5	7	2	6	3	9	8
1	2	4	9	3	8	5	6	7
5	9	3	6	7	2	8	4	1
6	7	8	5	1	4	9	2	3
8	5	1	2	6	7	4	3	9
2	6	9	8	4	3	1	7	5
3	4	7	1	5	9	6	8	2

507

2	9	5	4	3	7	6	1	8
7	8	6	2	1	9	4	3	5
4	3	1	6	5	8	2	9	7
1	4	8	3	7	2	9	5	6
3	6	2	9	8	5	7	4	1
5	7	9	1	4	6	3	8	2
6	1	7	8	9	4	5	2	3
8	2	4	5	6	3	1	7	9
9	5	3	7	2	1	8	6	4

508

7	4	1	6	8	5	3	2	9
2	3	6	4	9	1	8	5	7
5	9	8	3	7	2	1	4	6
4	2	7	1	3	8	6	9	5
8	6	3	5	2	9	4	7	1
1	5	9	7	4	6	2	8	3
9	1	5	8	6	4	7	3	2
6	7	4	2	5	3	9	1	8
3	8	2	9	1	7	5	6	4

509

3	1	6	4	2	5	8	9	7
5	8	4	7	9	1	3	6	2
9	7	2	6	8	3	5	4	1
1	2	8	9	4	7	6	3	5
7	4	3	1	5	6	9	2	8
6	5	9	2	3	8	7	1	4
4	3	5	8	1	9	2	7	6
8	6	1	3	7	2	4	5	9
2	9	7	5	6	4	1	8	3

510

2	1	6	9	4	3	7	5	8
9	3	5	7	8	1	6	2	4
4	7	8	2	5	6	3	1	9
8	9	3	6	1	4	2	7	5
7	4	1	8	2	5	9	3	6
5	6	2	3	7	9	8	4	1
3	2	4	1	6	8	5	9	7
1	8	9	5	3	7	4	6	2
6	5	7	4	9	2	1	8	3

511

4	9	6	2	7	5	1	3	8
7	3	2	9	8	1	6	5	4
8	5	1	6	3	4	2	7	9
3	1	4	7	2	8	9	6	5
9	6	7	5	4	3	8	1	2
5	2	8	1	9	6	3	4	7
6	4	5	8	1	9	7	2	3
1	7	9	3	5	2	4	8	6
2	8	3	4	6	7	5	9	1

512

1	7	9	5	6	4	2	8	3
6	5	2	3	8	7	4	1	9
8	4	3	9	2	1	5	6	7
4	8	7	1	3	2	6	9	5
2	1	5	4	9	6	3	7	8
3	9	6	7	5	8	1	2	4
5	3	1	6	7	9	8	4	2
9	2	4	8	1	3	7	5	6
7	6	8	2	4	5	9	3	1

513

4	8	3	6	7	1	9	5	2
9	6	1	2	3	5	7	8	4
5	7	2	4	9	8	1	3	6
2	3	9	5	1	7	4	6	8
6	4	8	9	2	3	5	7	1
1	5	7	8	6	4	3	2	9
8	1	4	7	5	2	6	9	3
3	9	5	1	8	6	2	4	7
7	2	6	3	4	9	8	1	5

514

2	9	3	6	1	7	4	5	8
4	1	5	9	8	2	7	6	3
8	6	7	4	3	5	9	1	2
7	2	1	5	6	3	8	4	9
6	4	8	7	2	9	1	3	5
3	5	9	1	4	8	6	2	7
1	3	2	8	9	6	5	7	4
5	8	6	3	7	4	2	9	1
9	7	4	2	5	1	3	8	6

515

4	7	3	2	9	1	6	5	8
9	5	6	8	7	3	1	2	4
8	1	2	5	6	4	3	7	9
7	3	9	1	5	6	8	4	2
1	2	4	7	8	9	5	3	6
6	8	5	3	4	2	9	1	7
2	6	7	9	1	5	4	8	3
3	9	1	4	2	8	7	6	5
5	4	8	6	3	7	2	9	1

516

5	9	6	3	4	8	7	2	1
1	2	8	7	5	6	3	4	9
7	3	4	2	1	9	8	5	6
4	5	1	9	6	7	2	3	8
2	6	7	1	8	3	5	9	4
9	8	3	4	2	5	6	1	7
6	7	9	5	3	1	4	8	2
8	4	5	6	9	2	1	7	3
3	1	2	8	7	4	9	6	5

517

4	7	6	1	3	2	5	8	9
2	5	3	8	4	9	6	7	1
8	1	9	6	5	7	3	2	4
1	6	2	4	9	3	8	5	7
5	8	4	7	2	1	9	3	6
3	9	7	5	6	8	4	1	2
7	3	1	9	8	4	2	6	5
9	2	5	3	1	6	7	4	8
6	4	8	2	7	5	1	9	3

518

8	9	3	6	2	4	1	5	7
5	2	1	7	3	8	4	6	9
4	7	6	1	9	5	2	3	8
3	6	7	9	8	1	5	4	2
9	1	8	4	5	2	6	7	3
2	4	5	3	6	7	9	8	1
7	3	9	2	4	6	8	1	5
6	8	2	5	1	3	7	9	4
1	5	4	8	7	9	3	2	6

519

1	7	9	6	8	4	3	5	2
6	3	4	2	1	5	7	8	9
2	5	8	3	7	9	1	4	6
9	2	7	5	6	1	4	3	8
8	6	5	4	9	3	2	1	7
3	4	1	8	2	7	9	6	5
7	8	2	1	4	6	5	9	3
4	9	3	7	5	8	6	2	1
5	1	6	9	3	2	8	7	4

520

7	6	3	4	1	2	9	5	8
4	5	2	8	6	9	1	3	7
1	8	9	3	7	5	4	2	6
5	2	1	9	3	8	7	6	4
3	4	8	6	2	7	5	1	9
6	9	7	1	5	4	3	8	2
9	7	5	2	8	1	6	4	3
2	1	6	7	4	3	8	9	5
8	3	4	5	9	6	2	7	1

521

9	7	5	3	2	8	1	4	6
2	4	8	5	1	6	3	9	7
1	3	6	7	4	9	2	8	5
3	5	4	8	6	7	9	1	2
6	2	9	1	3	4	5	7	8
7	8	1	2	9	5	6	3	4
4	6	7	9	5	1	8	2	3
5	1	2	4	8	3	7	6	9
8	9	3	6	7	2	4	5	1

522

3	7	1	4	8	5	6	2	9
4	5	6	9	2	1	8	3	7
9	8	2	3	6	7	4	5	1
6	3	4	1	5	9	2	7	8
2	9	7	6	3	8	5	1	4
8	1	5	7	4	2	9	6	3
5	6	3	8	1	4	7	9	2
7	2	8	5	9	3	1	4	6
1	4	9	2	7	6	3	8	5

523

9	3	2	4	7	6	8	1	5
8	1	6	5	2	3	9	7	4
4	5	7	9	1	8	6	3	2
3	9	5	7	4	1	2	6	8
2	6	1	8	3	9	5	4	7
7	8	4	6	5	2	3	9	1
5	4	3	2	6	7	1	8	9
1	7	8	3	9	5	4	2	6
6	2	9	1	8	4	7	5	3

524

4	1	9	2	5	7	8	6	3
2	6	5	8	4	3	1	9	7
7	3	8	1	9	6	2	4	5
6	9	7	5	8	1	4	3	2
5	4	1	3	6	2	7	8	9
8	2	3	4	7	9	5	1	6
1	7	6	9	2	8	3	5	4
3	5	2	6	1	4	9	7	8
9	8	4	7	3	5	6	2	1

525

7	3	2	6	4	5	9	1	8
8	1	5	9	3	7	2	4	6
9	4	6	1	8	2	3	7	5
3	2	9	5	1	4	6	8	7
6	7	4	8	2	9	1	5	3
5	8	1	3	7	6	4	9	2
1	6	7	4	5	3	8	2	9
2	9	8	7	6	1	5	3	4
4	5	3	2	9	8	7	6	1

526

5	8	3	1	6	4	9	7	2
4	2	7	9	5	8	6	1	3
1	9	6	7	2	3	4	5	8
7	1	2	8	4	6	5	3	9
6	4	9	5	3	1	8	2	7
8	3	5	2	9	7	1	6	4
3	7	1	6	8	9	2	4	5
9	5	4	3	1	2	7	8	6
2	6	8	4	7	5	3	9	1

527

7	8	1	3	2	5	6	9	4
9	5	3	4	6	1	7	2	8
4	6	2	9	7	8	1	5	3
1	7	5	8	9	2	3	4	6
6	3	8	5	1	4	9	7	2
2	4	9	7	3	6	5	8	1
8	2	7	1	5	3	4	6	9
5	1	4	6	8	9	2	3	7
3	9	6	2	4	7	8	1	5

528

6	2	9	7	3	5	1	4	8
4	3	7	8	1	2	9	5	6
8	5	1	9	6	4	2	3	7
1	6	3	5	2	7	8	9	4
7	4	5	3	8	9	6	1	2
9	8	2	1	4	6	5	7	3
3	9	4	6	5	8	7	2	1
5	1	6	2	7	3	4	8	9
2	7	8	4	9	1	3	6	5

529

2	4	3	5	6	9	1	8	7
5	1	7	4	2	8	9	3	6
6	9	8	7	3	1	2	5	4
1	2	9	6	5	7	8	4	3
4	7	5	2	8	3	6	9	1
8	3	6	9	1	4	5	7	2
3	5	1	8	4	6	7	2	9
7	6	2	3	9	5	4	1	8
9	8	4	1	7	2	3	6	5

530

7	3	1	8	4	5	9	6	2
6	9	5	2	1	3	7	4	8
2	4	8	7	6	9	5	3	1
1	5	4	3	2	8	6	7	9
9	7	6	1	5	4	2	8	3
3	8	2	9	7	6	1	5	4
8	6	9	5	3	1	4	2	7
4	1	7	6	8	2	3	9	5
5	2	3	4	9	7	8	1	6

531

7	8	1	9	4	6	5	3	2
5	2	9	1	7	3	8	6	4
4	6	3	8	2	5	1	9	7
8	4	7	3	9	1	6	2	5
3	9	2	6	5	4	7	1	8
1	5	6	7	8	2	3	4	9
2	3	4	5	1	8	9	7	6
9	1	5	4	6	7	2	8	3
6	7	8	2	3	9	4	5	1

532

1	4	7	5	2	6	9	3	8
3	8	5	1	9	7	4	6	2
2	9	6	4	8	3	7	1	5
4	5	1	6	3	2	8	9	7
6	7	8	9	4	5	3	2	1
9	2	3	8	7	1	6	5	4
7	1	9	2	6	8	5	4	3
5	3	4	7	1	9	2	8	6
8	6	2	3	5	4	1	7	9

533

1	9	5	7	8	6	4	3	2
6	7	4	1	3	2	8	5	9
8	2	3	4	5	9	1	7	6
5	3	2	8	1	7	6	9	4
7	1	9	5	6	4	2	8	3
4	8	6	9	2	3	5	1	7
9	5	7	2	4	8	3	6	1
3	4	1	6	9	5	7	2	8
2	6	8	3	7	1	9	4	5

534

4	3	5	2	6	8	7	1	9
8	6	7	1	9	4	3	5	2
2	9	1	7	5	3	6	8	4
9	1	6	8	4	7	2	3	5
3	4	8	5	2	9	1	6	7
7	5	2	3	1	6	9	4	8
1	2	9	6	8	5	4	7	3
5	7	4	9	3	1	8	2	6
6	8	3	4	7	2	5	9	1

535

6	8	1	3	9	7	2	4	5
3	2	7	5	8	4	9	6	1
5	4	9	1	2	6	7	8	3
9	7	5	4	6	2	3	1	8
8	1	3	9	7	5	4	2	6
4	6	2	8	1	3	5	7	9
2	9	4	6	5	1	8	3	7
1	3	8	7	4	9	6	5	2
7	5	6	2	3	8	1	9	4

536

2	1	7	4	8	9	6	3	5
6	4	9	3	1	5	2	8	7
3	8	5	7	6	2	4	1	9
1	6	8	2	4	7	5	9	3
9	5	2	6	3	8	1	7	4
7	3	4	5	9	1	8	2	6
5	2	1	9	7	4	3	6	8
4	7	6	8	2	3	9	5	1
8	9	3	1	5	6	7	4	2

537

4	1	6	3	2	7	5	8	9
3	9	7	1	8	5	2	6	4
8	2	5	6	9	4	1	3	7
1	6	2	9	4	8	3	7	5
5	4	3	7	1	6	8	9	2
7	8	9	5	3	2	4	1	6
9	5	4	8	7	3	6	2	1
2	7	8	4	6	1	9	5	3
6	3	1	2	5	9	7	4	8

538

8	9	5	4	1	7	6	2	3
2	3	4	6	9	8	5	7	1
6	7	1	3	5	2	4	8	9
9	5	6	1	7	4	2	3	8
4	2	8	9	3	5	7	1	6
7	1	3	2	8	6	9	5	4
5	8	9	7	6	1	3	4	2
1	6	2	5	4	3	8	9	7
3	4	7	8	2	9	1	6	5

539

9	8	5	4	2	6	1	7	3
4	2	7	1	3	5	9	8	6
6	3	1	9	8	7	2	4	5
1	5	8	6	7	4	3	2	9
3	4	6	8	9	2	5	1	7
7	9	2	3	5	1	4	6	8
8	6	3	2	4	9	7	5	1
2	7	9	5	1	8	6	3	4
5	1	4	7	6	3	8	9	2

540

2	9	6	1	7	3	5	8	4
3	4	5	8	9	6	7	1	2
8	7	1	4	5	2	9	6	3
5	6	9	2	3	4	1	7	8
1	2	7	9	8	5	4	3	6
4	8	3	6	1	7	2	5	9
9	3	2	7	6	1	8	4	5
7	5	4	3	2	8	6	9	1
6	1	8	5	4	9	3	2	7

541

2	8	9	5	3	6	4	1	7
6	5	7	4	8	1	2	9	3
4	3	1	2	9	7	5	8	6
1	2	6	7	5	8	3	4	9
9	4	3	1	6	2	8	7	5
5	7	8	9	4	3	1	6	2
8	9	2	3	7	4	6	5	1
3	6	5	8	1	9	7	2	4
7	1	4	6	2	5	9	3	8

542

1	2	9	7	6	4	8	5	3
7	6	3	1	8	5	9	2	4
8	5	4	2	9	3	6	1	7
9	3	8	5	4	7	1	6	2
6	4	1	8	3	2	7	9	5
5	7	2	9	1	6	3	4	8
3	8	5	6	2	1	4	7	9
2	9	6	4	7	8	5	3	1
4	1	7	3	5	9	2	8	6

543

2	4	6	3	5	7	1	9	8
3	9	7	8	1	6	4	5	2
1	5	8	2	4	9	6	3	7
9	8	2	5	6	3	7	4	1
5	6	4	7	8	1	9	2	3
7	3	1	4	9	2	5	8	6
6	2	3	9	7	4	8	1	5
8	1	9	6	3	5	2	7	4
4	7	5	1	2	8	3	6	9

544

5	1	4	8	3	9	7	2	6
3	2	7	1	6	5	8	9	4
8	6	9	2	7	4	5	1	3
4	9	8	6	2	3	1	7	5
1	5	3	9	8	7	6	4	2
2	7	6	4	5	1	3	8	9
9	8	5	3	1	2	4	6	7
6	3	2	7	4	8	9	5	1
7	4	1	5	9	6	2	3	8

545

7	5	3	9	6	1	8	2	4
2	1	6	8	3	4	7	9	5
4	8	9	2	5	7	1	3	6
8	7	5	6	4	3	2	1	9
1	9	4	7	8	2	6	5	3
6	3	2	1	9	5	4	7	8
9	2	8	3	7	6	5	4	1
3	4	1	5	2	8	9	6	7
5	6	7	4	1	9	3	8	2

546

7	8	1	9	6	5	2	3	4
3	4	9	2	1	8	5	6	7
5	2	6	4	3	7	8	1	9
6	5	2	1	7	4	9	8	3
8	1	7	5	9	3	4	2	6
9	3	4	6	8	2	7	5	1
2	6	8	3	4	9	1	7	5
4	7	3	8	5	1	6	9	2
1	9	5	7	2	6	3	4	8

547

3	9	7	2	5	6	1	8	4
6	1	4	3	8	9	5	2	7
5	2	8	1	4	7	9	6	3
7	3	5	9	6	8	4	1	2
1	8	2	5	3	4	6	7	9
9	4	6	7	2	1	8	3	5
4	7	1	8	9	2	3	5	6
8	5	9	6	7	3	2	4	1
2	6	3	4	1	5	7	9	8

548

9	7	8	3	6	4	1	5	2
4	1	2	7	5	8	3	9	6
5	6	3	2	1	9	8	7	4
7	5	1	8	4	3	6	2	9
2	4	6	1	9	5	7	8	3
3	8	9	6	7	2	5	4	1
8	9	4	5	3	1	2	6	7
1	2	7	4	8	6	9	3	5
6	3	5	9	2	7	4	1	8

549

9	3	1	6	8	7	4	2	5
4	8	2	5	3	1	6	7	9
5	7	6	4	9	2	8	3	1
7	9	4	2	6	3	1	5	8
6	2	8	1	5	4	3	9	7
3	1	5	9	7	8	2	4	6
2	5	9	3	1	6	7	8	4
1	4	7	8	2	9	5	6	3
8	6	3	7	4	5	9	1	2

550

9	7	4	6	3	2	5	8	1
3	1	6	5	9	8	7	2	4
2	5	8	7	1	4	9	3	6
6	3	5	2	4	9	1	7	8
4	9	1	8	5	7	2	6	3
8	2	7	3	6	1	4	9	5
1	4	3	9	2	6	8	5	7
7	6	2	1	8	5	3	4	9
5	8	9	4	7	3	6	1	2

551

7	8	9	3	2	4	6	1	5
5	3	2	6	7	1	4	8	9
4	1	6	5	9	8	3	7	2
8	9	7	2	4	5	1	6	3
2	6	4	7	1	3	9	5	8
1	5	3	9	8	6	2	4	7
9	2	1	8	6	7	5	3	4
6	7	5	4	3	2	8	9	1
3	4	8	1	5	9	7	2	6

552

2	3	7	4	9	1	5	6	8
5	8	6	2	7	3	1	9	4
1	9	4	8	6	5	3	7	2
9	4	8	5	1	7	2	3	6
3	7	2	6	4	8	9	5	1
6	1	5	3	2	9	8	4	7
8	6	3	7	5	2	4	1	9
7	5	1	9	8	4	6	2	3
4	2	9	1	3	6	7	8	5

553

7	1	4	8	6	3	5	2	9
6	5	9	1	7	2	4	8	3
3	8	2	4	5	9	7	6	1
1	6	8	2	3	7	9	5	4
2	3	5	9	4	1	8	7	6
9	4	7	6	8	5	3	1	2
4	7	3	5	1	6	2	9	8
5	9	6	3	2	8	1	4	7
8	2	1	7	9	4	6	3	5

554

9	8	6	1	2	4	5	7	3
7	4	1	8	5	3	2	9	6
2	5	3	6	9	7	4	1	8
6	1	4	3	7	5	8	2	9
5	9	7	2	1	8	6	3	4
8	3	2	4	6	9	7	5	1
4	2	9	5	8	1	3	6	7
3	7	5	9	4	6	1	8	2
1	6	8	7	3	2	9	4	5

555

3	2	5	8	7	6	9	1	4
7	9	1	3	2	4	5	6	8
6	4	8	5	9	1	2	3	7
8	1	7	2	4	3	6	9	5
5	6	2	7	1	9	8	4	3
9	3	4	6	8	5	1	7	2
1	7	9	4	5	2	3	8	6
2	8	6	9	3	7	4	5	1
4	5	3	1	6	8	7	2	9

556

5	9	7	2	4	1	8	3	6
8	6	2	5	9	3	1	7	4
3	1	4	6	8	7	9	5	2
6	3	1	4	5	8	2	9	7
2	7	9	3	1	6	4	8	5
4	5	8	7	2	9	3	6	1
9	8	5	1	6	4	7	2	3
7	4	6	9	3	2	5	1	8
1	2	3	8	7	5	6	4	9

557

2	4	3	1	9	6	8	7	5
7	8	5	3	4	2	1	9	6
6	1	9	5	8	7	4	3	2
8	9	7	4	5	1	6	2	3
1	6	2	8	7	3	9	5	4
3	5	4	6	2	9	7	1	8
9	3	8	2	1	4	5	6	7
4	2	1	7	6	5	3	8	9
5	7	6	9	3	8	2	4	1

558

7	3	6	8	1	5	4	2	9
2	9	5	4	6	7	1	3	8
8	4	1	3	2	9	5	6	7
9	1	8	2	5	3	7	4	6
3	2	7	6	8	4	9	1	5
5	6	4	7	9	1	3	8	2
4	8	3	5	7	2	6	9	1
1	5	2	9	3	6	8	7	4
6	7	9	1	4	8	2	5	3

559

9	2	5	8	3	7	6	4	1
7	3	1	2	4	6	8	5	9
4	8	6	1	5	9	7	3	2
1	9	4	5	6	2	3	7	8
8	6	7	4	1	3	9	2	5
3	5	2	9	7	8	1	6	4
5	1	3	7	8	4	2	9	6
6	4	9	3	2	1	5	8	7
2	7	8	6	9	5	4	1	3

560

6	5	9	1	8	2	4	7	3
7	1	8	4	5	3	2	6	9
2	3	4	6	9	7	1	8	5
5	9	1	8	3	4	6	2	7
8	7	2	5	6	9	3	1	4
3	4	6	2	7	1	9	5	8
1	2	3	7	4	5	8	9	6
4	8	7	9	1	6	5	3	2
9	6	5	3	2	8	7	4	1

561
```
6 7 8 2 5 4 1 9 3
5 9 2 7 1 3 4 6 8
3 1 4 9 8 6 5 2 7
7 3 5 8 2 1 9 4 6
2 4 1 3 6 9 7 8 5
8 6 9 4 7 5 3 1 2
9 5 6 1 3 2 8 7 4
4 2 7 5 9 8 6 3 1
1 8 3 6 4 7 2 5 9
```

562
```
7 5 3 2 9 1 8 4 6
9 1 6 7 4 8 2 3 5
2 4 8 5 6 3 7 1 9
3 2 7 8 1 6 9 5 4
6 9 5 4 3 7 1 8 2
4 8 1 9 2 5 3 6 7
5 6 9 1 8 2 4 7 3
8 3 2 6 7 4 5 9 1
1 7 4 3 5 9 6 2 8
```

563
```
2 5 8 9 6 4 1 3 7
7 9 1 8 3 5 4 2 6
4 6 3 2 7 1 5 9 8
6 1 5 4 2 3 8 7 9
9 3 4 7 5 8 6 1 2
8 7 2 1 9 6 3 5 4
1 2 6 5 8 7 9 4 3
3 4 7 6 1 9 2 8 5
5 8 9 3 4 2 7 6 1
```

564
```
1 4 3 2 5 8 9 6 7
5 9 8 1 6 7 4 2 3
7 6 2 4 9 3 5 1 8
3 5 1 9 4 6 8 7 2
9 2 7 3 8 1 6 4 5
4 8 6 7 2 5 3 9 1
6 3 9 5 7 2 1 8 4
2 1 4 8 3 9 7 5 6
8 7 5 6 1 4 2 3 9
```

565
```
5 9 2 6 3 4 7 1 8
8 3 1 2 5 7 9 4 6
6 7 4 1 8 9 5 3 2
9 2 7 5 6 3 4 8 1
3 5 8 7 4 1 2 6 9
1 4 6 9 2 8 3 7 5
7 8 9 4 1 2 6 5 3
2 6 3 8 7 5 1 9 4
4 1 5 3 9 6 8 2 7
```

566
```
3 6 7 4 8 1 5 2 9
8 4 1 5 9 2 6 7 3
5 2 9 6 3 7 4 1 8
2 8 6 7 4 9 3 5 1
1 3 5 2 6 8 7 9 4
7 9 4 3 1 5 2 8 6
4 5 8 1 7 6 9 3 2
9 7 3 8 2 4 1 6 5
6 1 2 9 5 3 8 4 7
```

567
```
9 7 5 4 3 2 1 8 6
6 3 8 7 1 5 2 4 9
4 1 2 9 6 8 7 3 5
3 8 6 5 7 9 4 1 2
7 5 4 1 2 6 3 9 8
1 2 9 8 4 3 5 6 7
2 4 7 6 8 1 9 5 3
5 6 3 2 9 4 8 7 1
8 9 1 3 5 7 6 2 4
```

568
```
9 5 6 3 1 4 2 8 7
8 4 7 5 6 2 9 1 3
2 3 1 9 7 8 4 6 5
3 7 9 2 8 6 5 4 1
4 6 8 1 9 5 7 3 2
5 1 2 7 4 3 6 9 8
1 9 3 4 5 7 8 2 6
6 2 5 8 3 9 1 7 4
7 8 4 6 2 1 3 5 9
```

569
```
8 4 5 3 1 2 9 7 6
1 6 9 5 7 4 3 8 2
7 3 2 8 6 9 5 1 4
2 1 4 9 5 6 8 3 7
6 5 8 1 3 7 4 2 9
9 7 3 4 2 8 6 5 1
5 8 6 2 9 1 7 4 3
3 2 7 6 4 5 1 9 8
4 9 1 7 8 3 2 6 5
```

570
```
2 9 5 6 8 3 4 7 1
8 4 7 5 2 1 6 3 9
3 1 6 9 7 4 2 5 8
9 2 1 3 6 7 5 8 4
6 5 4 8 9 2 3 1 7
7 8 3 1 4 5 9 2 6
1 7 2 4 3 9 8 6 5
5 6 9 2 1 8 7 4 3
4 3 8 7 5 6 1 9 2
```

571
```
6 7 5 3 9 8 1 4 2
8 1 4 5 2 7 6 9 3
2 3 9 4 6 1 8 7 5
5 6 2 7 4 9 3 8 1
9 8 7 1 5 3 2 6 4
3 4 1 6 8 2 7 5 9
7 2 6 9 3 5 4 1 8
1 9 8 2 7 4 5 3 6
4 5 3 8 1 6 9 2 7
```

572
```
5 1 9 4 6 8 7 3 2
6 3 2 1 9 7 4 5 8
4 7 8 3 2 5 6 9 1
8 6 5 2 1 4 9 7 3
7 4 3 9 8 6 1 2 5
2 9 1 7 5 3 8 4 6
1 2 6 5 4 9 3 8 7
9 8 7 6 3 2 5 1 4
3 5 4 8 7 1 2 6 9
```

573
```
5 8 3 9 1 4 6 7 2
9 1 6 7 3 2 5 4 8
2 4 7 8 5 6 9 1 3
3 5 9 1 7 8 4 2 6
8 6 1 4 2 5 3 9 7
7 2 4 6 9 3 1 8 5
1 9 8 3 6 7 2 5 4
6 7 5 2 4 1 8 3 9
4 3 2 5 8 9 7 6 1
```

574
```
4 6 1 7 8 2 3 5 9
2 5 8 9 1 3 7 4 6
9 7 3 5 6 4 2 8 1
3 1 5 8 2 7 6 9 4
8 9 2 4 3 6 1 7 5
7 4 6 1 5 9 8 3 2
6 2 9 3 7 5 4 1 8
1 3 4 6 9 8 5 2 7
5 8 7 2 4 1 9 6 3
```

575
```
2 5 4 1 6 9 3 8 7
3 7 6 4 2 8 5 1 9
8 1 9 7 5 3 6 4 2
6 3 5 9 1 2 8 7 4
7 9 2 6 8 4 1 5 3
4 8 1 5 3 7 2 9 6
5 4 3 2 9 1 7 6 8
9 6 8 3 7 5 4 2 1
1 2 7 8 4 6 9 3 5
```

576
```
8 6 1 7 4 9 3 2 5
5 2 7 8 3 1 9 6 4
4 3 9 2 6 5 1 8 7
6 9 3 5 2 4 8 7 1
7 8 4 1 9 6 5 3 2
1 5 2 3 7 8 6 4 9
2 1 5 6 8 7 4 9 3
3 4 6 9 5 2 7 1 8
9 7 8 4 1 3 2 5 6
```

577
```
6 5 3 8 2 9 7 1 4
2 1 7 6 4 3 9 5 8
8 9 4 1 7 5 6 3 2
3 7 8 5 9 2 4 6 1
4 6 5 7 1 8 2 9 3
9 2 1 3 6 4 8 7 5
5 8 2 9 3 6 1 4 7
1 3 6 4 8 7 5 2 9
7 4 9 2 5 1 3 8 6
```

578
```
9 6 4 2 8 3 5 7 1
8 3 5 6 1 7 9 4 2
1 2 7 4 5 9 6 3 8
2 7 8 1 6 5 3 9 4
6 4 3 7 9 2 1 8 5
5 9 1 3 4 8 7 2 6
3 8 9 5 2 6 4 1 7
4 5 2 9 7 1 8 6 3
7 1 6 8 3 4 2 5 9
```

579
```
2 7 3 8 1 5 9 4 6
8 6 4 9 3 7 5 1 2
9 1 5 4 2 6 7 3 8
5 3 2 7 6 8 1 9 4
6 8 9 5 4 1 2 7 3
7 4 1 2 9 3 8 6 5
4 9 8 6 7 2 3 5 1
3 5 7 1 8 4 6 2 9
1 2 6 3 5 9 4 8 7
```

580
```
9 5 1 3 2 4 7 6 8
8 4 6 1 5 7 2 3 9
7 3 2 6 8 9 4 1 5
5 8 3 7 1 6 9 2 4
4 2 7 5 9 3 6 8 1
6 1 9 2 4 8 3 5 7
2 9 4 8 3 5 1 7 6
3 6 8 4 7 1 5 9 2
1 7 5 9 6 2 8 4 3
```

581

5	4	9	3	7	1	8	2	6
8	2	3	6	4	9	1	7	5
1	6	7	2	5	8	4	9	3
4	8	2	1	3	6	7	5	9
6	9	5	7	2	4	3	1	8
7	3	1	8	9	5	6	4	2
9	1	4	5	8	3	2	6	7
2	5	8	4	6	7	9	3	1
3	7	6	9	1	2	5	8	4

582

2	8	7	9	6	5	3	4	1
6	4	3	7	8	1	5	9	2
1	5	9	2	4	3	8	7	6
7	2	6	3	1	9	4	5	8
8	9	5	4	2	6	7	1	3
3	1	4	5	7	8	2	6	9
9	7	8	1	3	4	6	2	5
4	6	1	8	5	2	9	3	7
5	3	2	6	9	7	1	8	4

583

4	3	2	5	6	9	8	1	7
5	8	9	1	7	4	2	3	6
6	7	1	3	2	8	9	5	4
9	2	5	7	4	6	3	8	1
3	4	8	9	5	1	6	7	2
1	6	7	2	8	3	5	4	9
7	5	4	8	9	2	1	6	3
2	1	6	4	3	5	7	9	8
8	9	3	6	1	7	4	2	5

584

1	5	3	8	7	2	6	9	4
2	6	7	4	5	9	3	1	8
4	8	9	1	6	3	7	5	2
8	9	4	5	3	1	2	7	6
7	2	1	6	8	4	5	3	9
5	3	6	2	9	7	8	4	1
6	4	8	7	1	5	9	2	3
9	7	2	3	4	8	1	6	5
3	1	5	9	2	6	4	8	7

585

5	9	8	6	1	2	3	4	7
7	6	3	9	4	5	8	2	1
1	4	2	8	3	7	9	6	5
3	2	1	5	6	9	7	8	4
9	7	6	3	8	4	1	5	2
4	8	5	2	7	1	6	3	9
2	3	7	1	5	8	4	9	6
6	5	4	7	9	3	2	1	8
8	1	9	4	2	6	5	7	3

586

4	8	3	2	1	9	5	6	7
6	1	2	3	5	7	9	8	4
5	7	9	6	4	8	2	1	3
8	6	1	4	7	5	3	9	2
3	5	7	9	2	6	8	4	1
2	9	4	1	8	3	6	7	5
1	4	6	8	3	2	7	5	9
7	3	8	5	9	1	4	2	6
9	2	5	7	6	4	1	3	8

587

2	9	8	1	7	3	4	6	5
1	5	4	6	2	9	7	8	3
3	7	6	4	5	8	2	1	9
6	8	2	5	1	7	9	3	4
7	4	9	3	8	6	1	5	2
5	3	1	2	9	4	6	7	8
9	1	5	7	3	2	8	4	6
8	6	7	9	4	5	3	2	1
4	2	3	8	6	1	5	9	7

588

8	7	9	1	3	6	4	2	5
2	4	6	8	9	5	1	7	3
1	5	3	4	2	7	6	9	8
5	6	8	3	7	2	9	1	4
9	1	2	5	6	4	8	3	7
4	3	7	9	8	1	2	5	6
3	8	5	6	1	9	7	4	2
7	9	4	2	5	8	3	6	1
6	2	1	7	4	3	5	8	9

589

9	4	6	3	8	7	5	2	1
1	7	5	2	6	9	8	3	4
2	3	8	1	4	5	9	6	7
7	8	4	9	2	6	3	1	5
5	1	9	7	3	4	2	8	6
3	6	2	5	1	8	4	7	9
8	9	7	6	5	3	1	4	2
6	2	3	4	9	1	7	5	8
4	5	1	8	7	2	6	9	3

590

4	8	1	2	5	9	7	6	3
5	6	2	7	4	3	1	8	9
3	7	9	1	6	8	4	5	2
8	1	5	4	7	2	3	9	6
6	9	7	3	1	5	8	2	4
2	3	4	8	9	6	5	7	1
7	2	3	9	8	1	6	4	5
9	4	6	5	3	7	2	1	8
1	5	8	6	2	4	9	3	7

591

3	1	2	8	6	9	5	7	4
6	9	4	7	5	2	8	3	1
5	8	7	4	1	3	2	9	6
7	4	3	6	9	8	1	2	5
8	2	5	3	7	1	4	6	9
1	6	9	5	2	4	3	8	7
2	7	8	1	4	6	9	5	3
9	5	1	2	3	7	6	4	8
4	3	6	9	8	5	7	1	2

592

5	1	3	9	4	7	6	8	2
8	6	4	3	2	5	1	7	9
7	2	9	1	6	8	3	4	5
4	3	5	8	7	6	9	2	1
6	8	7	2	9	1	4	5	3
2	9	1	5	3	4	8	6	7
1	5	2	6	8	9	7	3	4
3	7	8	4	1	2	5	9	6
9	4	6	7	5	3	2	1	8

593

2	7	3	1	8	4	9	6	5
5	4	8	6	9	3	7	2	1
6	1	9	7	2	5	4	3	8
3	2	6	5	4	1	8	9	7
8	5	7	2	3	9	1	4	6
4	9	1	8	7	6	2	5	3
1	3	2	4	6	8	5	7	9
9	8	4	3	5	7	6	1	2
7	6	5	9	1	2	3	8	4

594

7	5	4	9	2	8	1	3	6
3	1	2	6	5	7	4	8	9
8	9	6	1	3	4	7	2	5
4	8	9	2	7	6	5	1	3
6	7	5	3	8	1	9	4	2
2	3	1	5	4	9	6	7	8
1	2	8	4	6	5	3	9	7
5	4	7	8	9	3	2	6	1
9	6	3	7	1	2	8	5	4

595

1	5	2	8	6	9	4	7	3
9	8	4	3	7	5	2	1	6
7	6	3	4	2	1	9	5	8
4	1	7	9	3	6	5	8	2
5	3	6	1	8	2	7	4	9
2	9	8	5	4	7	6	3	1
8	4	5	6	9	3	1	2	7
3	7	9	2	1	4	8	6	5
6	2	1	7	5	8	3	9	4

596

3	2	7	5	8	1	6	9	4
4	6	5	3	2	9	8	1	7
1	9	8	6	4	7	3	2	5
6	5	1	2	9	3	4	7	8
9	8	2	4	7	5	1	3	6
7	3	4	1	6	8	2	5	9
2	1	9	8	5	6	7	4	3
5	4	6	7	3	2	9	8	1
8	7	3	9	1	4	5	6	2

597

8	4	1	2	9	7	5	6	3
5	9	6	3	1	4	2	8	7
7	2	3	5	6	8	4	1	9
9	3	7	8	2	1	6	4	5
2	6	8	4	5	3	7	9	1
4	1	5	6	7	9	8	3	2
6	8	2	1	3	5	9	7	4
3	7	4	9	8	2	1	5	6
1	5	9	7	4	6	3	2	8

598

5	6	7	3	1	8	9	2	4
4	1	9	2	5	6	8	3	7
2	3	8	4	9	7	6	1	5
7	4	3	1	2	9	5	8	6
8	5	2	7	6	4	3	9	1
1	9	6	8	3	5	4	7	2
6	7	1	9	4	3	2	5	8
9	8	5	6	7	2	1	4	3
3	2	4	5	8	1	7	6	9

599

5	3	6	2	4	7	8	1	9
9	7	1	5	3	8	4	6	2
8	4	2	1	9	6	7	3	5
7	5	3	8	2	9	1	4	6
6	1	9	4	7	5	3	2	8
2	8	4	3	6	1	5	9	7
3	9	7	6	5	4	2	8	1
4	6	8	7	1	2	9	5	3
1	2	5	9	8	3	6	7	4

600

2	1	5	8	3	9	6	4	7
3	6	9	5	4	7	1	8	2
7	4	8	1	6	2	3	9	5
6	7	4	2	9	3	8	5	1
1	8	2	4	5	6	7	3	9
5	9	3	7	8	1	4	2	6
9	2	6	3	7	8	5	1	4
8	5	1	6	2	4	9	7	3
4	3	7	9	1	5	2	6	8

601

7	9	2	8	1	6	5	3	4
4	5	3	7	2	9	1	6	8
1	8	6	5	3	4	7	9	2
9	1	8	6	5	3	4	2	7
3	7	5	4	8	2	9	1	6
2	6	4	9	7	1	8	5	3
8	3	9	2	4	5	6	7	1
6	4	1	3	9	7	2	8	5
5	2	7	1	6	8	3	4	9

602

6	3	1	5	4	8	7	2	9
8	7	2	3	9	1	5	6	4
5	4	9	6	7	2	1	8	3
4	6	8	1	2	9	3	5	7
1	2	3	7	5	6	4	9	8
9	5	7	4	8	3	6	1	2
7	8	4	9	1	5	2	3	6
3	9	5	2	6	7	8	4	1
2	1	6	8	3	4	9	7	5

603

3	2	1	7	5	8	9	6	4
5	8	9	2	6	4	3	7	1
4	6	7	1	9	3	8	5	2
6	3	5	8	2	1	7	4	9
7	1	2	5	4	9	6	3	8
8	9	4	3	7	6	1	2	5
2	5	3	9	8	7	4	1	6
1	4	8	6	3	2	5	9	7
9	7	6	4	1	5	2	8	3

604

1	8	3	9	4	6	2	5	7
4	6	5	3	2	7	9	8	1
2	7	9	1	8	5	6	4	3
6	5	2	4	9	3	1	7	8
7	4	8	6	5	1	3	2	9
9	3	1	8	7	2	5	6	4
5	1	4	7	6	9	8	3	2
8	9	6	2	3	4	7	1	5
3	2	7	5	1	8	4	9	6

605

1	5	2	8	3	7	4	9	6
6	4	7	2	9	5	8	3	1
9	8	3	4	6	1	2	5	7
8	6	5	1	4	3	9	7	2
7	3	1	9	5	2	6	4	8
2	9	4	7	8	6	5	1	3
3	2	6	5	1	4	7	8	9
4	1	9	6	7	8	3	2	5
5	7	8	3	2	9	1	6	4

606

8	7	9	1	2	6	3	4	5
6	5	1	3	4	7	2	8	9
4	2	3	9	8	5	1	6	7
7	6	5	8	1	2	4	9	3
9	1	4	5	6	3	7	2	8
2	3	8	7	9	4	6	5	1
3	8	2	6	7	9	5	1	4
5	9	6	4	3	1	8	7	2
1	4	7	2	5	8	9	3	6

607

1	9	5	8	7	3	4	2	6
7	2	8	6	1	4	9	3	5
4	6	3	9	2	5	1	8	7
5	8	1	2	4	9	6	7	3
3	7	9	5	8	6	2	1	4
2	4	6	1	3	7	5	9	8
9	3	2	4	6	8	7	5	1
8	1	4	7	5	2	3	6	9
6	5	7	3	9	1	8	4	2

608

9	8	6	3	1	4	5	7	2
1	2	4	5	7	8	3	9	6
3	5	7	9	6	2	4	1	8
5	3	8	7	2	9	6	4	1
4	6	9	1	8	5	7	2	3
2	7	1	4	3	6	9	8	5
8	4	5	2	9	3	1	6	7
6	1	3	8	4	7	2	5	9
7	9	2	6	5	1	8	3	4

609

9	6	1	4	2	8	7	3	5
2	7	4	1	3	5	9	8	6
5	8	3	6	9	7	1	2	4
4	1	9	3	6	2	8	5	7
6	2	8	5	7	1	3	4	9
3	5	7	9	8	4	2	6	1
7	9	2	8	4	6	5	1	3
8	4	5	7	1	3	6	9	2
1	3	6	2	5	9	4	7	8

610

9	6	1	7	8	5	3	4	2
5	8	4	3	9	2	7	1	6
3	2	7	4	1	6	9	5	8
1	4	8	6	5	7	2	3	9
6	9	5	2	3	1	8	7	4
2	7	3	8	4	9	1	6	5
8	5	2	1	7	4	6	9	3
4	1	6	9	2	3	5	8	7
7	3	9	5	6	8	4	2	1

611

9	2	7	6	4	1	3	8	5
6	1	8	5	3	7	9	2	4
5	3	4	9	2	8	6	7	1
3	4	5	1	6	2	8	9	7
1	6	9	7	8	5	4	3	2
7	8	2	4	9	3	1	5	6
8	7	3	2	1	6	5	4	9
4	5	1	8	7	9	2	6	3
2	9	6	3	5	4	7	1	8

612

5	7	9	6	1	4	3	8	2
6	4	3	8	2	7	5	9	1
8	1	2	5	9	3	7	4	6
3	5	7	2	4	1	8	6	9
4	2	8	7	6	9	1	3	5
9	6	1	3	8	5	4	2	7
1	3	6	9	7	8	2	5	4
7	9	5	4	3	2	6	1	8
2	8	4	1	5	6	9	7	3

613

1	7	6	4	8	9	3	2	5
9	2	3	5	1	6	4	8	7
5	4	8	7	3	2	9	6	1
3	6	7	2	9	1	8	5	4
8	1	9	3	4	5	6	7	2
4	5	2	8	6	7	1	3	9
6	3	5	1	7	4	2	9	8
2	9	1	6	5	8	7	4	3
7	8	4	9	2	3	5	1	6

614

4	5	9	1	7	3	2	8	6
7	8	6	4	9	2	3	5	1
2	1	3	8	5	6	4	7	9
8	2	1	3	4	9	7	6	5
6	3	7	2	8	5	9	1	4
5	9	4	6	1	7	8	2	3
3	6	8	9	2	1	5	4	7
1	7	2	5	3	4	6	9	8
9	4	5	7	6	8	1	3	2

615

3	2	5	9	8	6	7	1	4
9	8	4	3	7	1	6	2	5
7	1	6	2	4	5	8	3	9
5	6	1	4	9	3	2	8	7
2	3	7	6	5	8	9	4	1
4	9	8	7	1	2	5	6	3
1	4	9	8	6	7	3	5	2
6	5	2	1	3	9	4	7	8
8	7	3	5	2	4	1	9	6

616

6	8	4	2	7	3	1	5	9
3	2	9	8	1	5	7	4	6
7	1	5	4	6	9	3	2	8
1	7	2	9	4	6	5	8	3
4	5	6	1	3	8	2	9	7
8	9	3	7	5	2	4	6	1
2	3	1	6	8	4	9	7	5
9	6	7	5	2	1	8	3	4
5	4	8	3	9	7	6	1	2

617

2	4	8	7	3	5	9	6	1
1	7	3	9	6	8	4	2	5
5	9	6	2	1	4	7	8	3
4	3	9	1	5	2	6	7	8
8	5	1	6	4	7	3	9	2
6	2	7	8	9	3	5	1	4
3	1	2	4	7	6	8	5	9
7	8	5	3	2	9	1	4	6
9	6	4	5	8	1	2	3	7

618

1	8	4	9	2	5	3	6	7
7	9	2	1	3	6	8	5	4
5	6	3	7	8	4	1	9	2
2	4	1	6	9	3	5	7	8
3	7	8	5	4	1	6	2	9
9	5	6	8	7	2	4	3	1
8	2	5	3	1	9	7	4	6
4	3	7	2	6	8	9	1	5
6	1	9	4	5	7	2	8	3

619

9	1	4	8	7	6	3	5	2
5	8	3	9	1	2	4	7	6
6	2	7	5	4	3	8	1	9
1	3	9	2	8	5	6	4	7
2	4	5	7	6	1	9	8	3
7	6	8	4	3	9	5	2	1
4	7	2	3	9	8	1	6	5
8	9	6	1	5	7	2	3	4
3	5	1	6	2	4	7	9	8

620

1	3	2	6	5	7	8	4	9
5	6	4	9	8	3	1	2	7
7	9	8	1	4	2	6	5	3
2	5	3	7	1	8	9	6	4
8	7	6	5	9	4	2	3	1
4	1	9	2	3	6	5	7	8
3	8	1	4	6	5	7	9	2
6	4	7	8	2	9	3	1	5
9	2	5	3	7	1	4	8	6

621

```
5 7 3 8 4 2 1 6 9
9 1 2 7 3 6 4 5 8
8 4 6 5 9 1 2 3 7
4 9 8 1 6 5 3 7 2
6 3 7 9 2 8 5 4 1
1 2 5 3 7 4 8 9 6
3 8 1 6 5 7 9 2 4
2 6 9 4 1 3 7 8 5
7 5 4 2 8 9 6 1 3
```

622

```
4 6 1 5 7 9 3 8 2
3 8 9 4 2 6 5 1 7
2 5 7 1 8 3 6 9 4
5 9 3 7 6 2 1 4 8
7 1 2 8 3 4 9 5 6
6 4 8 9 1 5 7 2 3
8 7 4 3 9 1 2 6 5
9 2 5 6 4 7 8 3 1
1 3 6 2 5 8 4 7 9
```

623

```
6 5 1 2 7 4 8 9 3
7 4 8 9 3 6 5 1 2
2 3 9 8 5 1 7 4 6
3 6 4 1 8 7 2 5 9
9 1 7 4 2 5 3 6 8
8 2 5 6 9 3 4 7 1
1 7 2 3 4 9 6 8 5
5 9 3 7 6 8 1 2 4
4 8 6 5 1 2 9 3 7
```

624

```
4 8 7 9 6 5 3 2 1
1 3 9 2 7 4 6 5 8
5 6 2 1 3 8 7 9 4
7 5 3 8 2 9 4 1 6
2 1 8 4 5 6 9 3 7
6 9 4 7 1 3 2 8 5
9 2 6 5 8 7 1 4 3
8 7 1 3 4 2 5 6 9
3 4 5 6 9 1 8 7 2
```

625

```
4 1 3 9 7 6 2 8 5
9 6 2 1 5 8 3 4 7
5 7 8 3 2 4 6 9 1
7 3 5 6 8 1 9 2 4
6 8 9 2 4 5 1 7 3
1 2 4 7 9 3 5 6 8
3 4 7 5 6 9 8 1 2
8 5 6 4 1 2 7 3 9
2 9 1 8 3 7 4 5 6
```

626

```
6 4 7 5 3 1 8 2 9
1 5 3 9 2 8 6 4 7
9 2 8 7 4 6 5 1 3
3 6 1 2 5 7 9 8 4
5 9 2 6 8 4 3 7 1
8 7 4 3 1 9 2 5 6
4 1 9 8 6 2 7 3 5
2 3 6 4 7 5 1 9 8
7 8 5 1 9 3 4 6 2
```

627

```
9 3 6 7 5 8 2 1 4
7 2 8 1 3 4 9 6 5
5 1 4 2 9 6 7 3 8
2 7 5 6 4 1 8 9 3
6 4 9 8 7 3 1 5 2
3 8 1 9 2 5 6 4 7
1 5 7 4 8 9 3 2 6
8 6 3 5 1 2 4 7 9
4 9 2 3 6 7 5 8 1
```

628

```
5 9 1 6 8 3 7 2 4
2 4 3 5 1 7 8 6 9
7 6 8 9 4 2 1 5 3
9 8 6 3 5 1 2 4 7
1 7 5 2 6 4 9 3 8
3 2 4 7 9 8 6 1 5
4 1 9 8 3 6 5 7 2
8 3 7 1 2 5 4 9 6
6 5 2 4 7 9 3 8 1
```

629

```
9 6 5 1 3 4 2 8 7
2 4 7 6 9 8 3 5 1
8 1 3 2 5 7 6 9 4
6 3 1 7 2 5 9 4 8
5 2 8 9 4 1 7 3 6
4 7 9 3 8 6 1 2 5
1 8 2 4 6 3 5 7 9
3 5 6 8 7 9 4 1 2
7 9 4 5 1 2 8 6 3
```

630

```
5 3 7 9 6 1 2 4 8
1 8 2 3 4 5 9 7 6
6 4 9 7 8 2 3 5 1
4 9 1 2 5 8 6 3 7
8 7 5 4 3 6 1 2 9
3 2 6 1 7 9 5 8 4
2 6 3 8 1 4 7 9 5
7 1 8 5 9 3 4 6 2
9 5 4 6 2 7 8 1 3
```

631

```
2 1 8 6 7 9 4 5 3
9 6 3 5 2 4 1 8 7
5 7 4 3 8 1 2 6 9
4 2 6 9 5 7 8 3 1
7 8 5 1 4 3 9 2 6
3 9 1 8 6 2 5 7 4
6 5 9 4 3 8 7 1 2
1 3 7 2 9 5 6 4 8
8 4 2 7 1 6 3 9 5
```

632

```
9 7 5 6 3 1 4 2 8
2 1 4 7 5 8 3 9 6
8 6 3 9 2 4 7 5 1
3 4 2 8 7 5 6 1 9
6 5 7 2 1 9 8 3 4
1 8 9 3 4 6 5 7 2
5 2 1 4 6 3 9 8 7
4 3 8 1 9 7 2 6 5
7 9 6 5 8 2 1 4 3
```

633

```
9 8 2 1 3 4 7 6 5
1 4 6 7 2 5 3 9 8
7 5 3 6 8 9 4 1 2
5 6 4 2 9 1 8 7 3
3 1 8 5 6 7 2 4 9
2 7 9 3 4 8 6 5 1
8 9 1 4 7 3 5 2 6
6 3 7 9 5 2 1 8 4
4 2 5 8 1 6 9 3 7
```

634

```
2 4 6 9 3 7 5 8 1
8 3 7 1 4 5 9 2 6
1 9 5 8 2 6 7 4 3
3 6 8 2 9 4 1 7 5
5 1 2 3 7 8 4 6 9
4 7 9 5 6 1 2 3 8
6 2 1 4 5 3 8 9 7
7 8 4 6 1 9 3 5 2
9 5 3 7 8 2 6 1 4
```

635

```
5 2 9 4 1 6 7 3 8
3 7 6 2 8 9 1 4 5
8 4 1 7 5 3 6 9 2
6 3 4 1 2 7 5 8 9
9 1 8 3 6 5 4 2 7
2 5 7 8 9 4 3 6 1
4 6 2 9 7 1 8 5 3
7 9 5 6 3 8 2 1 4
1 8 3 5 4 2 9 7 6
```

636

```
2 1 8 7 6 4 9 3 5
6 3 5 8 9 2 4 1 7
9 7 4 3 5 1 8 2 6
7 2 9 6 1 3 5 4 8
5 8 3 9 4 7 1 6 2
1 4 6 2 8 5 7 9 3
4 5 2 1 3 8 6 7 9
8 6 7 4 2 9 3 5 1
3 9 1 5 7 6 2 8 4
```

637

```
7 6 3 9 2 4 1 5 8
4 2 5 8 7 1 6 3 9
9 1 8 3 6 5 2 7 4
1 3 4 7 8 6 5 9 2
6 8 9 4 5 2 3 1 7
2 5 7 1 3 9 8 4 6
5 9 6 2 4 3 7 8 1
8 4 2 5 1 7 9 6 3
3 7 1 6 9 8 4 2 5
```

638

```
3 2 4 8 9 5 7 1 6
9 7 8 3 6 1 2 4 5
5 1 6 7 2 4 8 9 3
4 9 7 2 1 3 6 5 8
8 3 1 4 5 6 9 2 7
6 5 2 9 7 8 1 3 4
1 8 5 6 4 9 3 7 2
7 4 3 1 8 2 5 6 9
2 6 9 5 3 7 4 8 1
```

639

```
3 1 2 9 6 5 7 4 8
9 5 8 4 7 1 3 2 6
6 4 7 2 3 8 5 9 1
4 2 3 5 1 9 6 8 7
7 6 9 3 8 2 1 5 4
1 8 5 6 4 7 2 3 9
2 7 4 8 5 6 9 1 3
5 3 6 1 9 4 8 7 2
8 9 1 7 2 3 4 6 5
```

640

```
3 1 8 7 2 9 5 4 6
4 5 9 8 1 6 3 2 7
7 6 2 5 4 3 8 9 1
5 9 6 2 7 4 1 3 8
8 4 3 9 6 1 7 5 2
1 2 7 3 8 5 9 6 4
6 3 1 4 9 8 2 7 5
9 7 4 1 5 2 6 8 3
2 8 5 6 3 7 4 1 9
```

641

4	3	9	2	1	8	5	6	7
2	5	8	7	6	3	9	1	4
6	1	7	5	4	9	8	2	3
3	9	2	4	5	6	7	8	1
5	4	6	1	8	7	3	9	2
7	8	1	3	9	2	6	4	5
9	2	5	8	7	4	1	3	6
1	6	3	9	2	5	4	7	8
8	7	4	6	3	1	2	5	9

642

4	7	5	3	9	8	1	6	2
9	2	6	7	1	4	8	5	3
3	1	8	6	5	2	7	9	4
7	5	4	9	3	1	6	2	8
2	9	3	8	6	5	4	1	7
8	6	1	4	2	7	9	3	5
6	3	7	2	8	9	5	4	1
1	4	9	5	7	3	2	8	6
5	8	2	1	4	6	3	7	9

643

4	2	9	6	5	8	1	3	7
8	1	3	4	7	9	6	2	5
5	7	6	2	3	1	8	4	9
7	9	4	1	6	3	5	8	2
2	5	8	9	4	7	3	6	1
6	3	1	8	2	5	9	7	4
1	4	5	7	8	6	2	9	3
3	6	2	5	9	4	7	1	8
9	8	7	3	1	2	4	5	6

644

9	1	5	3	7	6	2	8	4
3	4	8	9	1	2	7	5	6
2	7	6	8	5	4	3	1	9
8	9	3	2	6	1	4	7	5
5	2	1	7	4	8	9	6	3
7	6	4	5	3	9	8	2	1
6	3	7	4	8	5	1	9	2
4	5	9	1	2	7	6	3	8
1	8	2	6	9	3	5	4	7

645

9	5	3	7	8	2	1	4	6
8	1	6	9	4	3	7	2	5
2	7	4	6	5	1	3	9	8
5	4	2	3	1	8	6	7	9
7	8	9	5	6	4	2	3	1
3	6	1	2	9	7	5	8	4
4	2	5	1	3	9	8	6	7
6	9	7	8	2	5	4	1	3
1	3	8	4	7	6	9	5	2

646

5	4	3	1	8	6	2	9	7
8	6	9	2	5	7	1	4	3
1	2	7	3	4	9	6	5	8
4	8	2	5	6	1	3	7	9
7	3	5	4	9	2	8	1	6
6	9	1	8	7	3	5	2	4
9	5	4	6	1	8	7	3	2
2	7	6	9	3	5	4	8	1
3	1	8	7	2	4	9	6	5

647

4	7	5	2	3	8	6	1	9
2	3	9	6	1	5	4	8	7
8	6	1	4	9	7	2	5	3
1	8	7	3	4	2	9	6	5
9	5	3	8	7	6	1	2	4
6	4	2	1	5	9	3	7	8
5	2	8	9	6	4	7	3	1
7	1	4	5	2	3	8	9	6
3	9	6	7	8	1	5	4	2

648

8	9	2	7	1	5	4	6	3
3	1	4	8	9	6	5	7	2
7	6	5	4	2	3	8	9	1
5	7	1	3	6	4	2	8	9
4	8	9	2	5	7	1	3	6
2	3	6	1	8	9	7	4	5
6	4	8	5	3	2	9	1	7
1	5	3	9	7	8	6	2	4
9	2	7	6	4	1	3	5	8

649

7	2	3	6	8	9	5	4	1
8	9	5	3	1	4	2	7	6
4	1	6	2	5	7	3	9	8
6	5	1	7	2	8	4	3	9
2	4	9	1	3	6	7	8	5
3	8	7	9	4	5	6	1	2
5	3	2	8	7	1	9	6	4
9	7	8	4	6	2	1	5	3
1	6	4	5	9	3	8	2	7

650

6	8	9	5	3	4	7	2	1
1	4	5	7	2	8	3	6	9
3	7	2	9	6	1	8	4	5
5	6	1	8	4	2	9	7	3
7	9	8	6	5	3	4	1	2
4	2	3	1	7	9	6	5	8
9	3	7	4	1	5	2	8	6
2	1	4	3	8	6	5	9	7
8	5	6	2	9	7	1	3	4

651

8	2	4	3	5	7	6	1	9
7	9	3	6	1	2	5	8	4
1	6	5	4	9	8	2	3	7
6	3	8	1	7	9	4	5	2
2	4	7	5	3	6	8	9	1
5	1	9	8	2	4	7	6	3
4	5	2	9	6	1	3	7	8
3	7	1	2	8	5	9	4	6
9	8	6	7	4	3	1	2	5

652

7	5	9	8	3	1	2	6	4
4	6	2	7	5	9	1	3	8
3	1	8	4	6	2	9	5	7
8	7	4	3	2	6	5	1	9
5	3	1	9	8	4	6	7	2
2	9	6	1	7	5	4	8	3
1	4	7	6	9	3	8	2	5
9	8	5	2	1	7	3	4	6
6	2	3	5	4	8	7	9	1

653

8	1	3	5	7	2	9	6	4
4	7	2	6	3	9	5	8	1
9	6	5	8	1	4	2	3	7
3	4	6	7	9	1	8	2	5
1	9	7	2	5	8	3	4	6
2	5	8	4	6	3	1	7	9
6	2	9	3	4	5	7	1	8
7	3	1	9	8	6	4	5	2
5	8	4	1	2	7	6	9	3

654

3	2	4	9	7	1	6	5	8
7	9	6	5	8	2	3	4	1
8	5	1	6	4	3	9	7	2
9	3	8	1	6	7	5	2	4
1	7	2	3	5	4	8	9	6
4	6	5	2	9	8	1	3	7
6	1	7	4	3	9	2	8	5
2	8	3	7	1	5	4	6	9
5	4	9	8	2	6	7	1	3

655

6	3	9	5	7	2	1	4	8
2	5	8	4	6	1	3	7	9
1	7	4	9	3	8	5	2	6
4	9	3	6	2	7	8	1	5
5	1	7	8	9	4	6	3	2
8	2	6	3	1	5	7	9	4
3	6	2	1	8	9	4	5	7
9	8	5	7	4	3	2	6	1
7	4	1	2	5	6	9	8	3

656

6	2	1	9	7	4	8	5	3
8	3	4	5	1	2	6	7	9
9	7	5	3	8	6	4	2	1
7	8	3	2	9	1	5	6	4
1	5	9	6	4	8	7	3	2
4	6	2	7	3	5	1	9	8
5	9	8	1	6	3	2	4	7
2	4	7	8	5	9	3	1	6
3	1	6	4	2	7	9	8	5

657

5	3	9	4	6	1	8	2	7
1	7	8	2	9	5	3	6	4
4	2	6	3	8	7	9	1	5
2	4	3	6	5	9	1	7	8
6	5	1	7	3	8	2	4	9
9	8	7	1	4	2	5	3	6
7	6	5	8	2	3	4	9	1
3	9	4	5	1	6	7	8	2
8	1	2	9	7	4	6	5	3

658

6	9	4	5	8	2	1	3	7
7	1	2	9	6	3	5	8	4
8	5	3	4	1	7	9	2	6
3	6	7	2	4	9	8	1	5
1	4	8	6	3	5	7	9	2
5	2	9	8	7	1	6	4	3
2	3	6	7	9	8	4	5	1
4	8	5	1	2	6	3	7	9
9	7	1	3	5	4	2	6	8

659

1	5	8	4	3	7	9	2	6
6	4	9	5	1	2	7	8	3
3	2	7	8	9	6	1	4	5
2	7	5	3	6	1	8	9	4
8	6	3	9	7	4	5	1	2
9	1	4	2	8	5	6	3	7
7	3	1	6	4	8	2	5	9
5	9	6	1	2	3	4	7	8
4	8	2	7	5	9	3	6	1

660

8	3	2	4	6	9	1	7	5
1	9	6	5	7	8	2	4	3
7	5	4	3	1	2	8	9	6
5	2	1	7	4	6	9	3	8
6	8	7	1	9	3	4	5	2
3	4	9	8	2	5	6	1	7
9	1	8	6	3	7	5	2	4
4	7	5	2	8	1	3	6	9
2	6	3	9	5	4	7	8	1

661

1	3	9	5	6	4	8	2	7
4	5	7	3	2	8	1	9	6
6	8	2	9	7	1	4	5	3
8	2	5	4	3	7	9	6	1
3	6	4	1	9	2	5	7	8
7	9	1	8	5	6	3	4	2
2	4	3	6	8	5	7	1	9
9	1	6	7	4	3	2	8	5
5	7	8	2	1	9	6	3	4

662

7	4	5	3	8	6	1	9	2
1	8	9	5	2	4	7	3	6
6	3	2	1	9	7	5	4	8
5	9	4	8	6	1	2	7	3
8	6	3	9	7	2	4	5	1
2	1	7	4	5	3	6	8	9
4	5	8	6	1	9	3	2	7
9	7	6	2	3	5	8	1	4
3	2	1	7	4	8	9	6	5

663

7	2	5	1	9	4	6	3	8
8	3	4	5	6	7	2	1	9
6	9	1	2	3	8	7	5	4
2	5	8	3	7	1	9	4	6
3	1	7	9	4	6	5	8	2
9	4	6	8	2	5	3	7	1
4	8	2	7	5	9	1	6	3
5	6	3	4	1	2	8	9	7
1	7	9	6	8	3	4	2	5

664

9	3	4	7	2	1	6	8	5
2	8	5	3	6	4	1	7	9
6	7	1	5	8	9	3	4	2
8	6	7	2	1	5	4	9	3
5	2	9	6	4	3	7	1	8
1	4	3	8	9	7	2	5	6
3	5	8	1	7	6	9	2	4
4	1	2	9	3	8	5	6	7
7	9	6	4	5	2	8	3	1

665

5	8	7	4	6	1	2	9	3
2	1	4	9	7	3	8	5	6
9	3	6	2	8	5	7	1	4
8	6	3	1	4	9	5	2	7
4	9	5	8	2	7	6	3	1
1	7	2	3	5	6	9	4	8
6	2	8	5	1	4	3	7	9
7	4	9	6	3	2	1	8	5
3	5	1	7	9	8	4	6	2

666

7	2	8	6	5	1	4	9	3
4	9	1	8	2	3	6	7	5
6	3	5	9	4	7	1	2	8
8	5	9	1	3	2	7	4	6
3	4	7	5	9	6	8	1	2
1	6	2	4	7	8	5	3	9
2	7	6	3	8	4	9	5	1
9	1	4	2	6	5	3	8	7
5	8	3	7	1	9	2	6	4

667

5	3	1	4	6	9	8	2	7
9	6	7	2	1	8	4	3	5
2	8	4	7	3	5	6	1	9
8	4	5	6	2	3	9	7	1
6	2	3	1	9	7	5	8	4
1	7	9	5	8	4	3	6	2
4	1	8	9	7	6	2	5	3
3	9	2	8	5	1	7	4	6
7	5	6	3	4	2	1	9	8

668

6	7	9	1	2	5	3	8	4
5	3	1	9	8	4	2	7	6
4	2	8	3	6	7	5	1	9
3	4	6	7	9	2	8	5	1
7	1	2	6	5	8	4	9	3
8	9	5	4	3	1	7	6	2
9	5	4	2	7	6	1	3	8
2	8	3	5	1	9	6	4	7
1	6	7	8	4	3	9	2	5

669

3	2	1	7	6	9	5	4	8
4	8	7	1	2	5	9	3	6
6	9	5	4	3	8	1	7	2
7	5	8	6	1	2	4	9	3
1	6	9	5	4	3	8	2	7
2	4	3	8	9	7	6	1	5
5	1	2	3	8	4	7	6	9
8	3	6	9	7	1	2	5	4
9	7	4	2	5	6	3	8	1

670

3	6	5	2	8	7	1	4	9
2	9	7	4	6	1	8	3	5
1	4	8	3	5	9	6	7	2
4	7	9	1	2	3	5	6	8
5	1	3	8	4	6	2	9	7
8	2	6	9	7	5	4	1	3
6	3	4	5	9	2	7	8	1
9	8	2	7	1	4	3	5	6
7	5	1	6	3	8	9	2	4

671

1	8	2	5	7	6	9	3	4
6	9	4	3	2	1	7	8	5
5	7	3	9	4	8	6	2	1
9	5	6	1	3	4	2	7	8
4	3	7	8	5	2	1	6	9
2	1	8	7	6	9	4	5	3
7	4	9	2	8	3	5	1	6
8	6	5	4	1	7	3	9	2
3	2	1	6	9	5	8	4	7

672

7	9	4	3	2	8	5	6	1
2	1	5	4	9	6	7	3	8
3	8	6	7	1	5	9	4	2
1	4	2	8	6	7	3	5	9
6	5	8	1	3	9	2	7	4
9	7	3	5	4	2	1	8	6
5	2	7	6	8	1	4	9	3
4	6	9	2	5	3	8	1	7
8	3	1	9	7	4	6	2	5

673

6	7	2	5	8	4	3	1	9
9	8	3	6	1	7	5	2	4
1	4	5	2	9	3	7	6	8
2	5	9	1	3	8	4	7	6
4	6	1	7	2	9	8	3	5
7	3	8	4	6	5	1	9	2
5	1	7	9	4	2	6	8	3
3	2	4	8	7	6	9	5	1
8	9	6	3	5	1	2	4	7

674

4	3	6	1	2	8	9	5	7
8	5	2	3	9	7	1	4	6
9	7	1	6	4	5	2	8	3
5	2	9	4	1	3	7	6	8
3	1	8	5	7	6	4	9	2
7	6	4	9	8	2	3	1	5
6	9	5	7	3	1	8	2	4
2	4	7	8	5	9	6	3	1
1	8	3	2	6	4	5	7	9

675

7	5	2	8	4	1	9	6	3
6	4	1	2	3	9	7	8	5
3	8	9	6	5	7	2	1	4
1	9	4	7	8	6	3	5	2
2	3	8	5	1	4	6	9	7
5	7	6	3	9	2	8	4	1
4	1	7	9	6	3	5	2	8
8	6	3	4	2	5	1	7	9
9	2	5	1	7	8	4	3	6

676

2	7	5	9	6	1	4	8	3
6	8	9	3	4	5	2	7	1
3	4	1	8	2	7	5	6	9
9	6	2	1	8	3	7	5	4
4	1	7	2	5	6	3	9	8
5	3	8	4	7	9	1	2	6
8	5	3	6	1	2	9	4	7
7	9	4	5	3	8	6	1	2
1	2	6	7	9	4	8	3	5

677

4	2	3	9	5	7	6	1	8
6	5	7	4	1	8	9	3	2
9	1	8	2	3	6	7	5	4
1	6	2	5	9	3	8	4	7
5	8	4	6	7	2	3	9	1
7	3	9	1	8	4	5	2	6
3	9	6	7	4	1	2	8	5
2	4	5	8	6	9	1	7	3
8	7	1	3	2	5	4	6	9

678

3	4	2	5	6	1	9	7	8
6	5	8	2	9	7	3	1	4
9	1	7	4	3	8	6	2	5
7	9	5	6	4	3	2	8	1
1	6	3	7	8	2	4	5	9
8	2	4	1	5	9	7	3	6
5	3	1	9	7	6	8	4	2
2	8	6	3	1	4	5	9	7
4	7	9	8	2	5	1	6	3

679

7	9	1	5	2	8	6	4	3
5	3	4	1	6	7	8	2	9
2	8	6	9	3	4	1	5	7
6	1	8	4	9	3	2	7	5
3	2	9	7	5	6	4	8	1
4	7	5	8	1	2	3	9	6
8	4	3	6	7	5	9	1	2
1	6	7	2	8	9	5	3	4
9	5	2	3	4	1	7	6	8

680

1	2	5	3	9	4	6	7	8
9	8	3	2	6	7	1	4	5
6	4	7	1	8	5	2	3	9
2	7	6	8	3	1	5	9	4
3	9	8	4	5	6	7	1	2
4	5	1	9	7	2	8	6	3
5	1	4	7	2	9	3	8	6
7	3	2	6	4	8	9	5	1
8	6	9	5	1	3	4	2	7

681

1	2	3	5	4	6	7	9	8
7	6	9	1	2	8	4	5	3
5	8	4	7	9	3	1	2	6
4	3	6	9	7	2	5	8	1
2	9	1	6	8	5	3	7	4
8	5	7	4	3	1	2	6	9
3	1	5	2	6	9	8	4	7
6	4	2	8	1	7	9	3	5
9	7	8	3	5	4	6	1	2

682

3	7	2	4	5	9	6	1	8
5	6	4	1	8	2	3	7	9
1	9	8	6	3	7	2	5	4
2	5	9	8	6	3	7	4	1
7	8	6	9	4	1	5	3	2
4	3	1	7	2	5	9	8	6
6	4	5	2	7	8	1	9	3
8	1	3	5	9	6	4	2	7
9	2	7	3	1	4	8	6	5

683

1	6	3	8	4	5	2	7	9
9	7	4	2	6	3	5	1	8
8	5	2	1	9	7	3	4	6
7	1	9	6	2	8	4	5	3
6	4	5	3	7	9	1	8	2
3	2	8	5	1	4	9	6	7
2	9	1	4	8	6	7	3	5
5	8	7	9	3	1	6	2	4
4	3	6	7	5	2	8	9	1

684

8	5	7	3	1	6	9	4	2
1	2	4	8	9	7	6	5	3
3	9	6	4	5	2	7	1	8
5	4	8	2	7	1	3	9	6
2	1	9	6	3	4	8	7	5
6	7	3	5	8	9	4	2	1
4	3	2	7	6	5	1	8	9
9	6	5	1	4	8	2	3	7
7	8	1	9	2	3	5	6	4

685

7	3	2	4	8	6	1	5	9
5	1	8	9	2	3	6	4	7
6	9	4	7	1	5	2	3	8
8	4	5	6	9	1	3	7	2
1	7	3	2	5	8	4	9	6
9	2	6	3	7	4	8	1	5
3	5	7	8	4	2	9	6	1
4	8	1	5	6	9	7	2	3
2	6	9	1	3	7	5	8	4

686

4	8	2	7	3	6	1	5	9
9	3	7	5	4	1	2	6	8
6	1	5	8	9	2	4	3	7
7	4	3	9	2	5	8	1	6
5	2	9	1	6	8	3	7	4
1	6	8	3	7	4	9	2	5
8	7	4	2	5	3	6	9	1
2	9	1	6	8	7	5	4	3
3	5	6	4	1	9	7	8	2

687

5	2	7	6	8	1	9	3	4
8	9	3	7	5	4	1	6	2
6	1	4	3	9	2	7	5	8
4	6	5	8	7	3	2	9	1
3	7	2	5	1	9	4	8	6
1	8	9	4	2	6	3	7	5
2	5	1	9	3	8	6	4	7
9	4	8	1	6	7	5	2	3
7	3	6	2	4	5	8	1	9

688

3	6	8	5	2	9	1	7	4
2	5	9	4	1	7	3	6	8
1	4	7	8	6	3	5	2	9
8	2	6	3	4	1	7	9	5
4	3	5	9	7	6	2	8	1
9	7	1	2	8	5	6	4	3
7	9	2	1	5	4	8	3	6
5	8	3	6	9	2	4	1	7
6	1	4	7	3	8	9	5	2

689

3	4	6	5	9	2	8	7	1
7	2	8	1	4	6	5	3	9
5	1	9	8	3	7	4	6	2
8	9	1	6	2	4	7	5	3
6	7	4	3	1	5	9	2	8
2	5	3	9	7	8	1	4	6
1	3	5	4	6	9	2	8	7
9	8	7	2	5	3	6	1	4
4	6	2	7	8	1	3	9	5

690

7	2	6	4	1	9	8	5	3
5	1	3	2	7	8	6	4	9
4	9	8	3	5	6	2	1	7
9	6	1	5	8	4	7	3	2
3	5	7	1	6	2	4	9	8
8	4	2	9	3	7	1	6	5
6	3	4	7	2	5	9	8	1
1	7	9	8	4	3	5	2	6
2	8	5	6	9	1	3	7	4

691

2	8	4	3	7	1	6	5	9
5	1	9	8	2	6	3	4	7
3	6	7	4	5	9	1	2	8
6	3	5	2	4	8	9	7	1
8	4	1	9	6	7	2	3	5
7	9	2	5	1	3	4	8	6
9	2	3	6	8	5	7	1	4
1	5	6	7	3	4	8	9	2
4	7	8	1	9	2	5	6	3

692

7	9	3	5	1	8	6	4	2
1	2	4	6	3	7	8	5	9
6	5	8	4	2	9	1	3	7
8	3	1	9	5	4	2	7	6
4	7	5	2	8	6	9	1	3
9	6	2	1	7	3	4	8	5
3	4	9	7	6	1	5	2	8
2	8	6	3	4	5	7	9	1
5	1	7	8	9	2	3	6	4

693

3	5	8	4	2	1	9	7	6
4	1	2	9	7	6	8	5	3
6	9	7	8	3	5	1	2	4
9	2	4	5	6	3	7	1	8
5	6	3	7	1	8	4	9	2
7	8	1	2	9	4	3	6	5
8	7	9	3	5	2	6	4	1
2	3	6	1	4	9	5	8	7
1	4	5	6	8	7	2	3	9

694

4	3	8	5	2	1	9	6	7
9	5	7	6	3	8	2	4	1
2	1	6	7	4	9	5	8	3
6	9	3	2	1	7	8	5	4
1	4	5	3	8	6	7	9	2
8	7	2	9	5	4	3	1	6
5	6	9	4	7	2	1	3	8
7	8	4	1	9	3	6	2	5
3	2	1	8	6	5	4	7	9

695

4	9	8	3	1	2	5	7	6
6	3	1	7	5	8	9	4	2
7	5	2	6	9	4	3	1	8
8	6	7	9	3	5	4	2	1
9	1	3	2	4	7	6	8	5
2	4	5	1	8	6	7	9	3
1	8	9	4	6	3	2	5	7
5	2	6	8	7	9	1	3	4
3	7	4	5	2	1	8	6	9

696

2	8	6	3	7	1	9	4	5
4	7	9	2	5	6	1	8	3
1	5	3	4	9	8	6	2	7
8	4	2	7	6	3	5	1	9
3	6	5	8	1	9	4	7	2
9	1	7	5	4	2	8	3	6
6	9	4	1	3	7	2	5	8
7	2	1	6	8	5	3	9	4
5	3	8	9	2	4	7	6	1

697

1	4	7	3	8	2	5	9	6
5	6	9	7	4	1	8	3	2
3	8	2	6	5	9	4	1	7
7	9	1	4	2	8	6	5	3
8	2	6	5	1	3	7	4	9
4	3	5	9	6	7	2	8	1
6	1	3	8	7	4	9	2	5
9	7	8	2	3	5	1	6	4
2	5	4	1	9	6	3	7	8

698

7	1	3	4	8	5	9	2	6
4	6	2	7	1	9	8	5	3
9	8	5	6	3	2	4	7	1
3	2	4	9	5	8	6	1	7
8	7	1	2	6	4	3	9	5
5	9	6	1	7	3	2	8	4
2	5	9	3	4	7	1	6	8
1	4	8	5	2	6	7	3	9
6	3	7	8	9	1	5	4	2

699

8	3	4	1	5	9	2	6	7
1	6	2	4	7	8	9	3	5
5	9	7	6	2	3	8	4	1
7	2	1	3	9	4	6	5	8
9	5	6	2	8	7	4	1	3
3	4	8	5	6	1	7	2	9
6	1	9	7	3	2	5	8	4
2	8	3	9	4	5	1	7	6
4	7	5	8	1	6	3	9	2

700

6	4	1	7	9	5	3	2	8
3	5	8	2	4	6	7	9	1
9	2	7	8	1	3	4	5	6
8	6	9	3	2	1	5	7	4
2	7	4	6	5	9	1	8	3
5	1	3	4	7	8	9	6	2
7	8	2	9	3	4	6	1	5
4	9	5	1	6	2	8	3	7
1	3	6	5	8	7	2	4	9

701

8	3	2	5	9	4	7	1	6
5	7	4	1	8	6	9	3	2
9	6	1	3	2	7	8	4	5
2	1	5	7	6	3	4	9	8
4	9	7	8	1	5	6	2	3
6	8	3	9	4	2	1	5	7
7	4	6	2	5	1	3	8	9
1	2	8	6	3	9	5	7	4
3	5	9	4	7	8	2	6	1

702

7	1	2	3	6	8	4	5	9
5	8	4	7	9	2	3	1	6
9	6	3	1	4	5	8	7	2
3	4	6	9	5	1	2	8	7
2	7	1	6	8	4	5	9	3
8	5	9	2	7	3	6	4	1
4	9	7	8	2	6	1	3	5
1	2	8	5	3	9	7	6	4
6	3	5	4	1	7	9	2	8

703

3	7	1	2	5	9	6	4	8
2	5	9	6	4	8	3	1	7
4	8	6	1	7	3	2	5	9
7	9	4	3	8	2	1	6	5
1	2	5	9	6	7	8	3	4
8	6	3	5	1	4	7	9	2
9	1	8	7	3	5	4	2	6
5	3	7	4	2	6	9	8	1
6	4	2	8	9	1	5	7	3

704

6	3	4	7	2	5	8	1	9
5	8	7	3	1	9	2	6	4
2	1	9	6	4	8	5	7	3
8	9	6	5	7	4	3	2	1
4	2	1	9	6	3	7	8	5
3	7	5	1	8	2	4	9	6
7	4	3	2	9	6	1	5	8
1	6	8	4	5	7	9	3	2
9	5	2	8	3	1	6	4	7

705

3	9	7	6	1	2	5	4	8
8	5	1	9	3	4	7	6	2
4	6	2	8	5	7	1	3	9
2	8	3	5	7	1	4	9	6
6	7	5	4	9	3	8	2	1
9	1	4	2	8	6	3	5	7
1	3	9	7	6	5	2	8	4
5	4	8	1	2	9	6	7	3
7	2	6	3	4	8	9	1	5

706

2	3	8	6	4	5	1	9	7
9	6	4	3	7	1	2	8	5
1	7	5	8	9	2	3	6	4
3	8	2	1	5	7	9	4	6
5	4	6	2	8	9	7	3	1
7	1	9	4	6	3	5	2	8
4	9	1	5	3	8	6	7	2
8	2	3	7	1	6	4	5	9
6	5	7	9	2	4	8	1	3

707

9	1	7	6	3	8	4	5	2
8	3	2	1	5	4	6	9	7
4	5	6	2	9	7	1	8	3
3	6	9	4	2	1	5	7	8
2	4	8	5	7	6	3	1	9
1	7	5	9	8	3	2	6	4
5	2	4	8	1	9	7	3	6
6	9	3	7	4	5	8	2	1
7	8	1	3	6	2	9	4	5

708

7	9	6	3	5	2	1	8	4
8	3	2	1	9	4	6	5	7
4	1	5	7	8	6	3	9	2
1	8	3	9	4	7	5	2	6
5	7	9	6	2	3	4	1	8
2	6	4	5	1	8	9	7	3
9	4	7	8	6	1	2	3	5
6	5	8	2	3	9	7	4	1
3	2	1	4	7	5	8	6	9

709

9	1	3	7	6	2	5	4	8
7	8	4	1	3	5	6	9	2
6	5	2	9	8	4	3	1	7
5	2	9	4	1	3	8	7	6
8	6	7	5	2	9	4	3	1
3	4	1	6	7	8	2	5	9
4	3	6	2	9	7	1	8	5
1	7	8	3	5	6	9	2	4
2	9	5	8	4	1	7	6	3

710

9	5	7	8	3	6	1	2	4
3	2	8	4	1	9	5	7	6
6	4	1	7	5	2	8	3	9
2	7	3	6	4	5	9	1	8
5	8	4	1	9	3	2	6	7
1	6	9	2	8	7	3	4	5
8	1	5	3	7	4	6	9	2
4	9	6	5	2	1	7	8	3
7	3	2	9	6	8	4	5	1

711

9	2	6	8	3	4	5	1	7
8	1	5	2	7	6	3	9	4
3	4	7	5	9	1	6	2	8
4	6	2	9	1	5	8	7	3
1	8	3	4	2	7	9	6	5
7	5	9	6	8	3	1	4	2
5	3	1	7	4	9	2	8	6
6	7	8	1	5	2	4	3	9
2	9	4	3	6	8	7	5	1

712

7	3	8	9	2	6	4	5	1
1	6	4	5	7	8	3	9	2
2	9	5	1	4	3	6	8	7
5	1	2	4	6	9	8	7	3
6	7	9	8	3	5	2	1	4
4	8	3	2	1	7	9	6	5
3	4	6	7	9	1	5	2	8
8	2	1	6	5	4	7	3	9
9	5	7	3	8	2	1	4	6

713

7	6	2	9	4	5	1	8	3
4	3	8	7	2	1	6	5	9
9	1	5	3	6	8	7	2	4
5	2	4	1	3	7	8	9	6
8	7	6	5	9	4	2	3	1
1	9	3	2	8	6	5	4	7
2	5	9	6	7	3	4	1	8
3	4	7	8	1	2	9	6	5
6	8	1	4	5	9	3	7	2

714

9	1	4	7	3	8	2	5	6
6	5	8	2	4	1	9	7	3
3	2	7	9	5	6	4	8	1
5	7	3	6	1	4	8	9	2
8	4	9	3	7	2	1	6	5
2	6	1	5	8	9	3	4	7
1	3	6	8	9	5	7	2	4
7	9	2	4	6	3	5	1	8
4	8	5	1	2	7	6	3	9

715

9	8	1	6	4	2	7	3	5
5	4	7	9	1	3	6	8	2
3	6	2	5	8	7	9	4	1
2	5	8	3	6	9	1	7	4
7	9	3	1	5	4	2	6	8
4	1	6	2	7	8	5	9	3
6	2	9	4	3	1	8	5	7
8	3	5	7	2	6	4	1	9
1	7	4	8	9	5	3	2	6

716

9	4	5	3	7	2	1	6	8
2	6	8	9	4	1	5	3	7
7	1	3	8	6	5	9	2	4
4	3	2	1	5	8	6	7	9
5	9	7	2	3	6	4	8	1
6	8	1	4	9	7	3	5	2
1	5	6	7	2	4	8	9	3
3	2	4	5	8	9	7	1	6
8	7	9	6	1	3	2	4	5

717

6	5	9	7	3	2	1	8	4
7	4	1	8	6	9	5	3	2
8	2	3	1	4	5	6	9	7
1	6	8	4	9	3	7	2	5
4	9	2	5	7	8	3	6	1
3	7	5	6	2	1	9	4	8
2	1	6	9	5	4	8	7	3
9	8	4	3	1	7	2	5	6
5	3	7	2	8	6	4	1	9

718

3	7	6	2	9	8	4	5	1
1	9	5	4	7	3	2	8	6
4	2	8	5	1	6	9	3	7
2	5	7	9	6	1	8	4	3
6	1	3	8	2	4	7	9	5
9	8	4	7	3	5	1	6	2
7	6	9	3	8	2	5	1	4
5	3	2	1	4	9	6	7	8
8	4	1	6	5	7	3	2	9

719

4	8	3	9	5	7	1	2	6
9	1	6	8	3	2	7	4	5
7	5	2	4	1	6	3	9	8
8	3	1	6	7	4	2	5	9
5	6	7	3	2	9	8	1	4
2	9	4	1	8	5	6	7	3
1	4	5	2	6	8	9	3	7
6	2	9	7	4	3	5	8	1
3	7	8	5	9	1	4	6	2

720

8	4	2	1	5	6	3	7	9
5	1	3	2	7	9	8	6	4
7	6	9	4	3	8	2	5	1
9	7	5	6	2	3	1	4	8
2	8	6	9	4	1	5	3	7
1	3	4	7	8	5	9	2	6
3	2	1	8	6	7	4	9	5
6	5	8	3	9	4	7	1	2
4	9	7	5	1	2	6	8	3

721

7	8	6	9	3	1	2	5	4
9	2	4	7	6	5	8	1	3
5	3	1	2	8	4	7	6	9
3	1	2	5	4	9	6	8	7
6	5	8	3	1	7	4	9	2
4	7	9	6	2	8	1	3	5
2	9	5	8	7	6	3	4	1
1	6	7	4	5	3	9	2	8
8	4	3	1	9	2	5	7	6

722

1	9	5	7	3	6	4	8	2
2	8	3	1	9	4	7	5	6
7	6	4	8	5	2	9	1	3
6	2	7	9	8	3	1	4	5
8	3	9	4	1	5	6	2	7
4	5	1	2	6	7	3	9	8
9	4	2	6	7	8	5	3	1
5	1	6	3	2	9	8	7	4
3	7	8	5	4	1	2	6	9

723

2	1	9	8	4	7	3	6	5
6	3	7	9	2	5	1	8	4
4	8	5	6	3	1	2	7	9
1	6	8	2	7	4	9	5	3
9	4	3	1	5	6	7	2	8
5	7	2	3	8	9	4	1	6
3	2	6	4	1	8	5	9	7
7	9	4	5	6	2	8	3	1
8	5	1	7	9	3	6	4	2

724

9	8	6	7	1	2	4	3	5
7	3	5	6	8	4	9	1	2
2	4	1	3	5	9	6	7	8
8	5	3	4	9	7	2	6	1
1	9	7	2	6	8	3	5	4
4	6	2	1	3	5	8	9	7
3	1	8	5	2	6	7	4	9
6	2	4	9	7	1	5	8	3
5	7	9	8	4	3	1	2	6

725

2	7	1	9	5	8	6	3	4
8	6	3	1	4	2	7	5	9
5	4	9	3	6	7	8	1	2
4	5	7	2	1	6	3	9	8
3	1	6	5	8	9	4	2	7
9	2	8	7	3	4	5	6	1
7	9	4	6	2	3	1	8	5
6	8	5	4	9	1	2	7	3
1	3	2	8	7	5	9	4	6

726

4	8	9	6	5	7	3	1	2
1	3	7	9	4	2	8	5	6
6	5	2	8	1	3	9	4	7
7	2	3	4	6	5	1	8	9
8	4	6	1	3	9	2	7	5
9	1	5	2	7	8	6	3	4
3	6	1	5	9	4	7	2	8
2	9	4	7	8	1	5	6	3
5	7	8	3	2	6	4	9	1

727

5	6	3	4	7	2	8	9	1
8	4	1	6	9	3	2	5	7
7	9	2	5	1	8	6	3	4
3	5	7	9	2	1	4	6	8
6	2	4	8	5	7	9	1	3
1	8	9	3	6	4	7	2	5
2	7	8	1	3	9	5	4	6
4	1	6	2	8	5	3	7	9
9	3	5	7	4	6	1	8	2

728

8	7	3	4	2	5	9	6	1
1	6	5	7	3	9	4	2	8
4	2	9	6	8	1	7	3	5
6	9	1	2	5	7	3	8	4
7	4	8	3	9	6	1	5	2
3	5	2	1	4	8	6	9	7
9	3	4	5	7	2	8	1	6
5	8	6	9	1	4	2	7	3
2	1	7	8	6	3	5	4	9

729

2	4	7	8	3	1	6	9	5
8	9	6	4	7	5	2	3	1
1	5	3	2	9	6	7	8	4
4	7	5	9	2	3	8	1	6
6	3	8	1	5	7	4	2	9
9	1	2	6	4	8	3	5	7
5	2	4	3	6	9	1	7	8
3	8	9	7	1	4	5	6	2
7	6	1	5	8	2	9	4	3

730

7	9	6	4	3	5	1	8	2
4	3	8	2	6	1	9	5	7
1	2	5	7	9	8	6	3	4
3	5	1	6	7	9	2	4	8
8	4	9	3	5	2	7	6	1
2	6	7	1	8	4	5	9	3
9	1	3	5	4	7	8	2	6
6	8	2	9	1	3	4	7	5
5	7	4	8	2	6	3	1	9

731

2	4	6	8	1	7	3	9	5
9	8	1	4	5	3	6	7	2
5	7	3	2	9	6	1	8	4
7	3	5	1	4	2	9	6	8
4	1	8	5	6	9	2	3	7
6	9	2	3	7	8	5	4	1
8	6	9	7	2	5	4	1	3
3	2	4	9	8	1	7	5	6
1	5	7	6	3	4	8	2	9

732

8	4	5	3	9	1	2	6	7
2	6	9	8	4	7	5	3	1
3	7	1	5	2	6	9	8	4
4	3	7	9	1	8	6	5	2
9	2	6	7	3	5	4	1	8
1	5	8	2	6	4	7	9	3
7	1	4	6	8	9	3	2	5
5	9	2	1	7	3	8	4	6
6	8	3	4	5	2	1	7	9

733

9	7	5	4	2	1	6	3	8
6	4	2	9	8	3	7	5	1
8	3	1	5	6	7	2	4	9
5	8	9	6	7	4	3	1	2
4	1	7	8	3	2	5	9	6
3	2	6	1	5	9	4	8	7
7	5	4	2	1	8	9	6	3
2	9	8	3	4	6	1	7	5
1	6	3	7	9	5	8	2	4

734

5	6	7	4	3	9	1	2	8
8	3	4	2	6	1	5	9	7
9	1	2	7	8	5	6	3	4
3	2	8	6	5	4	7	1	9
6	5	1	9	7	3	4	8	2
7	4	9	1	2	8	3	5	6
1	9	5	8	4	6	2	7	3
2	8	6	3	1	7	9	4	5
4	7	3	5	9	2	8	6	1

735

5	3	2	9	1	4	8	6	7
1	6	9	8	2	7	5	4	3
8	4	7	6	5	3	9	2	1
3	8	1	4	9	5	2	7	6
9	2	6	7	8	1	4	3	5
7	5	4	3	6	2	1	8	9
6	1	3	5	4	8	7	9	2
4	9	5	2	7	6	3	1	8
2	7	8	1	3	9	6	5	4

736

6	3	8	4	2	1	7	9	5
2	1	7	5	9	8	4	6	3
9	5	4	7	3	6	1	8	2
3	2	5	8	4	9	6	7	1
7	8	9	6	1	5	2	3	4
4	6	1	3	7	2	9	5	8
5	7	6	2	8	4	3	1	9
1	4	3	9	5	7	8	2	6
8	9	2	1	6	3	5	4	7

737

5	3	4	9	6	7	2	8	1
7	1	8	4	2	3	5	9	6
9	2	6	1	5	8	7	3	4
8	4	2	3	1	6	9	7	5
3	9	7	5	8	4	1	6	2
1	6	5	7	9	2	8	4	3
2	7	1	6	4	9	3	5	8
4	5	9	8	3	1	6	2	7
6	8	3	2	7	5	4	1	9

738

6	8	9	4	2	7	3	5	1
2	3	7	5	6	1	4	8	9
4	5	1	3	8	9	7	2	6
3	1	4	2	5	6	9	7	8
5	7	6	8	9	4	2	1	3
8	9	2	7	1	3	5	6	4
9	2	8	1	4	5	6	3	7
1	6	3	9	7	2	8	4	5
7	4	5	6	3	8	1	9	2

739

8	5	7	6	4	3	9	2	1
4	2	3	1	7	9	5	6	8
9	1	6	2	5	8	3	4	7
7	8	9	5	2	6	4	1	3
2	3	1	7	9	4	6	8	5
5	6	4	8	3	1	7	9	2
3	4	8	9	1	7	2	5	6
6	9	5	3	8	2	1	7	4
1	7	2	4	6	5	8	3	9

740

3	2	8	7	4	9	1	5	6
7	6	9	5	1	2	8	3	4
1	4	5	6	3	8	9	7	2
8	9	4	1	5	3	2	6	7
6	5	3	9	2	7	4	1	8
2	1	7	4	8	6	3	9	5
9	8	2	3	7	5	6	4	1
5	3	1	8	6	4	7	2	9
4	7	6	2	9	1	5	8	3

741
```
4 7 2 1 5 9 3 6 8
6 1 5 8 3 2 7 9 4
8 9 3 6 4 7 5 2 1
2 6 1 3 7 8 4 5 9
3 8 9 4 2 5 6 1 7
5 4 7 9 6 1 8 3 2
1 5 4 2 8 3 9 7 6
7 2 8 5 9 6 1 4 3
9 3 6 7 1 4 2 8 5
```

742
```
4 8 6 3 5 9 7 1 2
7 1 5 4 2 8 6 9 3
3 9 2 7 6 1 8 5 4
1 7 4 8 9 2 3 6 5
2 3 8 5 4 6 1 7 9
5 6 9 1 3 7 4 2 8
6 4 3 2 7 5 9 8 1
8 5 7 9 1 4 2 3 6
9 2 1 6 8 3 5 4 7
```

743
```
5 6 9 1 8 4 7 2 3
2 1 7 3 5 9 6 8 4
3 4 8 7 2 6 5 1 9
4 2 1 6 3 8 9 7 5
8 3 5 2 9 7 4 6 1
9 7 6 5 4 1 2 3 8
6 8 3 9 7 5 1 4 2
1 9 2 4 6 3 8 5 7
7 5 4 8 1 2 3 9 6
```

744
```
5 1 6 8 4 2 3 7 9
8 2 9 3 5 7 4 1 6
3 7 4 6 1 9 5 2 8
2 4 3 7 9 5 6 8 1
9 5 8 4 6 1 7 3 2
7 6 1 2 3 8 9 4 5
1 3 7 5 8 6 2 9 4
4 9 5 1 2 3 8 6 7
6 8 2 9 7 4 1 5 3
```

745
```
1 2 5 6 4 8 3 9 7
9 7 6 5 2 3 8 4 1
3 8 4 1 9 7 2 6 5
6 4 8 3 5 9 1 7 2
5 3 1 7 6 2 9 8 4
2 9 7 8 1 4 6 5 3
8 1 3 9 7 5 4 2 6
4 5 9 2 3 6 7 1 8
7 6 2 4 8 1 5 3 9
```

746
```
6 4 1 3 5 7 8 9 2
3 8 2 4 1 9 7 5 6
7 5 9 8 6 2 1 4 3
2 9 5 7 3 1 4 6 8
1 6 3 5 8 4 2 7 9
4 7 8 9 2 6 5 3 1
9 2 4 6 7 8 3 1 5
8 3 7 1 9 5 6 2 4
5 1 6 2 4 3 9 8 7
```

747
```
5 4 1 3 8 7 2 9 6
3 2 7 4 9 6 8 1 5
8 9 6 5 1 2 7 3 4
7 5 2 6 4 1 9 8 3
6 8 4 2 3 9 1 5 7
1 3 9 7 5 8 4 6 2
9 7 3 1 2 5 6 4 8
4 6 8 9 7 3 5 2 1
2 1 5 8 6 4 3 7 9
```

748
```
6 5 9 1 4 3 2 7 8
7 4 1 2 6 8 9 3 5
2 3 8 5 9 7 4 1 6
5 7 2 3 1 4 6 8 9
3 8 4 6 5 9 1 2 7
1 9 6 8 7 2 3 5 4
9 2 5 4 8 1 7 6 3
4 6 3 7 2 5 8 9 1
8 1 7 9 3 6 5 4 2
```

749
```
3 8 9 4 1 6 7 5 2
5 2 6 3 7 9 1 8 4
1 4 7 8 2 5 3 9 6
6 5 2 1 9 3 8 4 7
7 3 4 5 8 2 9 6 1
9 1 8 6 4 7 5 2 3
8 6 3 7 5 4 2 1 9
2 7 5 9 6 1 4 3 8
4 9 1 2 3 8 6 7 5
```

750
```
2 4 7 8 1 6 5 3 9
9 8 5 3 2 7 6 1 4
3 1 6 4 9 5 2 8 7
8 6 3 1 4 2 9 7 5
1 7 2 5 3 9 8 4 6
5 9 4 7 6 8 3 2 1
7 5 9 2 8 1 4 6 3
4 2 1 6 5 3 7 9 8
6 3 8 9 7 4 1 5 2
```

751
```
6 3 2 1 7 5 9 8 4
7 8 5 6 9 4 3 1 2
4 1 9 3 2 8 5 7 6
5 2 7 8 4 3 6 9 1
8 4 6 2 1 9 7 3 5
3 9 1 5 6 7 4 2 8
1 6 4 7 3 2 8 5 9
9 7 8 4 5 1 2 6 3
2 5 3 9 8 6 1 4 7
```

752
```
6 7 9 2 4 1 5 8 3
4 5 3 6 9 8 7 1 2
2 1 8 5 3 7 6 9 4
7 3 5 1 8 9 4 2 6
9 2 4 7 5 6 8 3 1
8 6 1 3 2 4 9 5 7
1 8 2 4 7 5 3 6 9
5 4 6 9 1 3 2 7 8
3 9 7 8 6 2 1 4 5
```

753
```
9 5 7 4 2 6 3 8 1
8 1 4 7 3 5 2 9 6
6 3 2 1 8 9 5 7 4
4 8 9 3 6 7 1 2 5
3 7 6 5 1 2 9 4 8
1 2 5 9 4 8 7 6 3
5 9 1 6 7 4 8 3 2
2 6 3 8 9 1 4 5 7
7 4 8 2 5 3 6 1 9
```

754
```
2 3 8 1 5 7 9 4 6
4 9 1 6 2 3 8 5 7
6 7 5 8 9 4 3 2 1
7 4 9 5 3 6 2 1 8
1 2 6 4 7 8 5 3 9
5 8 3 9 1 2 7 6 4
9 6 4 3 8 5 1 7 2
8 5 2 7 6 1 4 9 3
3 1 7 2 4 9 6 8 5
```

755
```
9 1 8 5 4 3 2 6 7
4 5 3 7 2 6 1 8 9
6 2 7 8 9 1 5 4 3
2 4 1 3 8 5 9 7 6
7 6 9 2 1 4 3 5 8
8 3 5 6 7 9 4 1 2
1 7 2 4 3 8 6 9 5
5 8 4 9 6 2 7 3 1
3 9 6 1 5 7 8 2 4
```

756
```
2 6 4 5 3 8 9 7 1
3 8 5 9 1 7 6 2 4
7 1 9 2 6 4 3 5 8
5 7 3 8 4 6 2 1 9
8 9 2 1 7 5 4 3 6
1 4 6 3 9 2 7 8 5
9 2 7 6 8 1 5 4 3
6 5 1 4 2 3 8 9 7
4 3 8 7 5 9 1 6 2
```

757
```
2 6 5 7 9 1 8 4 3
8 9 7 4 6 3 5 2 1
1 3 4 8 2 5 7 9 6
9 1 6 3 5 8 2 7 4
4 8 2 9 7 6 3 1 5
7 5 3 2 1 4 6 8 9
6 4 8 1 3 7 9 5 2
5 7 9 6 4 2 1 3 8
3 2 1 5 8 9 4 6 7
```

758
```
8 6 4 7 1 2 3 5 9
5 7 3 6 9 8 4 2 1
2 9 1 4 5 3 7 8 6
3 4 8 1 6 9 2 7 5
6 1 2 3 7 5 9 4 8
7 5 9 2 8 4 6 1 3
1 3 6 8 4 7 5 9 2
9 2 7 5 3 1 8 6 4
4 8 5 9 2 6 1 3 7
```

759
```
6 1 5 3 7 9 8 4 2
7 9 3 8 4 2 6 1 5
4 2 8 6 1 5 3 7 9
9 7 6 4 5 3 1 2 8
5 8 1 7 2 6 9 3 4
2 3 4 1 9 8 7 5 6
3 4 9 2 6 1 5 8 7
8 6 2 5 3 7 4 9 1
1 5 7 9 8 4 2 6 3
```

760
```
2 7 1 5 6 4 8 9 3
8 9 4 3 1 7 6 5 2
3 6 5 9 8 2 7 4 1
7 2 9 8 4 5 3 1 6
1 4 3 7 9 6 2 8 5
6 5 8 2 3 1 4 7 9
5 3 7 4 2 9 1 6 8
4 8 6 1 5 3 9 2 7
9 1 2 6 7 8 5 3 4
```

761

3	5	1	7	2	8	6	9	4
6	9	2	3	1	4	7	8	5
7	8	4	9	5	6	3	2	1
8	6	5	4	9	7	2	1	3
9	2	3	1	6	5	4	7	8
1	4	7	2	8	3	5	6	9
4	3	9	6	7	1	8	5	2
2	7	8	5	3	9	1	4	6
5	1	6	8	4	2	9	3	7

762

9	2	8	6	7	3	5	4	1
6	7	4	8	1	5	2	9	3
3	1	5	9	2	4	6	8	7
1	5	9	4	3	8	7	6	2
2	6	3	5	9	7	8	1	4
4	8	7	1	6	2	9	3	5
7	9	2	3	4	6	1	5	8
8	3	6	7	5	1	4	2	9
5	4	1	2	8	9	3	7	6

763

4	1	3	9	5	6	8	2	7
6	7	5	8	2	4	1	9	3
2	9	8	1	3	7	6	4	5
7	4	6	2	8	1	3	5	9
5	2	9	4	6	3	7	8	1
3	8	1	5	7	9	2	6	4
9	6	2	7	1	5	4	3	8
1	3	4	6	9	8	5	7	2
8	5	7	3	4	2	9	1	6

764

9	2	7	4	3	6	8	5	1
6	5	8	7	9	1	2	4	3
4	1	3	8	5	2	7	9	6
2	7	4	5	1	3	6	8	9
3	6	5	9	4	8	1	7	2
8	9	1	6	2	7	5	3	4
1	8	9	2	7	4	3	6	5
5	3	6	1	8	9	4	2	7
7	4	2	3	6	5	9	1	8

765

1	6	2	3	7	8	4	9	5
4	5	7	1	9	2	6	3	8
8	3	9	6	4	5	2	7	1
6	8	1	9	3	4	5	2	7
5	7	3	2	8	6	1	4	9
9	2	4	7	5	1	3	8	6
3	4	8	5	6	7	9	1	2
2	9	6	8	1	3	7	5	4
7	1	5	4	2	9	8	6	3

766

4	6	9	1	8	7	5	3	2
1	7	5	3	2	6	9	8	4
3	8	2	9	5	4	1	7	6
6	9	7	5	3	8	2	4	1
5	3	1	2	4	9	8	6	7
8	2	4	7	6	1	3	5	9
9	5	3	6	7	2	4	1	8
7	1	8	4	9	5	6	2	3
2	4	6	8	1	3	7	9	5

767

3	1	5	7	2	4	6	8	9
6	4	2	9	3	8	5	7	1
7	8	9	1	6	5	4	3	2
1	9	6	5	8	3	2	4	7
2	7	8	4	9	1	3	5	6
4	5	3	6	7	2	9	1	8
8	3	1	2	5	9	7	6	4
9	6	4	3	1	7	8	2	5
5	2	7	8	4	6	1	9	3

768

9	8	1	3	7	4	2	5	6
5	6	7	9	8	2	4	3	1
3	2	4	1	6	5	7	9	8
4	9	8	6	5	3	1	7	2
2	7	3	4	1	8	5	6	9
1	5	6	7	2	9	8	4	3
6	1	5	2	9	7	3	8	4
8	4	9	5	3	1	6	2	7
7	3	2	8	4	6	9	1	5

769

1	6	4	3	2	8	7	9	5
9	2	8	6	7	5	4	1	3
7	5	3	9	1	4	2	8	6
4	1	7	2	8	6	3	5	9
8	3	5	1	4	9	6	7	2
2	9	6	5	3	7	8	4	1
6	7	1	8	9	2	5	3	4
3	4	2	7	5	1	9	6	8
5	8	9	4	6	3	1	2	7

770

6	9	3	8	5	2	7	4	1
5	4	2	7	6	1	8	9	3
1	7	8	9	3	4	5	2	6
4	2	5	3	1	8	6	7	9
3	1	6	4	7	9	2	5	8
9	8	7	6	2	5	3	1	4
8	3	1	2	4	7	9	6	5
7	5	9	1	8	6	4	3	2
2	6	4	5	9	3	1	8	7

771

6	5	7	4	9	1	2	8	3
9	2	4	8	3	5	1	7	6
8	3	1	7	2	6	4	9	5
3	4	2	5	1	7	9	6	8
5	7	8	2	6	9	3	4	1
1	6	9	3	8	4	5	2	7
2	1	5	9	7	8	6	3	4
7	9	6	1	4	3	8	5	2
4	8	3	6	5	2	7	1	9

772

2	4	5	9	8	1	3	7	6
9	3	6	5	2	7	1	8	4
7	1	8	4	6	3	2	5	9
8	5	7	3	4	2	9	6	1
4	9	1	8	5	6	7	2	3
6	2	3	1	7	9	8	4	5
3	8	2	6	9	5	4	1	7
1	6	4	7	3	8	5	9	2
5	7	9	2	1	4	6	3	8

773

3	9	5	8	7	6	2	4	1
8	2	1	9	3	4	5	6	7
7	6	4	5	2	1	9	3	8
5	8	2	7	1	3	6	9	4
1	3	6	2	4	9	8	7	5
9	4	7	6	5	8	1	2	3
6	7	9	3	8	5	4	1	2
2	1	8	4	6	7	3	5	9
4	5	3	1	9	2	7	8	6

774

1	6	5	3	7	4	9	2	8
4	2	9	1	8	6	7	3	5
3	8	7	9	5	2	4	6	1
6	9	3	5	4	8	1	7	2
8	4	2	7	6	1	3	5	9
7	5	1	2	3	9	8	4	6
5	1	4	8	2	3	6	9	7
9	7	6	4	1	5	2	8	3
2	3	8	6	9	7	5	1	4

775

9	7	4	8	5	2	1	6	3
5	6	2	4	1	3	7	9	8
1	3	8	9	7	6	2	5	4
7	1	6	3	4	9	8	2	5
2	4	5	7	6	8	3	1	9
3	8	9	5	2	1	6	4	7
8	5	1	2	9	7	4	3	6
4	2	7	6	3	5	9	8	1
6	9	3	1	8	4	5	7	2

776

9	6	2	4	5	1	3	7	8
8	4	3	7	6	9	2	1	5
7	5	1	2	8	3	4	6	9
1	7	8	9	3	6	5	4	2
5	9	4	8	2	7	6	3	1
3	2	6	5	1	4	8	9	7
6	1	5	3	7	8	9	2	4
2	3	9	1	4	5	7	8	6
4	8	7	6	9	2	1	5	3

777

4	5	1	2	9	6	8	3	7
8	2	3	5	7	1	6	9	4
9	6	7	8	4	3	1	5	2
5	1	4	7	6	9	2	8	3
6	3	2	4	1	8	5	7	9
7	8	9	3	5	2	4	1	6
2	4	8	9	3	5	7	6	1
1	9	5	6	2	7	3	4	8
3	7	6	1	8	4	9	2	5

778

6	2	7	3	1	9	4	5	8
4	3	5	7	2	8	9	1	6
8	9	1	5	6	4	7	3	2
3	7	4	1	9	6	8	2	5
5	8	6	4	7	2	1	9	3
9	1	2	8	3	5	6	4	7
7	5	8	9	4	3	2	6	1
1	6	9	2	5	7	3	8	4
2	4	3	6	8	1	5	7	9

779

3	6	4	1	8	9	2	5	7
8	5	9	2	4	7	1	3	6
1	7	2	3	6	5	9	4	8
9	4	6	5	1	2	8	7	3
7	3	8	4	9	6	5	1	2
2	1	5	7	3	8	4	6	9
4	2	1	9	7	3	6	8	5
6	9	3	8	5	1	7	2	4
5	8	7	6	2	4	3	9	1

780

7	4	1	2	9	6	8	5	3
5	3	2	1	8	4	6	9	7
6	8	9	7	5	3	4	1	2
4	2	3	6	1	5	7	8	9
1	6	7	9	2	8	3	4	5
9	5	8	4	3	7	1	2	6
2	1	6	3	4	9	5	7	8
8	7	4	5	6	2	9	3	1
3	9	5	8	7	1	2	6	4

781

```
7 9 3 2 8 4 6 1 5
1 5 8 7 6 3 9 2 4
2 6 4 5 1 9 7 3 8
9 1 2 4 7 6 5 8 3
5 4 6 9 3 8 2 7 1
8 3 7 1 2 5 4 9 6
3 7 1 6 5 2 8 4 9
6 2 9 8 4 1 3 5 7
4 8 5 3 9 7 1 6 2
```

782

```
7 2 8 6 1 3 4 9 5
1 9 6 4 5 7 3 2 8
4 5 3 9 2 8 1 7 6
9 6 5 1 4 2 8 3 7
8 1 4 7 3 9 5 6 2
3 7 2 8 6 5 9 1 4
6 8 9 3 7 4 2 5 1
5 4 1 2 9 6 7 8 3
2 3 7 5 8 1 6 4 9
```

783

```
3 6 7 8 9 5 1 2 4
8 9 2 7 1 4 6 3 5
4 5 1 2 3 6 7 9 8
7 1 6 4 8 2 9 5 3
9 4 5 1 6 3 8 7 2
2 3 8 9 5 7 4 1 6
5 2 4 6 7 1 3 8 9
6 7 9 3 2 8 5 4 1
1 8 3 5 4 9 2 6 7
```

784

```
3 7 2 8 5 4 1 9 6
5 8 4 9 6 1 2 7 3
6 9 1 7 3 2 4 8 5
2 6 3 1 4 9 8 5 7
9 4 7 3 8 5 6 1 2
8 1 5 6 2 7 3 4 9
4 3 9 5 1 6 7 2 8
1 5 8 2 7 3 9 6 4
7 2 6 4 9 8 5 3 1
```

785

```
9 8 2 1 5 4 3 6 7
7 1 5 3 9 6 8 2 4
4 6 3 2 7 8 5 9 1
6 5 4 9 3 7 1 8 2
2 9 7 6 8 1 4 3 5
8 3 1 5 4 2 9 7 6
3 2 6 8 1 5 7 4 9
5 7 8 4 2 9 6 1 3
1 4 9 7 6 3 2 5 8
```

786

```
3 4 7 5 1 2 9 8 6
8 1 2 9 6 4 3 5 7
5 9 6 3 8 7 2 4 1
6 3 1 4 9 8 5 7 2
2 5 9 7 3 6 8 1 4
4 7 8 1 2 5 6 9 3
7 8 3 6 5 1 4 2 9
1 6 5 2 4 9 7 3 8
9 2 4 8 7 3 1 6 5
```

787

```
6 4 7 8 9 5 2 1 3
5 1 9 7 3 2 6 8 4
2 8 3 4 1 6 9 7 5
3 9 2 1 6 7 5 4 8
7 5 4 3 2 8 1 6 9
8 6 1 9 5 4 3 2 7
1 3 8 6 4 9 7 5 2
9 7 5 2 8 1 4 3 6
4 2 6 5 7 3 8 9 1
```

788

```
8 9 1 3 4 7 5 6 2
3 2 5 9 6 1 4 7 8
7 4 6 2 8 5 3 9 1
2 3 7 5 1 6 8 4 9
1 5 4 8 2 9 7 3 6
6 8 9 4 7 3 1 2 5
4 1 3 6 9 8 2 5 7
9 7 2 1 5 4 6 8 3
5 6 8 7 3 2 9 1 4
```

789

```
8 4 7 5 3 6 1 2 9
6 1 3 8 9 2 7 4 5
9 2 5 1 7 4 6 3 8
2 6 9 3 1 8 4 5 7
5 7 4 6 2 9 8 1 3
3 8 1 7 4 5 9 6 2
4 3 2 9 8 1 5 7 6
1 5 8 2 6 7 3 9 4
7 9 6 4 5 3 2 8 1
```

790

```
6 3 2 7 1 9 4 5 8
7 4 5 3 2 8 1 9 6
1 9 8 5 6 4 3 2 7
4 5 6 9 8 3 2 7 1
9 2 1 6 5 7 8 4 3
3 8 7 1 4 2 5 6 9
5 7 9 4 3 1 6 8 2
8 1 4 2 7 6 9 3 5
2 6 3 8 9 5 7 1 4
```

791

```
8 2 4 3 5 1 9 7 6
9 3 1 7 4 6 5 8 2
7 5 6 8 9 2 3 4 1
5 9 7 2 3 8 6 1 4
6 4 3 1 7 5 2 9 8
1 8 2 4 6 9 7 3 5
4 6 5 9 1 3 8 2 7
3 7 8 6 2 4 1 5 9
2 1 9 5 8 7 4 6 3
```

792

```
1 2 8 9 7 3 4 6 5
3 4 5 1 6 8 7 2 9
7 9 6 2 4 5 1 3 8
5 6 2 8 9 4 3 1 7
4 3 9 7 1 6 8 5 2
8 1 7 5 3 2 9 4 6
2 5 1 3 8 7 6 9 4
6 8 3 4 2 9 5 7 1
9 7 4 6 5 1 2 8 3
```

793

```
6 5 9 1 8 4 2 7 3
1 3 2 7 5 9 4 8 6
7 8 4 3 6 2 5 9 1
4 9 8 6 7 3 1 2 5
3 2 1 5 9 8 7 6 4
5 6 7 4 2 1 9 3 8
2 4 3 9 1 6 8 5 7
8 1 5 2 3 7 6 4 9
9 7 6 8 4 5 3 1 2
```

794

```
8 2 3 4 9 5 7 6 1
5 6 4 7 3 1 9 2 8
9 1 7 6 2 8 5 4 3
3 8 2 5 1 7 4 9 6
1 4 5 9 6 2 8 3 7
6 7 9 8 4 3 1 5 2
4 9 8 3 7 6 2 1 5
2 5 6 1 8 9 3 7 4
7 3 1 2 5 4 6 8 9
```

795

```
4 2 5 3 1 7 8 6 9
8 7 9 6 5 2 1 3 4
1 3 6 8 4 9 5 2 7
3 8 7 5 6 1 9 4 2
2 5 1 9 7 4 6 8 3
6 9 4 2 3 8 7 5 1
7 1 3 4 8 5 2 9 6
5 6 2 1 9 3 4 7 8
9 4 8 7 2 6 3 1 5
```

796

```
8 7 1 9 3 2 6 5 4
2 4 9 6 5 1 3 8 7
5 3 6 7 8 4 1 2 9
4 1 7 5 2 6 8 9 3
3 9 5 1 7 8 4 6 2
6 2 8 3 4 9 7 1 5
1 5 4 8 9 3 2 7 6
7 8 3 2 6 5 9 4 1
9 6 2 4 1 7 5 3 8
```

797

```
1 8 7 4 3 6 9 2 5
4 3 2 9 8 5 7 6 1
9 6 5 2 7 1 4 8 3
8 5 6 3 2 4 1 7 9
7 2 4 6 1 9 5 3 8
3 1 9 8 5 7 6 4 2
2 9 1 7 6 3 8 5 4
6 4 8 5 9 2 3 1 7
5 7 3 1 4 8 2 9 6
```

798

```
2 5 3 1 8 7 6 4 9
4 6 8 9 2 5 3 7 1
9 7 1 4 6 3 5 2 8
8 2 5 7 1 6 4 9 3
7 1 4 3 9 8 2 6 5
3 9 6 2 5 4 8 1 7
5 3 9 6 7 2 1 8 4
6 8 7 5 4 1 9 3 2
1 4 2 8 3 9 7 5 6
```

799

```
1 5 6 9 8 2 7 4 3
2 9 4 5 7 3 8 6 1
7 8 3 1 4 6 5 9 2
8 3 5 7 1 9 4 2 6
9 7 2 3 6 4 1 8 5
4 6 1 8 2 5 9 3 7
5 4 9 2 3 1 6 7 8
3 1 8 6 9 7 2 5 4
6 2 7 4 5 8 3 1 9
```

800

```
7 1 3 9 5 4 8 6 2
2 6 5 8 7 1 9 3 4
4 9 8 3 6 2 7 1 5
1 8 7 4 9 6 2 5 3
3 2 9 5 1 8 6 4 7
5 4 6 2 3 7 1 9 8
8 5 2 6 3 9 4 7 1
6 3 4 1 8 7 5 2 9
9 7 1 2 4 5 3 8 6
```

801

1	8	7	3	5	2	6	9	4
4	3	9	6	1	7	8	2	5
5	2	6	8	4	9	3	1	7
7	1	8	9	2	3	4	5	6
2	5	4	1	7	6	9	3	8
6	9	3	5	8	4	2	7	1
9	7	5	2	6	8	1	4	3
8	4	2	7	3	1	5	6	9
3	6	1	4	9	5	7	8	2

802

8	6	5	7	3	4	9	2	1
4	9	1	8	5	2	6	3	7
3	2	7	1	9	6	8	5	4
9	1	4	6	7	5	3	8	2
5	3	8	4	2	1	7	9	6
6	7	2	3	8	9	4	1	5
2	5	6	9	4	8	1	7	3
1	8	3	2	6	7	5	4	9
7	4	9	5	1	3	2	6	8

803

3	6	9	2	4	1	8	7	5
7	4	2	5	8	3	9	6	1
1	5	8	7	9	6	3	4	2
5	7	4	3	6	8	2	1	9
9	3	6	1	2	5	7	8	4
8	2	1	4	7	9	5	3	6
2	9	7	8	1	4	6	5	3
4	8	5	6	3	2	1	9	7
6	1	3	9	5	7	4	2	8

804

2	1	5	8	4	7	6	3	9
4	3	9	2	6	5	1	7	8
6	7	8	9	1	3	5	2	4
9	2	3	5	8	6	4	1	7
1	5	7	4	9	2	8	6	3
8	6	4	3	7	1	2	9	5
5	4	1	6	3	9	7	8	2
7	9	2	1	5	8	3	4	6
3	8	6	7	2	4	9	5	1

805

9	8	2	1	4	7	6	3	5
5	7	6	3	2	9	8	4	1
1	3	4	6	5	8	2	9	7
6	9	1	4	3	5	7	2	8
3	5	8	9	7	2	1	6	4
2	4	7	8	6	1	3	5	9
8	1	5	2	9	3	4	7	6
7	6	3	5	8	4	9	1	2
4	2	9	7	1	6	5	8	3

806

9	2	6	5	7	8	1	3	4
3	8	5	1	4	9	7	2	6
4	7	1	6	3	2	9	5	8
2	1	7	8	6	3	4	9	5
6	4	8	9	5	7	3	1	2
5	3	9	2	1	4	6	8	7
1	5	3	7	8	6	2	4	9
8	6	2	4	9	1	5	7	3
7	9	4	3	2	5	8	6	1

807

7	8	9	1	2	4	3	5	6
6	4	2	5	8	3	7	1	9
1	3	5	7	6	9	8	2	4
2	1	4	9	7	6	5	8	3
5	6	8	3	1	2	9	4	7
3	9	7	8	4	5	2	6	1
8	7	3	6	5	1	4	9	2
4	5	6	2	9	7	1	3	8
9	2	1	4	3	8	6	7	5

808

2	4	6	8	5	9	3	1	7
1	8	9	3	7	2	6	4	5
7	5	3	6	1	4	2	8	9
4	3	7	9	2	1	8	5	6
6	9	2	5	4	8	1	7	3
5	1	8	7	3	6	9	2	4
8	2	5	4	9	3	7	6	1
9	7	1	2	6	5	4	3	8
3	6	4	1	8	7	5	9	2

809

5	8	6	7	2	9	1	3	4
4	7	1	3	5	6	2	9	8
9	3	2	8	1	4	5	7	6
6	5	8	1	4	7	9	2	3
2	1	9	5	8	3	6	4	7
7	4	3	9	6	2	8	1	5
8	9	5	4	7	1	3	6	2
1	2	4	6	3	5	7	8	9
3	6	7	2	9	8	4	5	1

810

3	7	1	4	2	9	8	6	5
6	4	9	3	8	5	2	7	1
8	5	2	7	1	6	3	4	9
5	6	3	9	7	2	1	8	4
9	2	7	1	4	8	5	3	6
1	8	4	6	5	3	9	2	7
2	1	5	8	6	4	7	9	3
4	9	8	5	3	7	6	1	2
7	3	6	2	9	1	4	5	8

811

4	1	3	8	5	2	6	7	9
5	9	2	4	6	7	8	1	3
6	7	8	3	9	1	4	5	2
8	5	4	2	3	9	1	6	7
7	6	9	5	1	4	3	2	8
3	2	1	7	8	6	5	9	4
2	3	5	6	7	8	9	4	1
9	4	6	1	2	3	7	8	5
1	8	7	9	4	5	2	3	6

812

5	6	1	2	9	8	3	4	7
7	8	2	4	6	3	5	1	9
9	3	4	7	5	1	6	8	2
4	2	5	3	7	9	8	6	1
6	1	7	8	2	5	9	3	4
3	9	8	1	4	6	7	2	5
1	7	3	5	8	2	4	9	6
8	5	6	9	1	4	2	7	3
2	4	9	6	3	7	1	5	8

813

2	3	4	5	8	9	6	7	1
7	6	5	3	1	4	9	8	2
9	8	1	7	2	6	5	3	4
5	9	6	2	4	7	3	1	8
1	4	7	9	3	8	2	5	6
3	2	8	1	6	5	7	4	9
8	5	3	6	9	1	4	2	7
4	7	9	8	5	2	1	6	3
6	1	2	4	7	3	8	9	5

814

4	6	9	5	1	7	2	3	8
8	7	3	9	4	2	1	5	6
2	1	5	6	8	3	7	9	4
6	8	4	3	5	1	9	7	2
5	9	1	7	2	8	4	6	3
7	3	2	4	6	9	5	8	1
3	2	6	1	9	5	8	4	7
9	4	8	2	7	6	3	1	5
1	5	7	8	3	4	6	2	9

815

8	9	5	7	4	1	3	6	2
3	7	2	5	8	6	9	1	4
1	6	4	3	9	2	5	7	8
4	2	7	6	3	9	8	5	1
6	5	3	8	1	7	4	2	9
9	8	1	2	5	4	7	3	6
7	3	6	9	2	8	1	4	5
5	1	8	4	6	3	2	9	7
2	4	9	1	7	5	6	8	3

816

4	8	6	5	3	2	1	9	7
2	3	7	9	8	1	5	6	4
5	1	9	4	6	7	3	2	8
1	9	2	6	5	8	7	4	3
7	5	3	2	9	4	6	8	1
8	6	4	7	1	3	9	5	2
6	7	1	8	4	9	2	3	5
3	4	5	1	2	6	8	7	9
9	2	8	3	7	5	4	1	6

817

3	5	6	9	7	4	2	1	8
9	8	2	5	1	6	4	3	7
4	7	1	2	8	3	5	9	6
8	9	5	1	3	7	6	4	2
6	3	4	8	2	5	9	7	1
1	2	7	4	6	9	8	5	3
7	6	9	3	4	8	1	2	5
2	4	3	6	5	1	7	8	9
5	1	8	7	9	2	3	6	4

818

8	5	1	3	2	6	9	7	4
2	4	7	8	9	5	1	6	3
6	3	9	4	1	7	8	5	2
1	8	5	6	7	4	2	3	9
4	7	2	5	3	9	6	1	8
3	9	6	2	8	1	7	4	5
7	1	3	9	5	8	4	2	6
9	2	4	1	6	3	5	8	7
5	6	8	7	4	2	3	9	1

819

7	4	9	3	8	6	2	5	1
5	8	3	2	4	1	9	7	6
6	1	2	9	7	5	3	4	8
9	6	5	8	1	3	7	2	4
2	7	8	4	5	9	6	1	3
4	3	1	7	6	2	8	9	5
1	5	7	6	2	8	4	3	9
3	2	6	5	9	4	1	8	7
8	9	4	1	3	7	5	6	2

820

8	6	5	1	3	9	7	4	2
3	1	7	2	8	4	9	6	5
9	2	4	7	5	6	8	3	1
5	9	8	4	7	3	2	1	6
2	4	6	5	9	1	3	7	8
7	3	1	8	6	2	5	9	4
4	5	9	6	1	8	7	2	3
1	8	3	9	4	5	6	2	7
6	7	2	3	1	8	4	5	9

821
```
3 1 8 9 2 4 6 7 5
9 7 6 1 3 5 2 4 8
2 5 4 6 8 7 1 3 9
7 4 1 8 9 3 5 2 6
6 3 5 7 1 2 9 8 4
8 2 9 4 5 6 3 1 7
1 6 3 5 7 8 4 9 2
4 9 7 2 6 1 8 5 3
5 8 2 3 4 9 7 6 1
```

822
```
7 5 8 9 3 6 2 1 4
4 3 9 1 7 2 8 5 6
6 1 2 8 5 4 7 3 9
1 7 6 2 8 5 9 4 3
8 2 4 3 6 9 5 7 1
3 9 5 7 4 1 6 8 2
5 4 7 6 2 3 1 9 8
9 6 3 5 1 8 4 2 7
2 8 1 4 9 7 3 6 5
```

823
```
5 6 2 4 8 3 9 7 1
1 4 8 5 9 7 3 2 6
9 3 7 2 1 6 8 4 5
4 2 9 7 5 8 6 1 3
7 8 3 9 6 1 2 5 4
6 1 5 3 2 4 7 9 8
3 5 1 6 7 9 4 8 2
8 9 4 1 3 2 5 6 7
2 7 6 8 4 5 1 3 9
```

824
```
3 8 9 4 5 7 6 1 2
2 6 7 9 8 1 4 3 5
4 1 5 2 6 3 8 9 7
1 2 6 8 7 4 9 5 3
8 9 4 3 2 5 1 7 6
5 7 3 1 9 6 2 8 4
6 3 2 5 1 9 7 4 8
9 5 8 7 4 2 3 6 1
7 4 1 6 3 8 5 2 9
```

825
```
9 3 7 2 6 1 8 5 4
4 5 2 8 9 7 6 3 1
8 1 6 3 4 5 7 2 9
1 9 8 7 3 6 5 4 2
5 7 4 1 2 9 3 8 6
2 6 3 5 8 4 9 1 7
3 4 5 9 7 2 1 6 8
7 2 1 6 5 8 4 9 3
6 8 9 4 1 3 2 7 5
```

826
```
1 6 7 9 2 4 3 5 8
5 2 3 7 8 1 6 9 4
4 8 9 6 3 5 1 2 7
9 3 8 1 5 6 4 7 2
2 7 1 3 4 8 9 6 5
6 5 4 2 7 9 8 3 1
7 1 6 4 9 2 5 8 3
8 4 2 5 6 3 7 1 9
3 9 5 8 1 7 2 4 6
```

827
```
6 7 8 3 2 5 1 9 4
3 4 5 9 8 1 2 6 7
1 9 2 4 7 6 8 3 5
8 1 3 5 9 2 4 7 6
4 5 7 1 6 8 9 2 3
9 2 6 7 3 4 5 8 1
2 6 4 8 5 3 7 1 9
5 3 9 2 1 7 6 4 8
7 8 1 6 4 9 3 5 2
```

828
```
4 3 2 5 9 6 1 8 7
8 5 6 7 1 4 9 2 3
1 7 9 2 8 3 5 6 4
5 9 4 6 3 2 8 7 1
3 6 8 1 7 5 4 9 2
2 1 7 9 4 8 3 5 6
7 8 5 3 2 1 6 4 9
9 4 3 8 6 7 2 1 5
6 2 1 4 5 9 7 3 8
```

829
```
8 2 3 7 1 4 6 9 5
6 9 5 3 8 2 1 7 4
1 4 7 9 6 5 8 2 3
9 5 1 6 3 8 7 4 2
7 6 8 2 4 9 5 3 1
4 3 2 5 7 1 9 8 6
5 1 9 4 2 7 3 6 8
3 7 4 8 5 6 2 1 9
2 8 6 1 9 3 4 5 7
```

830
```
8 1 6 5 4 2 9 7 3
3 5 2 6 7 9 1 4 8
4 7 9 1 8 3 2 5 6
6 4 3 8 9 5 7 1 2
5 8 1 7 2 4 3 6 9
9 2 7 3 1 6 4 8 5
1 3 5 9 6 7 8 2 4
2 6 8 4 3 1 5 9 7
7 9 4 2 5 8 6 3 1
```

831
```
6 7 1 9 5 2 4 8 3
3 5 2 4 1 8 6 9 7
9 8 4 7 6 3 5 2 1
4 1 9 6 2 5 3 7 8
5 6 3 8 7 1 9 4 2
7 2 8 3 9 4 1 6 5
2 4 5 1 8 9 7 3 6
8 3 7 5 4 6 2 1 9
1 9 6 2 3 7 8 5 4
```

832
```
3 8 1 4 7 2 5 9 6
4 7 5 9 3 6 1 2 8
9 6 2 8 1 5 4 3 7
1 5 9 6 2 8 3 7 4
8 2 3 7 4 9 6 5 1
7 4 6 3 5 1 2 8 9
6 9 4 2 8 3 7 1 5
5 3 7 1 9 4 8 6 2
2 1 8 5 6 7 9 4 3
```

833
```
3 6 1 7 5 9 8 4 2
2 9 7 1 8 4 6 5 3
4 5 8 2 3 6 1 9 7
5 7 4 9 1 3 2 6 8
6 3 9 4 2 8 7 1 5
1 8 2 5 6 7 4 3 9
8 1 6 3 7 5 9 2 4
7 4 5 6 9 2 3 8 1
9 2 3 8 4 1 5 7 6
```

834
```
7 8 5 6 4 9 1 3 2
6 4 3 5 1 2 7 9 8
1 9 2 8 7 3 4 5 6
2 3 8 7 6 4 5 1 9
5 7 6 3 9 1 8 2 4
9 1 4 2 8 5 3 6 7
4 6 1 9 5 7 2 8 3
3 5 9 4 2 8 6 7 1
8 2 7 1 3 6 9 4 5
```

835
```
9 7 2 1 4 8 3 5 6
4 8 5 6 2 3 9 1 7
3 6 1 5 7 9 8 2 4
5 2 9 8 3 4 6 7 1
6 1 8 7 9 5 4 3 2
7 4 3 2 6 1 5 9 8
8 5 4 3 1 7 2 6 9
1 3 6 9 8 2 7 4 5
2 9 7 4 5 6 1 8 3
```

836
```
2 1 5 8 9 3 6 7 4
6 4 9 2 5 7 3 8 1
3 7 8 1 4 6 5 2 9
1 5 7 3 2 9 4 6 8
4 8 2 6 1 5 7 9 3
9 3 6 4 7 8 1 5 2
7 9 3 5 8 4 2 1 6
5 6 1 9 3 2 8 4 7
8 2 4 7 6 1 9 3 5
```

837
```
5 3 9 7 6 1 8 4 2
4 2 6 3 8 5 9 7 1
8 7 1 2 9 4 5 6 3
7 1 4 6 5 2 3 9 8
2 9 3 8 1 7 6 5 4
6 5 8 9 4 3 2 1 7
9 8 2 1 7 6 4 3 5
3 4 7 5 2 9 1 8 6
1 6 5 4 3 8 7 2 9
```

838
```
2 4 8 7 3 5 6 1 9
1 5 9 8 4 6 7 3 2
3 7 6 1 9 2 5 8 4
5 8 3 6 1 4 9 2 7
9 1 4 3 2 7 8 6 5
6 2 7 9 5 8 1 4 3
8 3 1 4 7 9 2 5 6
4 9 2 5 6 1 3 7 8
7 6 5 2 8 3 4 9 1
```

839
```
6 1 2 8 5 3 7 4 9
4 5 9 1 7 2 8 3 6
7 3 8 6 4 9 2 1 5
3 2 5 4 9 7 1 6 8
9 8 6 5 2 1 4 7 3
1 7 4 3 6 8 9 5 2
2 9 3 7 1 5 6 8 4
5 6 7 2 8 4 3 9 1
8 4 1 9 3 6 5 2 7
```

840
```
9 4 3 6 1 5 7 2 8
2 8 1 3 7 9 4 6 5
5 6 7 4 2 8 1 9 3
6 5 8 2 3 4 9 1 7
7 2 9 5 8 1 6 3 4
3 1 4 9 6 7 5 8 2
8 3 5 7 9 6 2 4 1
1 7 6 8 4 2 3 5 9
4 9 2 1 5 3 8 7 6
```

841

9	4	8	1	6	5	3	7	2
1	3	2	7	9	8	5	4	6
5	6	7	4	2	3	9	8	1
3	7	4	6	5	1	2	9	8
8	9	6	3	7	2	4	1	5
2	1	5	9	8	4	7	6	3
6	5	1	2	4	9	8	3	7
7	8	9	5	3	6	1	2	4
4	2	3	8	1	7	6	5	9

842

5	8	1	7	2	3	9	6	4
3	6	4	9	1	5	7	2	8
7	9	2	6	8	4	3	1	5
4	5	8	2	3	9	1	7	6
2	1	6	5	4	7	8	3	9
9	3	7	1	6	8	5	4	2
6	7	3	8	9	2	4	5	1
1	4	9	3	5	6	2	8	7
8	2	5	4	7	1	6	9	3

843

4	1	2	5	3	8	7	6	9
9	3	7	6	1	4	8	5	2
8	5	6	2	7	9	4	3	1
5	9	8	7	6	2	3	1	4
7	6	4	1	8	3	2	9	5
1	2	3	9	4	5	6	7	8
6	8	5	3	2	1	9	4	7
3	4	9	8	5	7	1	2	6
2	7	1	4	9	6	5	8	3

844

9	8	4	6	3	7	1	5	2
6	7	2	5	4	1	3	9	8
1	3	5	2	9	8	4	7	6
2	1	9	4	8	5	6	3	7
5	6	8	3	7	2	9	1	4
3	4	7	1	6	9	8	2	5
7	5	6	8	1	3	2	4	9
8	2	3	9	5	4	7	6	1
4	9	1	7	2	6	5	8	3

845

1	4	7	3	9	8	2	5	6
5	8	3	6	2	7	4	1	9
2	6	9	1	5	4	3	8	7
7	1	4	5	3	9	6	2	8
3	5	8	4	6	2	7	9	1
6	9	2	8	7	1	5	4	3
9	7	5	2	1	6	8	3	4
4	2	1	7	8	3	9	6	5
8	3	6	9	4	5	1	7	2

846

1	3	8	5	2	7	6	4	9
6	2	4	8	3	9	1	5	7
7	9	5	1	4	6	3	8	2
4	6	1	2	7	5	9	3	8
3	8	7	9	6	1	4	2	5
2	5	9	3	8	4	7	6	1
8	7	6	4	9	2	5	1	3
9	1	3	6	5	8	2	7	4
5	4	2	7	1	3	8	9	6

847

3	9	7	4	2	5	6	8	1
8	1	5	6	7	9	2	4	3
6	2	4	3	1	8	9	7	5
1	6	8	2	5	3	7	9	4
4	7	3	1	9	6	8	5	2
2	5	9	7	8	4	1	3	6
7	8	2	5	4	1	3	6	9
9	4	6	8	3	2	5	1	7
5	3	1	9	6	7	4	2	8

848

2	4	3	8	7	9	5	6	1
9	5	8	6	1	4	2	7	3
7	6	1	3	5	2	4	9	8
1	7	4	9	2	6	3	8	5
5	3	6	1	4	8	7	2	9
8	9	2	5	3	7	6	1	4
3	1	7	2	8	5	9	4	6
4	8	9	7	6	3	1	5	2
6	2	5	4	9	1	8	3	7

849

2	4	1	3	9	8	5	6	7
7	3	5	6	1	4	8	2	9
8	6	9	5	2	7	3	1	4
5	7	4	2	8	6	9	3	1
9	1	8	7	5	3	2	4	6
3	2	6	9	4	1	7	5	8
4	8	2	1	3	9	6	7	5
1	5	7	8	6	2	4	9	3
6	9	3	4	7	5	1	8	2

850

9	3	4	7	1	2	8	6	5
1	2	6	8	4	5	9	3	7
8	5	7	3	6	9	4	1	2
7	8	5	1	9	4	6	2	3
3	6	9	2	8	7	5	4	1
2	4	1	6	5	3	7	8	9
6	9	8	5	2	1	3	7	4
5	7	2	4	3	8	1	9	6
4	1	3	9	7	6	2	5	8

851

1	5	9	8	6	2	3	7	4
3	2	8	7	1	4	9	5	6
7	4	6	9	3	5	2	8	1
6	3	4	5	7	1	8	2	9
9	8	7	4	2	6	5	1	3
5	1	2	3	8	9	4	6	7
2	7	3	6	4	8	1	9	5
8	6	5	1	9	3	7	4	2
4	9	1	2	5	7	6	3	8

852

6	7	9	1	3	5	2	8	4
2	8	4	6	7	9	5	1	3
3	5	1	8	4	2	7	9	6
4	9	2	7	5	1	6	3	8
1	6	5	9	8	3	4	7	2
8	3	7	4	2	6	1	5	9
9	2	3	5	1	4	8	6	7
7	1	6	2	9	8	3	4	5
5	4	8	3	6	7	9	2	1

853

5	7	3	2	4	8	1	9	6
9	2	8	1	6	5	3	4	7
4	6	1	9	3	7	5	2	8
2	5	7	8	1	9	4	6	3
8	1	6	4	2	3	9	7	5
3	4	9	5	7	6	8	1	2
6	9	2	3	8	1	7	5	4
7	8	5	6	9	4	2	3	1
1	3	4	7	5	2	6	8	9

854

2	4	9	6	1	3	8	5	7
1	6	3	7	8	5	2	4	9
7	5	8	9	4	2	3	1	6
9	3	2	8	7	1	5	6	4
4	8	5	2	6	9	1	7	3
6	7	1	5	3	4	9	2	8
8	2	4	1	9	7	6	3	5
3	1	6	4	5	8	7	9	2
5	9	7	3	2	6	4	8	1

855

7	5	4	8	3	2	1	6	9
6	3	8	1	4	9	2	5	7
9	2	1	5	6	7	8	3	4
3	4	6	2	7	5	9	8	1
2	8	7	3	9	1	5	4	6
5	1	9	4	8	6	7	2	3
1	7	3	6	5	8	4	9	2
8	6	2	9	1	4	3	7	5
4	9	5	7	2	3	6	1	8

856

4	7	2	1	5	3	8	9	6
6	1	3	8	9	4	5	2	7
9	5	8	6	2	7	4	3	1
7	2	6	4	3	5	9	1	8
1	9	5	7	6	8	3	4	2
8	3	4	9	1	2	6	7	5
3	4	7	5	8	1	2	6	9
5	6	1	2	4	9	7	8	3
2	8	9	3	7	6	1	5	4

857

6	9	3	7	4	5	8	2	1
5	8	4	3	2	1	7	6	9
7	2	1	8	6	9	3	5	4
8	5	9	2	3	4	6	1	7
3	1	6	5	9	7	2	4	8
2	4	7	1	8	6	9	3	5
4	7	2	6	1	8	5	9	3
1	6	5	9	7	3	4	8	2
9	3	8	4	5	2	1	7	6

858

1	9	2	7	3	5	8	6	4
6	8	4	1	2	9	3	5	7
3	7	5	4	8	6	1	9	2
9	2	6	8	5	3	7	4	1
8	4	1	2	6	7	9	3	5
5	3	7	9	1	4	2	8	6
7	1	3	5	4	8	6	2	9
4	6	9	3	7	2	5	1	8
2	5	8	6	9	1	4	7	3

859

3	6	5	7	2	1	4	9	8
9	1	2	4	6	8	5	7	3
4	7	8	5	9	3	6	2	1
2	4	1	6	8	7	9	3	5
7	9	3	2	1	5	8	4	6
5	8	6	9	3	4	7	1	2
6	3	7	8	4	2	1	5	9
8	2	4	1	5	9	3	6	7
1	5	9	3	7	6	2	8	4

860

1	4	3	7	2	5	9	6	8
9	7	2	8	1	6	3	4	5
5	8	6	4	3	9	2	7	1
2	9	5	3	6	4	1	8	7
6	3	4	1	7	8	5	2	9
8	1	7	9	5	2	6	3	4
3	6	1	5	4	7	8	9	2
4	5	8	2	9	3	7	1	6
7	2	9	6	8	1	4	5	3

861

```
3 2 7 8 9 1 5 4 6
9 8 5 6 4 3 1 7 2
4 6 1 2 7 5 3 9 8
1 5 4 9 8 6 7 2 3
2 9 3 5 1 7 6 8 4
6 7 8 4 3 2 9 5 1
5 1 2 7 6 4 8 3 9
8 4 6 3 5 9 2 1 7
7 3 9 1 2 8 4 6 5
```

862

```
2 5 9 3 4 6 8 7 1
7 1 8 9 5 2 6 3 4
4 3 6 1 8 7 9 5 2
9 7 1 2 3 5 4 6 8
5 4 3 6 1 8 7 2 9
8 6 2 4 7 9 3 1 5
6 8 4 5 2 3 1 9 7
3 2 7 8 9 1 5 4 6
1 9 5 7 6 4 2 8 3
```

863

```
8 1 5 9 6 4 7 2 3
4 2 7 3 5 8 1 9 6
3 9 6 7 2 1 8 5 4
1 5 8 6 4 2 9 3 7
9 6 4 1 7 3 2 8 5
7 3 2 8 9 5 6 4 1
2 7 3 4 1 9 5 6 8
6 8 9 5 3 7 4 1 2
5 4 1 2 8 6 3 7 9
```

864

```
6 8 2 4 1 9 3 7 5
4 7 9 3 8 5 2 1 6
1 5 3 6 2 7 4 9 8
2 1 4 9 5 6 8 3 7
7 3 5 1 4 8 6 2 9
8 9 6 2 7 3 5 4 1
5 4 8 7 3 1 9 6 2
9 2 7 5 6 4 1 8 3
3 6 1 8 9 2 7 5 4
```

865

```
1 4 8 5 9 2 7 6 3
5 9 6 4 7 3 8 1 2
3 2 7 8 6 1 9 4 5
2 5 4 9 1 7 6 3 8
8 3 1 6 2 5 4 9 7
6 7 9 3 4 8 2 5 1
9 8 3 2 5 6 1 7 4
7 6 5 1 8 4 3 2 9
4 1 2 7 3 9 5 8 6
```

866

```
6 3 1 4 7 2 8 5 9
9 4 8 5 6 1 3 7 2
2 5 7 9 3 8 4 6 1
7 6 9 3 2 5 1 8 4
3 1 4 8 9 6 7 2 5
5 8 2 7 1 4 6 9 3
1 7 6 2 4 9 5 3 8
4 2 5 6 8 3 9 1 7
8 9 3 1 5 7 2 4 6
```

867

```
5 2 7 9 3 6 1 4 8
3 4 6 5 8 1 9 7 2
1 9 8 4 7 2 3 5 6
2 7 4 1 5 8 6 3 9
6 3 5 7 2 9 4 8 1
9 8 1 3 6 4 7 2 5
4 5 9 8 1 7 2 6 3
8 1 2 6 4 3 5 9 7
7 6 3 2 9 5 8 1 4
```

868

```
4 1 7 8 3 2 5 6 9
9 6 3 7 4 5 2 8 1
8 5 2 9 1 6 3 4 7
5 9 1 3 6 7 4 2 8
2 3 8 1 9 4 6 7 5
6 7 4 5 2 8 9 1 3
7 2 5 6 8 9 1 3 4
3 8 6 4 5 1 7 9 2
1 4 9 2 7 3 8 5 6
```

869

```
3 4 6 7 5 2 9 1 8
2 7 8 1 9 3 4 5 6
9 1 5 4 6 8 7 3 2
8 3 4 2 7 9 5 6 1
6 5 1 3 8 4 2 9 7
7 2 9 6 1 5 3 8 4
4 6 2 9 3 1 8 7 5
1 8 3 5 2 7 6 4 9
5 9 7 8 4 6 1 2 3
```

870

```
7 4 1 8 9 3 6 2 5
2 5 3 1 6 7 9 4 8
9 6 8 4 5 2 7 3 1
8 3 5 6 2 9 4 1 7
1 7 9 5 3 4 8 6 2
6 2 4 7 8 1 3 5 9
3 9 7 2 1 6 5 8 4
5 1 6 9 4 8 2 7 3
4 8 2 3 7 5 1 9 6
```

871

```
9 3 4 2 7 1 6 8 5
6 8 7 4 9 5 2 1 3
5 1 2 3 6 8 4 9 7
3 6 5 8 1 2 7 4 9
2 9 8 7 4 3 1 5 6
4 7 1 6 5 9 3 2 8
1 4 3 5 8 7 9 6 2
8 2 9 1 3 6 5 7 4
7 5 6 9 2 4 8 3 1
```

872

```
4 2 7 6 3 5 9 8 1
5 6 1 9 8 7 3 4 2
3 9 8 1 2 4 5 6 7
8 4 3 7 6 9 2 1 5
6 7 2 8 5 1 4 3 9
9 1 5 2 4 3 6 7 8
1 8 4 3 9 2 7 5 6
2 5 6 4 7 8 1 9 3
7 3 9 5 1 6 8 2 4
```

873

```
1 6 4 5 2 9 7 3 8
9 3 2 7 6 8 1 5 4
5 8 7 3 1 4 6 2 9
8 1 5 2 7 3 9 4 6
2 4 9 6 8 5 3 1 7
3 7 6 9 4 1 5 8 2
4 9 8 1 5 7 2 6 3
7 2 1 8 3 6 4 9 5
6 5 3 4 9 2 8 7 1
```

874

```
9 5 4 7 2 3 8 6 1
2 1 8 5 6 9 4 7 3
3 6 7 4 1 8 5 9 2
5 4 9 2 7 1 3 8 6
7 2 3 6 8 5 1 4 9
6 8 1 9 3 4 7 2 5
4 7 5 1 9 6 2 3 8
8 9 2 3 5 7 6 1 4
1 3 6 8 4 2 9 5 7
```

875

```
2 7 3 8 4 5 1 9 6
9 5 6 7 2 1 3 4 8
4 8 1 9 6 3 5 2 7
7 6 5 2 9 4 8 1 3
8 1 4 5 3 6 9 7 2
3 9 2 1 7 8 6 5 4
5 4 9 6 8 7 2 3 1
6 2 7 3 1 9 4 8 5
1 3 8 4 5 2 7 6 9
```

876

```
4 8 2 7 9 1 3 6 5
3 1 6 4 5 8 9 7 2
7 5 9 3 6 2 1 8 4
1 4 3 6 8 9 2 5 7
6 9 7 2 3 5 4 1 8
8 2 5 1 4 7 6 3 9
9 6 1 5 7 4 8 2 3
5 3 8 9 2 6 7 4 1
2 7 4 8 1 3 5 9 6
```

877

```
2 5 1 4 3 7 9 8 6
4 3 6 8 1 9 2 7 5
8 9 7 6 5 2 4 1 3
9 6 4 7 2 5 1 3 8
1 7 3 9 6 8 5 4 2
5 8 2 3 4 1 6 9 7
6 2 9 1 7 3 8 5 4
3 4 8 5 9 6 7 2 1
7 1 5 2 8 4 3 6 9
```

878

```
4 2 7 3 8 9 5 6 1
6 9 1 7 5 4 3 2 8
3 5 8 2 1 6 7 4 9
2 6 5 8 4 7 9 1 3
1 7 9 5 6 3 2 8 4
8 4 3 1 9 2 6 7 5
7 8 2 4 3 5 1 9 6
5 1 6 9 7 8 4 3 2
9 3 4 6 2 1 8 5 7
```

879

```
4 3 6 1 7 8 5 2 9
1 5 9 2 3 4 6 7 8
7 8 2 5 9 6 3 1 4
5 9 4 7 8 3 1 6 2
6 2 7 4 1 9 8 5 3
3 1 8 6 5 2 4 9 7
8 4 5 9 2 1 7 3 6
2 6 1 3 4 7 9 8 5
9 7 3 8 6 5 2 4 1
```

880

```
2 3 1 9 8 5 6 4 7
8 9 7 6 3 4 5 1 2
4 6 5 2 7 1 3 8 9
3 8 9 1 5 6 7 2 4
1 2 4 7 9 3 8 5 6
5 7 6 8 4 2 9 3 1
9 5 2 4 6 8 1 7 3
6 1 3 5 2 7 4 9 8
7 4 8 3 1 9 2 6 5
```

881

2	7	6	4	1	3	9	5	8
1	5	9	8	6	7	2	4	3
3	4	8	5	2	9	1	7	6
7	9	1	3	8	5	6	2	4
4	6	3	1	9	2	7	8	5
8	2	5	7	4	6	3	9	1
6	3	2	9	5	8	4	1	7
5	1	7	2	3	4	8	6	9
9	8	4	6	7	1	5	3	2

882

3	6	2	4	7	8	9	1	5
9	7	1	2	3	5	6	8	4
8	4	5	9	1	6	7	3	2
7	2	3	8	4	1	5	6	9
6	9	4	7	5	3	8	2	1
1	5	8	6	9	2	3	4	7
4	3	6	5	2	9	1	7	8
5	8	7	1	6	4	2	9	3
2	1	9	3	8	7	4	5	6

883

1	6	8	5	9	4	7	2	3
3	5	7	8	6	2	1	9	4
2	4	9	3	1	7	8	5	6
7	9	6	4	3	5	2	1	8
5	2	3	1	8	9	6	4	7
4	8	1	2	7	6	5	3	9
8	3	5	7	4	1	9	6	2
6	1	4	9	2	8	3	7	5
9	7	2	6	5	3	4	8	1

884

6	8	2	1	3	7	9	5	4
9	3	4	2	8	5	1	6	7
5	7	1	4	9	6	2	8	3
2	9	7	3	5	1	6	4	8
8	4	5	7	6	9	3	1	2
1	6	3	8	2	4	5	7	9
4	5	8	9	1	2	7	3	6
7	1	9	6	4	3	8	2	5
3	2	6	5	7	8	4	9	1

885

3	8	6	5	1	2	4	9	7
5	2	1	4	7	9	3	8	6
7	4	9	8	3	6	2	1	5
6	9	4	1	5	8	7	3	2
1	3	5	6	2	7	9	4	8
2	7	8	9	4	3	6	5	1
9	1	2	7	8	4	5	6	3
4	5	3	2	6	1	8	7	9
8	6	7	3	9	5	1	2	4

886

7	6	2	4	1	3	9	8	5
1	3	5	9	2	8	4	6	7
4	9	8	6	7	5	2	1	3
9	5	3	8	6	2	1	7	4
6	1	4	5	9	7	8	3	2
8	2	7	1	3	4	5	9	6
2	8	9	7	5	6	3	4	1
5	7	1	3	4	9	6	2	8
3	4	6	2	8	1	7	5	9

887

9	1	8	5	4	7	3	2	6
4	7	6	3	8	2	1	5	9
3	2	5	9	1	6	4	7	8
2	9	4	6	5	3	8	1	7
6	5	7	8	2	1	9	3	4
1	8	3	7	9	4	2	6	5
5	3	2	4	6	8	7	9	1
7	4	9	1	3	5	6	8	2
8	6	1	2	7	9	5	4	3

888

4	2	7	1	6	5	3	9	8
5	1	8	3	4	9	2	7	6
3	6	9	2	7	8	1	5	4
7	5	1	4	3	6	8	2	9
2	9	6	7	8	1	4	3	5
8	4	3	9	5	2	7	6	1
9	8	2	6	1	7	5	4	3
6	3	5	8	2	4	9	1	7
1	7	4	5	9	3	6	8	2

889

3	1	5	2	6	9	4	8	7
2	8	7	1	4	5	6	3	9
6	4	9	7	3	8	1	2	5
1	2	8	3	9	7	5	4	6
5	9	6	4	8	1	3	7	2
7	3	4	6	5	2	9	1	8
8	6	3	9	7	4	2	5	1
4	5	2	8	1	6	7	9	3
9	7	1	5	2	3	8	6	4

890

1	6	2	7	3	9	8	5	4
9	8	7	4	5	1	2	6	3
3	5	4	6	2	8	7	9	1
5	1	9	8	4	2	3	7	6
2	7	8	3	1	6	9	4	5
6	4	3	5	9	7	1	8	2
7	9	5	2	6	3	4	1	8
8	2	6	1	7	4	5	3	9
4	3	1	9	8	5	6	2	7

891

2	4	5	3	9	8	6	7	1
3	8	7	4	6	1	2	9	5
1	6	9	7	5	2	8	3	4
5	2	4	8	3	9	7	1	6
8	7	3	2	1	6	4	5	9
9	1	6	5	4	7	3	8	2
4	9	1	6	7	3	5	2	8
7	5	8	9	2	4	1	6	3
6	3	2	1	8	5	9	4	7

892

8	4	9	7	3	6	1	2	5
3	5	2	1	4	9	7	6	8
1	6	7	2	8	5	4	3	9
5	2	4	8	6	7	3	9	1
7	1	6	9	5	3	8	4	2
9	8	3	4	1	2	5	7	6
6	3	1	5	2	4	9	8	7
2	9	5	3	7	8	6	1	4
4	7	8	6	9	1	2	5	3

893

7	1	4	9	8	2	5	3	6
6	8	5	3	7	1	9	4	2
3	9	2	5	6	4	8	1	7
4	5	7	8	1	6	2	9	3
8	3	1	4	2	9	7	6	5
9	2	6	7	3	5	4	8	1
1	6	8	2	9	7	3	5	4
2	4	3	6	5	8	1	7	9
5	7	9	1	4	3	6	2	8

894

9	5	8	4	2	6	1	7	3
2	6	1	3	7	5	9	8	4
3	7	4	8	9	1	6	2	5
8	3	9	6	5	7	4	1	2
4	2	7	9	1	3	8	5	6
6	1	5	2	8	4	7	3	9
5	8	2	7	4	9	3	6	1
1	4	3	5	6	8	2	9	7
7	9	6	1	3	2	5	4	8

895

6	1	4	8	5	3	9	2	7
3	5	7	9	2	6	8	1	4
2	9	8	7	1	4	5	6	3
8	3	1	2	6	9	4	7	5
9	7	5	4	3	1	6	8	2
4	2	6	5	7	8	1	3	9
5	4	3	6	8	2	7	9	1
1	6	9	3	4	7	2	5	8
7	8	2	1	9	5	3	4	6

896

9	6	3	8	5	7	2	1	4
7	5	2	4	1	3	6	8	9
8	4	1	6	9	2	5	3	7
5	3	8	7	2	6	9	4	1
4	9	6	1	8	5	3	7	2
1	2	7	3	4	9	8	6	5
6	7	5	9	3	4	1	2	8
2	8	4	5	6	1	7	9	3
3	1	9	2	7	8	4	5	6

897

5	8	1	7	6	3	2	9	4
4	2	6	8	9	1	5	3	7
9	3	7	4	2	5	6	8	1
1	7	5	3	8	4	9	2	6
6	4	3	9	1	2	7	5	8
8	9	2	6	5	7	4	1	3
7	5	4	2	3	8	1	6	9
3	1	9	5	4	6	8	7	2
2	6	8	1	7	9	3	4	5

898

7	8	9	1	6	3	2	4	5
3	5	1	8	4	2	6	7	9
6	2	4	9	5	7	1	8	3
5	3	7	6	2	9	8	1	4
8	9	2	4	1	5	3	6	7
1	4	6	3	7	8	5	9	2
2	1	5	7	8	4	9	3	6
9	7	8	5	3	6	4	2	1
4	6	3	2	9	1	7	5	8

899

8	1	6	3	7	5	9	2	4
5	7	2	4	8	9	6	1	3
3	4	9	1	6	2	8	7	5
6	3	8	7	5	4	2	9	1
4	2	7	8	9	1	5	3	6
9	5	1	2	3	6	7	4	8
2	9	5	6	1	3	4	8	7
1	8	4	5	2	7	3	6	9
7	6	3	9	4	8	1	5	2

900

3	2	7	1	8	5	6	4	9
1	6	8	4	7	9	2	3	5
9	4	5	6	3	2	7	8	1
6	5	2	8	4	7	9	1	3
8	7	9	3	5	1	4	6	2
4	1	3	9	2	6	5	7	8
5	3	6	2	1	4	8	9	7
7	9	1	5	6	8	3	2	4
2	8	4	7	9	3	1	5	6

901

5	6	7	8	2	9	4	3	1
1	8	3	5	7	4	2	6	9
2	9	4	3	6	1	7	8	5
3	2	9	1	4	6	8	5	7
6	7	5	9	3	8	1	4	2
8	4	1	7	5	2	6	9	3
9	5	2	6	8	7	3	1	4
7	3	6	4	1	5	9	2	8
4	1	8	2	9	3	5	7	6

902

1	5	3	4	8	6	9	2	7
7	8	2	1	9	3	4	5	6
4	6	9	5	2	7	1	3	8
6	4	7	2	3	9	8	1	5
8	2	5	6	7	1	3	9	4
9	3	1	8	4	5	7	6	2
3	7	4	9	6	2	5	8	1
2	1	8	3	5	4	6	7	9
5	9	6	7	1	8	2	4	3

903

9	2	5	4	8	1	6	7	3
6	7	1	2	3	9	4	5	8
3	8	4	5	7	6	9	1	2
1	4	7	3	5	2	8	6	9
8	6	2	9	1	7	5	3	4
5	3	9	6	4	8	7	2	1
2	1	6	7	9	4	3	8	5
4	5	8	1	6	3	2	9	7
7	9	3	8	2	5	1	4	6

904

4	1	9	5	2	3	7	6	8
8	2	3	7	4	6	9	1	5
6	5	7	9	8	1	2	3	4
5	4	2	1	3	9	6	8	7
9	8	1	6	7	4	3	5	2
3	7	6	8	5	2	1	4	9
2	9	5	3	6	8	4	7	1
1	3	8	4	9	7	5	2	6
7	6	4	2	1	5	8	9	3

905

4	2	7	1	9	6	8	3	5
6	9	8	5	3	4	1	2	7
3	5	1	2	7	8	4	9	6
2	8	5	9	6	3	7	4	1
1	6	9	7	4	2	5	8	3
7	4	3	8	5	1	9	6	2
5	7	4	6	2	9	3	1	8
9	1	6	3	8	7	2	5	4
8	3	2	4	1	5	6	7	9

906

3	9	1	6	2	5	4	8	7
6	7	8	3	1	4	9	5	2
5	4	2	9	8	7	1	6	3
7	6	4	1	5	8	2	3	9
2	5	9	7	4	3	8	1	6
1	8	3	2	9	6	7	4	5
9	2	5	4	6	1	3	7	8
8	1	7	5	3	9	6	2	4
4	3	6	8	7	2	5	9	1

907

8	1	7	3	6	4	2	5	9
6	2	9	5	7	1	3	4	8
5	4	3	2	8	9	6	7	1
2	7	6	9	1	5	4	8	3
9	3	8	4	2	6	5	1	7
4	5	1	8	3	7	9	2	6
1	9	2	7	4	3	8	6	5
3	6	4	1	5	8	7	9	2
7	8	5	6	9	2	1	3	4

908

3	6	8	1	7	5	4	9	2
1	4	5	6	9	2	8	3	7
2	9	7	4	8	3	6	1	5
6	1	2	7	3	4	9	5	8
9	5	4	8	2	1	7	6	3
8	7	3	5	6	9	2	4	1
7	2	9	3	1	6	5	8	4
5	3	6	2	4	8	1	7	9
4	8	1	9	5	7	3	2	6

909

9	4	5	2	8	3	7	1	6
3	1	7	5	4	6	8	2	9
2	6	8	7	9	1	3	5	4
1	3	9	8	7	2	4	6	5
6	8	4	3	1	5	2	9	7
7	5	2	4	6	9	1	8	3
5	2	1	6	3	7	9	4	8
8	7	6	9	2	4	5	3	1
4	9	3	1	5	8	6	7	2

910

3	6	7	8	9	2	4	5	1
5	4	2	6	1	7	9	8	3
8	1	9	3	4	5	6	7	2
7	8	1	9	2	6	5	3	4
2	3	4	5	8	1	7	6	9
9	5	6	4	7	3	1	2	8
1	7	5	2	3	9	8	4	6
4	9	3	7	6	8	2	1	5
6	2	8	1	5	4	3	9	7

911

6	8	7	9	4	1	2	3	5
5	9	2	3	8	7	6	1	4
3	4	1	6	2	5	9	8	7
8	5	9	4	3	6	1	7	2
4	7	3	2	1	9	8	5	6
2	1	6	7	5	8	3	4	9
7	2	8	5	9	3	4	6	1
9	3	5	1	6	4	7	2	8
1	6	4	8	7	2	5	9	3

912

1	3	6	8	7	2	4	9	5
2	8	5	9	1	4	7	3	6
4	7	9	5	3	6	2	1	8
6	4	3	1	2	9	5	8	7
7	2	8	4	5	3	1	6	9
9	5	1	7	6	8	3	4	2
5	1	4	6	8	7	9	2	3
3	6	7	2	9	1	8	5	4
8	9	2	3	4	5	6	7	1

913

7	9	8	4	3	6	5	1	2
4	2	1	9	5	7	6	8	3
6	5	3	8	2	1	4	9	7
9	1	2	3	7	5	8	6	4
5	8	6	2	4	9	3	7	1
3	4	7	6	1	8	2	5	9
8	6	4	7	9	2	1	3	5
2	7	5	1	8	3	9	4	6
1	3	9	5	6	4	7	2	8

914

9	3	5	1	8	7	6	4	2
1	4	8	2	6	5	7	9	3
7	2	6	3	9	4	1	5	8
5	1	9	8	7	6	2	3	4
2	8	3	5	4	1	9	7	6
4	6	7	9	2	3	5	8	1
8	7	1	4	5	2	3	6	9
3	5	4	6	1	9	8	2	7
6	9	2	7	3	8	4	1	5

915

6	2	4	7	1	3	9	5	8
8	3	9	5	4	6	1	2	7
7	1	5	9	8	2	4	3	6
3	5	8	6	7	4	2	9	1
2	9	6	1	3	8	7	4	5
1	4	7	2	9	5	8	6	3
9	6	3	8	2	7	5	1	4
4	8	2	3	5	1	6	7	9
5	7	1	4	6	9	3	8	2

916

9	6	4	8	7	5	2	3	1
8	7	2	6	1	3	5	9	4
5	1	3	9	4	2	6	8	7
6	9	5	3	2	1	4	7	8
3	4	8	7	9	6	1	2	5
7	2	1	4	5	8	9	6	3
4	5	7	2	8	9	3	1	6
1	3	9	5	6	7	8	4	2
2	8	6	1	3	4	7	5	9

917

8	6	7	5	3	9	1	2	4
2	3	1	4	8	7	9	5	6
4	5	9	2	1	6	7	3	8
9	4	3	8	2	1	5	6	7
1	7	6	9	5	4	3	8	2
5	2	8	6	7	3	4	9	1
6	1	5	3	4	2	8	7	9
3	9	4	7	6	8	2	1	5
7	8	2	1	9	5	6	4	3

918

9	5	7	2	1	4	8	3	6
4	6	1	9	8	3	5	2	7
3	2	8	6	7	5	9	4	1
2	8	5	1	6	7	4	9	3
1	4	9	3	2	8	6	7	5
7	3	6	5	4	9	2	1	8
8	1	2	7	9	6	3	5	4
5	9	4	8	3	1	7	6	2
6	7	3	4	5	2	1	8	9

919

9	2	7	1	6	5	3	4	8
3	1	5	9	4	8	2	6	7
6	4	8	3	7	2	9	1	5
4	5	3	7	2	1	8	9	6
2	7	6	8	9	4	5	3	1
8	9	1	5	3	6	4	7	2
7	6	2	4	8	3	1	5	9
1	3	9	2	5	7	6	8	4
5	8	4	6	1	9	7	2	3

920

5	9	4	6	2	3	8	7	1
7	8	2	9	1	4	6	3	5
1	6	3	8	5	7	9	2	4
2	1	7	3	6	9	5	4	8
3	5	6	4	1	8	7	9	2
8	4	9	5	7	2	3	1	6
6	7	5	2	9	4	1	8	3
9	2	8	1	3	5	4	6	7
4	3	1	7	8	6	2	5	9

921

```
5 3 9 6 4 1 7 2 8
7 6 8 2 9 5 1 4 3
1 4 2 3 7 8 9 6 5
3 8 4 5 2 7 6 1 9
2 1 6 8 3 9 5 7 4
9 5 7 4 1 6 3 8 2
8 7 3 1 5 4 2 9 6
6 9 5 7 8 2 4 3 1
4 2 1 9 6 3 8 5 7
```

922

```
9 4 5 6 8 1 3 7 2
7 6 8 2 9 3 5 1 4
2 3 1 5 7 4 8 6 9
6 1 4 8 3 7 9 2 5
8 7 9 4 5 2 6 3 1
5 2 3 9 1 6 7 4 8
1 5 7 3 4 8 2 9 6
3 9 6 1 2 5 4 8 7
4 8 2 7 6 9 1 5 3
```

923

```
3 5 6 9 4 7 8 2 1
2 9 7 8 6 1 5 4 3
1 4 8 3 2 5 7 9 6
5 6 9 4 7 3 2 1 8
4 3 1 2 8 9 6 5 7
7 8 2 5 1 6 9 3 4
9 2 4 6 3 8 1 7 5
6 1 3 7 5 2 4 8 9
8 7 5 1 9 4 3 6 2
```

924

```
4 7 3 1 8 9 6 5 2
1 2 9 6 4 5 8 7 3
8 6 5 2 3 7 9 4 1
9 4 2 5 1 6 7 3 8
3 1 8 7 2 4 5 6 9
6 5 7 8 9 3 2 1 4
2 8 6 4 7 1 3 9 5
7 3 4 9 5 8 1 2 6
5 9 1 3 6 2 4 8 7
```

925

```
8 5 9 6 2 7 1 3 4
2 3 7 1 9 4 5 6 8
6 4 1 5 8 3 9 7 2
3 1 8 2 5 6 7 4 9
5 6 4 9 7 8 3 2 1
9 7 2 3 4 1 8 5 6
4 2 3 7 1 9 6 8 5
7 9 5 8 6 2 4 1 3
1 8 6 4 3 5 2 9 7
```

926

```
3 9 7 1 2 5 6 8 4
2 8 6 4 7 9 5 1 3
5 1 4 6 3 8 2 9 7
4 5 9 3 8 1 7 6 2
7 2 8 9 5 6 4 3 1
1 6 3 7 4 2 9 5 8
8 4 1 5 6 7 3 2 9
9 3 5 2 1 4 8 7 6
6 7 2 8 9 3 1 4 5
```

927

```
6 7 5 8 9 2 4 3 1
9 1 2 4 6 3 5 8 7
4 3 8 7 5 1 9 6 2
3 2 4 5 7 9 8 1 6
7 8 6 1 3 4 2 9 5
5 9 1 6 2 8 7 4 3
1 6 9 2 8 7 3 5 4
8 4 7 3 1 5 6 2 9
2 5 3 9 4 6 1 7 8
```

928

```
4 8 9 2 1 3 5 7 6
3 1 2 5 7 6 4 9 8
5 7 6 9 8 4 3 1 2
9 2 4 1 3 7 6 8 5
6 3 7 8 5 2 1 4 9
1 5 8 6 4 9 7 2 3
8 6 3 7 2 1 9 5 4
7 9 5 4 6 8 2 3 1
2 4 1 3 9 5 8 6 7
```

929

```
9 4 2 8 5 6 3 1 7
5 1 7 3 4 2 6 9 8
8 6 3 7 9 1 4 2 5
4 7 6 2 8 9 5 3 1
3 2 9 4 1 5 7 8 6
1 8 5 6 3 7 2 4 9
2 5 8 9 6 4 1 7 3
7 3 1 5 2 8 9 6 4
6 9 4 1 7 3 8 5 2
```

930

```
2 1 8 9 6 7 4 3 5
5 4 7 2 8 3 1 9 6
3 6 9 4 1 5 8 2 7
8 2 5 1 7 4 9 6 3
7 3 4 6 2 9 5 1 8
1 9 6 3 5 8 2 7 4
4 7 3 8 9 2 6 5 1
6 8 2 5 3 1 7 4 9
9 5 1 7 4 6 3 8 2
```

931

```
3 5 7 4 9 6 1 8 2
8 9 1 2 5 3 7 6 4
4 6 2 8 7 1 5 9 3
7 8 6 3 4 5 9 2 1
5 2 9 6 1 7 3 4 8
1 3 4 9 8 2 6 5 7
2 4 5 1 3 9 8 7 6
9 1 8 7 6 4 2 3 5
6 7 3 5 2 8 4 1 9
```

932

```
1 4 9 3 8 2 6 5 7
5 8 7 4 6 9 3 1 2
2 6 3 5 1 7 8 4 9
3 7 8 6 5 1 9 2 4
4 1 6 2 9 3 7 8 5
9 5 2 7 4 8 1 6 3
6 3 5 1 7 4 2 9 8
7 9 1 8 2 5 4 3 6
8 2 4 9 3 6 5 7 1
```

933

```
9 1 5 4 8 2 7 3 6
4 7 6 3 5 9 2 8 1
3 2 8 7 1 6 4 5 9
8 9 7 5 4 1 3 6 2
2 3 4 9 6 7 5 1 8
5 6 1 2 3 8 9 4 7
7 8 3 6 9 4 1 2 5
1 5 2 8 7 3 6 9 4
6 4 9 1 2 5 8 7 3
```

934

```
7 9 3 4 1 2 6 8 5
4 2 6 9 8 5 7 3 1
8 1 5 6 7 3 4 9 2
2 5 1 7 3 8 9 4 6
6 4 7 1 2 9 8 5 3
3 8 9 5 6 4 1 2 7
1 3 8 2 9 6 5 7 4
9 6 4 3 5 7 2 1 8
5 7 2 8 4 1 3 6 9
```

935

```
5 8 4 2 6 9 1 3 7
1 9 7 4 3 8 6 2 5
3 6 2 7 1 5 9 4 8
6 4 5 1 8 7 2 9 3
2 7 8 6 9 3 5 1 4
9 1 3 5 4 2 7 8 6
7 5 9 8 2 4 3 6 1
8 2 1 3 7 6 4 5 9
4 3 6 9 5 1 8 7 2
```

936

```
5 6 2 4 1 9 8 3 7
3 9 8 5 6 7 1 4 2
1 4 7 2 3 8 5 6 9
6 3 4 1 2 5 9 7 8
8 7 1 9 4 3 2 5 6
9 2 5 8 7 6 3 1 4
7 8 6 3 5 2 4 9 1
2 1 3 7 9 4 6 8 5
4 5 9 6 8 1 7 2 3
```

937

```
7 5 8 6 3 2 1 9 4
6 2 4 9 7 1 3 8 5
3 1 9 5 8 4 6 2 7
1 6 7 3 4 9 2 5 8
5 9 3 8 2 6 7 4 1
8 4 2 1 5 7 9 6 3
9 8 1 7 6 5 4 3 2
2 7 5 4 9 3 8 1 6
4 3 6 2 1 8 5 7 9
```

938

```
7 9 2 6 5 3 4 8 1
4 6 1 8 2 7 5 9 3
5 3 8 1 9 4 2 7 6
9 8 6 2 7 1 3 5 4
1 4 7 5 3 9 6 2 8
3 2 5 4 6 8 9 1 7
6 5 4 7 8 2 1 3 9
8 1 3 9 4 5 7 6 2
2 7 9 3 1 6 8 4 5
```

939

```
2 3 7 9 5 1 8 4 6
8 9 4 7 6 2 3 5 1
1 5 6 8 4 3 2 7 9
9 1 3 5 8 6 4 2 7
7 4 5 2 1 9 6 8 3
6 2 8 3 7 4 1 9 5
4 7 2 1 3 5 9 6 8
5 6 1 4 9 8 7 3 2
3 8 9 6 2 7 5 1 4
```

940

```
6 5 9 8 4 2 7 1 3
3 4 2 5 7 1 6 9 8
7 8 1 3 6 9 5 4 2
8 9 4 2 1 7 3 5 6
2 1 6 4 3 5 9 8 7
5 7 3 6 9 8 4 2 1
4 6 8 9 2 3 1 7 5
1 3 5 7 8 4 2 6 9
9 2 7 1 5 6 8 3 4
```

941

2	4	1	9	6	7	5	3	8
3	5	7	4	8	2	6	9	1
6	8	9	1	5	3	4	7	2
7	9	2	8	3	4	1	5	6
5	6	3	2	1	9	7	8	4
8	1	4	6	7	5	3	2	9
4	3	8	5	2	6	9	1	7
9	2	5	7	4	1	8	6	3
1	7	6	3	9	8	2	4	5

942

1	6	9	8	4	5	3	7	2
8	2	4	3	7	1	9	6	5
3	7	5	6	9	2	8	4	1
9	4	8	5	1	6	2	3	7
7	1	6	4	2	3	5	8	9
2	5	3	9	8	7	6	1	4
5	8	2	7	3	4	1	9	6
4	3	1	2	6	9	7	5	8
6	9	7	1	5	8	4	2	3

943

1	5	3	6	4	2	9	8	7
2	8	4	9	5	7	6	1	3
6	7	9	1	8	3	4	5	2
3	4	6	7	9	5	1	2	8
8	1	5	2	6	4	3	7	9
7	9	2	3	1	8	5	6	4
5	3	7	4	2	1	8	9	6
4	6	1	8	7	9	2	3	5
9	2	8	5	3	6	7	4	1

944

8	5	6	4	2	3	7	9	1
1	3	7	6	9	8	2	5	4
4	9	2	5	7	1	6	8	3
7	6	5	1	8	4	9	3	2
9	2	4	3	5	7	1	6	8
3	8	1	2	6	9	5	4	7
2	1	8	9	4	5	3	7	6
5	7	3	8	1	6	4	2	9
6	4	9	7	3	2	8	1	5

945

6	1	4	5	3	9	7	2	8
8	7	3	2	4	6	5	9	1
9	2	5	1	8	7	6	4	3
2	4	7	8	6	1	3	5	9
1	3	9	7	2	5	8	6	4
5	6	8	3	9	4	2	1	7
3	5	6	9	1	8	4	7	2
7	9	2	4	5	3	1	8	6
4	8	1	6	7	2	9	3	5

946

2	5	8	1	7	3	4	6	9
7	6	1	9	4	2	8	5	3
3	4	9	8	5	6	1	7	2
4	2	5	3	6	9	7	8	1
1	8	3	7	2	5	6	9	4
9	7	6	4	1	8	2	3	5
5	9	4	2	8	7	3	1	6
6	1	7	5	3	4	9	2	8
8	3	2	6	9	1	5	4	7

947

6	8	3	1	5	9	7	4	2
5	1	7	2	4	3	9	8	6
9	2	4	8	7	6	3	5	1
1	5	8	9	6	2	4	7	3
4	9	6	5	3	7	1	2	8
7	3	2	4	8	1	6	9	5
3	4	9	6	2	5	8	1	7
8	7	5	3	1	4	2	6	9
2	6	1	7	9	8	5	3	4

948

2	9	8	6	7	5	1	4	3
1	4	7	3	2	9	6	8	5
6	5	3	1	8	4	9	7	2
4	3	9	7	1	8	5	2	6
7	2	6	4	5	3	8	1	9
5	8	1	9	6	2	7	3	4
9	6	4	8	3	1	2	5	7
8	7	2	5	4	6	3	9	1
3	1	5	2	9	7	4	6	8

949

4	9	1	2	8	3	6	5	7
6	2	3	1	5	7	8	9	4
5	8	7	9	6	4	3	1	2
1	4	5	3	2	8	7	6	9
3	7	2	6	9	5	1	4	8
8	6	9	4	7	1	2	3	5
7	5	6	8	1	9	4	2	3
2	3	8	5	4	6	9	7	1
9	1	4	7	3	2	5	8	6

950

3	9	5	7	2	1	4	8	6
2	8	4	5	6	9	1	7	3
1	6	7	8	3	4	5	2	9
5	2	9	3	1	7	8	6	4
8	1	3	2	4	6	7	9	5
4	7	6	9	5	8	3	1	2
6	3	1	4	8	2	9	5	7
9	5	8	6	7	3	2	4	1
7	4	2	1	9	5	6	3	8

951

3	6	9	1	4	2	5	8	7
1	4	7	6	8	5	2	9	3
5	8	2	3	7	9	1	6	4
7	9	6	5	1	4	3	2	8
4	2	5	9	3	8	7	1	6
8	1	3	7	2	6	4	5	9
9	3	4	2	6	1	8	7	5
6	7	1	8	5	3	9	4	2
2	5	8	4	9	7	6	3	1

952

1	6	4	2	8	9	3	7	5
2	5	9	1	3	7	4	6	8
7	3	8	6	4	5	2	9	1
8	2	5	4	7	6	9	1	3
4	9	7	3	1	2	8	5	6
3	1	6	9	5	8	7	4	2
6	8	1	7	2	4	5	3	9
9	7	2	5	6	3	1	8	4
5	4	3	8	9	1	6	2	7

953

7	4	6	2	3	5	8	1	9
9	1	3	4	7	8	5	2	6
5	8	2	1	6	9	4	7	3
8	9	4	5	2	7	6	3	1
6	5	1	9	4	3	2	8	7
2	3	7	8	1	6	9	5	4
1	6	8	3	9	2	7	4	5
3	7	5	6	8	4	1	9	2
4	2	9	7	5	1	3	6	8

954

3	4	7	8	6	2	1	5	9
5	8	2	1	7	9	4	6	3
9	1	6	3	5	4	2	8	7
7	2	8	9	3	5	6	1	4
1	5	9	4	2	6	7	3	8
4	6	3	7	1	8	9	2	5
6	3	5	2	9	7	8	4	1
8	7	1	6	4	3	5	9	2
2	9	4	5	8	1	3	7	6

955

8	5	3	6	7	4	2	1	9
2	6	4	9	1	8	3	5	7
7	1	9	2	5	3	4	8	6
4	3	1	5	2	7	9	6	8
6	2	7	4	8	9	1	3	5
5	9	8	1	3	6	7	4	2
3	8	6	7	9	1	5	2	4
9	4	2	3	6	5	8	7	1
1	7	5	8	4	2	6	9	3

956

7	3	4	2	6	1	9	5	8
6	8	1	9	5	4	2	7	3
5	9	2	8	3	7	4	1	6
9	5	6	1	7	2	8	3	4
3	2	7	4	8	5	6	9	1
4	1	8	3	9	6	5	2	7
1	6	3	5	2	8	7	4	9
8	4	5	7	1	9	3	6	2
2	7	9	6	4	3	1	8	5

957

4	7	1	2	8	6	3	9	5
3	9	8	5	1	7	2	4	6
2	5	6	4	3	9	8	7	1
8	1	9	6	7	5	4	2	3
5	2	3	1	4	8	7	6	9
6	4	7	9	2	3	5	1	8
1	3	5	7	9	4	6	8	2
7	8	2	3	6	1	9	5	4
9	6	4	8	5	2	1	3	7

958

2	6	3	8	4	9	7	1	5
5	8	1	3	7	2	4	9	6
4	9	7	6	1	5	3	8	2
7	4	5	1	3	6	8	2	9
8	3	6	9	2	4	1	5	7
9	1	2	7	5	8	6	4	3
6	2	9	4	8	7	5	3	1
3	5	4	2	6	1	9	7	8
1	7	8	5	9	3	2	6	4

959

3	9	5	7	2	4	8	6	1
2	6	7	3	1	8	9	5	4
1	8	4	9	5	6	3	2	7
7	1	3	4	8	2	6	9	5
5	4	9	6	3	7	1	8	2
8	2	6	1	9	5	7	4	3
4	7	1	2	6	9	5	3	8
9	3	8	5	4	1	2	7	6
6	5	2	8	7	3	4	1	9

960

6	8	5	3	2	7	4	9	1
4	2	9	1	6	8	7	3	5
7	3	1	4	9	5	8	6	2
1	5	2	9	3	4	6	7	8
8	4	3	6	7	2	1	5	9
9	7	6	8	5	1	2	4	3
5	6	8	2	4	9	3	1	7
3	1	7	5	8	6	9	2	4
2	9	4	7	1	3	5	8	6

961

7	5	4	2	3	8	1	9	6
3	6	8	5	1	9	4	7	2
2	1	9	6	7	4	5	3	8
4	3	1	7	5	6	8	2	9
9	8	2	3	4	1	7	6	5
5	7	6	9	8	2	3	1	4
8	2	3	4	6	7	9	5	1
6	4	7	1	9	5	2	8	3
1	9	5	8	2	3	6	4	7

962

8	9	6	3	2	7	5	4	1
4	2	1	8	5	9	3	7	6
5	7	3	4	6	1	9	2	8
3	4	9	1	8	2	6	5	7
6	1	5	7	9	3	2	8	4
2	8	7	6	4	5	1	9	3
1	5	4	9	7	6	8	3	2
7	3	2	5	1	8	4	6	9
9	6	8	2	3	4	7	1	5

963

5	4	8	1	2	9	6	3	7
7	2	1	3	6	5	8	4	9
9	3	6	8	7	4	2	1	5
3	5	9	6	8	1	7	2	4
6	8	4	2	9	7	1	5	3
2	1	7	4	5	3	9	8	6
1	9	2	5	4	6	3	7	8
8	7	5	9	3	2	4	6	1
4	6	3	7	1	8	5	9	2

964

7	9	3	2	8	4	5	6	1
8	4	1	5	9	6	2	7	3
6	5	2	7	1	3	4	9	8
3	2	8	6	5	9	7	1	4
5	6	7	3	4	1	9	8	2
9	1	4	8	2	7	3	5	6
1	3	9	4	7	8	6	2	5
4	7	5	1	6	2	8	3	9
2	8	6	9	3	5	1	4	7

965

4	2	7	8	5	3	9	6	1
6	1	3	4	2	9	7	5	8
8	5	9	6	1	7	2	3	4
9	3	1	2	7	4	6	8	5
2	4	6	5	8	1	3	9	7
7	8	5	3	9	6	4	1	2
5	6	2	9	4	8	1	7	3
3	7	4	1	6	5	8	2	9
1	9	8	7	3	2	5	4	6

966

4	5	7	2	1	6	3	9	8
8	6	3	4	9	7	2	5	1
9	2	1	3	8	5	4	7	6
2	4	8	7	6	1	5	3	9
1	3	5	9	4	2	8	6	7
7	9	6	8	5	3	1	4	2
5	1	9	6	2	4	7	8	3
6	7	4	1	3	8	9	2	5
3	8	2	5	7	9	6	1	4

967

4	3	2	1	8	5	9	6	7
7	1	9	2	3	6	4	5	8
6	5	8	9	7	4	3	2	1
1	7	6	4	5	9	2	8	3
8	9	5	3	2	7	1	4	6
2	4	3	8	6	1	5	7	9
3	6	1	7	4	2	8	9	5
9	2	7	5	1	8	6	3	4
5	8	4	6	9	3	7	1	2

968

3	1	8	6	4	2	5	9	7
9	2	7	8	3	5	6	4	1
5	6	4	1	7	9	2	8	3
7	4	2	5	1	6	9	3	8
8	9	6	7	2	3	1	5	4
1	5	3	4	9	8	7	6	2
6	3	5	2	8	7	4	1	9
2	8	1	9	5	4	3	7	6
4	7	9	3	6	1	8	2	5

969

7	1	8	5	3	9	4	2	6
3	2	6	4	7	1	9	5	8
9	4	5	8	2	6	1	7	3
8	6	4	2	1	7	3	9	5
1	7	3	9	8	5	6	4	2
5	9	2	3	6	4	7	8	1
4	8	9	6	5	3	2	1	7
2	3	7	1	9	8	5	6	4
6	5	1	7	4	2	8	3	9

970

2	8	6	4	1	3	5	9	7
4	9	5	6	7	2	3	1	8
7	3	1	9	8	5	4	6	2
3	1	4	7	2	6	9	8	5
5	7	8	3	9	4	6	2	1
6	2	9	8	5	1	7	3	4
1	4	2	5	3	9	8	7	6
8	5	3	1	6	7	2	4	9
9	6	7	2	4	8	1	5	3

971

9	7	4	5	8	1	6	3	2
2	8	5	7	3	6	4	1	9
6	3	1	4	2	9	7	5	8
1	4	7	2	6	5	9	8	3
3	9	2	8	1	7	5	6	4
5	6	8	3	9	4	2	7	1
4	2	6	1	7	8	3	9	5
7	1	3	9	5	2	8	4	6
8	5	9	6	4	3	1	2	7

972

5	1	9	8	3	4	6	2	7
2	4	7	6	5	1	9	8	3
8	3	6	9	2	7	4	1	5
3	7	2	4	8	9	5	6	1
6	8	4	3	1	5	2	7	9
9	5	1	7	6	2	8	3	4
4	2	3	5	7	6	1	9	8
1	9	8	2	4	3	7	5	6
7	6	5	1	9	8	3	4	2

973

1	8	9	7	6	2	3	4	5
7	4	2	5	3	9	8	6	1
6	3	5	1	8	4	7	9	2
9	1	7	2	5	8	4	3	6
3	5	6	4	1	7	2	8	9
8	2	4	3	9	6	5	1	7
2	7	1	6	4	3	9	5	8
5	9	3	8	7	1	6	2	4
4	6	8	9	2	5	1	7	3

974

8	1	3	7	4	5	2	9	6
5	4	7	6	9	2	3	8	1
6	9	2	1	8	3	4	5	7
2	8	1	5	6	4	9	7	3
7	3	9	2	1	8	6	4	5
4	6	5	9	3	7	1	2	8
9	2	8	3	5	1	7	6	4
1	7	4	8	2	6	5	3	9
3	5	6	4	7	9	8	1	2

975

8	2	5	9	4	3	1	7	6
9	3	4	7	6	1	2	5	8
1	7	6	5	8	2	4	3	9
6	9	2	8	3	5	7	4	1
3	4	8	2	1	7	9	6	5
5	1	7	4	9	6	3	8	2
7	8	9	6	2	4	5	1	3
2	5	3	1	7	8	6	9	4
4	6	1	3	5	9	8	2	7

976

1	7	3	2	5	8	4	6	9
4	6	8	1	9	3	7	2	5
5	2	9	6	7	4	3	1	8
6	3	7	9	1	5	2	8	4
9	8	4	3	2	7	1	5	6
2	5	1	8	4	6	9	3	7
7	9	2	5	8	1	6	4	3
3	1	5	4	6	9	8	7	2
8	4	6	7	3	2	5	9	1

977

4	7	9	2	8	5	1	6	3
3	2	6	1	4	7	8	5	9
1	8	5	9	3	6	7	2	4
9	6	3	7	2	8	4	1	5
5	4	8	3	9	1	6	7	2
2	1	7	6	5	4	9	3	8
6	9	2	8	7	3	5	4	1
7	3	4	5	1	9	2	8	6
8	5	1	4	6	2	3	9	7

978

9	6	5	1	8	3	4	7	2
4	7	3	6	2	9	8	1	5
2	8	1	5	4	7	9	6	3
7	5	8	3	9	4	1	2	6
1	9	2	8	6	5	3	4	7
3	4	6	2	7	1	5	8	9
5	2	9	4	1	6	7	3	8
8	1	7	9	3	2	6	5	4
6	3	4	7	5	8	2	9	1

979

8	5	3	4	6	9	2	7	1
6	9	2	1	3	7	5	8	4
7	4	1	8	2	5	3	6	9
9	3	4	6	1	2	7	5	8
2	7	8	5	9	4	1	3	6
1	6	5	7	8	3	4	9	2
5	8	9	3	4	1	6	2	7
3	1	6	2	7	8	9	4	5
4	2	7	9	5	6	8	1	3

980

8	4	1	5	9	7	2	6	3
6	3	9	2	4	1	5	8	7
7	5	2	6	8	3	9	1	4
1	7	3	9	6	8	4	2	5
9	8	4	1	2	5	7	3	6
2	6	5	3	7	4	8	9	1
5	2	7	8	1	6	3	4	9
3	9	6	4	5	2	1	7	8
4	1	8	7	3	9	6	5	2

981

6	2	8	5	9	3	1	4	7
5	7	9	8	1	4	2	6	3
4	3	1	2	6	7	8	9	5
1	9	3	6	8	2	7	5	4
7	6	5	3	4	1	9	8	2
8	4	2	7	5	9	3	1	6
9	5	7	1	2	6	4	3	8
2	8	4	9	3	5	6	7	1
3	1	6	4	7	8	5	2	9

982

3	5	8	6	2	4	9	7	1
1	4	9	5	7	3	8	2	6
7	6	2	1	9	8	3	5	4
2	8	4	3	5	7	1	6	9
9	7	6	4	1	2	5	3	8
5	1	3	9	8	6	2	4	7
4	9	5	2	6	1	7	8	3
8	3	1	7	4	5	6	9	2
6	2	7	8	3	9	4	1	5

983

2	3	6	8	7	1	9	4	5
7	5	9	6	4	3	2	1	8
1	8	4	5	2	9	3	6	7
9	6	5	2	1	8	4	7	3
8	1	3	4	9	7	5	2	6
4	7	2	3	6	5	8	9	1
6	9	8	7	3	4	1	5	2
3	4	7	1	5	2	6	8	9
5	2	1	9	8	6	7	3	4

984

2	3	9	8	5	7	6	4	1
8	5	6	4	9	1	7	2	3
4	1	7	2	6	3	9	5	8
5	8	2	9	4	6	3	1	7
9	4	1	3	7	2	5	8	6
7	6	3	5	1	8	2	9	4
1	2	4	7	3	9	8	6	5
3	9	5	6	8	4	1	7	2
6	7	8	1	2	5	4	3	9

985

8	4	1	3	5	2	7	6	9
7	2	3	9	6	4	8	1	5
5	6	9	7	1	8	4	2	3
6	5	8	1	7	9	3	4	2
9	1	2	5	4	3	6	8	7
4	3	7	8	2	6	9	5	1
3	7	6	2	8	5	1	9	4
1	8	5	4	9	7	2	3	6
2	9	4	6	3	1	5	7	8

986

5	6	4	2	8	9	7	1	3
9	7	1	5	6	3	4	8	2
3	2	8	1	4	7	5	6	9
1	4	9	3	5	6	8	2	7
7	5	3	9	2	8	1	4	6
2	8	6	4	7	1	3	9	5
6	3	7	8	9	4	2	5	1
4	1	2	6	3	5	9	7	8
8	9	5	7	1	2	6	3	4

987

9	4	5	3	8	2	7	1	6
1	7	8	9	4	6	3	5	2
6	3	2	5	7	1	9	8	4
7	6	1	2	5	9	4	3	8
8	2	3	7	6	4	5	9	1
4	5	9	1	3	8	6	2	7
3	8	6	4	2	5	1	7	9
2	1	7	6	9	3	8	4	5
5	9	4	8	1	7	2	6	3

988

8	7	4	3	2	6	9	5	1
2	1	5	8	9	4	3	6	7
9	6	3	7	1	5	8	2	4
1	3	9	5	7	2	4	8	6
7	4	2	9	6	8	1	3	5
5	8	6	4	3	1	2	7	9
4	5	1	6	8	3	7	9	2
3	2	7	1	5	9	6	4	8
6	9	8	2	4	7	5	1	3

989

2	8	4	5	7	1	9	3	6
9	7	5	3	6	8	2	4	1
3	6	1	4	2	9	7	5	8
6	1	8	9	3	4	5	7	2
5	4	9	7	8	2	1	6	3
7	2	3	1	5	6	8	9	4
4	5	7	8	1	3	6	2	9
1	3	6	2	9	5	4	8	7
8	9	2	6	4	7	3	1	5

990

6	9	7	5	3	4	8	1	2
8	4	3	2	1	7	6	5	9
5	2	1	8	6	9	4	3	7
3	7	5	6	2	8	1	9	4
4	6	8	1	9	3	2	7	5
9	1	2	4	7	5	3	8	6
1	5	9	3	4	2	7	6	8
2	8	6	7	5	1	9	4	3
7	3	4	9	8	6	5	2	1

991

6	8	4	9	5	1	7	2	3
1	2	7	6	3	4	5	8	9
5	9	3	8	7	2	4	6	1
4	3	1	5	6	7	2	9	8
9	7	6	3	2	8	1	5	4
2	5	8	4	1	9	6	3	7
3	4	2	7	8	6	9	1	5
7	1	5	2	9	3	8	4	6
8	6	9	1	4	5	3	7	2

992

8	4	5	9	7	6	3	2	1
1	7	2	4	5	3	8	9	6
6	3	9	2	1	8	7	4	5
2	5	1	8	6	4	9	7	3
3	9	7	5	2	1	6	8	4
4	8	6	3	9	7	1	5	2
5	2	8	1	3	9	4	6	7
9	6	3	7	4	5	2	1	8
7	1	4	6	8	2	5	3	9

993

8	6	3	1	5	9	2	4	7
5	1	7	2	4	3	8	6	9
4	2	9	7	6	8	5	3	1
1	9	2	6	3	4	7	8	5
3	5	6	9	8	7	4	1	2
7	4	8	5	2	1	6	9	3
2	3	5	8	9	6	1	7	4
9	8	1	4	7	2	3	5	6
6	7	4	3	1	5	9	2	8

994

4	3	8	2	9	1	6	7	5
2	7	9	3	6	5	1	4	8
1	6	5	8	4	7	2	9	3
8	9	1	5	2	4	3	6	7
6	2	3	7	8	9	4	5	1
5	4	7	1	3	6	8	2	9
3	1	6	9	7	2	5	8	4
7	8	2	4	5	3	9	1	6
9	5	4	6	1	8	7	3	2

995

6	8	9	2	4	7	5	3	1
5	3	7	6	1	9	2	8	4
2	4	1	3	5	8	6	9	7
1	7	5	4	9	2	3	6	8
8	6	2	7	3	1	9	4	5
4	9	3	5	8	6	7	1	2
3	2	6	1	7	4	8	5	9
7	1	8	9	6	5	4	2	3
9	5	4	8	2	3	1	7	6

996

5	1	8	6	7	2	4	9	3
4	7	2	3	9	8	6	1	5
3	9	6	1	5	4	8	2	7
6	5	4	2	1	7	9	3	8
1	2	9	4	8	3	7	5	6
7	8	3	5	6	9	2	4	1
9	4	1	7	3	6	5	8	2
8	3	7	9	2	5	1	6	4
2	6	5	8	4	1	3	7	9

997

2	5	3	7	4	6	8	9	1
8	4	6	1	9	3	7	2	5
7	9	1	2	8	5	6	4	3
3	2	5	6	7	9	4	1	8
6	1	4	3	2	8	9	5	7
9	7	8	5	1	4	3	6	2
1	3	9	8	6	2	5	7	4
4	8	2	9	5	7	1	3	6
5	6	7	4	3	1	2	8	9

998

7	8	9	1	5	3	4	6	2
2	3	4	6	8	7	5	1	9
5	1	6	9	2	4	7	8	3
4	2	1	7	3	8	9	5	6
9	5	7	2	1	6	8	3	4
8	6	3	4	9	5	1	2	7
3	9	2	5	7	1	6	4	8
6	7	5	8	4	2	3	9	1
1	4	8	3	6	9	2	7	5

999

6	2	4	1	3	7	9	5	8
7	8	3	9	4	5	1	6	2
9	5	1	6	8	2	4	3	7
8	6	2	5	1	3	7	4	9
4	3	9	7	6	8	5	2	1
5	1	7	4	2	9	3	8	6
1	7	6	8	5	4	2	9	3
3	4	8	2	9	1	6	7	5
2	9	5	3	7	6	8	1	4

1000

5	9	7	4	3	2	1	8	6
3	8	4	5	1	6	2	7	9
1	2	6	9	7	8	4	5	3
8	3	9	6	5	1	7	2	4
7	5	1	2	9	4	3	6	8
4	6	2	3	8	7	5	9	1
2	7	3	1	6	9	8	4	5
6	4	5	8	2	3	9	1	7
9	1	8	7	4	5	6	3	2